ISRAEL IN THE THIRD WORLD

Edited by
Michael Curtis and
Susan Aurelia Gitelson

Transaction Books
New Brunswick, New Jersey

Library of Congress Catalog Number: 75-44817.
ISBN: 0-87855-130-1(cloth); 0-87855-603-6(paper).
Printed in the United States of America.

Library of Congress Cataloging in Publication Data
Main entry under title:

Israel in the Third World.

Includes index.
    1. Israel—Foreign relations—Addresses, essays,
lectures.   2. Technical assistance, Israeli—Addresses, essays,
lectures.   3. Underdeveloped areas—Foreign relations—Addresses,
essays, lectures.   I. Curtis, Michael, 1923- II. Gitelson, Susan Aurelia,
1941-
DS119.6.I77   327.5694'0272'4   75-44817
ISBN 0-87855-130-1
ISBN 0-87855-603-6 pbk.

ISRAEL
IN THE
THIRD WORLD

CONTENTS

To our parents in appreciation and love

INTRODUCTION

Israel has had an unusual experience as both a recipient of foreign aid and as a donor country. Although it is small in area and population, it has developed the political, economic and military capacities of a middle-range power. It has thus been able to offer expertise to others while it has continued to develop at a rapid pace. In terms of location and ethnic background of the majority of the population, Israel belongs to Asia and therefore is an integral part of the Third World of Asia, Africa and Latin America. Yet because of particular historical circumstances, Israel is a creation of the Western world, a product of the European Enlightenment, the burgeoning of nationalism and the destruction of six million Jews in the Holocaust. Israel also has deep ties with Jewish communities in the United States, Europe, Latin America, South Africa and Australia.

This volume focuses on Israel's economic, cultural and political interactions with the Third World. The establishment of the state in 1948 was greatly assisted by Latin American votes in the General Assembly of the United Nations. As Israel sought to cope with the myriad problems of its development, absorbing immigrants with a wide variety of backgrounds and defending its borders against constant attack, it evolved useful techniques that could be adapted to the needs of other countries. Israeli leaders also felt the need to expand relations with Asian and African countries in an effort to enhance Israel's political legitimacy through formal and informal ties. This was an absolute necessity in order to counter Arab enmity which, when not expressed directly in hostile attacks, often took the form of economic and political pressures on other states. Thus the necessity to counteract negative Arab efforts reinforced Israel's close identification with the development process shared by new states to create a positive international cooperation program with many Third World countries. The socialist idealism of many Israeli leaders promoted early contacts and harmonious relations with some Asian countries. Its social system, its modern economy, its scientific accomplishments and its efforts in nation building have attracted admiration from many emerging countries.

Although Israel's natural resources are limited, it has been able to develop and share with other states some of the techniques and approaches evolved through its experience. Israel has taken the initiative in making contacts with developing countries, offering technical assistance and inaugurating joint economic programs. It has established training institutes for students from other countries and has sent technical assistance experts to many states to provide advice in the field.

In addition to these constructive bilateral relations, Israel has also tried to widen its political relations and actively participate in various international forums, such as the Afro-Asian groupings, nonaligned conferences and the United Nations General Assembly and specialized agencies such as Food and Agricultural Organization and World Health Organization. However, since the Arab countries have been more extensively represented in regional and world organizations, Israel has sometimes been forced into a defensive position. Despite such obstacles, Israel has tried to maintain at least a minimal presence in the Third World and to emphasize its affinities with developing countries.

The articles in this book reflect the evolution of Israel's position in the Third World, the range of its programs and activities and the problems and constraints of its international relations. The contributors indicate the contrasting conditions that have affected interchanges with Asian, African and Latin American states. Of these countries only Latin America has extensive Jewish communities. At the other extreme, few Jews live in Asia, and not many Asians have had extensive contacts with the Judeo-Christian tradition. The authors also trace the changes in Israel's Third World relations. Israel's ties with black Africa, which included its most extensive diplomatic representation network and technical assistance programs in the developing countries, evolved from enthusiastic early contacts to a growing mutual awareness of both successes and problems, and finally to the termination of most diplomatic and technical assistance links, mainly the result of external political and economic pressures. Where possible, attempts have been made to view the situation from the perspective of both Israel and the interacting countries.

Many of the contributors are Israelis who have been personally connected with diplomatic, economic or technical assistance activities. In addition to this practical treatment, Israeli and American scholars have tried to offer a more detached and objective view of the situation.

Taken in perspective, these views of Israel's interchanges with Asian, African and Latin American countries indicate the possibilities and limitations of a small or middle-range power engaged in a persistent regional conflict to interact normally with other developing countries and share with them the benefits of its development experiences.

We are grateful for the cooperation of Rivka Hadary, Helen Rivkin and Anne Sinai of the American Academic Association for Peace in the Middle East and Danielle Salti for assistance in the preparation of this book.

I
ISRAEL AND DEVELOPMENT

1

D.V. Segre

THE PHILOSOPHY
AND PRACTICE
OF ISRAEL'S INTERNATIONAL
COOPERATION

One of the unexpected consequences of the process of decolonization that has taken place in the second part of this century, and more particularly since 1960, has been the efforts made by underdeveloped states to supply aid to other states, even where these latter—though not yet developed—were potentially rich. The motivation of some underdeveloped states to help other underdeveloped states is usually political, often ideological, sometimes psychological, but never disinterested. Whatever the reason, the ability to give aid is not necessarily linked to the possession of means. At the same time, it has not been proved that the organization of poverty by the poorer is more effective than through the help of the wealthy.

The Soviet Union and communist China have often been suggested as examples of "self-development" and of successful aid by the underdeveloped of yesterday to the underdeveloped of today. This claim is preposterous. The Soviet Union and China were indeed underdeveloped countries at the time of their respective revolutions but they were not lacking in indigenous culture or in basic economic, social and political infrastructures. The Tsarist and Kuomintang regimes may have been corrupt and ineffective, but they were the (removable) social and political expression of otherwise compact and self-conscious national entities. This is not the case in most newly independent nations in Africa and, to a lesser extent, in Asia, where aid is often given to and accepted by governments acting on behalf of populations bundled together in territorial units which were demarcated by previous foreign colonial regimes with little concern for their ethnic, religious, social or cultural unity.

Other Communist countries like Poland and Hungary claim special knowledge in handling problems of development. In a sense they are right, since they were, until very recently, backward agricultural societies that have made great efforts to develop. Taking just two examples of innovations introduced by communist regimes, namely workers' enterprises and the collectivization of agriculture, one sees that these are very specific features not easily exportable. There is no evidence to substantiate the claim of some Marxist economists that the Eastern European brand of socialism provides more appropriate tools to solve problems of development outside Europe.[1] This claim to a knowledge of how to develop made by "poor nations who have made good" sounds rather like the claim of the peddler who became a millionaire to possess the secret of success. This proves that a peddler can become rich, not that his system is transferable.

There are other small countries (Formosa, Tunisia, Yugoslavia and Israel, for example) run by different types of political regimes, still asking for and receiving foreign aid for their own development while offering aid to more underdeveloped countries and claiming to possess special qualifications— not necessarily ideological—for so doing. One common feature is that they operate under constant political stress; another, that they are located at the periphery of large ideological "empires."[2] Formosa's foreign policy is dictated by its uncomfortable situation on the edge of the Maoist empire; Yugoslavia's by its relations with the Soviet empire. Israel stands, and acts, in conformity with its situation as a border country with the Arab world in Asia. Tunisia suffers from the shortcomings of being in a similar, though far less antagonistic, situation vis-à-vis the Arab world in Africa.

For marginal countries of this type, to engage in aid activities means, first and foremost, an attempt to transform the liability of their being a border state into an asset. This is particularly true when the situation of marginality is not a temporary one but is permanent and rooted in history. Contemporary political, ideological or cultural marginality is thus nourished on the geopolitical, cultural or religious marginality of the past. It contributes to the consolidation of the country's self-image as a go-between, thus legitimizing and rationalizing situations of ambivalence as features of national character. The Yugoslavs, for instance, are not simply Slavs; they are Slavs who stand between the Western Roman Empire, mainly Catholic, and the Eastern Empire, Byzantine, Ottoman or Muscovite.

Tunisia is marginal both to the Arab empire and to black Africa as well as to Mediterranean Europe. Living at the crossroads of continents, empires and cultures is no new experience for Tunisians. It is a geopolitical situation that can be traced back to the time of Carthage, and even more, to Kairawan, the major army base built in North Africa in the eighth century by conquering eastern Arab armies. The tug-of-war of influence over Tunisia was also felt along the north-south axis. To and from Tunisia came, through the centuries, merchants, soldiers and scholars of Europe, Islam and Byzantium, carrying their loads of salt, weapons, gold, slaves and ostrich feathers to and from black Africa.[3]

As for Israel, the middleman role of Jews throughout history, both inside and outside that low land of the Middle East which is Palestine needs no demonstration. It seems only natural that a people that has succeeded for generations in coping with its marginal situation, should consider itself better equipped than others to contribute to the exchange, diffusion and integration of cultures, in the widest sense of the word.

Israel is marginal to the three continents it borders: Europe, Africa and the Arab Middle East. It is the traditional route for the trade and armies of all three continents. The cultural marginality of its Jewish population vis-à-vis both Islamic and Christian civilization is evident. Political and ideological strife with the Arab world makes Israel an island in the Middle East, despite geographical contiguity. Its economic, technological and institutional structure differentiates Israel from all the so-called Third World. It is a Western society without being Christian, despite the fact that the majority of its population is non-European by birth. It is an Oriental society in terms of languages, climate, religion and origin of much of the population, without any of the economic or institutional structures of the East, or of Eastern social habits of thought.

This very marginal and special country has engaged, since the end of the fifties, in a constant effort to extend aid to underdeveloped countries in Asia, Africa and, more recently, Central and South America. The motivation has been mainly, though not exclusively, political, and the expression "enlightened self-interest" currently employed by Israeli officials in charge of international cooperation seems a fair description of the situation.

Whether this cooperation has been something original and new or just a variation on older themes is a matter of argument. Three facts are beyond doubt: that through efforts to participate in the battle against underdevelopment Israel has achieved a reputation superior to the means invested in this battle; that Israel has become identified, especially in Africa, as a power in the field of international cooperation, with the advantages, shortcomings, expectations and disillusions that such a paradoxical situation is bound to produce in donor, recipients and competitors; and that feedbacks of Israeli efforts in the field of international cooperation have deeply influenced the development of Israel itself, in terms of mentality, social patterns of thought and aid techniques.

It is beyond the scope of this article to retrace in detail the history, the nature and the consequences of Israel's activities in the frame of its own development and that of other countries.[4] I propose only to briefly describe the main facts concerning Israel's activities in the field of international cooperation and attempt to analyze some of their consequences at home and in the field of international relations.

Israel's international cooperation program was born in 1958, when a small department was first established in the Foreign Office in Jerusalem to deal with aid to underdeveloped countries. This has since developed into the largest section of that ministry, comprising a large number of offices in Jerusalem and elsewhere, with a budget which has grown from a modest beginning to a figure of IL 16,000,000 ($3.5 million) per year. By the end of 1970, some 4,000 Israelis had served abroad on missions of various types, varying in duration from a few weeks to a few years. Conversely, 15,000 trainees had been to Israel for short visits or longer periods of study. In all, an Israeli presence had been established in 60 countries, in some of which—Mali, for example—relations had been broken off. Those looking for statistics could add more figures: An Israeli expert costs $6-7,000 a year ($13,000 if accompanied by his family), which is more or less the same as a European cooperation expert, but less than half the cost of an American one.[5] Of these experts, one-third came from kibbutz or moshav[6] and more than half originated from European countries.

This statistical material is only now being submitted to close scientific scrutiny[7] and definite conclusions have not yet been reached as to why certain types of Israelis go abroad and why some succeed better than others. On the whole, studies so far carried out suggest that as Israel's aid program develops in scope and in area, the spectrum of motivations and abilities of Israeli experts tends to become increasingly similar to that of experts from other countries. In other words, the secret of Israeli success in technical cooperation does not lie in the quality of men engaged in various programs. Outstanding personalities may, particularly in initial stages, have given the whole project a special impulse, but this impulse could not last forever, nor has it crystallized into a body of definite doctrines. What has kept and still keeps Israel's cooperation programs strong is the feeling of legitimacy and authority that these experts carry abroad with them and the acceptance of this legitimacy and authority by foreign trainees in Israel. These two qualities, legitimacy and authority, are not the products of a special type of man in Israel, but of a special type of society, which because of its very particular history, development and internal (often paradoxical) logic, made its people sensitive and alert to problems of change. This seems particularly true of the first diplomats and experts sent abroad by Israel to carry out programs of technical cooperation, who were mostly drawn from the "plantocratic" elite of collective and cooperative settlements.[8]

These emissaries were not experts in their own branch of activity but had a vast amount of experience in development, combined with long personal experience of physical labor. The social ideology of the kibbutz made them honest "prophets" of labor; their belonging to a collective movement which was also a collective aristocracy, gave them a background of self-assurance and inborn authority. This was needed both for the people abroad and for their own people at home, who had to be educated in the new and difficult task of accepting and providing the means and proper machinery required by multiple aid activities.

However important the initial contribution of this group, it was soon replaced by professionals. These were less powerful and articulate personalities but generally shared with the men of the first group the belief that international cooperation was a good, flexible approach to any type of change and innovation, and also the best tool with which to break political isolation. This political belief was the outcome of a very specific event. In 1955 the Arabs succeeded in preventing the participation of Israel in the first big Afro-Asian gathering of ex-colonial peoples, and in branding Israel as a bridgehead of Western colonialism. This was a shock for many responsible people in Israel; it forced them to consider for the first time the magnitude of Israel's isolation among rising nations of the Third World. The Bandung shock of 1955 was made more painful by Israeli participation in the Anglo-French colonialist adventure at Suez in 1956. One of Israel's most brilliant diplomats in Asia,[9] after attending the Asian Socialist Conference in Rangoon in 1956, commented: "Even our best friends were liable under pressure of circumstances to join our opponents and to expel us unceremoniously from the organization we ourselves had helped to create."

If the Bandung Conference and the Suez affair were diplomatic disasters, the results of the 1956 war against Egypt had a number of considerable advantages Israel could exploit in the Third World (quite apart from the temporary security it brought to its frontiers). Israel could now use the newly acquired direct access to the Red Sea and the Indian Ocean, through the Straits of Akaba, to develop economic, cultural and political ties with East Africa and Southeast Asia, two areas still outside the influence of the Arabs and totally virgin from the point of view of an Israeli presence. Israel could establish friendly relations with African countries on the verge of independence and with others where French and British colonial administrations had, for political reasons, limited the presence of foreign interests. Israel could present its own experience in development as a successful example to be imitated of a national struggle against colonial backwardness in the Third World. It could offer technical aid to anyone in the developing world who wished to acquire it, with no strings attached.

Political necessity and national experience thus joined hands to promote the policy of international cooperation, linking one of the smallest countries in the world with some of the largest. This policy paid royal dividends in diplomatic, political, and economic terms, and also produced important feedbacks into the social, economic and ideological texture and structure of the Jewish state itself. Among other things, it helped to mature the concepts and train the men who, ten years later, were to be faced with the problem of developing the territories which the Arab-Israeli war of 1967 brought under

Israel's direct military control. Israel's ability to extend aid to other under-developed countries derived less from the availability of experienced man-power (or funds) than from three factors linked with the history of Zionism: pragmatic activism, immigration and geopolitical situation.

Israel's pragmatism is both the outcome of necessity and of culture. Judaism is not a religion of dogmas; it is a way of life based on morally inspired actions. Translated into terms of social and religious behavior, this means that a Jew should be judged by his actions. More important, it means that wheresoever reality and theory clash, the spontaneous reaction of traditional Judaism is to try to adapt theory to practice and not vice versa. In modern Israel, this traditional way of thinking has grown into an attitude of permanent activism, so strong, that a passion for action looks, at times, like a dangerous substitute for a willingness to think.

When it came in contact with the adaptation problems of mass immigra-tion, this activism usually turned into flexible pragmatism, especially when dealing with social and political ideologies and their day by day adaptation to the work of institutions. In a country of immigration, adaptation means more than simple compromise. It very often means searching deeply into other people's cultures to find the bases for establishing common denominators. Psychologists and anthropologists had to be called in by bureaucrats and politicians to solve cases which would normally be solved in a socialist country by ideological interpretation. For instance, when Yemenite workers stopped work, claiming that they had been "bewitched" by party officials or factory foremen, there was no point in appealing to their sense of class solidarity. Their claim had to be first accepted, then analyzed in terms of their own cultural values, and finally translated into appropriate modern (ideological or psychological) terminology, such as psychological stress, character incompatibility, cultural misunderstanding, and so on.[10]

This is only one of the many problems which Israel, as a country of immigrant population, had to face. Others were linked with the need to blend different communities into one nation. Techniques of nation building were a common topic of discussion and experiment long before the problem came to the forefront of political and sociological preoccupation of experts dealing with development in the Third World. But again, these techniques were based less on ideologies than on the belief that the problems of Jews were very special ones. There was considerable truth in this, but at the same time the practice of looking at human problems only through Jewish spectacles restricted nationbuilding experience in Israel to very parochial proportions. It concealed from the outside world, and for a long time from Israelis themselves, the human, international value of some of their nation-building and integration tools, such as the concept of *madrich* (guide).

A madrich is a particular type of person created in the pre-Israel, Zionist youth movements. A madrich combines the functions of group leader, adviser and teacher, in practical work and education. The madrich has been prominent in all trends of the pioneering movement linked with Zionism but has become institutionalized in the organized Jewish immigration movement known as Youth Aliyah. Between 1934 and 1954, this movement brought some 100,000 immigrants below the age of 18 to Israel, and had to provide for the physical welfare of its protégés, uprooted from their families at an early age, as well as for their moral and psychological care in a family-less environment.

The madrich had a manifold role: boss, teacher, protector, leader, confidant. He had to develop a thorough knowledge of technical know-how, deep psychological insight, and a quick understanding of a continously changing situation—changing both as the result of young people's maturation, and of environmental changes in Jewish society. He not only represented "the stable authoritative link between the newcomer and his strange new surroundings, but also [became] the principal interpreter of the new environment, the channel through which the environment influences and changes the attitude of the newcomer."[11]

Thus the madrichim were, by profession as well as by age, insider-outsiders to the people they had to teach and lead. Their technical abilities and certainly their professional credentials were secondary to their ability to get totally involved with both their pupils and their work, and to set a human rather than a professional example. It is this type of person—produced in vast numbers by the Israeli immigrant society—who was entrusted with the task of teaching trainees in development, sent to Israel by Third World countries. This in turn, partly because of government budget restrictions, constituted the bulk of Israeli cooperation activities at home rather than abroad, a situation which enabled planners to make the fullest use of the country's geopolitical and social circumstances.

One of the points in Israeli society where social pragmatism and immigration met successfully was cooperative agriculture. It is common knowledge that the moshav and moshav *shitufi*[12] are one of the main channels through which the Zionist dream of the return of Jews to their ancestral homeland was expressed. These differed from the early style of colonization, based on private property and hired (mainly Arab) labor, as well as from the more radical and utopian form of collectivism—the kibbutz. The moshav combined socialist aspirations with varying degrees of individualism. It had to compete fiercely with both the private village and the kibbutz, in terms of numbers of farms and areas of tilled land, until after the creation of the State of Israel.[13]

After independence, when between 1948 and 1953 Israel was flooded with a million immigrants for whom lodging, food and work had to be provided as rapidly as possible, the compact and highly selective society of the kibbutz was unable to provide a practical solution. The kibbutzim (whose population between 1948 and 1958 rose by only 20 percent as against 120 percent in the rest of the country) refused to allow themselves to be flooded by newcomers, with whom they had no ideological, cultural and social interests in common. The vast majority of immigrants, especially those from Islamic countries for whom the traditional extended family represented the main social institution to which they were accustomed, refused to adapt to the very specialized type of collectivism in the kibbutz. The private village was also incapable of offering rapid opportunities for immigrant absorption, leaving the task of individual integration to the towns. For the thousands who did not find jobs in towns, who could not or did not want to join a kibbutz, who did not have sufficient capital, skill or initiative to make an independent living, the moshav became the best available alternative.

Between 1949 and 1959 the number of cooperative villages in Israel rose sharply, together with their total population.[14] The agricultural cooperative movement also changed in character: its technical functionalism, originally aimed at promoting development for its own sake, became far more important than its cooperative ideology, which aimed at promoting a just society relatively apolitical and free of ideology. It turned into a valuable tool for planners of agricultural development in those areas—usually arid—which the creation of Israel had brought under the control of the Palestinian Jewish community. It also acted as a "train-as-you-go" system to help immigrants take root in their new environment and switch over from the traditional skills and trades brought from their own (colonial) societies to those of a rapidly changing Westernized state.

In development areas like B'sor or Lachish,[15] fitting the cooperative village system into a balanced framework of preplanned services and regional industries proved successful. It solved immediate local problems of economic absorption, and developed original techniques of comprehensive planning, in which as much attention was devoted to the psychological and educational problems as to economic and technical needs.

It was in these development areas that the new generation of madrichim discovered both the general, human relevance of their work—as distinct from parochial Jewish values—and the fallacies inherent in "single solution" approaches to development. Later on many of them saw this type of approach causing numerous failures in the work of foreign experts with whom they collaborated in bilateral or multilateral aid schemes in the underdeveloped countries of Asia, Africa and Latin America.[16] From these moshav-based, comprehensive, regional development programs, many Israeli experts learned that the accepted alternative to the single solution approach, namely the "technological package approach," could only become operational with an appropriate institutional package: that price incentives cannot change the trends of traditional production unless accompanied by appropriate provision of services; that the promotion of comprehensive development called for more supple, intelligent and thoughtful ways of "manipulation of men", certainly quite different from those used in the manipulation of capital and instruments. Such manipulation could never be the treatment of isolated individuals, taken out of their milieu: to be successful it had to be applied within the setting of the original social milieu, not outside and not against it.

The moshav, and the comprehensive development schemes which accompanied it, provided Israel, well before it started its overseas policy of technical cooperation, with one of the most important tools for the realization of such a policy: the blueprints for comprehensive agricultural development. Men who had acquired at home the skills to deal with both technological and institutional "package" approaches to change, had also acquired the self-assurance and professional pride necessary to tackle problems of development abroad, and to test the experience acquired through trial, error and success at home.

Agricultural achievements in Israel were used as a showpiece for the moshav movement, for the benefit of foreign experts and trainees. In spite of bitter criticism to which it was often subjected at home,[17] the moshav acquired a favorable image abroad. To many people it was a comprehensive tool of progress with something to offer to all three models of underdevelopment included in Galbraith's classification: (1) the sub-Saharan African model, (2) the Latin American model and (3) the Southern Asian model.[18]

The moshav could serve the first of the three as a demonstration prototype of an agricultural village system. With its comprehensive combination of advanced techniques, integrated social and cultural services and participation by the villagers in the responsibilities of running all stages of local planning implementation, it seemed able to provide an answer which could overcome the main barrier to development in Model 1 countries: the absence of a society's minimal cultural base, and the lack of practical consensus towards development within the elite supposed to deal with cooperative administration. The Israeli experience had proved that the moshav system could produce such an elite even among new immigrants lacking agricultural or technical experience and common cultural ties. The situation which Israeli agricultural experts later found in the Central African Republic, in Senegal, in Dahomey, in West and East Nigeria, was not very different, from this point of view, from the situation with which they had struggled at home.

To Galbraith's second model—the Latin American model—the moshav could offer two things: (1) an alternative policy of development based on microtechniques to be incorporated into macrotechniques of development (usually in the form of politically inspired land reform) and options in the absence of lack of appropriate planning or personnel; and (2) the possibility of adding to macrodevelopment plans which had little appeal for the individual farmer, "personalized," microdevelopment schemes capable of firing and sustaining the enthusiasm of individuals for local development, while the wider infrastructure of national plans was being created.

Galbraith claimed that in Model 2 countries the main obstacle to development was the traditional social structure of societies. One classic solution which the establishment of almost any country disliked most, was an effort to bring about a more or less revolutionary disentanglement from the rural community by nonfunctional groups whose income and political power remained in most cases without real proportion to the services they rendered to the local society. Another solution was the equally classic evolutionary implementation of reforms, aimed at achieving a better distribution of income and eventually of political power among the groups most discriminated and primarily among farmers.

The former system has both the appeal and the shortcomings of radicalism. Its shortcomings are the price to be paid and the disillusion of seeing anticipated advantages of political change often obliterated by the poverty of what there is to be shared after political change has taken place. The evolutionary system has very little personal appeal to the hungry people concerned, the "pie" to be recut by the establishment being either so small or distributed with such parsimony that no one is satisfied, everyone made suspicious, while appetites grow beyond hope of appeasement.

The moshav system had nothing to offer revolutionaries: its declared aim was not to change man, but to allow those who wished to improve their economic and social status to do this reasonably quickly within any society. It stressed the principles and values of social pragmatism more than those of historical or ideological determinism. To a government interested in social evolution it offered two valuable solutions: first, it suggested some clusters of practical and tested solutions for the implementation of agricultural reforms. In many countries these stumbled not because authorities lacked good intentions, but because the country lacked trained personnel and appropriate techniques to carry them out. Second, the moshav possessed sufficient experience and self-confidence (acquired during its long fight with both collective and private systems in Israel) to back its own theory of (Marxist) microdevelopment against the theories of capitalist and communist macrodevelopment. The basic idea behind the moshav doctrine was the belief that farmers' enthusiasm could be sustained long enough to promote local dynamism and civic pride, if individuals involved in development schemes could be offered quick material incentives combined with understandable ideological rationalization of their newly planned activities. This theory has proved successful in a number of development projects initiated by Israel in Latin America within larger government schemes of agrarian reform, as in the case of El Sisal Development Project in Azua Province of the Dominican Republic,[19] or the Puno Scheme in Peru;[20] so successful, that Israel is now beginning to apply the moshav techniques to other areas of development, in Asia and Africa, where it was previously thought they could be tested only within the frame of limited prototypes of a new agricultural village.[21]

With regard to Galbraith's Model 3 countries, like India or Pakistan, where progress is hampered mainly by a disproportion among the various branches of production, the moshav system could only be of lesser relevance. The difficult ratio between land and population, coupled with the problem of small-size holdings made its impact almost nil.[22]

Turning now to the geopolitical factor, its importance is illustrated by the Israeli development experts' claim that "Africa [or Latin America or Asia] begins at home." This is an underlying belief of Israeli technical aid programs. The corollary is not how to make foreign realities fit the Israeli model, but how to adapt Israeli techniques to foreign realities.

Some of Israel's geographical features are well adapted to reducing the hiatus between home and abroad. Like many underdeveloped countries, Israel suffers from natural shortcomings: a hot climate, a tendency to soil erosion, drought, and an unequal distribution of rain throughout the year. There is also a diversity of agricultural cultures, some belonging to cold climates and others to tropical ones. Politically Israel has experienced colonial (British) rule and has had a taste of the French colonial system (through the immigration of a considerable portion of population from North Africa). Whatever influence may have been felt, these experiences have helped Israelis become familiar with colonial and anticolonial lingo. From the social angle, Israel sports a mosaic of immigrant groups comparable in many respects to tribal structures. This situation has heightened sensitivity, if not understanding, for problems of coexistence between traditional social structures (the patriarchal family of Asian and African immigrants or the traditional Arab village) and more modern ones, as well as problems of coexistence between different stages of agricultural development and various stages of industrial development.

Israel's social structure also seems particularly congenial for the transfer of know-how to foreign trainees. In a society where cabinet ministers can be seen washing dishes in a kibbutz; where farmers exude the confidence of upper classes; where clothing, cars or housing are not status symbols—it is easier for an instructor to persuade his foreign pupils to work with their own hands than it would be in a society where manual work is synonymous with social inferiority. Foreign trainees in Israel usually assimilate the teaching they receive more quickly and more easily than elsewhere.

A further factor contributing to sharpening Israel's pedagogic abilities in the field of technical cooperation is the chronic budget shortage and the relative abundance of multilingual instructors. Turning these two factors to its advantage, Israel has specialized in technical training of noncommissioned officers rather than generals, a characteristic which has made Israeli programs particularly attractive to foreign governments plagued by the problem of unemployed intellectuals and in dire need of low-rank cadres.

One of the results has been Israel's ability to provide training out of all proportion to the size of its population, when compared with that of other aid-giving countries. Between 1958 and 1969, 13,025 foreign trainees came to Israel from African, Asian, Latin American and Mediterranean countries. This is a very large number even in absolute terms; it is the highest percentage in the world if one considers the proportion of foreign trainees to the total national population. By comparison, the number of experts which Israel has sent abroad is limited. The official figure of 3,500 in the period 1958-69 is somewhat misleading. In 1969, for instance, 341 experts provided 2,332 man months of work, which means that the average stay of an expert was 6.5 months. In fact, the number of experts who served for much shorter periods abroad is considerably larger than the figure of those who served the statistical average of 6.5 months.

There are several explanations for this imbalance between experts and trainees. One is lack of money: it is understandable that a small country like Israel, itself engaged in development and bearing heavy security responsibilities, should not be in a position to dispose of the capital which usually goes with the expatriate expert and is often a condition for his acceptance by foreign governments. Another reason is the relative shortage of personnel. The best and most deeply rooted people in any society do not usually go abroad to serve; they stay at home. A large country whose political future does not depend on the reputation of its citizens abroad, can perhaps afford to care relatively little about their public conduct. But the image of Israel— upon which the diplomatic behavior of new countries towards her often depends—can be radically affected by personal misconduct of its citizens abroad or by lack of professional abilities of its experts. The basic purpose of Israel's policy of overseas aid is political, namely to counteract the Arab and Communist accusation of colonialism, imperialism, and so on. It thus became imperative for those responsible for technical cooperation to ensure that only the best qualified people were sent abroad.

The recruiting potential of a country of 2,500,000 (no Arab Israelis have been sent out on technical aid missions) is extremely limited and forces Israel to give preference to short-term missions abroad (for which leading local experts can be mobilized). This always works in favor of quick "indigenization" of any joint enterprises established abroad.

There is one last political advantage in Israeli offers of aid: they come from a small country which does not appear as a dangerous political friend. The case of Uganda, where Israel has been accused of political machinations, has proved inter alia that the smallest African (not to speak of Latin American or Asian) country can easily dispense with Israeli aid from one day to the next without political risk (Burma did so in 1962, Tanzania in 1965, and Congo Brazzaville in 1966).

Israel's aid projects had to fulfil a number of basic conditions. They had to be of interest to recipient countries in order that the financial burden could be shared with or carried by the recipient; they had to fit in with the technical capabilities of Israel to provide services for the length of time required; they had to be big enough to create a visible impact; they had to be manageable— from the point of view of overall responsibility and rapidity of their realization—in order to take full advantage of initial interest and enthusiasm and to sustain them along the way with tangible results.[23]

Not all programs filled these requirements. Some suffered from improper planning and unjustified ambition. Examples were Solel Boneh's (Israel's big socialist contracting firm) joint construction ventures in West Africa in the sixties. Their aim was to create a "national building contractor" more responsible and more "patriotic" than existing private firms. The two ventures in question—Ghana National Construction Company and Sonitra (a joint construction venture in the Ivory Coast)—have been the object of a detailed and critical analysis.[24] The conclusions are worth quoting: "These two ventures were the most successful in Africa from the financial point of view . . . [but] a national contractor is not just one more contractor—there were enough contracting firms both in Ghana and in the Ivory Coast . . . the national contractor must be capable of executing major works whether on his own behalf or as a partner to world-wide firms. It must, therefore, possess the ability to negotiate, on an equal footing, with governments, banks, international agencies and firms. Its management must possess not only the necessary high professional qualifications, but also extensive experience, knowledge, skills and political consciousness." This meant that the qualities which Solel Boneh possessed in Israel as a national contracting company could not be reproduced by the same Israeli firm in West Africa, where the feeling of identity of Israelis engaged in the operation with the host country was different from the feeling they had at home towards their own country and society.

In the Bobo Dijolasso area of Upper Volta, Israeli advisors established in 1963 a Multi-Purpose Agricultural Center at Matourkou. An ambitious scheme, financed largely by the UN Special Fund and intended, inter alia, to train native agricultural foremen. The Final Report prepared by the center's director R. Agmon,[25] reads like a manual on "how to fail for the wrong reasons," namely, the "fundamental changes of social structure, attitudes and mentality of farmers and of their society"[26] which the Israelis were unable to carry out but which they learned to identify as the common root of any "technical" problem.

Americans could send tractors to Upper Volta, teach local drivers how to use them and replace them if they came to a quick standstill through improper maintenance. Israelis could not imitate them. Lacking material and financial means, they were obliged to concentrate on human problems in development, and progressively less on technical and environmental ones. At Bobo Dijolasso many "tricks" were tried. Israeli advisors discovered that their presence in the field during practical demonstrations of new ploughing techniques by the center's native instructors to farmers, reduced the status of instructors in the eyes of farmers. They therefore devised curricula of private tutoring in sowing and ploughing, making a point of being absent when their pupils turned into instructors.

In Western Nigeria Israelis in charge of an ambitious palm oil reclamation scheme[27] found themselves handicapped by facilities (e.g. too much pocket money) granted to farmers by the government. These facilities reduced the feeling of responsibility and ownership of farmers, who could not grasp the aims of the government. Farm plots were soon invaded again by weeds, trees were left untended, pocket money used to hire unskilled labor while the farmers went back to the city. A solution was found when all the plantation trees were mapped and individual trees allocated to individual farmers, with payment of allowances conditional on the health and good appearance of palm trees. The personification of plants, the establishment of a direct connection—both visual and financial—between the tree and the farmer, helped to overcome the feeling of strangeness which these same trees, seen as part of a large plantation, had produced previously in the minds of farmers who had not planted them.

In South America, Israeli innovations in technical aid were more successful from the outset. One of the most popular is the system of scaled agricultural credits, tied to planned agricultural performance. This system was tested in Israel as an incentive for new immigrants in development areas, and was to be developed into a coherent pattern of incentives in agricultural development in Latin America. In Venezuela, for instance, a supervised credit system helped to double the agricultural production of 134 villages in one of the most depressed zones of the country, in less than 3 years.[28] This compares well with the work of the Citrus Development Scheme in Ecuador,[29] or the establishment of chicken farms in West Africa, where Israeli efforts were never more than a "prestige operation" intended to establish Israel on the international cooperation map rather than to provoke an enduring economic or social transformation in the local society.

We come now to the crux of the matter. The introduction of new techniques—commercial, political, scientific or other—useful as they may be to the recipients, always provokes one major question: how can these new techniques be absorbed, not in terms of their efficiency or practical utility, but in terms of their integration into local patterns of thought or action? Just as with an organ transplant, it was soon realized by Israeli advisers that there was no point in proposing an innovation without at the same time providing the social, educational and psychological "antitoxins" which would prevent rejection.

Some experts thought that these antitoxins could be artificially increased by the use of proper aid techniques. They called this the "microcooperation" approach (as opposed to current "macrocooperation"), and it was founded on the belief that development is more easily brought about by aiding agriculturists rather than agriculture, by changing men prior to changing their environment. To put these ideas into practice they needed an overall authority which they could not have in a foreign land. They had to wait for the opportunity to reorganize the agriculture of the West Bank before they could speak conclusively—as they now do—of a special Israeli way to development.

NOTES

1. Jossef Bognar, *Economic Policy on Planning in Developing Countries* (Budapest: 1968). Akademiai Kiado,

2. D.V. Avni-Segre, "Quelques Aspects du Marginalisme dans le Transfert de Culture," *Acta Africana Geneva-Africa* 6, no. 2 (1967) :216-23.

3. E. Gauthier, *L'Islamisation de L'Afrique du Nord: Les Siècles Obscurs du Mashrch* (Paris, 1927).

4. These subjects have been discussed in many books and articles, though no attempt has so far been made to study the implications—other than political and economic—of Israel's aid to development for Israel's own development.

5. Leopold Laufer, *Israel and the Developing Countries: New Approaches to Cooperation* (New York, 1967), p. 50. In a Pakistani government report of 1958, the average cost of an American expert was put at $40,000 a year. See G. Myrdal, *The Challenge of World Poverty: A World Anti-Poverty Program in Outline* (New York, 1970), p. 350.

6. Laufer, *Israel and the Developing Countries*, p. 55. For a detailed description of the organization of the Israeli International Cooperation setup, see Z.Y. Hershlag, *Israel-Africa Cooperation Research Project, Progress Report* (Tel Aviv University [restricted circulation], 1970, p. 2, chap. 5).

7. See Tables 1, 2 and 4.

8. The Role of the Plantocracy in Israel has been discussed in D.V. Segre, *Israel: A society in transition* London: O.U.P., 1972).

9. David Hacohen, former Israel; Ambassador to Burma. *Jerusalem Post*, August 8, 1965.

10. I am grateful to anthropologist Phyllis Palghi of Tel Aviv University for the information on the subject with which she kindly supplied me.

11. Laufer, *Israel and the Developing Countries*, pp. 65-68.

12. The *moshav* (settlement) is a cooperative settlement, with each family organizing its own private life, but linked with the others through common ownership of land and means of production, and by the common marketing of products. Stress is laid on the elitist element and on ideological identity. Immigrants from Germany in the late 1930s evolved a mixture of kibbutz (collective settlement) and moshav, called *moshav shitufi*, in which the community's ideological control over its members was greater than in the moshav, economy and ownership collective as in the kibbutz, but each family had its own house and was responsible for its own cooking, laundry, and care of children, as in the moshav, while work and pay were adjusted to individual circumstances. In addition, the moshav shitufi, like the kibbutz, tends to develop industry in addition to agriculture.

13. There were 115 kibbutzim in Palestine on the eve of independence, and almost the same number of moshavim. In 1970 the figures were 235 and 344, respectively, (and 22 moshavim shitufiim) with populations of about 80,000 and 130,000.

14. Albert Meiser, *Principes et Tendences de la Planification Rurale en Israel* (Paris: Lahaye, 1962); H. Darin-Drabkin, *Planification Rurale en Israel, Un Aspect Regional* (Jerusalem, 1960 [roneotyped]; H. Halperin, *Changing Pattern in Israel Agriculture* (London, 1957; and Paris: Agrindus, 1966).

15. *Background Data on the Lachish Region* (Ministry of Agriculture, Jerusalem).

16. Frank Michael, *Cooperative Land Settlements in Israel and their Relevance to African Countries* (Basle, 1968).

17. Maxwell I. Klayman, *The Moshav in Israel. A Case Study of Institution Building for Agricultural Development* (New York, 1970), ch. 10. D. Weintraub, H. Lissak, and Y. Azmon, *Moshava, Kibbutz and Moshav* (Ithaca, N.Y., 1969); J. Ben David, ed., *Agricultural Planning and Village Community in Israel* (UNESCO, 1964); R. Weitz, *Hakfar Haisraeli Beidan Hatechnologica* (Tel-Aviv, 1967).

18. J.K. Galbraith, *Underdevelopment–An Approach to Classification* (paper presented to the Rehovot Conference on Fiscal and Monetary Problems in Developing Countries, edited by D. Krivine, New York, 1967).

19. Ministry of Agriculture Center for Agricultural Cooperation with Developing Countries, The El-Sisal Development Project, Azva Province, Dominican Republic, A Joint OEA-Israel-BID Project—*A Synopsis of the Rural-Development Plan* (Rehovot, Israel: December 1970).

20. For a summary of Israel's cooperation activities in Latin America, see Division de Cooperacion International, Ministerior de Relaciones Exteriories, *Sumario de los Programas de Cooperacion International en las Americas* (Jerusalem, 1971).

21. For instance, in Laos, in Nepal, and in Zambia.

22. Some attempts have, indeed, been made to apply the moshav model to programs even in this type of country, but without concrete results, and the causes have not been fully investigated. The failure may possibly be attributed to the fact that Galbraith's model 3 countries also happen to be those with whom Israel has either very cool (e.g., India) or no diplomatic relations (Pakistan and Indonesia), or because their development problems are of an immensity that a small country like Israel cannot tackle.

23. Not all Israeli projects had, of necessity, to fit in with these requirements. For instance, the military cooperation that Israel extended to many African countries—

starting with Congo Kinshasa in 1962, at the request of the United Nations—had a logic of its own. It had to be effective and professional. The Israeli military trainers might have been able to do their job more quickly and better than their counterparts from other countries because of Israel's experience in modern warfare, but there was nothing particularly new or special in the training of soldiers. Israel's asset in this field was her high level of professionalism together with her lack of military interests outside the Arab Middle East.

24. Ministry for Foreign Affairs, Division for International Cooperation, *Israel's Programme of International Cooperation* (Jerusalem, 1970), ch. 14 and 15.

25. R. Agmon, Project Manager, "Final Report," Agricultural Training and Demonstration Center, Bebo-Dijolasso (Upper Volta), UNDP/SF—FAO, Project No. 79/UPU/RU (April 1968, mimeographed).

26. Ibid., p. 224.

27. West Nigeria Scheme.

28. See Table 4.

29. State of Israel, Ministry for Foreign Affairs, and Ministry of Agriculture, *Israel's Agricultural Cooperation with Developing Countries, Concepts, Objectives, Projects* (Jerusalem, 1970), Table 25. For a concise and very pertinent description of Israel's basic approach to aid to development, see Dr. Itzhak Abt, *Israel's Agricultural Cooperation with Developing Countries* (The Harry S. Truman Research Institute of the Hebrew University of Jerusalem, Truman International Conference on Technical Assistance and Development, Jerusalem, 23-31 May 1970).

TABLE 1 Israeli Experts Assignments and Trainees in Israel (by continent)

	Experts Assignments		Trainees in Israel	
Continent	1974	1958– 1974	1974	1958– 1974
Latin America	329	1,397	383	3,586
Asia, the Mediterranean Area and Oceania	105	1,225	431	7,241
Africa	51	3,304	88	7,627
Total	485	5,926	902	18,454

TABLE 1A Israeli Experts in the Service of International Organizations

Long-term Field Assignments	77
Short-term Field Assignments	30
In Secretariats	37
Total	144
Total—Israeli Experts Assignments	629

TABLE 2 Israeli Cooperation Projects Abroad—1974 (by subject and continent)

	Latin America	Asia, The Mediterranean Area & Oceania	Africa	Total
Agriculture	21	5	3	29
Comprehensive Regional Planning & Development	3	2	—	5
Cooperation and Labor Studies	6	—	—	6
Industry, Construction and Economic Services	13	—	—	13
Science & Technology	8	2	—	10
Administration and Public Services	1	—	—	1
Community Development and Education	—	1	—	1
Medicine and Health Service	—	—	3	3
Youth Program	6	—	3	9
Total	58	10	9	77

TABLE 3 Israeli Experts Assignments and Trainees in Israel (by subject)

	Experts Assignments		Trainees in Israel	
Subjects	1974	1958-1974	1974	1958-1974
Agriculture	162	2,141	135	6,645
Comprehensive Regional Planning & Development	55	131	119	293
Cooperation and Labor Studies	33	188	274	3,915
Industry, Construction & Economic Services	10	301	29	467
Science and Technology	85	273	106	1,226
Administration and Public Services	29	419	31	660
Community Development and Education	28	478	166	2,062
Medicine and Public Health Services	32	508	26	1,089
Youth Programs	51	953	16	1,141
Various	—	534	—	956
Total	485	5,926	902	18,454

TABLE 4 Israeli Program of International Cooperation

	Expert Assignments Abroad (Long- and Short-Term)	Trainees and Students in Israel	Trainees and Students in On-the-Spot Courses and Seminars
A. 1974			
Latin America	329	383	730
Asia, the Mediterranean Area and Oceania	105	431	355
Africa	51	88	88
Total	485	902	1,173
Israeli Experts in the Service of International Organizations. Total	144		
	629		
B. 1958–1974			
Latin America	1,397	3,586	
Asia, the Mediterranean Area and Oceania	1,225	7,241	
Africa	3,304	7,627	
Total	5,926	18,454	

2

Netanel Lorch

AN ISRAELI VIEW
OF THE THIRD WORLD

DEFINITION OF THE *THIRD WORLD*

An Israeli view of the Third World is undoubtedly suspect. With Israel's frustrations, disappointments, rejected advances and unheeded wooings, anything positive will be condemned as undignified flattery and anything negative shrugged off as sour grapes. If in spite of this obvious—and justified—suspicion I venture some reflections on the subject, it is in the hope that I shall be able to overcome my bias, and the reader conquer his suspicion.

As one considers the Third World today, one cannot help repeating what the late President Johnson supposedly observed when he heard De Gaulle speaking grandiloquently about *les quatre*: "And who the hell are the other two?" It is as difficult today to visualize the Western, free, democratic, NATO-oriented "world" as one, as it is to consider the Soviet bloc and the People's Republic of China as another. The bipolarity of the Northern Hemisphere is a thing of the past; the global pentagon is a much more adequate description of the shifting realities in that part of the world than the duality used to describe it at the height of the cold war. Has the Third World then been demoted to the grade of Sixth? This may sound like an absurd term, yet not inadequate to denote a doubtful reality.

The first attempt to organize the Third World was at Bandung in 1955. At that time the main thrust was anticolonial; a colonial or quasi-colonial past (Chou En-lai was one of the pillars of the conference) was one of the prerequisites for membership. The program planks for the future were anticolonial with few exceptions—Africa was still a continent of colonies, and it was only natural that the primarily Asian leaders who met at Bandung should direct their attention to that continent. Less natural was the fact that

27

vast Russian possessions in Europe and Asia, incorporated into the Soviet Union without benefit of prior consultations, were not included in the Third World, and have so far escaped that attention of anticolonial leaders. By 1974 the colonial question, in the strict sense of overseas territories controlled by Western metropolises, has been almost completely resolved. With Portugal, the last of the metropolitan powers, recognizing the right of self-determination of its African colonies, with that halved right being granted even to ministates like Grenada (pop. 100,000) or the Maldive Islands (pop. 80,000), anticolonialism has run its course. Whether because of the political will galvanized at Bandung, or the absence of such will in former colonial powers, or the divisions within the Western world, or Soviet machinations or any combination of these, by 1974 the winds of anticolonial change have lost their momentum, leaving behind a harvest of newly independent nations and much debris besides.

Anticolonialism was soon to be complemented and later replaced by nonalignment as the political cement holding the Third World together. It suited the three founding fathers, each for reasons of his own: Tito, as a result of his quarrel with his Soviet comrades; Nasser, in his attempt to play the United States and the Soviet Union against each other in order to obtain the best bargain from each; and Nehru, attempting to reconcile his anti-Western stance with Western-type democracy. Nonalignment in its virginal purity did not last long. As early as 1956, Indian supported the Soviets in their crushing of Hungary; soon afterwards it had to resort to Western arms in its struggle against China. Tito gradually veered back toward the Soviet camp, and Cuba, which had never left it, was accepted as an honored member at a price to be mentioned later. Nonalignment received a boost when Latin American countries increasingly came to join. Anti-Yankeeism was a direct result of their geographical location, while political alignment with U.S. adversaries was an impossibility for precisely the same reason. The U.S. would be reluctant to accept nonalignment on its southern threshold; it was unlikely to stand by idly whilst Soviet bases were established in the Western Hemisphere.

Latin American countries gave renewed impetus to another ideological interpretation of nonalignment: the idea of a socioeconomic structure that was neither capitalist nor Communist, but was mixed, or cooperative. The Peruvian foreign minister stated that his was one of the few countries whose external and internal policies were mutually consistent: political nonalignment with neither of the major power blocs, externally; ideological nonalignment with them, internally. However, his own emphasis on the singularity of the Peruvian experience would indicate that it was the exception rather than the rule, and therefore unlikely to constitute the mortar that could hold the political grouping together.

Thus we come to the last, most prominent *raison d'être* for the group of 77, as it was originally called: the developing nations, the nonindustrial countries primarily in the Southern Hemisphere. To the extent that consistent political-economic programs, have been elaborated and supported by the group, they were primarily in the field of closing the gap between the rich of the North and the poor of the South. This has been attempted in UNCTAD (UN Conference on Trade and Development) and UNIDO (UN Industrial Development Organization). The First and Second Development Decades were largely the fruit of Third World endeavors and of attitudes originated in developed nations through concern for the Third World. However, here too a moment of truth seems to be at hand. Development has lost a good deal of its lustre (someone suggested recently that developing countries should call themselves the nonpolluted countries, and be proud and contented); the various conferences and stratagems designed to close the gap witnessed its increase. Finally, the recent energy crisis has demonstrated the artificiality of the concept, which put countries like Kuwait in one basket with Chad; underdeveloped countries with immense wealth in high-priced raw materials and minerals alongside others who had to import the very lifeblood of their economy. Some of the 77 enjoy the highest per capita income in the world; others suffer from the lowest. What do they have in common? Which is their common political denominator, a policy to which they are equally committed, a cause for which they are equally willing to struggle? The disillusionment manifested recently, particularly in Africa with the ruthless application of new oil prices that added millions to expenses, does not merely constitute an awakening to the real meaning of Arab brotherhood with Africans, it casts grave shadows on the economic and political unity of the Third World.

Although never categorically articulated, the Third World concept has undergone significant mutations since it was first enunciated in the early 1950s. Ironically, the country that has been consistently blackballed by the club is also one of the few that by any criterion should have best qualified for membership, that is, Israel. Its anticolonial struggle was more bitter and prolonged than that of almost any other former colonial territory; its commitment to anticolonialism has been consistent, even at times when such a posture involved grave political risks, particularly during the French-Israeli honeymoon in the late 1950s and early 1960s. Long before nonalignment became a Third World slogan, Israel had defined its foreign policy as one of nonidentification. Israel has never belonged to a power bloc and never been the location for foreign military bases. Its ideological credentials are above reproof; its economy is mixed; the cooperative and collective sectors are larger than in Yugoslavia. A socialist party has been in the center of government since the state's inception. Israel is a developing nation: it started out with little industry; it has few raw materials to call its own. Yet owing to Arab blackmail, it was blackballed at Bandung and later on ostracized and condemned. In fact, condemnation and breaking of relations with Israel became a virtue, a fig leaf to cover other sins. When Colonel Qaddafi of Libya attacked Cuba on account of its Soviet links and bases, it was through breaking off of relations with Israel that Fidel Castro bought his way back to grace.

When Israel realized that neither what it was nor what it stood for was sufficient to bring it into the group, it embarked on an ambitious and, on the whole, successful program of technical cooperation with most Third World countries. Maybe what it did would ultimately count. However, to no avail. Arab numerical superiority manifested in cajoling and blackmail, bribery and threats, kept the door tightly shut, and many Third World countries broke off diplomatic relations at a time when psychologically and politically Israel was most vulnerable. In retrospect, technical assistance, although frequently beneficial to Israel's bilateral relations with many individual countries in Asia and Latin America, may have been counterproductive in relations with the group as a whole. The Third World is a platform for voicing demands, not of mutual self-help; it is a group of receivers, not of givers. Israel's willingness to give may have contributed to its being branded an outsider.

It has been said that the ultimate test of a national political system is its attitude toward Jews within its territory; that anti-Semitism is a disease of the haters no less than an affliction of those hated. Transplanted to a higher level, anti-Israelism may well be the ultimate touchstone of supranational organizations. Not because Israel is better than anybody else, but because its numerical inferiority makes condemnation so expedient. Its attitude toward Israel has served as a criterion of the sincerity and the genuiness of Third World commitment to its declared goals—and the Third World has failed that test.

Does the above constitute a message of doom for the Third World? Not necessarily. But it does spell a grave warning. From a cause in search of an organization, it has gradually turned into an organization in search of a cause. It may yet find it. The original cause of war on disease, hunger and illiteracy has as much raison d'être as ever. If the Third World should fight these, it may yet retrieve itself. Whether it is willing or able to do so remains to be seen; but I venture one guess: a genuine change of attitude toward the oil-rich Arab countries on the one hand, and Israel on the other, will be among the first preconditions for such a renewed dedication, and the first signals of its having come about.

3

Eli Ginzberg

MANPOWER POLICY IN NATION BUILDING: LESSONS FROM ISRAEL

Every community has unique characteristics, some of which can be turned into assets for development, and others become liabilities which will hobble modernization. The deep ties that bind Israel to the Diaspora represent an asset; the differences among Israelis about the role of religious observance are a liability to development.

Despite the idiosyncratic nature of Israeli development, a number of lessons can be extracted from a consideration of how Israel approached and dealt with manpower problems during the first quarter century of its existence which have relevance for countries of the Third World, particularly those similar in size and resource endowment.

It is impossible to separate, surely initially, Israel's success in implementing various manpower policies from its favorable capital inflows. Even though the latter materially and favorably influenced Israel's accomplishments in the development and utilization of its manpower resources, we may still be able to identify certain strands of policy that are relevant for countries with less financial resources.

SOME MANPOWER LESSONS

From the first day of its existence as an independent state, Israel has followed an open-door policy with respect to immigrants, especially with respect to Jews who desire to return to the land of their fathers. A reading of the record leaves little doubt that the substantial inflow of population has been a major source of stimulation to the economy. While many Third World nations would gain nothing from encouraging a large-scale inflow of immig-

31

rants, others would profit from increased immigration. This is especially true of several countries in North Africa and the Middle East which have a population base too small for effective development, particularly in light of their recently swollen resources from oil exports. Libya and Saudi Arabia are obvious examples of countries which could profit from having a larger population.

It is characteristic of most developed and developing countries to be only modestly concerned with discrepancies among different groups with respect to their income, standard of living and access to services. But not Israel, which early on committed itself to establishing a basic standard of living for the early settler and the immigrant, the professional and the laborer, the urbanite and the farmer. This was not a commitment to a policy of equality of income or wealth. But Israel did establish heavily subsidized housing for newcomers, a social welfare system for all employees not geared to the length of their employment, a relatively flat wage structure, and a highly progressive income tax system. Israel did a great deal to narrow, although not eliminate, gross discrepancies in the quality of life for different groups in its body politic. If it is morally wrong and politically dangerous for countries to tolerate wide differences in wealth and welfare among its people, other nations should find Israel's experience worth studying and possibly worth emulating.

A second major manpower commitment, perhaps Israel's most unique contribution to manpower policy, is the overriding importance its leadership has attached to full employment. Drawing on its labor ideology, from its inception the new state has pursued policies aimed at providing useful work for all adults. In the days of mass immigration in the late 1940s and early 1950s when there was no opportunity for many of the uneducated, unskilled, impoverished immigrants to be fitted into the economy immediately, public authorities saw to it that they were employed on public works such as building roads and planting trees. Questions of cost, productivity and efficiency were not to the fore: the emphasis was on putting every adult male to work to assure that everybody would be able to earn his own livelihood. The leadership recognized the dangers of establishing a system of welfare without work requirement.

Faced with the challenge of rapidly absorbing large numbers of immigrants, the authorities established a series of development towns which, in conception at least, were to house an admixture of early settlers and newcomers so that the processes of acculturation and assimilation, socially and economically, could be accelerated. In attempting to provide jobs for the newly swollen labor force in these towns, authorities opted in favor of textile manufacturing with its relatively high labor component and disregarded the outlook for long-term competitiveness of new industries. In later years, much criticism was leveled at this policy, but the fact remains that if new immigrants were not to be confined to a life-style of existing without

The following values have given shape and direction to this large-scale public effort to broaden and deepen the educational base. Israelis are deeply committed to the belief that their economic independence and survival rests on the development and utilization of their human power, since they know they have no other comparative advantage. They realized that, in this largescale expansion, they would run the risk of periodic imbalances in the supply and demand of trained manpower, particularly since certain immigrant groups, such as recent arrivals from the Soviet Union, include a high proportion of specialists. However, they believe and act on the assumption that even if some of their graduates must go abroad because of lack of jobs at home, the dangers of small-scale losses from a brain-drain are much less serious than the consequences of a constrained educational system.

There are many weaknesses in this broad-scale expansion of the educational system from nursery schools to medical schools. On balance, we must conclude that the effort has been basically sound. Israel recognized that it dare not risk having a labor force with limited education and skills. It saw the urgent necessity to avoid this trap and has mounted the resources to overcome it. The fact that it has not yet found how to bring adequate numbers of Orientals through high school and university to graduation, that its vocational efforts are flawed, and that it is operating too many medical schools are minor blemishes. The leadership recognized the challenges it faced on the educational front and has responded accordingly.

It has been belatedly admitted by most development economists that they and government planners in the Third World erred in downgrading the agricultural sector in development planning. Israeli experience stands in sharp contrast. Its agricultural achievements are outstanding. Twenty years ago Israel's farms did not produce enough to feed a much smaller population. Today, with a few exceptions such as the growing of wheat and the raising of beef, Israel is not only self-sufficient but exports a wide range of high quality agricultural products, exports that contribute significantly to reducing the trade deficit.

The heart of Israel's agricultural success story lies in the twin approaches of continuing modernization and the broadening and deepening of agricultural skills. Although most economists, including this writer, would not understand why Israelis in the early and mid-1950s, despite their surplus labor, made heavy investments in farm machinery, time revealed the soundness of their long-term strategy. A modern agricultural sector is a sine qua non for a progressive economy.

High-level technology is not enough; high-level skills are a necessary component. There were certain special conditions in the Israeli scene that contributed to the latter: the unique quality of the kibbutzim; the self-conversion of many gifted European immigrants into successful farm owners and operators; and the ease of diffusion of new methods in a small and closely linked population with high goals.

There is more to the story of Israel's agricultural success, but the determination of individual elements and their proper weighting is less important than the basic stance which made this success possible. In most developing countries the leadership neglects agriculture and concentrates its efforts on speeding the modernization of industry. Such an approach has many untoward consequences, from accelerating out-migration of rural population to consuming limited foreign exchange because of the necessity of importing essential foodstuffs. Of all the lessons Israel has to teach the Third World none is more important than the nurturing of agriculture.

The gun together with the plow hold the clue to Israel's development. Israel had to fight for its independence in 1948, and it had to go to war again in 1956, in 1967 and in 1973. Had its defense forces been unequal to the task, Israel could not have survived. The building of the Israel Defense Forces and assuring that they perform at a high level of capability is due in large measure to Israel's first prime minister, David Ben-Gurion, who appreciated better than most the need for an effective military organization well supplied and well led. It was Ben-Gurion who, during the country's critical formative years, stood between the military and the Labor party and fought off politicians who sought to keep all the power strings in their own hands.

There are several key lessons to be extracted from Israel's military manpower experience. The first has already been noted: an emphasis on professionalism, which insists on objective criteria for promotion, which are the sine qua non for effective organization. To provide opportunities for talented younger people, those high in rank must be moved out at an early age. Israel's chiefs of staff were sometimes in their late thirties, seldom older than the early forties. By providing good fringe benefits for those forced into early retirement, including two years of subsidized study in a foreign school of management, the military made an important indirect contribution to increasing the nation's limited pool of executive personnel.

Israel has conscripted both men and women for its armed forces. While married women and girls with religious scruples are exempted, almost the entire male population is drafted. The rejection rate for young men is in the 5 percent range compared to 20-25 percent in the United States in periods of partial or total mobilization. The high intake rate means that the Israel Defense Forces (IDF) have been able to serve as a major instrument for acculturating, socializing, educating and providing skill training for successive cohorts of young generations. Israel could not have successfully absorbed so many newcomers without the contribution of the IDF.

There remains one more manpower theme that warrants exploration. The Arab student at the Stanford University seminar who remarked on the ties of Israel to the Diaspora recognized an important and unique facet in Israel's experience. Israel has sought to maintain strong representation abroad. Its diplomatic corps is known to be able and hard-working; its intelligence agents have many coups to their credit; in extracting money from its coreligionists Israel has a unique record of accomplishment. Less visible but still important have been the many sources of help that Israel has been able to mobilize abroad when faced with new crises. In short, Israel provides unequivocal evidence of the importance that small countries establish and strengthen their links abroad at the same time that they seek progress at home.

IN PERSPECTIVE

Every country is unique by virtue of its people, its history, its conditions and aspirations. But every country shares to some degree a communality of challenges and responses with other countries because each is linked to others through international political and/or economic associations. All Third World nations should be able to extract some part of the manpower experience of Israel that has been in so many ways unusual. To recapitulate: Israel followed an open immigration policy for Jews desiring to return. Israel's social policies have been aimed at narrowing differences between newcomers and earlier settlers. Israel never deviated from a policy of work for all. Israel acted to expand its educational system on the assumption that this was essential for modernization and progress. Israel gave high priority to the modernization of its agriculture. Israel built its defense forces into a major socializing force for the entire population. Israel recognized the value of qualified representatives abroad as an advance phalanx of nation building. working, the leadership had few alternatives to moving as it did, although they may have missed that point in time when the employment objective should have been moderated by considerations of profitability.

The maintenance of a high level of employment is the most serious challenge facing every developing country. It is not surprising that most Third World governments, short of experience and trained personnel, have sought to avoid this challenge. The large underemployed and underutilized manpower resources that characterize most developing nations only increases the challenge. There may be no specific job creation programs pursued by the Israelis that can be easily exported and replicated, but that government's deep and unswerving commitment to a high employment policy is the critical lesson that should be learned.

The educational system plays a crucial role in the manpower system of every country. Israel started with an adequate system of elementary schools and one distinguished university, but with a thin secondary-school structure. At the end of the first twenty-five years of Israel's experience, there are six or seven universities, a small number of junior colleges, an expanded system of compulsory and free education for ten years, a much expanded system of academic secondary schools in which tuition is geared to parental income, and a considerable number of vocational schools. The state has recently paid increasing attention to compensatory education, in a belated effort to narrow gross differences in educational achievement between newcomers and the established population.

4

Shimeon Amir

TRADITIONAL LEADERSHIP AND MODERN ADMINISTRATION IN DEVELOPING COUNTRIES*

At an international meeting held some time ago in Israel, a distinguished Latin American stated: "Underdevelopment is like God: it exists everywhere." This is a great truth, and the condition of underdevelopment is characterized by a multiplicity of factors. To deal with any one of them in isolation, or to single out this or that possible corrective measure is to conduct an exercise in abstraction. Fully conscious of this constraint, the topic I have chosen is a simple and limited proposition related to the introduction of modern techniques in traditional societies: changes should be introduced only when necessary; new contents should be transferred to existing institutions; institutions, habits and patterns of life compatible with new techniques should be conserved; and changes should be gradual.

This simple outline can be justified on a number of grounds. One is reminded of Occam's celebrated razor and the dictum that "entities must not be multiplied without necessity." Similarly, a logician of the management sciences could propose a law to the effect that "changes must not be introduced without necessity." Far more pressing is the psychological consideration. Every major change presents an effort, and therefore creates tensions and difficulties. In order to conserve the limited individual and social forces as much as possible, one should limit their introduction to the minimum. Changes imply learning, and the learning process is carried out by assimilation of new and unknown elements of knowledge to those already familiar and known. To facilitate this process, the number and scope of new elements should be limited, and the pace of their introduction should be gradual.

No less significant is the political aspect. The introduction of changes

*Adapted from an article in *Kidma*, 1, no. 3 (1974).

inevitably creates new foci of influence, so that traditional leaders tend to become apprehensive as to their future standing and privileges. Concern for their status is a vital requirement, if gradual transformation is to be achieved. On the international scene the problem assumes major dimensions in confrontation between societies, nations and regions. The need for self-respect of emerging nations, for self-reliance, takes shape as philosophy, creed and symbol; it eventually leads to different groupings and thus affects international relations.

Let me illustrate these generalizations with a few specific instances drawn from Israel's own experience as well as from its experience in development cooperation. One of Israel's principal national objectives and ideals, and one which became almost a national symbol, is the ingathering of the Diaspora, the absorption of new immigrants and their transformation into a unified modern nation, devoid of differences of origin. The very growth of the Jewish population, especially during the first decade, is a feat unparalleled in modern history. Israel has grown from about half a million to more than three million, mainly as a result of massive immigration. Its absorption, economically, socially and culturally, presented tremendous challenges. Nation building was not an abstract or chauvinistic slogan: it was a daily routine, expressed in the creation of jobs, changes of skills, building houses, teaching a new language, creating new health habits and generally transforming behavioural patterns in a population which had doubled in the course of a single decade.

Soon after the first few years, techniques of immigrant absorption underwent a basic change. At the beginning, the practice was to form heterogeneous groups, settling together immigrants from various countries and of different backgrounds. The underlying belief was that the melting pot approach would produce quicker results, mixing together in one neighborhood individuals from Roumania, Yemen and North Africa. Soon afterwards, a basic change was introduced in the light of observations and suggestions of renowned sociologists, including Margaret Mead. Settlements, both rural and urban, started to become more homogeneous. Those responsible for absorption policy noted that the process of adaptation and assimilation in the new country could be greatly facilitated if the range of changes was less sweeping and if at least some of the former habits and milieux were preserved. It then became the practice to form neighborhoods, rural and urban, in homogeneous groups, according to mother tongues or countries of the inhabitants. The idea of forming a unified nation was not sacrificed, but instead of reaching that goal through the absorption of each individual, separately, the new approach is based on bringing together groups of similar origin.

Although this practice had already been followed empirically for many years, it was only in the last few years that there emerged a growing consciousness that not enough was being done to conserve. The particular characteristics of ethnic groups are important, both for their intrinsic values, as an expression of rich and colorful traditions, and also as a means of enhancing the self-respect of the various groups and their members. The national ideal of mores is not the disappearance of ethnic differences and particularities and the creation of a single set of values. What is desired is a composite mosaic incorporating habits and patterns of a wide variety of origins and traditions. An ongoing exhibition of Moroccan Jewry in the Israel Museum is a worthwhile expression (and example) of rich tradition of this important segment of Israel's population and of the will to extend the spectrum of formative cultural backgrounds.

The same phenomenon may be noted in other walks of life. In Israeli radio and television programs the arts of folklore of the country's non-European communities play a much greater role than they did some years ago. Soon after the production of a successful musical based upon the Hassidic tradition of East European Jews, there followed the creation and production of *Sephardic Garden*, warmly applauded and received by the entire Israeli public. In teaching Jewish history, more emphasis than before is being placed on the history of Jewish communities of North Africa, the Balkans and the Middle East, while previously education concentrated mainly on Jewish communities of Europe.

So much for change in the approach to modernization in Israel itself, for the growing consciousness of the need to conserve valuable elements of various ethnic traditions and to achieve national unity through incorporation of differing elements rather than through imposition of one or a few. It is much too early to consider this effort to have been completely successful, but there is a growing realization of a great and challenging problem.

Economic changes in the "administered areas," in Judaea, Samaria, and later also in the Gaza Strip, experienced since the Six-Day War in 1967, add up to an example of successful and purposeful modernization. Here I shall limit myself exclusively to a single aspect of transformation, in agriculture. All other aspects important as they are, and especially the political one, are outside the scope of the present discussion. A recent publication quotes some indicators of economic growth of the administered areas.[1]

The gross national product of the areas in 1968-71 has grown (in terms of fixed prices) by 67 percent. In the two years 1970-71, the real local product grew by 16 percent, in spite of a reduction in locally employed persons by 5 percent, a decrease caused by growing employmnent of such laborers in Israel itself, outside the administered areas. The increase of productivity per employed person in the administered areas in those years (1970-71) was therefore 21 percent. The main increase in productivity is to be found in agriculture. Although the percentage of employees in agriculture has decreased substantially, its product grew quickly, from IL 169 million in 1968 to IL235 million in 1971, i.e. by 38 percent.

The most important characteristic of Israel's administration in the occupied areas since the war was the policy of minimal interference in the process of local government. The policy of the minister of defense responsible for the administered areas was "don't govern them," meaning that local population should govern itself according to its own wishes, the only limitation being strict observance of security precautions and prohibition and prevention of hostile acts against the Israeli Government.

In agriculture, another element was present: love of rural life, animals, plants; and the pioneering vocation of Israelis, brought up with the ideal of the transformation of the desert. The officer in charge of agriculture in Samaria district, Eytan Israeli, describes how he handled the reconstruction of agriculture from the outset.[2] Even before the war ended he located and established contact with the ex-Jordanian officials of agriculture of the area, urging them to resume their functions immediately. The only radical change introduced was their new administrative independence, so different from the former centralized system of administration, when even trivial decisions had to be referred for approval to the head office in Amman. From the beginning, the Israelis suggested to local officials to draw upon Israeli experience and to introduce changes in techniques of cultivation and crops. The number of Israelis was limited at all times, not exceeding ten to twenty throughout the administered areas. The agent of change has always been, not the Israeli, but the local extension officer. He achieved status by additional knowledge and by additional means put at his disposal, enabling him to conduct experiments and demonstrations.

A conscious effort was made to involve local leaders and village elders in the process of modernization. Their fields were included among those selected for experimentation whenever possible and they served as heads of local planning and production committees. Whenever a radically new concept or idea was suggested, a long period of gestation was recommended, so as to enable those involved to familiarize themselves, to assimilate it as something of their own rather than as something utterly alien and new.

The transformation of agriculture in the administered areas is a good example of modernization in a well-defined sector, restricting changes to essentials, using local change agents, with minimal interference from outside. What was unique in Israel, was the proximity of its highly developed agriculture and of a steady market for additional produce. Similar approaches and ideas have been propounded by Israelis in their development projects abroad.[3] The concepts were taught in courses attended during the past fifteen years by some fifteen thousand trainees, half of them in agriculture. The main emphasis is invariably placed, not on specific techniques and professional issues, but on questions of general approach and changes in attitude. Some of the recommendations suggested to trainees on the general issue of transformation and modernization, in training programs for field personnel in agriculture, are worth noting: (1) changes to be introduced must be simple, inexpensive and of direct benefit to the farmer; (2) they have to be adapted to conditions in the particular locality; (3) local sources of information, resources and innovation should be used as much as possible; (4) the innovations suggested should be as far as possible consonant with local tradition and culture; (5) local persons should be used as agents of change; (6) additional support should be sought through the traditional hierarchy and existing administrative structure. These specific precepts reflect the underlying principle that changes should be kept to a minimum and local tradition preserved to the maximum. The Mount Carmel Centre for Training in Community Development specializes in courses aimed at assisting women in playing an active role in development processes of their societies. Some two thousand participants have attended courses and study tours since the start of the center's program some twelve years ago.

Some works presented by students reflect the concern in developing societies not to let the process of modernization adversely affect their own personalities. To cite a specific example, here is what a student from Uganda wrote in 1972 on adult education:

> The world has always been changing, and one of the most important recent changes which affect adult education is the consequent weakening or even disappearance of traditional cultures, especially in developing countries which are suddenly exposed to urbanization and industrialization. How does this change affect adult education?
>
> If a rich man has built his house and wants trees in his compound, he does not have to plant young seedlings, he can have already-big trees transplanted into his compound. I am imagining such a tree, suddenly removed from its usual surrounding forest into a completely new environment, with the wind blowing it this way and that way, and man shaping it any way he wants. The tree is the people, the forest is the culture and the man is the agent of change. It is now a tree without its cultural background. That is the way I see a people whose traditional culture has been weakened or removed, and yet is exposed to urbanization and industrialization.
>
> One has to stand firm if one is to lift something. If the ground on which one is standing is shaky or slippery, one just falls under the weight of what one is lifting. Our culture is the ground, firm and secure, on which we stand so as to be able to extend our hand to get

hold of new things. Adult education helps people to adjust to a changing world. It is easier to help a person who is firm, because then he can move, than to help a person who is shaky and does not even know where he is—in this case one has to teach him to stand firm first, before new knowledge can be added.

Another student, from Botswana, wrote about the function of an agent of change in a changing society:

To bring about change we have to know that we should not impose it on the people lest we get rejected. We must take our time so that the people can digest it and feel it is necessary for them.

As an agent of change, I still have a lot more to learn, especially the past history and customs, for this will help me to understand the community and to be able to help it. We have to remember that our past customs have been moulded over long periods of change and adaptation. Social changes also must be brought about gradually, whether in a family or in a community as a whole.

I have to find out the reasons why people behave in a certain way that I am not used to, so that whatever I do, I will not be very far from their line of thinking, so that I can help them make their decisions, whether to keep their old ways of living or not. I must see that when something new is started, it does not lead to abuse.

Traditional social attitudes should be modified to take new situations into account. We ourselves need to plan whenever we want to bring about change, lest we bring about something valueless. If we want to use machinery, for instance, we must be sure that we have skilled men to use it, or else it will be a white elephant.

We cannot achieve change overnight. There must be concern for social justice and equality of opportunity, and a commitment to achieve change by persuasion and consultation rather than compulsion for satisfaction.

The famous Arusha Declaration of 1967 of Tanzania's Policy on Socialism and Self-Reliance is one of the most important and original definitions of national and continental policy in recent years, and contains numerous references to the need to conserve values and self-respect within the process of modernization. In stating the reason for the need of a new approach to its development, it says:

> We have been oppressed a great deal, we have been exploited a
> great deal and we have been disregarded a great deal. It is our
> weakness that has led to our being oppressed, exploited and disre-
> garded. Now we want a revolution, a revolution which brings to an
> end our weakness, so that we are never again exploited, oppressed or
> humiliated .... Gifts which increase, or act as a catalyst to, our own
> efforts are valuable. But gifts which could have the effect of weaken-
> ing or distorting our own efforts should not be accepted until we have
> asked ourselves a number of questions.

These are very astute observations, coming from one of the most influential
and respected leaders in Africa. All those engaged in development cooperation should bear in mind the basic underlying precept: the self-respect of the
recipient country or society is a most valuable element per se; in no way
should it be damaged even for the sake of the achievement of material or
technological advancement. The transformation of the donor-recipient relation, stressing equality of duties and privileges on both sides, has long been
established and recognized in the development universe. It has even been
given formal recognition in the very title of the Pearson Report *Partners in
Development*.

An important element in preparing for modernization is the increase of
capacity for change. This forms a complex embracing awareness of new
needs, disposition to accept innovations and the skills to absorb them. One of
the important objectives of training must be preparation for flexibility. One
of the prerequisites of development is this capacity for change, so characteristic of the more developed societies (in addition to their richer resources).

To sum up: The objective of modern administration in a traditional society
should be to plan, implement and review programs primarily to train and
prepare the population for greater flexibility and better capacity to absorb
changes for modern development, while at the same time preserving local,
regional and national identities and characteristics and thus achieve a proper
interdependence between change and continuity. This makes it desirable to
introduce limited changes in well-defined areas. They should be gradual,
commensurate with the local capacity for change. Every effort should be
made to preserve identity and to maintain self-reliance and self-respect.
Traditional leaders and existing institutions should be incorporated into the
process of change. The formula here suggested is admittedly complex and
not clear-cut. But these strictures apply to life itself. Israel's experience at
home and abroad shows that, at its best, the process of modernization
consists of a combination of general principles and ad hoc compromises, of
vision and realism.

NOTES

1. S. Amir, "Employment in Israel: The Dynamic Element in the Economy in Administered Areas," *Labour and National Insurance* (monthly review of the Ministry of Labour, in Hebrew), May 15, 1973.

2. See S. Tevet, *The Cursed Blessing* (Jerusalem: Weidenfeld and Nicholson, 1968).

3. Macarov and Fradkin, *The Short Course in Development Training* (Massada, 1973) presents a summing-up of those ideas.

5

E. Kanovsky

CAN ISRAEL SERVE AS A MODEL FOR DEVELOPING COUNTRIES?

During the last twenty-five years a few countries succeeded in developing at a very rapid pace, raising living standards and steadily reducing the dimension of poverty. Those which have had the good fortune of possessing large petroleum reserves in relation to the size of their populations, such as Kuwait and Libya, require no explanation, nor can they serve as models for others to emulate. I am referring to such outstanding examples as Japan, Israel, and since the 1960s, Taiwan, South Korea, Singapore, and some others. With the exception of Japan, these countries have been beset with the problem of a high rate of population growth—Israel by design, the others as a result of natural increase—yet have nonetheless successfully developed their economies and rapidly raised the living standards of their populations.

When I was a graduate student in the Department of Economics at Columbia University in the 1950s, one of my professors attempted to explain the widening gap between rich and poor countries by arguing roughly as follows: "The reason these countries are poor is because they are poor." By that he meant that since production and income were so low, barely at the subsistence level, these countries were unable to save and invest in modern machinery, equipment, improved transportation and communications, and all the other prerequisites for rapid economic growth. The obvious conclusion was that only advanced countries can break this vicious circle of poverty through a large-scale program of economic and technical aid to underdeveloped countries. The United States and other countries did undertake a large-scale foreign aid program for underdeveloped countries in the early 1950s, but during the 1960s there was increasing disillusionment with the efficacy of these programs, when so many recipient countries failed to show significant economic improvement and in some instances even retrogressed.

Since the 1960s, the conventional wisdom has been that the crux of the problem was the rapid growth of population, which presumably wiped out

45

many or all gains resulting from foreign aid and economic development programs. Another school of thought emerged in the 1960s exemplified by the following quotation from a study of economic development by two economists: "The best economic plans or projects, even when accompanied by a high degree of economic mobilization of financial resources, have proved unavailing or insufficient to cause true and lasting economic development.... Both experience and research have shown that only part of economic progress can be attributed to the input of the material or physical factors of production. The social variable (i.e., the human factor) has, as yet, not been placed in its proper role, although one now notes among development economists a general awareness of the limits of strictly economic notions and of their applicability to developing nations." [1]

Emphasis began to shift from the accumulation of physical capital (machinery, equipment, etc.) to human capital, namely, the need to raise educational and health standards as well as other social factors which bear heavily on the process of economic development. The World Bank and its affiliates have significantly altered their policies and have begun to provide loans for these purposes. Yet one finds many countries in which there are surpluses of so-called highly educated manpower, and the problem of the brain drain has come to the fore. I am well aware of the various economic errors and failures in Israel. There were and are instances of inefficiency and waste. During the initial period following independence, economic policies were adopted which later had to be abandoned. Even currently, those familiar with the Israeli economy can cite various inefficiencies. But on an overall basis there has been considerable success by almost any criterion of international comparison: whether in terms of per capita economic growth; labor, capital and total productivity; development of the prime sectors, agriculture and industry; rapid growth of exports of both goods and services; rising living standards for the bulk of the population; as well as many other criteria. To what factors can we attribute the success of the Israeli experience, and what parts of that experience are transferable to other developing countries? I have always been wary of monistic explanations, and I would attribute the achievements of the Israeli economy primarily to the following factors.

1. Israeli leadership—and I use the term in its broadest context to include government leaders, the Histadrut, the major political parties, the Jewish Agency and others—has consistently emphasized the goal of economic development. Though there have been and are differences as to methods, there has been a broad consensus that economic growth requires some sacrifice of current benefits for the sake of future development.

2. Israeli leadership has increasingly adopted a policy of economic pragmatism favoring all forms of initiative and enterprise which might advance

development, whether they emanate from private local enterpreneurs, foreign capitalists, Histadrut enterprises or the public sector. Many enterprises are partnerships between various sectors, including some kibbutz and Histadrut enterprises owned jointly with local or foreign entrepreneurs. More recently the government has adopted a policy of selling some of its enterprises to the private sector. This is in sharp contrast with leadership in many Third World countries which advocates dogmatic socialism and discourages private enterprise, especially foreign.

3. At the time of Israel's independence in 1948, the new state possessed a very great advantage over other newly-independent countries, starting off with a Jewish community whose educational levels were almost the highest in the world. The mass immigration which followed independence reduced average educational levels considerably. However, the greatest emphasis was put upon education, and by the mid-1960s the country had succeeded in raising its educational levels to that which had obtained before 1948. Since that time, rapid growth in higher education and post-Six Day War immigration from Western countries and the Soviet Union have significantly advanced the "educational stock" of the population and the labor force. Unlike so many other developing countries, there was a greater balance between levels of education—elementary, secondary and higher education—between academic and vocational schooling, and between areas of specialization such as the natural sciences, the social sciences, the humanities, engineering, health sciences, and so on. In many developing countries the extreme unbalance leads to bottlenecks on the one hand and surpluses on the other. One finds a surplus of specialists in, say, law and political science, and shortages of engineers and medical personnel; or surpluses of engineers and Ph.D.'s in the sciences, and shortages of technical personnel at the intermediate levels.

4. There has generally been a better balance between investment in physical capital and investment in human capital, i.e., education in its broadest context. Except for the fortunately short-lived recession of 1966-67, economic development has been rapid enough to absorb almost all locally educated manpower as well as immigrants who were professionally trained abroad. The problem of brain drain—emigration of educated Israelis—has not been significant except for the 1966-67 period. Many, if not most, Israelis studying abroad have returned to their country following completion of their studies, unlike professionals of so many other developing countries. There are exceptions in Israel, such as in medicine, but by and large this seems to be the situation. No doubt Zionist ideology is a factor, but were it not for the balance between education and economic growth, brain drain would have affected Israel to a far greater extent, as indeed was the case during the 1966-67 recession.

5. Though the military effort borne by the country has few parallels elsewhere, and on balance is a serious deterrent to economic growth, Israeli leadership has ameliorated its negative economic impact through innovative methods. The military is utilized to enhance educational levels of soldiers as well as of civilian population. The development of Nachal settlements and the stationing of Nachal units in existing border settlements, serves both military and economic functions. The military provides many with skills which are subsequently useful in civilian occupations. Major expansion of military industries, including aircraft, electronics, and others, and military research and development expenditures, have had important spillover effects on civilian economic sectors, and have aided in the improvement of civilian production, enabling it to compete more successfully in foreign markets.

6. Of no less importance than the balance between educational improvements and economic growth, is the balance between social and economic development. The integration of highly diverse groups of immigrants has been a serious and difficult challenge. Whatever the motivations, Israeli leadership has been at all times aware of the dangers of extreme social and economic inequalities. That is not to say that this problem has been solved in Israel. But there has been a long-term effort to bridge the social and economic gap, especially between the Ashkenazim and Sephardim. Many critics contend that the effort is less than adequate, but the leadership and the population as a whole are in agreement that major resources must be devoted to dealing with these problems. Whether or not the gap between the two communal groups has narrowed is a matter of dispute among Israel's researchers and leaders, but that all segments of the population have made rapid economic and educational advances is indisputable. Among the Israeli-born, both of Ashkenazic or Sephardic parents, the gap is narrower, and, incidentally, intercommunal marriages are steadily increasing—an optimistic note for the future.

7. Israel has been innovative in the social and institutional realms. Technologically, though advanced, in many fields it still lags behind the most developed countries. However, the development of new socioeconomic institutions such as the kibbutz, the moshav, the moshav shitufi, the urban producer, consumer and marketing cooperatives, the large enterprises in manufacturing, construction and others directly owned by the Histadrut, the vast system of health care of the Histadrut, and many other unique institutions, have been a major factor in Israel's social and economic development. Of equal importance is the fact noted above, namely, that the ideologues who had at an earlier period viewed the Histadrut and its many affiliates as the precursor and instrument of a socialist commonwealth, have given way to the pragmatists who advocate a mixed economy and the

encouragement of all forms of economic enterprise. In recent years there has been far greater emphasis in Histadrut enterprises on efficiency, productivity and profitability.

8. By and large, the underdeveloped countries started out with an economy based on primitive agriculture. Their political leaders, often educated in the most advanced, highly industrialized Western countries, instinctively equated economic development with industrialization, usually to the detriment of the agricultural sector. Economic planners in these countries, often ill-advised by Western specialists, laid the greatest stress on construction of the most technologically advanced industrial plants. It soon became apparent that they lacked the necessary technical and managerial personnel as well as local markets for the products of these enterprises. Capital-intensive industries failed to provide significant employment opportunities for the masses of unemployed and underemployed. Investment in the agricultural sector, to the extent that it did take place, was in dams for irrigation and other major projects. The mundane task of training peasants in modern agricultural techniques was seriously neglected. Agronomists preferred their offices in the capital city, and sent directives to the countryside, rather than undertaking the tedious task of instructing farmers. The results are well-known: lagging agricultural production and a widening income gap between rural and urban sectors; serious underutilization of industrial plants that were built; high costs of production; aggravated foreign exchange shortages due to rising food imports and the failure to expand exports significantly; and the transfer of rural underemployment to urban congestion, slums, and overt unemployment. By contrast, Israel's policy was initially to strongly emphasize agricultural development and production. This was motivated by security, political, and ideological considerations. The end result was a vast network of new agricultural settlements, and even surpluses of many farm products. Investment in large irrigation projects, and modern plant and equipment was essential. But the large-scale program of on-the-spot training of farmers by many agronomists who went out daily to farms and showed untrained new settlers how to farm was of crucial importance. Citriculture has been a mainstay of Israel's exports for many decades, but most recently there has been a major diversification of farm exports including flowers, avocados and many vegetables, as well as processed foods from the industrial sector. The drive to develop industry began in earnest in the mid-1950s, and has gathered momentum since that time, except for the recession of 1966-67. Israel also had its share of "white elephants," but by and large production and productivity have shown consistently rapid increases, and the export drive has been an almost continuing one since the early 1960s. The large network of vocational high schools, and on-the-job training in factories, subsidized by the government, have been important

contributory factors towards achieving this success.

9. I have intentionally left the large-scale "foreign aid" Israel has received for the end of the list. Not that it is unimportant, but its importance has often been exaggerated as an explanatory factor. This would include both financial aid from Jewish communities abroad, and aid from the U.S. and West German governments. Offsetting this aid, was the neccessity to absorb an unusually large immigration, largely destitute, as well as an onerous defense burden. A recent study of Israel's economy prior to the Six Day War, made by an American economist, comes to rather unconventional conclusions. He estimated that during the 1954-64 period, in the absence of foreign aid, Israel's economy would have grown by an annual average rate of 9.3 percent, rather than the 11.4 percent rate actually achieved.[2] By international standards a 9.3 percent rate of growth is very high. This would not have been the case in Israel's immediate post-independence period of mass immigration in 1948-51, nor in the post-Six Day War period with its vast escalation in military expenditures. But it is interesting to note that in the period of relatively low—that is for Israel—military expenditures, foreign aid was of far less crucial importance than is generally believed.

What aspects of the Israeli experience might be applicable to developing countries? Much of Israel's technical aid program in many African, Asian and Latin American countries has been in agriculture, the area in which Israel has been most innovative. These countries are interested not only in Israel's advanced level of technical expertise in this sector, but in the adoption and adaptation of some of Israel's novel socioeconomic institutions, primarily the moshav, and other cooperative innovations in credit and marketing. Channeling the military establishment towards economic development, in particular the establishment of Nahal units, is another area of prime interest. The organization of trade unions which would enhance, rather than impede, economic development, is yet another field. Other than that there are the more usual technical aid programs where Israelis are engaged in military training, the establishment of medical centers, education, the training of personnel, and many others. It is difficult to assess the efficacy of these programs currently operating in over seventy countries. Israel has certain political and economic motivations for the advancement of its technical aid program. We recently witnessed that in some African countries Israel suffered political setbacks. In many of the countries local political leaders have their own motivations for the establishment of trade unions and Nahal units, namely the enhancement of their political power, rather than economic development. However, the overall growth of this program and the large number of requests received by Israel from many countries indicates a widespread interest in learning and gaining from the Israeli experience. But the fundamental lesson to be derived from Israel's development has not been learned—nor is it easily taught. It is that development requires an overall sophisticated balance. Some development economists have advocated what they call a "balanced growth" doctrine, namely, the concurrent development of many industries as well as agricultural improvements. Thus, they argue, a market would arise for the increasingly varied range and quantity of products, leading to higher incomes, enhanced purchasing power, further investment and continued growth. The Israeli experience indicates that the balanced growth doctrine must be far broader to include at least the following: a balance between agricultural and industrial development, as well as the infrastructure; a balanced educational and manpower training program geared to the needs of the economy; a balance between social and economic development; a singleminded devotion on the part of the political and economic leadership to the goal of development, unencumbered by ideological biases; and the mobilization of human and capital resources, both domestic and foreign, to further the goal of social and economic development. In 1963, Moshe Dayan, then minister of agriculture, visited five African countries to inspect Israel's aid program. He reported, among other things, on his discussions with the leaders of Cameroon. Within his list of proposals Dayan suggested: youth training in farm techniques and social organization along the lines of the moshav; chicken farming; and the settlement of graduates on new farms. Cameroon officials objected to the plans for chicken farms and doubted that educated youth could be persuaded to take up farming. Dayan replied that Israel had been a success because it had adopted a policy of "yet another *dunam* and yet another goat." Success required persistent painstaking efforts and government assistance on a wide front—credit, legislation, seeds, guidance, roads, power, etc.—and this for three generations. In other words, he said, there is no shortcut to economic development.[3] More recently, in an article published by the International Monetary Fund and the World Bank, an Indian economist evaluated technical aid programs of Israel and of some other countries. While highly laudatory of Israel's programs he concluded that "it is easier to transplant technical skills than institutions and values."[4] This is the crux of the problem. The Israeli experience can serve in many respects as a model for other developing countries, but for that, they would have to learn not only technical skills, but to adopt and adapt Israel's balanced growth approach in its broadest context.

NOTES

1. F.S. Schiavo-Campo and H.W. Singer, *Perspectives of Economic Development* Boston: Houghton Mifflin, 1970, p. 69.

2. H. Pack, *Structural Change and Economic Policy in Israel* (New Haven: Yale University Press, 1971), p. 220.

3. *Jerusalem Post Weekly*, November 22, 1963, p. 5.

4. A.G. Chandavarkar, "Technical Cooperation within the Third World," *Finance and Development* (December 1972): 21.

II
ECONOMIC RELATIONS
AND TECHNICAL ASSISTANCE

6

Mordechai E. Kreinin

ISRAEL AND AFRICA:

THE EARLY YEARS

This chapter surveys Israel's technical assistance to Africa during the late 1950s and early 1960s, the years in which the program was formed and took on its special character. Although some of the projects which seemed promising at the time were later drastically modified or discontinued, it is of interest to review these early beginnings in order to gain historical perspective.

EARLY CONTACTS

Political ties and technical cooperation between Israel and the Afro-Asian world were preceded by ideological contacts established through the socialist and labor movements. They can be traced back to the 1950 International Trade Unions Congress in Belgrade. At the invitation of R. Barkatt of the Israeli delgation, three Burmese delegates stopped in Israel on their way home from the congress as the guests of the General Federation of Trade Unions (Histadrut). The next step was taken two years later at the Asian Socialist Conference in Rangoon. Israel's delegation was headed by the foreign minister, Moshe Sharett, in his capacity as a leading member of the Socialist Labor party. His discussion with the Burmese government resulted in an exchange of ambassadors between the two countries. In addition, the Israeli delegation established initial contact with representatives from several Asian and African nations.

David Hacohen, first Israeli ambassador to Burma, was chosen for the assignment because of his extensive background in building the industrial empire of the Histadrut. It was decided to cultivate relations with Burma on the basis of possible Israeli contributions to Burmese economic development. Since Burma and Israel attained their independence from Britain in the same year, the new ambassador was able to draw economic and political parallels between the two countries in discussing with Burmese officials their development programs. Technical cooperation between the two countries was at first confined to the military field, with Israel training Burmese technicians in military industries and supplying maintenance crews for Burmese planes. But since 1954 Israel has dispatched to Burma a variety of agricultural, medical and industrial experts, many of whom have worked in the Defense Service Industries (the economic branch of Burma's armed forces). A joint Burmese-Israeli construction company was set up subsequently, and Israel's National Shipping Line (Zim) was invited to take over management of Burma's Five Star Line. Likewise, a succession of agricultural projects led to Israel's involvement in the army resettlement program in 1959-60. From Burma Israel's reputation spread throughout the Far East, and relations were established with Ceylon, Thailand and the Philippines. Although India does not recognize Israel, there is cooperation with private Indian groups.

Relations with one West African country commenced practically with the creation of Israel. Liberia voted in the United Nations for the partition of Palestine, and was the third nation to recognize Israel. Since the early fifties there has been an honorary Israeli consul in Monrovia, although diplomatic missions were not exchanged until 1957. And while a private Israeli construction firm began operating there in 1956, governmental assistance projects in such fields as agriculture and medicine only began in 1958.

Israel's cooperation with Ghana radiated all over the African continent. The seeds for that tie were sown in meetings between Ghanaian and Israeli leaders in international socialist conferences and at the International Confederation of Free Trade Unions. Subsequently, when Ghana's Minister of Labor (Kojo Botsio) met the Israeli representative to the 1956 inauguration ceremony of the Liberian president, he asked that a consulate be set up in Accra. Thus Hannan Yavor became the first Israeli consul in an African country (Ghana) one year prior to its independence; he was replaced a year later by Ambassador Ehud Avriel.

In Ghana, as in Burma, emphasis was placed on technical and economic cooperation. In the small hotel room which housed the consulate, plans were laid for the Black Star Shipping Line and the Ghana National Construction Company to be set up after independence as partnerships between Ghana and two Israeli firms. Subsequently, plans were developed for Ghana's flying school, assistance to the Kumasi College of Technology, and cooperation in the fields of agriculture and youth organization. In that fashion, two former segments of the British empire, unconnected by historic ties, traditions or habits, were brought together solely on the basis of newly developing mutual interests.

Contact with other African countries spread from there. Rashidi Kawawa, vice-premier of Tanganyika, was introduced to Israel's foreign minister by President Nkrumah at a Pan-African socialist meeting. At about the same time, Joseph Nyerere, brother of the first prime minister of Tanganyika, participated in a Socialist Youth League conference in Israel which led to his subsequent interest in Israel's youth organizations. Likewise, the Western Nigerian ministerial delegation was induced in 1957 to include Israel on its itinerary while studying foreign cooperative movements.

By that time Israel was facing an increasing flow of visitors from many lands, who were intent on observing its trade union and cooperative movements. To accommodate that interest, the Histadrut organized the first Afro-Asian Seminar in Cooperation in 1958, whose success resulted in the expansion of Israel's foreign training activities in both trade unionism and cooperation. Similar requests from several nations led the Israeli government to inaugurate such programs in a variety of other fields. Technical assistance ceased to be an idea expounded by a few "crazy individuals" and became an integral part of Israel's foreign policy.

In Israel's relations with Latin America, political ties preceded technical cooperation. Several Latin American countries supported the creation of Israel in 1947 and have constantly raised their voices in the United Nations for a peacefully negotiated solution to the Middle East conflict. To this favorable pattern of relations a new dimension was added in 1962—that of technical cooperation. It was Latin American visitors to Israel who first discovered specific achievements which offered possible solutions to some dominant problems in Latin America. Subsequently Latin American trainees participated in various courses in Israel, primarily in the field of agriculture. Under an agreement with Brazil (signed in Recife on March 12, 1962) Israel was to supply a staff of technicians to organize a search for underground water resources and to provide training in irrigation methods. Another group of technicians would help organize farming cooperatives on the San Francisco River. And hundreds of Latin American trainees would come to Israel to attend courses in agriculture, cooperation and youth organization.

SCOPE OF THE PROGRAM IN ITS EARLY YEARS

The unique social organizations evolved in Israel through decades of development—agricultural cooperatives, structure of the labor movement and youth organizations—first attracted the attention of Afro-Asian leaders. Their interest in modern techniques employed in Israel came later, but in most cases it was submerged in admiration for the social framework within which the techniques were practiced. This was one reason why the technical assistance program at first emphasized short courses and seminars in Israel. New techniques can be demonstrated anywhere, but exposure to social patterns can be accomplished only where such patterns exist. Another reason was pragmatic. Israelis had little knowledge of African ecological conditions, and a training program in Israel could be better controlled to assure success than activities in an unfamiliar country.

These are compelling reasons. But a program confined to such course work is subject to important limitations. Many of the courses could not impart knowledge in sufficient depth to achieve concrete results, and the students were not always adequately prepared to absorb material on a high enough level. Even when this was not the case, the average trainee could not transplant independently knowledge that he had gained outside his own country. Consequently, as Israel gained more experience, some of the training and service activities were shifted to Africa.

During the three years ending in August of 1962, about three thousand individuals from Afro-Asian countries completed training in special courses organized for them in Israel and taught in English and French. The number of Israeli technicians sent overseas by the government was about one-tenth of that, but in addition, some five hundred Israeli foremen and engineers worked abroad under the auspices of Israeli companies which had established partnerships with African and Asian governments. The various segments of Israel's foreign assistance program are outlined below:

Training in Israel

1. Short conferences of the survey type, usually designed for upper-echelon civil servants and professionals. They included seminars on rural planning and the role of women in a developing society, the latter leading to a series of specialized courses in community development.
2. Intensive courses in specialized subjects, lasting from three to ten months. Designed primarily for intermediate-level personnel, they constituted the bulk of the training program and included agriculture, youth organization, community development, cooperation, trade unionism, public and police administration, and vocational training.
3. Sub-academic courses lasting between one and three years, and including accelerated training of physical education teachers and nurses.
4. Individual training by means of practical work or observation tours ranging in duration from a month to a year.
5. Special academic courses—offered in English by Israeli universities—in agricultural engineering and medicine.
6. Training of a few individual students in Israel's institutions of higher learning. Intensive training in Hebrew, offered by special institutes

designed to teach the language to new immigrants (Ulpan), was a prerequisite for enrollment. In some cases graduates of the short courses stayed on for further academic work.

Israeli Assistance Abroad

1. Survey and fact-finding missions lasting from one to four months. These included general surveys of a branch of the economy, investigation of particular problems, or missions exploring the possibility of Israeli contributions to the country's development. Their value was in familiarizing Israelis with African problems and conditions as much as in recommendations supplied to the host government.
2. Experts working in Africa and Asia in advisory and planning capacities or carrying out specific assignments (one to four years of service).
3. Advisors under the auspices of United Nations agencies. Strictly speaking, these were not part of Israel's program.

Joint Commercial Ventures

Enterprises in various African and Asian countries, jointly owned by Israeli companies and a local government body, with the latter owning the controlling share. Key administrative and technical personnel were usually supplied by Israel, but the ultimate aim was gradual transfer of management to local hands.

TRAINING IN COOPERATION

An unusual feature of Israel's cooperative movement is its affiliation with the Histadrut. The Histadrut initiated the first three-month (November 15, 1958-February 15, 1959) Seminar in Cooperation for sixty participants from Asia and Africa. (It is also for this reason that some subsequent courses contained material on both trade unionism and cooperation.) This international seminar inaugurated Israel's formal instructional program, although many individual visits had preceded the seminar. The seminar in turn was the forerunner of additional courses in the field, and finally of the Afro-Asian Institute for Labor Studies and Cooperation.

Realizing that there can be no mechanical transplantation from one country to another, the purpose of the seminar was to place Israel's experience in cooperative activities at the disposal of people wishing to utilize it. The program consisted of an initial six weeks of classroom lectures and discussions which was followed by three weeks of active participation in three types of cooperative villages, and concluded with two weeks of special study in any type of cooperative which had particular interest for the individual student. Discussion sessions were broadened by contributions from six trainees, who discussed the cooperative movements in their own countries.

Most participants were enthusiastic about the seminar, feeling that this experience with Israel's cooperative movement would help them greatly in their work in their own countries. But like any initial experiment, the seminar had problems, most of which can be summed up under the heading of *diversity*. The sixty participants hailed from seventeen different countries, both English and French-speaking, and thus the seminar had to be conducted in both languages. While this variety of nationalities made for a valuable international experience, it also meant that there was no common level of cultural background among participants; their educational and occupational attainments were extremely diverse. Side by side in the classroom were college graduates and high school dropouts; veterans of cooperative movements and novices who had never been one in action; government officials shared lectures and discussions with trade unionists, teachers, farm representatives and cooperators.

The lecturers and guest speakers were chosen as experts in various areas of cooperative activity in Israel. An undesirable but inevitable corollary was their almost universal ignorance of conditions outside of Israel—a deficiency that was only partially rectified in subsequent seminars. Thus the students were given no help in relating the Israeli experience to African conditions. Most of the participants found the seminar, for survey purposes, much too long, the great number of topics covered in the curriculum deprived the seminar of a focus, and inadequate coordination resulted in considerable overlapping and, at times, conflicts. As a result, participants who had had no previous experience with cooperatives gained little from what was for them too diffuse and superficial a survey, and those whose future plans did not include actual engagement in cooperative work found the seminar's general value dissipated in a multiplicity of details. Trainees and lecturers alike joined in recommending for future seminars a greater concentration on specific subjects centered around two or three major themes, and felt that having fewer teachers would result in a more unified coverage of the subject matter.

Despite its drawbacks, the participants' tremendous eagerness to learn and the Israeli's willingness to show and teach made the seminar a considerable success. One of its important results was to whet the appetites of participating countries for additional training and greater exposure to Israel's cooperative movement. In response to their requests Israel organized further international seminars and courses designed for specific national groups. While certain elements of diversity continued to plague the international gatherings (though to a lesser extent than in the first seminar), groups who came for special courses were of a more uniform composition. These included a study tour by four Guinean labor leaders; two Indian study missions, one of them representing the Boodhan (land gift) movement; and student groups from various parts of Africa. Since 1960 the newly established Afro-Asian Institute for Cooperation and Trade Unionism has taken over the training in cooperation. For the most part its functions are carried out in four-month courses in which both cooperation and trade unionism are taught, although trainees are given some opportunity to specialize in specific subjects.

Was the Israeli cooperative experience, especially in agriculture, considered applicable to African conditions? In the early 1960s it was widely believed that the moshav could be usefully introduced in developing countries, especially in new settlement areas. The moshav combines individual farm ownership with cooperative marketing, financing and certain cultivation activities.

Most African countries had at least some experience with single-purpose cooperative societies, engaged either in credit extension or in marketing a single product. The one distinct advantage of such societies over the multipurpose variety is simplicity. They do not require a complex accounting system to allocate costs to the different activities of the society. Easier to manage, they avoid the bewildering problems that often cause dissension in multipurpose cooperatives. African cooperators were attracted to the moshav because of the numerous advantages they saw in the multipurpose society. Such a cooperative tends to have a larger turnover and lower overhead expenses, and can better afford to engage specialized staff. It has one administrative center, one account per member, and one worker for the accounts. Transport cost is one area in which savings can be effected. Trucks employed in shipping agricultural produce can return to the village with supplies when marketing and supply functions are combined in one cooperative. Also, the individual farmer delivers his crops to one packing center rather than to a different location for each product.

Availability of credit through the society can add markedly to its stability. Disloyalty to the marketing society often results from the need for cash which draws farmers to private dealers. Being well-informed of the farmer's overall financial position, the multipurpose society can provide credit on a basis suited to the farm economy. The farmer's anticipated returns on his crop are more important in assessing his repayment capacity than the amount of land he can put up as collateral. Finally, the multipurpose society, dealing with the peasant's economy as an entity, induces a higher degree of personal involvement in the farmer.

The attainment of multipurpose societies calls for capital, part of which must come from the government, as well as disciplined and somewhat sophisticated farmers. They must have confidence in, and loyalty to the society, and in African countries they often do not. Not the least important is the supply of well-trained cooperative managers. These prerequisites limit the ability of African cooperators to draw on Israel's experience. Although the level of sophistication of some Israeli settlers is often similar to that of the African villager, other conditions are totally different. Israel has an abundance of trained personnel as well as of foreign capital, and its new settlers immediately receive the support of strong central cooperative organizations. Above all, Israel started with a clean slate. Its problem was establishing new settlements, not trying to introduce cooperatives into existing villages, and therefore the settlement authority could aim from the start at multipurpose societies.

In certain Asian countries such as Ceylon and India, a fairly wide network of single-purpose cooperatives already existed and efforts were being made to convert them to multipurpose societies. Although such tasks are usually performed by the villagers themselves, inspiration was often gotten from Israel. On the other hand, most African countries did not appear ripe for the introduction of multipurpose societies in existing villages. The appetite created among African trainees in Israel for the establishment of moshavim had to be satisfied in new settlement areas. Graduates of Israel's courses in cooperation from Tanganyika, Mali, Rwunda, Burundi and perhaps Cyprus, were contemplating the establishment of new moshav-type settlements in their countries. Israel had already dispatched experts to Nigeria, Burma and Brazil to advise on the setting up of moshavim. In most cases settlers were of above average intelligence and education, which gave at least a minimum assurance of success. In western Nigeria new settlements were used to attract school dropouts to the farm, and for demonstration purposes in converting single- to multipurpose societies in old villages. In some experiments, new settlements were built in the context of a regional settlement scheme, patterned after the Lachish region in Israel.[1]

GHANA'S BUILDERS BRIGADE AND YOUNG PIONEERS

Ghana attempted to cope with its youth problems by setting up the Builders Brigade (now Workers Brigade) in 1957. Established originally under British command, the brigade was designed to absorb veterans, school dropouts, and other unemployed, and to prepare them for productive life.

In September of 1959, a high-ranking Ghanaian delegation paid a visit to Israel. Impressed by the accomplishments of the Nahal, the mission recommended that its pattern be adopted by the Builders Brigade. Shortly after the visit, John Tettegah, a member of the delegation, was named commander of the Brigade, and one of his first actions was to invite a team of four Nahal officers to advise and guide his organization. In addition to its head, the team consisted of specialists in education, agriculture and engineering.

Preliminary study revealed to the advisory group that the Brigade's main problem was lack of purpose. It was next to impossible to prepare an effective training program when no one knew what the training was for. The objectives of such a national organization must be determined by the economic planning or other governmental authority. Drawing on their own background and experience, the Israeli advisors proposed the goal of cooperative agricultural settlement, but although the Ghanaians did not accept the proposed objective, they offered no alternative in its place. Lacking a final objective toward which to guide the Brigade, the advisors had to content themselves with intermediate purposes. The program they instituted consisted mainly of work and training in modern agricultural techniques and fighting illiteracy. Training was also offered in various other useful vocations: construction and tractor operation and maintenance, and weaving, embroidery and other crafts for women. All courses were given at a central school, where group leaders were also trained.

Despite the absence of a clear-cut final objective, the Brigade could point to certain impressive achievements. It mobilized technically untrained and partly delinquent individuals, and converted them to disciplined and organized workers' groups, ready for any national task and very proud of their organization. It operated thirty well-administered farms employing modern methods and equipped with heavy machinery for which ample maintenance crews had been trained—its camp at Somaya became one of the show places to which visiting foreign dignitaries were brought. Among its members were people who had received training and experience in essential technical vocations. The Brigade's farms had a strong demonstration effect on surrounding villages and even on neighboring countries. Farmers in the vicinity of the camps attempted to put into practice new methods they had seen there. After seeing the results of the Brigade's work, many West African countries turned to Israel for assistance in youth organization.

PROVISION OF MEDICAL SERVICES

Israel's medical work in Africa ranged from setting up new operational clinics, service in existing medical institutions, to high-level planning and advice. Of all these methods of rendering assistance, the first has proved most effective. It enabled the Israeli expert to establish and function within a new organizational framework. Not bound by longstanding institutional traditions, he could introduce new practices and expect them to outlast his presence. Nothing demonstrates this point better than the case of the Monrovia eye clinic.

At the request of the Liberian government, Professor Michaelson of The Hebrew University conducted a survey of eye diseases in that country. He recommended the setting up in Monrovia of a twenty-bed well-equipped eye clinic with an outpatient department. An Israeli team consisting of two eye specialists and an optician was dispatched to open and run the clinic, and two Liberian nurses came to Israel for work in ophthalmology under Professor Michaelson. Famous all over West Africa, the clinic became a referral institution and performed many cataract and glaucoma operations. Work was well organized, and the staff became accustomed to promptness, night duty, and other practices which might be difficult to introduce in an already existing hospital. The head nurses, upon return from Israel, were performing their supervisory and training functions well, while the Israeli optician trained Liberian assistants to work with her. The team engaged in research in tropical eye diseases at the clinic and at the West African Research Institute for Tropical Medicine, in coordination with a parallel research program at the Hebrew University. This fruitful combination of treatment, teaching and research within a single framework should have a lasting effect after foreign assistance is phased out. It is an outstanding example of technical aid to be duplicated in other countries.

By contrast, five Israeli medical specialists working in Ghana functioned within existing government hospitals at Accra and Kumasi. Although the original plan anticipated that they would raise the professional level of the entire hospital, they were assigned upon arrival to routine medical tasks. Thus they had no authority to modify institutional practices or to raise the level of support of paramedical personnel. Such work is beneficial while it lasts, but it is unlikely to have an enduring impact.

In between these two extreme examples lie a variety of cases in which Israeli specialists were entrusted with the responsibility of introducing organizational and other changes in existing institutions. Israeli physicians directed a hospital in Massawa, Ethiopia; ran a tuberculosis clinic, an obstetric department and a psychiatric hospital in Monrovia; managed a maternity hospital in Freetown, Sierra Leone; and headed various hospital departments in Burma. Most of these doctors were well-qualified and rendered very satisfactory service. But the permanence of their contributions depended upon finding a good local successor—and as often as not such counterparts were not available.

VOCATIONAL TRAINING

Next to agricultural education, the promotion of technical training is a most important need in Africa. While high-level technical advice can usually be secured by employing foreign consultants, any developing nation needs to produce an indigenous core of intermediate-level personnel. In some

European countries technical training takes place in industry through an apprenticeship system. But in Africa, as in Israel, conditions for such training are lacking: well-developed industrial plants, and a tradition under which the interests of education and production are fully harmonized. Israel obtains its technicians from special technical schools at the secondary level; and since most African countries would have to do likewise, they can be helped by the Israeli experience. Its vast network of four-year vocational secondary schools enabled Israel to inaugurate a foreign training program. In so doing the government had the full cooperation of the Organization for Rehabilitation Training (ORT)—an organization devoted to the rehabilitation of Jewish children through vocational training. ORT has been operating training facilities throughout the world for more than eighty years, and has a network of schools in Israel. Of particular importance is ORT's experience in working with children from poor backgrounds, and with accelerated courses for new immigrants.

The center of activity in vocational education for African students in the early 1960s was an ORT technical high school situated near Natania, a medium-sized industrial town about twenty miles north of Tel-Aviv. In 1861, training and lodging facilities for about one hundred pupils were added to the school, and one-year accelerated courses were initiated in metal work, electrical work and carpentry. Altogether, forty-eight students from three English-speaking countries, and twenty-two from four French-speaking countries registered for the first year. Average class size was ten to fifteen pupils, and each class received twelve hours of theoretical instruction and thirty hours of practical training in the school's workshop per week—all taught by the same instructor. Studies were intensive and completely concentrated on the subject. Half of the students were to remain for two years of additional training, after which they could become foremen or instructors at an African trade center. At the same time, seventy new pupils would be accepted. Third-year students were expected to tutor freshmen as part of their training.

In addition to this permanent facility, Israel has sponsored ad hoc courses in a variety of subjects. These include automechanics, telecommunication, radio broadcasting, woodworking, linotype operation and printing, education for the blind, physical education and construction. While the arrangement (at the permanent facility) which kept the instructor continuously with the same class taxed the teacher's endurance to the limit, it also had important advantages. In addition to encouraging an intimate relationship between teacher and student, it assured complete coordination between theoretical and practical phases of the course. As a general rule African students were unaccustomed to abstract thinking, and consequently were better able to learn through practical work than absorption of theoretical material. Having the same teacher for both made it possible to get theoretical points across with the help of continuous demonstrations and observation. It may be questioned whether the training of semiskilled workers abroad can be justified on economic or educational grounds. Is it not more efficient to conduct such education in the trainees' home countries, bringing to Israel only selected graduates for advanced study? This is what was done with a foremen training course in construction. After an inauspicious beginning in Israel, it was shifted to Africa, to train foremen for joint construction companies.

GENERAL OBSERVATIONS ON TECHNICAL ASSISTANCE[2]

Criteria for Evaluating Technical Assistance

Technical assistance concerns the transfer across national boundaries of a most important factor of production: know-how. Despite its importance, and despite voluminous reports written every year on the subject, there is no explicit, universally accepted criterion by which to measure success in this field. Since a general standard by which performance may be evaluated is indispensable in any objective discussion of the issue, this section will formulate two complementary sets of criteria which technical assistance projects should ideally meet. The first set concerns the evaluation of an individual project on its own merits, and may be stated as follows: A successful technical assistance project is one which introduces a new product or brings about improved methods of producing existing products, coupled with attitudinal and/or social change, and where these changes survive the withdrawal of foreign technicians. The social and attitudinal effects of technical assistance are often no less important than its technological aspects, since they determine the viability of technical changes.

These conditions are not sufficient from a national point of view. Even a successful project can result in only a negligible contribution to the national economy if it ranks low in the country's priority list of development efforts. Each individual project should be related to the country's needs; it must never be examined in isolation. The second criterion by which technical assistance must be assessed is the extent to which the individual project is integrated into the country's development plan so as to make the greatest impact on its growth potential.

Broadly speaking, technical assistance consists of two types of activities: the assignment of foreign experts to work in underdeveloped countries in advisory or executive capacity; and the training of indigenous personnel within the country and abroad. The competence of experts and students alike is of absolute importance. A proper selection procedure, reasonable dispatch in formulating assignments, and the provision of a congenial environment in which experts and participants function (including all supporting activities) are necessary conditions for success. But they do not assure success. Neither are they the problems which concern us here. This section is devoted to two general, all-pervasive institutional problems which hamper the effectiveness of technical assistance into the country's development plan. The main source dedicated personnel.

Planning

The proliferation of aid-giving countries and agencies in the technical assistance field makes it difficult for both the aid-giving and aid-receiving countries to set up a well-planned operational framework. On the international level, the United Nations and its eight specialized agencies extend technical assistance to the entire underdeveloped world. On the regional level, organizations such as the Colombo plan in Asia and the Foundation for Technical Cooperation in Africa, South of the Sahara (FAMA) are active in the same field. Finally, a multitude of nations, many of them comparatively small, conduct bilateral programs of their own. There is nowhere a compilation of all the technical assistance projects, although such a list (accompanied by a short description of each project) would be very useful in coordinating the work of all concerned. The Technical Assistance Board of the United Nations could collect and publish such data on an annual or biennial basis, with information obtained for both giver and recipient. A standard functional classification system can be devised to make the list usable for any interested individual or agency. Agencies working in the field often know comparatively little about each other's activities in any one country. Planning and coordination of technical assistance is left to the recipient country. It is usually judged to be uncomprehensive and unsystematic.

An equally pressing and an even more difficult problem is the integration of tehcnical assistance into the country's development plan. The main source of technical advice in comprehensive economic planning is the International Bank Missions. Missions' reports exist now for several countries, but their main focus is investment opportunities rather than technical assistance needs.[3] The same thing can be said of economic planning missions financed by United Nations regional economic commissions and by such private agencies as the Ford Foundation. They are indispensable to the planning of technical assistance, but do not address themselves specifically to that problem. Integration is customarily left in the hands of the aid-receiving country, with the result that all too often technical assistance projects are not an integral part of the country's development plan. The absence of planning frequently results in waste and duplication, and in channeling resources to low priority projects. The cost of such inefficiency is often hidden, at least in the short run. It is extremely difficult to determine what would have been the ranking of certain services, advice or training programs, had a priority scheme been in existence. It is significant that elaborate projects in fields such as medicine or agriculture, costing millions of pounds, are often proposed without a hint at their importance in the country's development plan. The justification presented rests exclusively on the project's own merits, and no consideration is given to its contribution to the country's growth potential.

The most glaring incidents which point up complete disregard of overall priorities are found in foreign training programs. Cases can be cited where groups of up to fifty students from an African country, returned from a lengthy training period abroad (at government expense) and no one knew what to do with them. Participants interviewed during the training period often express uncertainty and anxiety concerning their future employment. Often they return to work in fields other than those for which they were trained.

Individual Projects

We turn now from overall planning to a discussion of the individual project. On the basis of factual observation, involving a close study of scores of projects, an important generalization may be offered: success of a technical assistance project depends on the existence of an independent organizational framework within which the project is pursued. A foreign expert thrown into an existing bureaucratic machinery almost invariably gets caught in a web of red tape, vested interests and traditional ways of approaching problems which militate against the modification of existing practices. It is impossible to bring about the all-important attitudinal or social change. Even in cases of partial success in the technical sphere, the improvements rarely prove to be of a lasting nature, and rarely do they survive withdrawal of the foreign technician. To the contrary, work routines often tend to lapse back into earlier habits and traditions.

The efficacy of foreign training opportunities for indigenous personnel is also subject to important limitations. Even when trainees are well selected, they are not always prepared to absorb knowledge in a foreign environment. Their instructors are usually not familiar with ecological and social conditions prevailing in their countries, and are unable to gear training programs to meet specific needs of the students' countries. Often trainees are unable to translate knowledge acquired under foreign conditions to their home environment. Finally, students tend to be quite low in the bureaucratic echelon so as not to be able to effect change. Frequently they get reabsorbed in the home atmosphere where much of what they had learned is all but forgotten.

In contrast with these cases, examples can be cited where a successful technical assistance project owed much of its success to an independent organizational framework. The Monrovia eye clinic is a case in point. In light of past experience, all or most technical aid should be extended within the framework of projects over which the aid giver has administrative jurisdiction. Training of a large number of foreign students at all levels, and the dispatch of experts abroad to work in isolation should be held to a bare minimum or eliminated altogether (not because they are useless, but because they do not effect change with maximum efficiency). Instead there should be well-conceived projects in high priority areas, which integrate advice, execution and training, each within one independent administrative framework.[4]

NOTES

1. For details see M.E. Kreinin, *Israel and Africa: A Study in Technical Cooperation* (New York: Praeger, 1964) chap. 4.

2. See M.E. Kreinin, "Planning and Continuity: Problems in Technical Assistance," *MSU Business Topics* (Summer 1965).

3. For a concise review of these reports see F.T. Moore, "The World Bank and Its Economic Missions," *Review of Economics and Statistics* (February 1960):81-93.

4. For a specific proposal along these lines see Kreinin, "Planning and Continuity."

7

Ehud Avriel

ISRAEL'S BEGINNINGS
IN AFRICA

With joy one remembers how we in Israel threw ouselves, with verve and boundless enthusiasm, into cooperation with the fledgling movement of emerging African nationalism. The latter half of the fifties was not a period of idealistic optimism regarding the future of our planet and society. The cold war was sobering to hopes entertained during the brief euphoria immediately following the victory over Hitler's Axis. Commercialism had replaced the magnanimous expectations engendered by the new beginning after the darkest interlude in human history; the war-time Alliance had disintegrated; European powers were on the verge of decline; the adjustment to life in the shade of the two giant superpowers was beginning to take its awkward shape.

The sound of cheerful drumming from remote Africa, announcing the stirrings of Nkrumah's national liberation movement and its scattered echoes from other parts of the black continent were the one encouraging message in an otherwise most unimaginative world. Israel was among the first to derive courage from these signs on the firmament: we were looking for kindred souls, people in hope for justice, equality, purposeful social development, unorthodox politics, daring foresight, readiness for sacrifice. We had just received an inkling of these from a different source. David Hacohen, Israel's first ambassador to Burma, had evolved unprecedented schemes for practical cooperation. Rather than content himself with the analysis of political trends in the country in which he represented us, he attempted to dig more deeply. His enthusiasm infected the leadership of The Burmese People's party. Soon Israeli technicians, advisers and experts arrived in faraway Burma to help avoid the repetition of mistakes we had made, just recently, when we began to develop our own country with the new elan that came with independence.

Our first encounter with the new Africa occurred thanks to one of Israel's most stable friends, President Tubman of Liberia. Ambassador Daniel Levin went in 1956 to the president's third inauguration to represent Israel. On the late president's pilgrimage to the American Congress in 1935 (for the resumption of relations) he was shunned by most and scorned by many. Congressman Emanuel Celler was the one person who comforted and encouraged President Tubman in his despair. Ever since Tubman remained a true friend of the Jewish people whom he regarded as equal only to Africans (and blacks in America) in terms of suffering and disdain on the part of the "superior races." At that inauguration Levin met two representatives of the Gold Coast. The Israeli and the Africans spent hours on end telling each other about their respective countries, comparing the underlying philosophies of the Zionist movement and of the Convention People's party, and found that they had much common ground.

In search for new sea routes—in view of the barring of the Suez Canal to Israeli shipping—a representative of the National Shipping Line (Zim) explored the West Coast of Africa at that time for suitable harbors. He found what he had looked for—and more—in Accra. Shalom Klinghofer returned from his search for new outlets for Zim's initiatives with glowing reports about the Convention People's party and their leaders: high-minded, dedicated young men who thought along much the same lines as the Haganah (volunteer defense forces before Israel became a state) and the pioneering movement in Israel.

Ambassador Levine, then in charge of African and Asian affairs in the Foreign Office, added a file inscribed "Gold Coast" to his lean archives and started to look around for an emissary to the newly discovered territory. As independence was still some way off, the first representative of Israel was to be a consul rather than an ambassador. Luckily, Levine was able to obtain the most suitable candidate for the mission into the unknown. Hanan Yavor, a kibbutznik without the protocol air but with devotion to the heritage of the pioneering movement that built Israel and love for exciting adventure. He went to Accra and planted the Israeli flag in the center of what was to be for a number of years the Jerusalem of African nationalism; Kwame Nkrumah's capital city, Accra.

During the winter of 1956-57 the Foreign Relations Department of the Histadrut received a telegram from four African trade unionists, who had attended an Asian trade union conference in Bandung. There they had heard so much invective against Israel that their curiousity was aroused: where there was so much smoke there must be some fire. If, they had argued, Arab countries with no free trade union movement whatsoever, inveighed so aggressively against the one country in their area that had a model trade union movement—they would like to have a look for themselves at the object of Arab tirades. Could they spend a few days as guests of the Histadrut on their way home? Barkatt was delighted and cabled immediate acceptance. They came, led by John Tettegah of the Ghana Trade Union Congress (TUC) and at that time a close aide of Kwame Nkrumah's, and stayed not for a few days but for a few weeks. They were overcome with admiration for the achievements of Israel during the short time that had elapsed since the end of "colonial rule" and overwhelmed by the warmth of their comradely reception. Also they were impressed by the fact that they were not exposed to anti-Arab polemics. Instead of hostile instigation against their nonaligned Arab friends, they were led from one serious discussion about the real problems concerning the social and technological development of their territories to another. As they returned to their respective countries (Ghana, Nigeria, Northern Rhodesia [later Zambia] and Upper Volta), human contacts had been established stronger than any vitriolic Arab incitement against the "Zionist imperialists." (Incidentally, one of the issues that remained unexplained during this crucial encounter, and was to remain a moot point throughout most of the ensuing relationship, was the speed of Israeli development: when we insisted that we had begun to lay the foundations for independent statehood right under the nose of the Mandate we were often judged overmodest or exaggerating unavoidable insignificant initiatives. How, the Africans asked, could you begin to build the infrastructure of your educational system, your agriculture, your industry, and moreover your armed services while foreign power is still all-prevasive. The fact that this attitude was the source of their weakness—as ours was the secret of our relative strength—remained clouded to the end.)

The proclamation of Ghana's independence was welcomed by high tides of warm love from all over the world. Delegations of all sovereign countries and of most underground movements still struggling for their freedom congregated in Accra. The emergence of the first black African state from colonial rule was regarded as a momentous event. The fact that this emergence had become possible by mutual consent and compromise between the British and the Ghanaians augured well for future relations. It was generally assumed though, that for quite a while Ghana would be alone. No other British colony and certainly no French dependency would soon follow the path of Ghana to independence.

At the end of the Ghanaian festivities, the Israeli delegation had a private audience with Kwame Nkrumah. He presented them (David Hacohen with his Burmese experience was a member) with exactly the same list of urgent requirements he expected from the older states: a shipping line to transport the countries' exports, mainly cocoa, to overseas markets, advice on modernization of agriculture, technical assistance in the production of import replacements, schools, frameworks for the mobilization of youth in the service of the new state's development.

Under Golda Meir's energetic leadership, the Israeli Foreign Office vastly expanded its technical assistance program that had just been installed. Ambassador Aharon Remez was given the task of coordinating Israeli government agencies, public and private entrepreneurs, universities, the Histadrut, the kibbutz movement and the Israeli Army in an effort to meet Ghana's demands.

Less than one year after Ghana's proclamation of independence, Israel had already installed an embassy in Accra. Before the first year was out, every single requirement on Nkrumah's list had become a subject for intensive cooperation between Ghana and Israel. We provided the top men. We received first-rate Ghanaians to understudy and serve as second-in-command to prepare to take over as soon as possible from our specialists. Ghana, still in possession of vast foreign exchange reserves, provided most of the capital necessary. Over two hundred Israelis were busy on the many schemes. As a matter of policy we very seldom seconded personnel to existing departments, in Ghana, and later, as cooperation expanded, in other African countries. We preferred to assist in the creation of new enterprises or new departments of public administration, better suited to the requirements of an independent state than the carry-overs of colonial structures.

India and Israel were at that early stage the countries closest to Nkrumah's mind. He venerated Nehru's continuous neutralism, antiimperialism and nationalistic pride that offered no favors to the technologically more advanced white nations. He admired Israel's tenacity in the face of widespread hostility, its military prowess in the face of more numerous and more heavily equipped, long-established armies, its success in "making the desert bloom" through hard work and the application of unorthodox technical and social devices. Nkrumah shrewdly calculated that his acceptance of our enthusiastically and massively offered aid would have to constitute sufficient reward for a people accustomed to dwell in solitude and unpampered by the support of likeminded power blocs.

It was in this spirit that major strides forward were made in our cooperation with Ghana during the initial period of our friendship. The Black Star Line—the first African shipping line ever—was founded on only a fraction of the investment deemed necessary by older (and more self-centered) seafarers than has Israel; a nautical college was installed to provide officers and engineers for the merchant navy when we discovered, to our consternation, that black Africans had been kept down to the level of unskilled deckhands. Chicken farming was most successfully introduced with negligible capital investment to overcome the trauma left along the West African coast by a grandiose but wholly inexpert scheme the British had tried out and which had left behind the myth that eggs cannot be produced in the tropics and that the few eggs necessary—only whites would need them anyway—would be forever imported from Northern Europe. Alumni of the Israeli pioneering movement, the kibbutz and the paramilitary defense-cum-settlement movement Nahal arrived in Ghana to instil patriotic dedication into the members of the Youth Brigade, established to take unemployed youngsters from idleness to productivity.

These and many other programs deepened the relationship between Israel and Africa's first decolonized model country. A major breakthrough into wider expanses was to occur on this background during the All-African-People's Conference, held in Accra in December 1958. This meeting of the movements of national liberation from all over Africa could have easily been overshadowed by extremist Arab incitement against recognition and cooperation with Israel. The competition between Nasser and Nkrumah for leadership of the oppressed was fierce. While Nasser had the necessary funds and ambition, Nkrumah knew well how to use his kinship and the uniqueness of his constitutional achievement in making Ghana the African symbol of decolonization.

Golda Meir was on a state visit to Ghana just as the conference convened and Accra abounded with resistance fighters from all corners of the continent. George Padmore, venerated father of Pan-Africanism, suggested that Nkrumah's guest, the foreign minister of Israel, meet in special session with the participants of his revolutionary gathering. With the president's blessing Golda Meir entered a conference hall containing mostly people who had little—or utterly negative—information about Israel. George Padmore acted as host and moderator. Mrs. Meir, in her outspoken simplicity, repelled the attack of Algeria, orchestrated by the immensely popular Algerian delegates. As they remonstrated against Israel's involvement with France (still our "friend and ally"), Mrs. Meir patiently and convincingly explained Israel's true philosophy to an increasingly interested and warmly affected audience. Padmore's affirmation of the Israeli position elevated her statements to a level beyond any possible doubt. Within that afternoon Israel had sown the seeds of future attachments with otherwise completely unattainable personalities. The pessimistic timetables of the leaders of decolonization were soon to be overturned by De Gaulle's ruse and by Britain's sudden awareness of "the winds of change." Within less than one year the subversive ringleaders who had congregated at Accra to prepare for a long-drawn struggle found themselves in positions of acknowledged legitimacy as heads of states. Many of those present who had listened to Mrs. Meir's talk, gladly grasped the hand of Israel profferred to initiate cooperation on the Ghana model.

When the lights went out in one Israeli embassy in Africa after another, many an Israeli was deeply saddened. Not only those who had actively participated in our cooperative effort; not only the diplomats and commentators whose business is the analysis of political events. The severance of diplomatic relations was—when it came right during the Yom Kippur war—a heavy blow: we felt abandoned by countries we had helped in their own hour of need and rejected by people for whom we felt great warmth.

The African decision to break relations with Israel is partly the result of the self-imposed law of unanimity that prevails at the Organization for African Unity: the Arabs of Northern Africa, shedding all pretense, forced the Middle Eastern conflict upon a forum designed mainly for the purpose of dealing with problems more directly pertinent to Africa's own survival in a troubled world.

Israel has no regrets concerning its role in the emergence of African independence. If we were privileged to add even the tiniest particle to the liberation of oppressed Africans and to the amelioration of their cruel living conditions, we shall always regard ourselves vastly rewarded for whatever efforts we may have invested in a great human enterprise.

8

Akiva Eger

HISTADRUT: PIONEER AND PILOT PLANT FOR ISRAEL'S INTERNATIONAL COOPERATION WITH THE THIRD WORLD

It is not astonishing, in light of the situation and necessities of the Third World and of the unique role of Histadrut in national development, that the latter attracted growing interest by the countries in development and especially of its labor and cooperative organizations.

Histadrut's structure and particularly its workers' villages were of specific significance in this process. It was only natural that the first attempts at courses and seminars, and later advisers and experts sent to a growing number of countries were organized by Histadrut. To a very large extent Histadrut was a pioneer and pilot plant for Israel's relations and practical cooperation with the Third World.

The activities of Israel in this field, mainly organized by the Department for International Cooperation of the Ministry of Foreign Affairs, established in 1960, followed the initiatives of Histadrut. The activities of Israel have greatly increased and intensified, mainly through the channels of various specialized frameworks dealing with agriculture, elementary and higher education, scientific research, youth, health, public administration, vocational training and development agencies. But even now, ten years after, the absolute share of Histadrut in these activities is considerable and of high specific value. Israel's program for technical assistance to needy countries cannot be imagined today without this mighty and specific contribution of

Histadrut, as Israel is difficult to be imagined without this its greatest voluntary organization of the working people and its contribution to the foundations and the development of the emerging state.

In 1950, early contacts with the Burmese delegation at the International Trade Union Congress in Belgrade led to its visit to Israel as guests of Histadrut which impressed them as the main bearer of socialist realisations in the emerging young state. A couple of years later these first contacts, initiated by Reuven Barkatt, then responsible for the International Relations Department of Histradrut and a leading figure of the Israeli Labor Party, Mapai, were followed by larger and deeper discussions during the Asian Socialist Conference in Rangoon, where Moshe Sharett, then Minister of Foreign Affairs of Israel and a central personality of Mapai, arrived at the exchange of ambassadors between the two countries. With the appointment of David Hacohen as Israel's first ambassador in Burma and in Asia at large, technical cooperation started with the Asian continent, first with Burma and later with Ceylon, Thailand and the Phillippines. Almost all cooperation was in the fields in which Histadrut took a most active part: joint construction company with Solel Boneh, Histadrut's building firm; management of Burma's Five Stars Line shipping company by ZIM, Israel's shipping line, in which Histadrut had its considerable share; an ex-soldiers' agricultural resettlement program; a variety of experts in the agricultural, medical and industrial fields, almost all from Histadrut's enterprises and institutions.

In Africa, relations developed somewhat later. After the establishment of contacts in Liberia in the early fifties by the Israeli representative Hanan Yavor, a member of Kibbutz Kfar Hamakkabi who had fulfilled many Histadrut missions abroad before, more intensive and comprehensive relations developed with Ghana. Here, like in Burma, joint enterprises were established with Solel Boneh (Ghana National Construction Company), with Zim (Black Star Shipping Line), and more projects followed in agricultural cooperation, technological training and in youth organization—from Liberia and Ghana relations developed with Tanganyika, Nigeria and Kenya. In these developments Ehud Avriel, Israel's first ambassador to Ghana, member of Kibbutz Neot Mordehai, played a dominant role. After the visit of John Tettegah, the general secretary of Ghana's Trade Union Council, and with the assistance of three successive Histadrut advisors, Ghana's Trade Union Organization was remodeled from the British TUC type to one similar to that of Histadrut in structure and aims, on industrial lines and by combining educational and economic activities with those of wage-earner's organization. This development had great impact on other African countries whose labor organizations were searching for new and genuine ways to tackle the many problems they were facing with political independence of their emerging states. Unfortunately, the centralized organization of Ghana's TUC was subsequently used by the Nkrumah regime as an efficient arm of government policy and no real free and voluntary organization of the workers in Ghana was ever established under his government.

While Histadrut's relations with Burma and Ghana grew and radiated to other countries in both continents, a steadily increasing stream of interested visitors came to Israel to observe the unique synthesis of trade unionism and labor economy within Histadrut and to understand its leading role in building the national economy and society of a young state. Of specific interest were the cooperative and collective villages of Israeli workers—the kibbutz, the moshav and the moshav shitufi. These visitors from many countries found that in a small and democratic country like Israel the development process could be easily observed: the process of national integration of "tribe," the transformation of nonworking people into productive workers, of urban elements into rural population of efficient farmers, the conquest of the desert by cooperative land cultivation and settlement—and all these under the guidance and with the ideological and economic initiatives of Histadrut. Israel and Histadrut became in their eyes a living laboratory of socioeconomic experiences in development. And to share these experiences in order to find out their own ways of development was the explicit desire of the trade union and cooperative leaders who were the guests of Histadrut in the second half of the fifties. This situation led to the initiative of Reuven Barkatt to call for an open Afro-Asian seminar on cooperation to take place between November 1958 and February 1959. This seminar became the pilot project of Histadrut in all its relations with the Third World. By many it is considered as the main cornerstone of all future initiatives of Israel in the field of international technical cooperation.

The seminar was based on an open invitation to trade union and cooperative movements as well as to a number of governments of already independent nations or to national liberation movements. This seminar was the prelude to a growing number of similar seminars which followed as a result of the first one's relative success. About a dozen other seminars on cooperation and labor problems in emerging countries took place during the following two years. Outstanding among these were the six-month course for the Bhoodan Movement in India, a special seminar for cooperative members from Guinea, two courses on rural cooperation for French-speaking Africa and a special large seminar for East African trade unionists and cooperative members. This led Histadrut, under the initiative of its secretary general Pinhas Lavon, to the idea of the establishment of a permanent institute which could operate these seminar activities on a national and planned basis. Encouragement to this initiative came from other labor organizations, especially from the AFL-CIO which granted a number of scholarships to permit qualifying candidates from Asian and African trade unions and cooperative movements to take part in the first courses of the Institute.

The Afro-Asian Institute was not established suddenly with a preconceived program, but gradually and organically came into being, by trial and error. The main objectives of the study-program were:

1. To explain that development was not only an economic problem and challenge, but had to be planned and undertaken on a comprehensive basis and under the assumption that the human individual, itself aim and target of every development, was the decisive element in moving towards higher levels of development. This meant that any planning of development must integrate health and hygiene, nutrition and baby care, family planning and housekeeping; education for all ages and on all levels, with particular accent on girls and women, workers' education and in all with particular accent on rural areas; application and adaptation of modern science and technological progress to local, regional and national levels; special efforts for more efficient and accelerated integration of women into the social progress.

2. To clarify that cooperation as a structure and method could be an excellent efficient and less expensive instrument for development while training manpower for management and qualified labor, because of the applied principle of organized mutual aid; would need relatively less investment per capita and lower general running expenses of enterprises, like any other large-scale undertaking; finally, it would guarantee application of modern methods, machinery and agro-mechanics, i.e. make modernization possible even for the poor equipped with a minimum of means in finances and of production.

3. To give evidence that the challenges of organized labor in the underdeveloped countries could not be limited to trade unionism and its necessarily vindicating character, as only a very small percentage of the working people is composed of wage earners while the bulk is self-employed in its own tiny farms. The social and economic involvement of labor organized in trade unions and its initiatives as regards this rural population is concerned, becomes imperative if they want to play a vital role in national development. That they could do so while building a labor economy, foremost in rural areas, is an historical opportunity and challenge of utmost value and practical importance.

In all these three points of study, Israel is serving as a living laboratory as it has gone and is still going through similar processes. To acquire more courage and self-confidence in tackling their own problems, paving their own way to development, to show that man can overcome the most gigantic obstacles if he is building in the right spirit—this is the main aim of the institute's study-program. Not only successes are shown and explained in Israel but the story of failures and shortcomings as well.

Since Histadrut started its activities in assisting to train labor leadership for countries of the Third World, more than two thousand graduates have gone through the Afro-Asian Institute and its forerunners. Almost one thousand more participated in eighteen courses held in Asia and Africa on request of organizations in which graduates of the Institute were active and responsible officers. For these courses initiatives are coming increasingly from international trade secretariats and other organizations interested in cooperating with the Institute.

The fact that the Institute is an independent educational institution, not supported or subventioned by government, but by Histadrut which does not interfere in its practical work while animating its basic approaches and dynamics, serves as a great advantage in dealing freely with labor, cooperative and government institutions and organizations, without any strings and in full freedom of decision and action.

JOINT ENTERPRISES

Most Israeli joint economic ventures with countries of the Third World were undertaken by the public sector. Here Histadrut's share was overwhelming. Solel Boneh, Histadrut's construction and building enterprise went into joint ventures with Ghana, Burma, Nigeria, Sierra Leone, Nigeria and Nepal. Among the projects were: parliament buildings in Sierra Leone and Nigeria; international airports in Accra and Katmandu; first-class hotels in Sierra Leone, Nigeria, Tanzania and Kenya; university buildings in Nigeria and Nepal; roads and bridges in Nigeria, Nepal and Turkey; and military installations in the Ivory Coast.

The Mekorot Water Resources Development Ltd. (Vered) went into joint undertakings in Western Nigeria, Iran, Ivory Coast, Peru, Honduras, Sierra Leone and a number of other countries. ZIM, in which Histadrut is a joint partner to a lesser extent than in Mekorot, established joint companies in Ghana (Black Star Line) and Burma (Five Stars Line). There were other projects in Tanzania (cooperative wholesale and consumer stores—Cossata, Amiran) and in Kenya (consumer cooperative), whose success was much less convincing.

On the whole, the joint enterprises contributed very much to give substance to Histadrut's relations with the countries to be developed. They were of mutual benefit, gave managerial, technical and vocational training to the African, Asian or Latin American partners, larger fields of activity to many Israelis to enrich and improve their experiences. The terms of agreements and contracts of these enterprises provided a majority of capital in the hands of Israel's partners, possibility to renounce the contract from their end before the period of contract was over, and systematic training of local personnel on the spot and/or in Israel in order to enable it to take over the Israeli part of the joint enterprise as soon as possible. This became the general pattern of all Israel's joint enterprises in the Third World.

By 1970, of all joint companies only one or two were left, all others transferred already into the exclusive management of the young states' enterprises. Solel Boneh and Mekorot-Vered continue to carry out a considerable number of projects in these countries, but as contractors and not in form of joint enterprises. Egged, Histadrut's passenger and goods transport cooperative, contributed to the development of an Ethiopian bus cooperative and some of its managers served as consultants in various South American countries. There was trial and error in this field, but no doubt in retrospect, the joint enterprises were an important contribution to development as well as to the relations of Histradrut with Third World countries.

The specific contribution of Histadrut within the international efforts of assistance to the Third World consists in the fact that a progressive labor organization of a developing country, meeting many problems similar to those experienced by others in Africa, Asia and Latin America, is sharing its experiences and lending its energies to learn together how to improve conditions to start and to accelerate development of underdeveloped areas and societies. The human and material laboratory of Israel's society and economy is an excellent ground for comparative studies, and from these living fields of practical experiences come those who are in a mental and technical position to cooperate in the efforts of others to overcome their difficulties and obstacles.

Israel has developed over the last decade a vast variety of activities on behalf of the Third World, mainly as coordinator of frameworks competent for the specific fields, but also as an initiator of new ideas and projects. Histadrut, in all its activities in this field, has contributed its own genuine efforts and will continue to do so, without losing its identity and peculiarity while concentrating on cooperative and labor projects, training and activities.

The very essence and aim of development is the fuller evolution of man everywhere and under all conditions, the growing equality between men, societies, economies and nations. True development efforts, as those of Histadrut, are therefore peace-building factors. Histadrut's intentions are to assist in the process of nation building of other peoples who ask for this cooperation. This is also the central task of Histadrut in Israel.

There is little doubt that here lies the main importance of Histadrut's international activities. The stronger and more effective Histadrut's impact on nation-building processes abroad, lending them a progressive social character, the more imposing will become those tendencies working for social and international peace in this tortured world. As far as Israel's position between three continents is concerned, surrounded by hostile regimes, any progress in this direction will increase chances for peace building with its neighbors, even if the road to final pacification of the region may be extremely difficult and hard to follow.

9

Samuel Decalo

AFRO-ISRAELI TECHNICAL COOPERATION: PATTERNS OF SETBACKS AND SUCCESSES

Few events in the field of international cooperation stirred as much attention and interest as the rapid escalation in Afro-Israeli technical cooperation in the late 1950s and early 1960s. From very modest roots and origins, mutual contacts and exchange of personnel and cadres mushroomed into what *Newsweek* somewhat exaggeratedly called "one of the strangest unofficial alliances in the world."[1] By 1963 the Israeli aid program had become an established fact in over a dozen African states, and hundreds of experts had been dispatched on a variety of consultative or developmental missions. Streaming in the reverse direction came thousands of Africans preparing to undertake training in Israel in a multitude of technical and cooperative fields. Israel's isolation in the world arena, vividly felt even before the 1956 war, appeared to have been irrevocably shattered. Its importance as a major laboratory for socioeconomic experimentation had finally been fully recognized as further underscored by the procession of foreign dignitaries and heads of state that made a visit to Jerusalem a sine qua non of their international itineraries.[2]

Israel's involvement with Africa sparked a deluge of articles in the scholarly and popular press, in Europe as well as in the United States. Israel had always shared the distinction, together with only a handful of other countries, of being a "newsworthy" country; its entry into Africa (and the Third World in general) only heightened editorial interest and the proclivities of writers and scholars.[3] Yet by the late 1960s the outpouring dried to a trickle, and the main sources of data on Afro-Israeli cooperation were reduced to specialized research bulletins.

There are several reasons for this dramatic decline in world interest in the Israeli effort in Africa. For one, the novelty had rapidly worn off, consequent to its early "overexposure." Israeli aid—crucial and dominant as it may have been in the early hectic days following Africa's independence[4]— began to tell its qualitative limitations as other assistance programs that took longer to set up began to overshadow what has always been a modest Israeli presence in the continent, and a financially limited assistance program.[5] More important was the growing gap between excessively heightened expectations of achievement of unrealistic goals with Israeli aid and the cruel reality of the resilience of poverty and the traditional socioeconomic order to anything short of sustained and comprehensive developmental assaults spearheaded by sincere and dedicated political elites commanding adequate financial and technical resources. In the absence of such dedication and resources in most African states, perception of the chasm between aspirations and realities became poignantly clear, accompanied by the belated realization that the Israeli effort in Africa, with all its dedication and ingenious developmental models and approaches was not the overnight panacea that many in Africa and Israel had so ardently sought. The problems of transferring cross-culturally to traditional, status quo oriented extended family societies in tropical Africa, techniques for rapid socioeconomic change developed in other sociocultural settings, was immensely more complicated than originally assumed, especially when African political hierarchies themselves were not often prepared to accept the burdens of a sustained drive in that direction.

Afro-Israeli cooperation in certain domains proceeded very smoothly and resulted in a variety of striking achievements of considerable value to the modernization and developmental aspirations of African states, negating prophecies of perpetual stagnation of these societies. In a sense the composite picture that emerges of fifteen years of Afro-Israeli cooperation is an intricate mosaic of advances and reverses, successes in some fields and setbacks in others, with attempts to adjust projects to better accomodate the lessons of past experience and the demands of a differently perceived reality. The multitude of Afro-Israeli programs of cooperation have been discussed at great length elsewhere:[6] the purpose of this article is to pinpoint several generic causes of success and failure.

PROGRAMS OF SOCIAL DEVELOPMENT AND THE AFRICAN CONTEXT

When attempting to evaluate Israel's technical assistance to Africa it is useful to distinguish for analytic purposes between programs aiming at social and agrarian development and those oriented at the importation of strictly technical skills and the creation of services and economic infrastructures. The distinction is somewhat arbitrary and superficial, and the boundary lines between the two are frequently blurred. Many programs mesh social development and the implantation of new skills and techniques. Yet the distinction is nevertheless crucial for any understanding of the nature of problems facing Israeli programs of social change in Africa. Programs of this nature are implicitly or explicitly aiming at a transformation of the social ethos, reorganizing social patterns of interaction, modernizing life-styles and reshaping perceptions of the world and the role of the self within it. Cultural change and psychological shifts in perceptions and attitudes are the bedrock of such programs. It is change of this kind which leads eventually to meaningful systemic change, and is an inevitable process on the road to economic takeoff. By the same token programs in this area will face the greatest difficulties and the stubborn resistance of ingrained and still largely functional traditional values to the trumpets heralding the appearance of the new order. Herein lies the first cluster of factors which interacts with the various Israeli programs in Africa.

A second set of considerations that has to be taken into account, both in planning programs and in their evaluation, is the economic and political background of recipient countries. The two most important factors here are the political and economic fragility of many African states, which may lead to hasty erection of programs with ambitious goals that are doomed in advance to remain empty shells, testimonials to good intentions but empty state coffers. The success or failure of a program frequently depends on whether the two partners in the venture have similar or different intentions regarding use of the final product. For example, various African varieties of the Nahal concept are often viewed by African elites as supplementary sources of political support for their shaky thrones, and as ideal forms of patronage, rather than as nation-building structures and agents for social and agrarian change. Joint commercial ventures and state farms, where profitability (or at least nonwastage of resources) is an important consideration, may turn into dumping grounds for political appointees leading to overstaffing and economic loss.[7]

THE TRADITIONAL SETTING

A large number of Israel's programs in Africa have to do with social development. Agrarian reorganization and resettlement (along whatever lines) aims not only at implanting new administrative and agricultural skills, but at the creation of upwardly mobile, individualistic and profit-inclined attitudes in the economic sphere, within boundaries of mutual cooperation. Model and state farms aim at creating a tangible visible example of what can be achieved with the right implements, fertilizers and seeds; through the spillover (or multiplier) effect other neighboring farmers, it is assumed, will attempt a replication of these new agricultural procedures—obviously, on a more modest scale—leading to a transformation of the agrarian sector. Finally, Nahal programs aim at eradication of tribalism, the inculcation of civic consciousness, new modern values and a zest for manual labor preparatory to resettlement on the land.

The cultural background of these bold experiments is hostile to rapid change. Even assuming successful completion of a training and resettlement project, new pioneers are both part of and at the mercy of the traditional host culture which surrounds them. Pierre Alexandre, former French Colonial Service administrator and distinguished scholar, vividly described traditional African society and values when he wrote:

> Seen from the angle of the individual's relationship with the group these societies were ... *collectivist, status-bound* and *absolutely functional*. Their collectivism ... embraces every activity of the individual including the physical life. It can even be said that there was, strictly speaking, no individual behavior or action but only fractional aspects of the collective life of the group. Moreover, any member who tended towards individualism should theoretically become divorced from the group and be outlawed as a social outcast. The individual, in order to remain integrated into the group had to conform. Nonconformism was to be condemned since, as has been seen, any questioning of the social order compromised the whole order of the cosmos.... The development of each individual's existence depended then, not so much on his own intrinsic qualities or his personal or individual peculiarities as on external factors which had little to do with his own efforts and which determined his *status*: sex, filiation, rank in the order of births, etc.[8]

These parameters are still very much part and parcel of the social context of much of Africa. There is wide variation, as in areas with a history of prolonged contact with European and modern influences (coastal regions), where traditional values have been partly broken down consequent to decades of sustained socioeconomic development (Ivory Coast, Gabon and parts of Kenya and Ghana) or in areas where traditional hierarchy was not so powerful to start with (as in Southern Nigeria and especially among the Ibo). Yet even in these areas ethnic exclusiveness (or tribalism) may still be high for it is now becoming evident that there is no necessary unilinear correlation between modernity and the growth of intertribal linkages.[9]

The practical implications of the traditional and tribal nature of African society for programs of social change such as Israel's are obvious. In

Dahomey, Togo and Ivory Coast, to cite but three instances, agrarian resettlement and Nahal-type projects have had to abandon a former sine qua non—the fusion of different tribal elements into cohesive "national" groups. The nation-building aspects of the Nahal concept, so much an integral and core part of the rationale of these programs and the raison d'être of their implantation in Africa, proved totally unmanageable within the context of acute regionalism and historic tribal animosities and suspicions—even when the subjects were, as at the outset, urban unemployed "transitionals" and not rural elements.[10] Continuous tension, friction and overt hostility among opposing tribal elements not only broke discipline and prevented the growth of national consciousness, but also contributed to high levels of desertion from the formations (up to 60 percent). In like manner tribal tensions were marked also in the training of the Ivory Coast's women's auxiliary corps in Bouake by officers of Israel's Chen (women's army), and in Sierra Leone where Mende-Temne friction was intense. With the shift from recruitment of disparate tribal elements to training and resettlement of socially and ethnically cohesive units in their own regions (again, a major deviation from original plans for national integration that called for the interspersing of such units all over the country), a reduction of this form of friction was accomplished though desertion still remained high.

The basic values of African traditional life have similarly created obstacles to programs of socioeconomic change. As Alexandre has noted, an individual's social status is largely determined by factors outside his immediate control; attempts at social and economic amelioration through individual efforts and new techniques (unless one moves to urban areas) may lead to ostracism of the individual concerned and his entire kinship group. In light of the importance to Africans in the traditional sector of their ties to their extended family—without which one has little influence or social status in a village community—Israeli-trained farmers returning to their native villages have often shied away from actions that might bring upon their heads the wrath of village elders and the social pressures of their kinfolk. Coexistence is often difficult (though this is slowly changing) between a traditional ethos that stresses egalitarianism in consumption and wealth, subordination of certain activities to dictates of ritual, and immemorial tradition and age as criteria for wisdom or status—and young farmers with new concepts and methods and an ethic that does not subordinate the product of their extra labor and knowledge to the aggregate needs of the village. Since the elders are not only the repository of accumulated wisdom but also the link between the ever-watchful lineage ancestors and their offspring, both living and yet unborn, acts of insubordination are seen as directly threatening the dependency linkages between the dead, the living and the yet unborn, with dire results for all. Quite apart from the social tensions inherent in a situation where the elders are not given their customary deference nor are they any longer the prime repositories of wealth or knowledge, pressures from relatives of newly trained farmers for a distribution of their increased crops can rend villages asunder.[11] The social security framework of traditional society cannot tolerate individuals who wish to partake of its psychological comforts without subordinating to its socioeconomic dictates.[12]

It is consequent to the factors noted above that resettlement of farmers trained in Nahal units or in other institutional frameworks has been marked by difficulties experienced in their native villages. Even resettlement a mile or two away may cause tensions and strife in social relationships as it has on several occasions in Dahomey and Ghana. This problem was so acute in Upper Volta that newly trained farmers have occasionally been allocated land in areas far away from their native villages. While this may appear as one possible way to break the social obligations expected of more successful farmers by their village kinsfolk, the psychological deprivation many of the former feel may lead to the collapse of the new settlement as new settlers drift back to their native villages forsaking their newly gained knowledge that had poisoned their social relations. This approach is only feasible in a few countries such as Upper Volta, where poor soil conditions, soil erosion, population pressure, pest invasions and frequent droughts have traditionally forced groups of villagers to found new settlements away from their native villages, or to migrate to the Ivory Coast in search of salaried work.[13]

It is also important to examine the motivations of those who are recruited into new agricultural programs. The Nahal-type formations, which existed in over twenty states in Africa alone, were originally aimed at soaking up unemployed youth in urban areas (where a 25-30 percent unemployed rate is common) recently arrived from the countryside.[14] Many of the original operative guidelines of these structures were not overly successful due to high desertion rates and lack of motivation or inclination for manual and agricultural labor on the part of urban recruits who were not suitable for cooperative work.[15] These youths had after all moved away from rural areas in order to escape both the social oppressiveness of traditional life and the drudgery of agricultural work. Inculcation of the zeal for manual work in Israel was a very unique process with strong emotional and ideological overtones which were already in existence as part of the country's political culture. The effort to acculturate African urban youth with this mystique in the absence of the sustaining cultural values that existed in Israel often resulted in failure. Even African governments trying to impose upon high school or university students a one or two-year period of national service in the countryside (not necessarily manual work) have faced virtual revolts from this segment of society which is for all practical purposes the future elite of the country.[16] After the largely unsatisfactory conclusion of several agricultural training programs, new directives were issued in many African countries to start recruiting uneducated, rural youth, and a certain improvement in the attrition rate was clearly visible. Even now, however, a significant percentage of ex-trainees, as in the Ivory Coast, for example, where many flatly refuse to join their villages, promptly move to urban areas with their newly acquired agricultural expertise. As one Israeli official in Abidjan noted, completion of a course of instruction in agricultural training camps is viewed by some recruits as an educational qualification—incongruous as it may be—for clerical work in the cities.[17]

POLITICAL AND ECONOMIC SETTING

The previous considerations which so obviously affect the nature and success of Israeli programs of social and agrarian development in Africa are rooted in the cultural milieu of African states. The economic and political background of these programs also affect their operation and chances of success.

The most important aspect of the economic setting is the scarcity of budgetary and developmental resources in most African states. This leads among other things to the erection of programs without any hope of successful completion due to financial considerations. In general Israeli experts in the field have been able to cope with this problem through improvisation, which has given the programs an added distinction and attraction. Occasionally, this is impossible, as when the Tadzewu cattle ranch was set up in Ghana in 1962 with an anticipated investment budget of $490,000 for superior cattle from Mali and machinery from Europe. Ghana's shortage of foreign funds delayed the project, which eventually commenced its activities with cannibalized machinery from various state farms and one-tenth of its anticipated herd of two thousand, largely inferior stock hastily culled from other Ghanaian sources. This inauspicious beginning together with political interference, immeasurable bureaucratic haggling between various Ghanaian ministries, lack of accounting and established administrative procedures, created a variety of problems to an inherently sound and eminently feasible project.

Shortage of funds, despite Israeli estimates which has been approved in advance, caused a temporary stalemate in the program to establish a Nahal-type formation in the Central African Republic (called Jeunesse Pionnière Nationale—JPN) in 1962. Criticism and opposition to it rapidly built up in the National Assembly consequent to the fact that the JPN had been allocated a modest budget, yet still larger than that of several ministries including the presidency itself.[18] Largely consequent to President Dacko's excellent relations with Israel, and the latter's interest in maintaining its presence in the Central African Republic, relevant treaties were renegotiated with Israel assuming a larger share of the financial burden. Similar parliamentary opposition arose in West Nigeria over the regional government's plan to allocate funds for the erection of five farm institutes to train school leavers who would be resettled with government loans of approximately six thousand dollars per family. Chief Akin Deko envisaged that through the spillover effect levels of productivity throughout the region would rise; the opposition argued that few farmers would be able to amass the financial resources needed to emulate the trainees, and that in terms of cost-benefits the program was totally irresponsible.[19] As an example of the relatively large cost of providing for a rural resettlement program one can note that Ivory Coast's two new villages set up in 1965 consumed over 55 percent of the entire budget of the Community Service. In like manner the Gadna-type Jeunesse et Travail program in Ivory Coast was greatly hampered by a low budget and a very high ratio of recruits per instructor (1 to 260)—both of which prevented the fulfillment of even an approximation of the program's goals.

A number of other projects in Africa have suffered either through criticism of their (relative) cost or more frequently consequent to financial overextension of African governments. This has inevitably delayed or truncated programs with adverse effects on productivity (in the case of State Farms, as in Ghana, where profitability was important), emulation effect (in the case of Model Farms, as in Upper Volta, Dahomey, the Central African Republic) and recruits (in the case of Nahal or cooperative projects in many countries). Budgetary limitations in Dahomey, for example, has meant that the central Service Civique training camp at Ouassa (near Bohicon) accommodated trainees in dilapidated dormitories with straw mats on the floor and few other facilities, while food and operating funds arrived very irregularly. On a few occasions when conditions were especially bad, trainees have had to fend for themselves, many deserting for good. And this in a program administered by the Dahomean army (the Service Civique was set up as a separate branch in 1971 under a senior officer) with which both the Israeli Embassy and the Israeli Military Training Mission had the best possible relations (at least until the 1972 coup). These harsh financial conditions have existed to some extent in the civil service as well; assembling the monetary outlay and meeting the deadline of each payday has been a never-ending part of the harrowing nightmares of most officials in the Finance Ministry. Its effect upon the Service Civique was an important contributing factor to the heavy desertion rate of recruits whose numbers have tended to drop from a high of two hundred at the outset of the nine-month course to a graduating class of approximately sixty. Training was frequently disrupted when recruits simply melted into the bush for various periods of time whenever their help was needed in their own native villages.[20]

Financial problems plagued the creation of the Central African Republic Nahal program and they continued even after the program was officially set up. The budget stipulated a monthly outlay per recruit of CFA Fr4500 ($16.66) of which $2.00 per month constituted pocket money. Delays in the transmission of these finds caused heavy resentment among recruits who had been asked to volunteer for the nation-building effort. In Tanzania poor preplanning and lack of resources prevented the deployment and resettlement in 1965 of national service units, despite the significant outlay of funds and efforts in creating and training them.[21] Such programs have also suffered from interministerial haggling over responsibilities and budgets, lack of accounting and bookkeeping procedures, red tape, overstaffing consequent to political appointments, overt attempts to transform them into personal political and patronage machines, and even an occasional embezzlement of funds.[22] The degree to which programs have been affected negatively has depended upon the extent of interference and the firmness, tact and improvisational abilities of Israeli experts in the host country. One of the best known examples of political penetration and interference occurred in the case of Ghana's Workers' Brigades. These, which in their heyday included over fifteen thousand Ghanaians, chaotically organized for poorly defined and continuously shifting developmental tasks,[23] served functionally as a patronage machine for the Nkrumah regime. With unemployment in most cities fluctuating between 25 and 30 percent, the removal off the streets of restless young elements and their integration into formations which at least provide for their sustenance becomes an action of considerable political importance.

In like manner the former Tanzanian minister, Oscar Kambona, attempted to spread his wings over the National Service units; and in the Central African Republic there was competition between the head of the army, Bokassa (currently the president) and Izamo, head of the police, over ultimate control of the units. Even in the Ivory Coast, which rapidly became the crowning jewel of Israel's multifaceted assistance program, there has been at least one instance of political interference and a recent trend to transform Civic Service units into a personal patronage machine and power source for the presidency.[24] One 1971 semirestricted Israeli report that evaluated the Israeli programs of social and agrarian change in the Ivory Coast warned that the Ghanaian pattern may be repeating itself again since the regime appeared to be more concerned with short-run solutions to political unrest than long-range social and agrarian transformation. Several Israeli officers in the country have suggested an Israeli pullout as more advisable than countenancing a repeat of the Ghanaian experience. Most probably here too, political considerations will assure continued Israeli participation in programs in this key state, just as political considerations impelled Israel to continue "showing the flag" even in the darkest days of Nkrumah's rule.

The above points should suffice to indicate the wide range of problems that programs of social and agrarian change face in Africa. All this is not to imply that every or most Israeli efforts in this domain have been unsuccessful or beset with problems that drastically curtailed their effectiveness. Such an interpretation would be far from the truth since many programs of agrarian training and settlement have been highly successful. However, a sizable number of Israeli programs in this specific area of technical cooperation, and especially in West Africa, have encountered the problems previously noted, resulting from the cultural, political and economic context within which they are established. Several of the same factors also exist in Asia and Latin America, where Israel has extensive programs of cooperation. There the cultural framework is quite different, and important progress has been achieved especially with Latin American peasantry. Some of the more important obstacles to successful social change are unique to Africa and do not allow for comparison with other regions.

Despite the above analysis of the state of some programs and their problems it is hard to reach any meaningful conclusions. It is extremely difficult to set criteria for the evaluation of programs aiming at social change, since some of the variables involved cannot be quantified. It is not simply a matter of counting the number of cadres trained and remaining on their farms, or the number of new settlements established; nor does it involve attempts to measure increased productivity and the application of new techniques of farming in villages where trained cadres have been implanted. Evaluating social change, which many of Israel's programs in Africa aim at, is a much more complex process than mere assessment of tangible manifestations of agrarian modernization and productivity. Success and failure are relative. The span of time over which programs have been operative is an important consideration. And though some of Israel's programs in this domain have been in existence for over ten years, their hybrids, established after years of experimentation, and currently more attuned to the limitations imposed by African conditions, have been operative in many cases for only five to six years, a far too short period of time to allow for valid generalizations beyond those already attempted.

It is safe to conclude that the limited scope of these programs—dictated by African budgetary considerations—greatly curtails their potential benefits; at the most—even taking into account the multiplier effect—they can only produce limited pockets of modernization which will have to be carefully nurtured by the host country lest they be drowned and overwhelmed by the surrounding traditional ethos. On the basis of past experience it can be argued that meaningful longlasting change depends upon the dedication and commitment of political elites. To date, with the one clear exception of Tanzania, and possibly a handful of other states, this has been sadly lacking in Africa.

TRANSFER OF SKILLS AND ERECTION OF SERVICE INFRASTRUCTURES

It is when one moves to an examination of Israeli programs which involve transfer of technical skills to Africa and the creation of joint companies and/or service infrastructures, that one encounters the most clear-cut successes of Afro-Israeli joint efforts. This is because the cultural variables noted previously are only marginally important, so that Israeli selection standards and quality control can be adhered to and hence Israeli control and influence are more marked. The profitability, or at least nonwastage of resources of the joint companies is of some importance to African political elites who might otherwise have to foot the bill. Paradoxically, training programs in Israel and Afro-Israeli joint companies usually based in urban areas, have earned less attention despite their importance and visibility. Technical training and joint companies in the construction area are less glamorous forms of international cooperation than programs of rural agrarian and social development. Though modernization of agriculture and the forging of a nation out of ethnicaly diverse elements is a key stage on the road to socioeconomic development, so is the process of expanding the service, technical and administrative sectors of an underdeveloped country.

Afro-Israeli cooperation in this field falls into three separate categories: transfer of technical and other skills through training programs (including those for Nahal leaders and agrarian cadres), short or long-term loans of Israeli experts, and the creation of joint companies or transfer of managerial skills to African enterprises. Tables 1-4 indicate the magnitude of the Israeli training programs and the number of Israeli experts serving in Africa. In 1970, the last year for which full statistics are available, 246 Israeli experts served in Africa a total of 1495 man/months—36.8 percent of the latter figure devoted to Nahal/Gadna activities, 26.6 percent to agricultural guidance and 13.8 percent to managerial and public service assistance. During the same year a total of 434 Africans came to Israel for 1724 study months: 120 studied agriculture, 99 cooperation activities and 59 community development.[25] The striking fact about Table 3 and projections through 1973 is that some 8000 Africans have been directly exposed to Israel and its developmental concepts and approaches in a continent where urban and rural modern or modernizing sectors are relatively small. This has important side benefits to Israel from the political standpoint,[26] and adds much needed middle-range technical and administrative personnel to Africa's pool of cadres involved in the developmental process.

Enthusiasm and satisfaction with training courses in Israel has been high judging by figures cited by Yannay based on a 1963 survey, despite pockets of criticism regarding length of courses and insufficient time devoted to practical work (see Table 5). Subsequent courses took into account these criticisms which stemmed, according to Israeli instructors, from the greater need of Africans for visual aids and/or more extensive practical demonstrations. Complaints have also been voiced by financially pressed African governments about the high cost of travel to Israel for training purposes (courses have been offered in Africa but this is not possible in many fields and the impact is enhanced by direct exposure to the Israeli context), or the considerable expenditures required to host and pay Israeli experts. Despite the fact that the latter are relatively cheaper than comparable non-Israeli experts (in fields where they are available), the Israeli government has at times quietly picked up the tab for expenses normally covered by recipients of such assistance.

On the Israeli side there have been some grumblings about occasional African students sent out to Israel on junkets consequent to their connections in various ministries, or of inadequate screening of prospective trainees who arrive without the barest of qualifications. Greater Israeli control over intake of trainees, exercised by Israeli embassies in Africa, has reduced the number of such cases. A more difficult problem to solve was the decline in the late 1960s of the number of experts available for work abroad. The gradual retirement of many older personnel sent in earlier years and the end of the brief recession in the Israeli economy dried up many sources of recruitment. Some of the "experts" recently sent abroad have been fresh young university graduates not all of whom were fired with the same zeal or possessed the same professional skills and experience so manifest in experts sent to Africa in earlier years. Agricultural experts in particular have had to cope with a variety of problems in the field not the least of which were soil conditions, pests and crops that they had not encountered before. Their adjustment to tropical conditions and crops has been remarkably smooth. The quality of Israeli personnel in Africa has in general been high.

JOINT COMPANIES

Of all Afro-Israeli joint ventures established since 1958 those formed by Solel Boneh with African public capital are probably best known abroad. Five such construction companies were established in Ghana (GNCC), Western Nigeria (Nigersol), Eastern Nigeria (ENCC), Sierra Leone (NCC)

TABLE 1 Israeli Experts Abroad 1958-1970

Africa	2483
Latin America & Caribbean	530
Mediterranean Area	504
Asia	431
Total	3,948

Source: Israel's Programme of International Cooperation, (Israel: Ministry for Foreign Affairs, 1971), p. 57.

TABLE 2 Israeli Experts Abroad by Specialization 1958-1967

Agriculture	916
Youth organization	354
Health	262
Education	238
Others	566
Total	2,582

Source: Ibid.

TABLE 3 Trainees in Israel 1958-1970

Africa	6,623
Asia	2,510
Mediterranean Area & Others	2,476
Latin America & Caribbean	2,181
Total	13,790

Source: Ibid.

TABLE 4 Trainees in Israel by Field 1958-1968

Agriculture	2,747
Study tours & seminars	1,582
Cooperative & labor studies	1,246
Community development	1,007
Academic, including medicine	729
Youth leadership	567
Vocational training	538
Individual trainees & miscellaneous	2,153
Total	10,569

Source: Ibid.

TABLE 5 Evaluations of Israeli-Trained Cadres

Question	% Yes	% No
Are you employed in the field in which you got training?	78	22
Has the training helped you in your work?	95	5
Have you been promoted since your return home?	48	52
Was the course well planned?	90	10
Were the lectures effective and was the level of theory adequate?	90	10
Was the practical work sufficient?	65	35
Was the course long enough?	41	59
Was there satisfactory written material to accompany the course?	74	26

Source: Y. Yannay, "Technical Cooperation between Israel and the Developing World," *International Development Review* 6, no. 3 (1964): 10-15.

---

and Ivory Coast (Sonitra). Of these only Sonitra remains as a de facto joint company, the others having been turned over to full African control. Altogether, up to the point when the Israeli connection was broken (and in the case of Sonitra up to 1970), a total of $107 million in works have been executed. Nine Solel Boneh branches, operating as expatriate construction companies, were also established in eight countries (two in Nigeria),[27] of which six are still operative today. Their total of works executed by 1970 amounted to $71 million. These operations of Solel Boneh cannot be considered technical cooperation. Several other Afro-Israeli joint companies have been established involving, on the Israeli side, Tahal and Water Resources Development International, a subsidiary of Mekorot. Also notable are the activities of private Israeli capital and management concerns such as the Federman group and the Mayer brothers.

While most joint companies have been successful financial ventures that have also contributed significantly to the development of Africa's infrastructure (roads, building complexes, dams, airports), there has been a trend among Israeli public companies not to get overly involved in new enterprises of this kind. With the new economic pickup in Israel, construction companies have sufficient work to occupy them at home and this in turn translates into a paucity of skilled personnel available for missions abroad.

Managerial fees and the share of profits that the Israeli partner gets in a joint company are quite low. Risks on the other hand are potentially high, whether consequent to political turmoil, as occurred in the regional government of West Nigeria with Nigersol caught in the middle, or as a result of premature and underhanded dissolution of the joint enterprise, as occurred in Ghana with GNCC. Joint companies have to contend with a variety of political pressures, interministerial bog-downs, cumbersome and tardy procedures for payments for services rendered to the government, and a host of intrigues sponsored by anti-Israeli groups—whether they be Lebanese, Syrian, French or British expatriate economic interests. The above points notwithstanding, Afro-Israeli joint companies have been ideal mechanisms for the transfer of technical, managerial and administrative skills, and useful devices for breaking the monopoly metropolitan companies possess in Africa.

To better illustrate both the kinds of problems Afro-Israeli joint companies have faced and their contributions to the transformation of the host country's landscape, the operations of Motoragri in Ivory Coast might be instructive—even though Motoragri is not a joint company in the strict sense of the term. Motoragri was set up in April 1966 following a survey conducted by Agridev[28] experts at President Houphouet-Boigny's request, to ascertain the best way to utilize some $4 million worth of agricultural machinery attained through an AID loan and already being unloaded at Abidjan's docks. Following the survey Agridev signed a managerial contract specifying an annual fee of $140,000 (in 1969 reduced to $85,000) in exchange for which it recruited Israeli managerial, technical, administrative and training personnel (at the outset twenty-four for the new company in the Ivory Coast.[29] Motoragri was given considerable autonomy in its activities, though it was ultimately responsible to a super-board of directors (in which French interests were indirectly represented) which included delegates of all ministries, the National Assembly and even the private sector. Motoragri's prime task was to engage in large-scale mechanized clearing of tropical forest and bush land for new agricultural or other use, under contracts from central and local authorities, village communities or private landowners. Other activities included construction of roads and irrigation of earth dams, clearing of projected village sites and plowing and subsoiling existing plots.

The company faced from the outset the opposition of entrenched interests (Ivorian as well as French) and inherited a wide assortment of incompatible new machinery since Houphouet-Boigny had allocated his AID loan purchases equally among the three main American manufacturers of machinery equipment. There was also a very acute shortage of skilled labor, foremen, tractor drivers and mechanists which necessitated an immediate crash training program. Other complications arose when the best applicants for jobs consistently turned out to be diligent and honest Mossi emigrants from Upper Volta, a fact which caused some resentment because it reduced the number of openings available to native Ivorians. There were also the usual attempts of local notables and politicians to exert influence upon Motoragri to recruit personnel from their own regions or to give priority to projects of personal interest to them.[30]

The Israeli team rapidly commenced activities with a headquarters, repair shop and spare parts manufacturing workhouses in Abidjan, and seven regional centers where the actual machinery and staff were concentrated. Tight control was exerted on the precise location of all equipment and its regular maintenance and repair—a fact which was commented upon favorably in the press[31] and which can be contrasted with the poor administration and maintenance of a larger (2000 machines) but similar Soviet venture in Ghana. Different price lists were calculated to assure amortization of equipment and capital on a nonprofit basis while allowing enterprising villages and/or medium landowners to avail themselves of Motoragri's services. While most of the work was contracted for by various ministries as part of their development plans, a significant number of projects were completed for local communities and individuals.[32] The initial April 1966 staff of 85 greatly expanded as the training programs—of extremely high standards[33]—churned out the skilled manpower needed. By the end of that year the staff numbered 250, and it more than doubled in 1967 to a total of 650 native employees and 31 Israelis. In 1969 further expansion commenced consequent to the addition of a new and big regional center and the acquisition of new machinery.

By 1971 Motoragri had completed contracts worth $16 million, including over 2170 miles of roads of all kinds and had cleared 17,500 hectares (43 million acres) of land. Its impact upon the development of Ivory Coast's infrastructure and its contributions in the field of expanding the size of available agricultural land have been immense. Through its training programs Motoragri has also created a sizable pool of skilled and semiskilled labor. Though the Africanization process has been slow an Ivorian was promoted to the post of managing director in 1969 and most Israeli personnel had practically from the outset Ivorian assistants who were being prepared to take over responsibilities once Israeli presence was no longer deemed necessary. The unqualified success of Motoragri in the Ivory Coast has led to several requests by other African states for similar joint ventures, even if on a more modest scale. Agridev (and Solel Boneh) has been hesitant to respond affirmatively to these invitations for reasons previously noted. Though Agridev's political vistas in Ivory Coast have been minimal, this has not been entirely the case with Sonitra (the Ivory Coast-Solel Boneh construction company) and Agridev's financial incentive ($85,000 a year) has been very small.[34]

There are a variety of other aspects of the Afro-Israeli history of technical cooperation that cannot be dealt with due to space limitations: military and internal security personnel training, loans of Israeli staff to African ministries, hospitals, national lotteries, etc.[35] In terms of scope and variety Afro-Israeli cooperation has been both unique and one of the most significant examples of international cooperation. Despite various problems that have afflicted several of these efforts, and despite intense international pressures by Arab states against overly close Afro-Israeli relations, these programs of cooperation have not altered and are continuing to contribute their share to social and economic development of the continent.

NOTES

1. "A Surplus of Brains," *Newsweek*, August 20, 1962.

2. These state visits not only shattered the hitherto parochial nature of Israeli civic events, but more than anything attested to Israel's coming of age. Prior to these African state visits (in 1960-61 alone there were seven) only one leader had deigned to visit Israel. For a discussion of the evolution of Israeli foreign policy vis-à-vis the Third World see Samuel Decalo, "Israeli Foreign Policy and the Third World," *Orbis* (Fall 1967): 724-45.

3. For a review of some of the literature see Samuel Decalo, "Israel and Africa: A Selected Bibliography," *Journal of Modern African Studies* 5, no. 3 (1967): 385-99.

4. In the "honeymoon" period of Ghanian-Israeli relations (1967-62) the Israeli Embassy in Accra and the Israeli technical assistance in Ghana were the most prestigious and influential bar none. The Israeli Ambassador was credited with having immediate access to Nkrumah at all times. The same was true in the Central African Republic (under Dacko) and in a couple of other states. See, for example, John B. Oakes, *The Edge of Freedom* (New York: Harper & Brothers, 1961), p. 45.

5. Among other external factors that worked to diminish Israel's role in Africa can be noted the Franco-Israeli break, which had significant repercussions in French Africa; the Arab-Soviet propaganda drive against Israel's activities in Africa; and, more recently, the Libyan financial juggernaut assault on several African states.

6. Mordechai Kreinin, *Israel and Africa: A Study in Technical Cooperation* (New York: Praeger, 1964); and Leopold Laufer, *Israel and the Developing Countries: New Approaches to Cooperation* (New York: Twentieth Century Fund, 1967).

7. See among others Victor Uchendu, "Socioeconomic and Cultural Determinants of Rural Change in East and West Africa," *Food Research Institute Studies*, no. 3 (1968): 225-42; Howard Schuman, "Economic Development and Individual Change: A Social-Psychological Study of the Comilla Experiment in Pakistan,". *Occasional Papers in International Affairs*, no. 15 (Cambridge: Harvard University Center for International Affairs, 1967); Philip Porter, "Environmental Potentials and Economic Opportunities; Background for Cultural Adaptation," *American Anthropologist* (April 1965): 409-20; Arthur Niehoff, "Peasant Fatalism and Socio-Economic Innovation," *Human Organization* (Winter 1966): 273-83; Philip Hauser, "Cultural and Personal Obstacles to Economic Development in Less Developed Areas," *Human Organization* (Summer 1959):pp. 78-84; and Development of Smallholder Agriculture in Eastern Nigeria," *Economic Development and Cultural Change* (April 1965): 278-92.

8. Pierre Alexandre, "The Problems of Chieftancies in French Speaking Africa,"

in *West African Chiefs*, ed. Michael Crowder and Obaro Ikime (Ile-Ife, Nigeria: University of Ife Press, 1970), p. 28.

9. See among others Robert Melson and Howard Wolpe, "Modernization and the Politics of Communalism: A Theoretical Perspective," *American Political Science Review* (December 1970):1112-30; and idem, *Nigeria: Modernization and the Politics of Communalism* (East Lansing: Michigan State University Press, 1974).

10. From interviews in Dahomey and Togo, 1971 and 1972. For the background and contemporary setting of these tensions see Samuel Decalo, "Regionalism, Politics and the Military in Dahomey," *Journal of Developing Areas* (April 1973): 1-47; and idem, "The Politics of Military Rule in Togo," *Geneve-Afrique* (January 1974).

11. For an example in a different geographical area see the illuminating article by Vaiao and Fay Ala'ilima, "Samoan Values and Economic Development," *East-West Center Review* 1, no. 3 (February 1965):3-18.

13. See also the pessimistic view of the possibilities of cooperative efforts in Africa contained in Xavier A. Flores, "Institutional Problems in the Modernization of African Agriculture," in *A Review of Rural Cooperation in Developing Areas* (Geneva: United Nations Research Institute for Social Development, 1969).

13. See Peter B. Hammond, *Yatenga: Technology in the Culture of a West African Kingdom* (New York: The Free Press, 1966); and Elliott P. Skinner, *The Mossi of Upper Volta* (Stanford: Stanford University Press, 1964).

14. See for example Walter Elkan, "Out of School Education and Training for Primary-School Leavers in Rural Kenya," *International Labour Review* (September 1971):205-16.

15. See Moshe Dayan's comments on Central African Republic's Nahal in "West African Diary," IV, *Jerusalem Post*, November 26, 1963.

16. For a recent example of this in Nigeria, see *West Africa*, March 12, 1973.

17. From interviews in Abidjan. See also Laufer, *Israel and the Developing Countries*, p. 117.

18. *Marchés Tropicaux et Méditerranéens*, January 5, 1963.

19. See M. Kreinin, "The Introduction of Israel's Land Settlement Plan to Nigeria," *Journal of Farm Economics* (August 1963):535-46; idem, Cooperative Farming: West Nigeria's Exciting 20 million Scheme," *Africa Trade and Development* (September 1961):12-13; idem, "Farm settlement schemes in Nigeria," *Nigerian Trade Journal* (January-March 1962):2-6; and idem, *West Africa*, February 24, 1962.

20. Interviews in Cotonou and Ouassa, July-August 1971. For further background on Dahomey's economy see Samuel Decalo, "The Politics of Instability in Dahomey," *Geneve-Afrique* 7, no. 2 (1968):5-32.

21. Laufer, Israel and the Developing Countries, p. 116.

22. An interesting case cropped up in the State Lottery of Dahomey, which was a different form of technical assistance than the one currently being discussed. There a ranking officer presented to the lottery a patently forged winning ticket. Despite representations of the Israeli director, the military junta then in power ordered payment of the prize.

23. In 1964 the brigades were separated into two sections—one for agricultural work and the other for construction. Though it is undeniable that the units performed some important work, productivity was low, discipline and control were lax and many members regarded their entry into the brigades as official sinecures.

24. Interviews in Jerusalem, Abidjan and Ouagadougou, June-August 1972.

25. Figures from Dan V. Segre, "The Philosophy and Practice of Israel's International Cooperation."

26. On several occasions in different countries a measure of pro-Israeli sentiment was visible even when the official governmental posture was neutral or hostile. This occurred, for example, in Nigeria following the 1967 war and in Mali during the Munich 1972 murders. In the latter instance the author was witness to several personal expressions of regret at the incident by civilians and soldiers who approached th Israeli Embassy in Bamako, at a time when the government-controlled press was taking a positive view of the incident. See L'Essor (Bamako), September 6, 1972.

27. In Ivory Coast, Kenya, Nigeria, Tanzania and Afar and Issa Territory, where they still operate, and formerly in Ethiopia, Zambia and Uganda.

28. Agridev is a subsidiary of Water Resources Development which in turn is a subsidiary of Mekorot, and had hitherto operated mostly in the Far East.

29. Hence Motoragri is different from the Ivory Coast-Solel Boneh joint company SONITRA insofar that in the latter the Israeli partner has a financial stake in the form of 45 percent of the shares.

30. Thus Motoragri acquiesced to rush certain work in Yamoussoukro, Houphouet-Boigny's native town and site of his country residence.

31. See issues of Fraternité (Abidjan) for December 7, 1966, March 31, 1967 and April 7, 1967; and L'Observateur Africain (Dakar) April 1968.

32. From interviews in Abidjan, August 1972.

33. Of 4000 applicants in 1966-67 only 650 were admitted and a further 40 percent of those were found unsuitable by the end of the training period. See Fraternité, December 7, 1966.

34. Its overheads have also been low, but according to sources in Abidjan much more agreeable terms are available practically anywhere else.

35. Israel has set up or helped reorganize the state lotteries of Cameroon, Dahomey, Togo, Sierra Leone and Ghana.

10

Moshe Alpan

ISRAELI TRADE
AND ECONOMIC RELATIONS
WITH AFRICA

There is no clear-cut reply to the question whether there is any uniqueness in the economic and trade relations between Israel and the new nations emerged in the last two decades on the African continent. There is certainly no trace of uniqueness in the volume of trade, either in absolute figures or relatively to other markets. Neither from the point of view of the trade balance of African states, nor from the side of the contribution to Israel's export activity, have impressive achievements been registered. In international terms the figures are infinitesimal.

If this is the case, where does the strong impact of these relations stem from? Why did world opinion regard Israel as a giant casting its light (or shadow) upon the African continent, south of the Sahara desert? Or is Israel's influence on social and economic development in Africa only imaginary or psychological?

In the eyes of its African friends—at least in the first years of warm and friendly relations—Israel was a state of infinite resourcefulness, a source of hidden powers, a model of successful independence and development that should be followed, the older loving brother, and a potential strong benefactor. If not all or part of these, then at least a spring of inspiration for a constructive struggle towards independence, a stockpile of ideas and recipes regarding conquest of the desert, a teacher to solve social and ethnic problems and to create a socialist substance on the ruins of a prefeudal colonial past.

In the minds of the Israeli public Africans appeared as a host of refreshing, new and likable friends. Most Israelis remember the Diaspora, persecution and anti-Semitism, and tend to show their hatred of racism and discrimination by expressing humanitarianism toward "man created in the image of God." The successful struggle and achievement of independence by other nations, mainly the Africans, were considered in Israel in the late fifties as one of the greatest phenomena of the century, comparable only with the resurrection of Israel.

In 1958, on the tenth anniversay of the State of Israel, the march of African independence had just begun. Until 1956, Ethiopia and Liberia were the only independent countries in Africa. Ghana, formerly the Gold Coast, followed suit, later others joined at a rapid pace, and by 1960 sixteen African states had achieved independence. Israel was celebrating the achievements of the first decade of independence, which by any account were enormous, and had just recovered from the Sinai war. The time and the spirit were ready to seek contacts with emerging Africa, and the Israeli public was watching with joy and enthusiasm the newly independent countries joining the family of nations and searching for ways and means of cooperation with these new prospective partners. Amidst the enthusiasm and celebrations of independence of black Africa, the government of Israel most probably also kept count of the voices joining the United Nations, in expectation that most of them would support Israel's case against the multitude of Arab votes. This "honeymoon atmosphere" did not even ebb much in January 1961, when the voices of the three "radical" states in West Africa (Ghana, Guinea and Mali) rose together with the United Arab Republic, Morocco and Algeria's Front of National Liberation (FLN) accusing Israel of being "a tool in the hands of African colonialism." The assistance given by Israel to African countries (amongst them the radical ones) remained unchanged in spite of this. In retrospect, Israel's decision not to object to good relations between the black countries of Africa and Arab countries, based on the desire to be an objective and constructive friend, may be regarded as naive optimism. These special relations were motivated mainly by humanitarian feelings. Nevertheless, to disregard geopolitical and political motivations such as the need for support in the international scene and the wish to secure free navigation through the Straits of Tiran to East Africa, a wish that followed the maritime blockade imposed by Egypt and put to an end in 1956, would certainly underestimate the maturity of Israeli politicians.

There was much talk as to the existence of an Israeli model regarding collaboration with African countries. As far as we could trace the development of economic and trade cooperation with these countries, it was difficult to discover a special Israeli pattern planned and outlined ahead. The beginning of cooperation was spontaneous. For example: establishment of the Black Star Line (with Zim Lines Ltd.) in 1957 with the government of Ghana as partner (three years later the whole shareholding was transferred to the government of Ghana, and Zim was appointed administrator of the company for five additional years); establishment of the Ghana National Constructor Company (GNCC), a partnership of Solel Boneh (40 percent) and the government of Ghana (60 percent); partnerships between Solel Boneh and Water Resources Development company (WRD) in Nigeria and that of Solel Boneh in Siera Leone; establishment of Dizengoff West Africa in 1958 (a subsidiary of the trading company, Alda, now Koor Foreign Trade Ltd.). All these partnerships were just first reflections of enthusiasm which, if taken along the correct path and carried on for sufficient time, could have led toward the creation of an entirely new model. If there is any special Israeli feature, it is characterized by the capability to improvise rapidly and bring the pioneering ideology to a fast realization, avoiding red tape and stumbling-blocks of bureaucracy. This was typical and unique of Israel's operation during the first years of activity in Africa.

Israel's straightforward and humane approach became more impressive the more the former colonial machinery became heavy and worn out. Large local colonial companies were rich and disliked. They were late in listening to the bells of a new era, in understanding the desire of natives to become genuinely independent—they could not believe that the new governments and their indigenous subjects could run any part of the economy on their own. They could also hardly face the fact that the new leadership was ready not only for self-government, but also keen to enjoy its fruits.

Great powers that had not been involved in colonial government in Africa were slow and late in recognizing the international importance of this continent. In the initial stages they believed that problems could be solved only by pouring in large amounts of money, especially from international sources.

The Third World had just made its first political steps, and in that stage its only activity was to publish political and anticolonial statements. Leaders did not have any interest at that phase in extending any constructive assistance to emerging African states that could, and later did, become allies. Only Yugoslavia, at later stages, entered into economic collaboration and trading relations with some African countries, on a strictly business basis without laying emphasis upon cooperation or assistance of any kind.

In such a situation, no wonder that the volunteering of Israel—a state just relieved of colonial yoke and having shown considerable success in self-development—was accepted gladly. Improvisation expressed in immediate and rapid response was exactly what fascinated Africans—who are generally of a pragmatic frame of mind.

Another feature that may have distinguished Israel from other countries—in the eyes of African states—was its political-economic-social structure. Economic growth does not often fall into line with organic development of society. This is a problem which is especially crucial in some

African countries. African leaders understand well that there is a wide gap between modern tools and means of planning and development, and the social structure of their countries. Israel was perhaps the only state that had to face similar problems: social integration of Jews arriving to Israel from different countries, from completely different social and cultural backgrounds, different socioeconomic pasts, and different levels of culture and education. On the one hand was the need for rapid economic growth, utilization of highly skilled manpower, talent, and readily available help of the world and the Jewish people in particular, including the availability of financial support; on the other hand the social cleft between two poles of the Jewish people: those who had survived the Nazi holocaust, and those who came from backward Arab countries. All this in a country poor of natural resources and water, and rich only in arid desert land and sand—seemed an unsurmountable task. Israel faced all these challenges successfully, and its new African friends were pleased to draw encouragement and hope that their own situation was not desperate and that their own enormous difficulties could be overcome.

Neither socialism nor capitalism have ever seriously dealt with problems of underdeveloped countries that achieved independence from colonial rule. No theory or empirical program have ever been established. How to deal with problems of lack of social and physical infrastructure; how to bring about radical reforms without jeopardizing social equilibrium; how to invest massively in development and increase the very low (sometimes not more than forty to fifty dollars per capita yearly) national income; how to change the subsistance-based tribal farming system into a modern marketing-oriented agriculture; how to industrialize with existing manpower and without uprooting the traditional structure of a tribal society; how to develop a network of communication; and how to reshape the human soul and mind to accept all these massive, radical and rapid changes. Nobody has ever given a satisfactory reply to any of these questions, let alone to their conglomeration. The leap from a feudal-tribal-colonial regime to a technology-based social system was never before considered as a realistic possibility.

The problem was not to transfer the means of production to national or public ownership, or to the hands of big private companies—the problem was to create them. The issue was not to change production relations, but to form a model of production structure under these specific conditions. The problem was to create a production function to fit both the abundance of manpower and the lack of necessary capital, modern technology and know-how. The challenge was not to satisfy demand but to create it. Socialist theory has never seriously considered these problems and has never offered any solutions, either political or economic. Socialism was suggesting solutions to problems of industrial countries in the stage of capitalism. The effort to solve the problems of capitalist countries by colonialism had obviously failed, hence there was no solution in this capitalist concept either. American capitalism with a national income per capita many times the national income of African natives was far off from African problems, without any possibility of bridging the distance.

In this situation, Israel came along with a message. A strong state- and public-owned economy fulfilling important developing and pioneering objectives side by side with a private economy; a well-developed cooperative sector, including a collective economy with various levels of cooperation, cooperation between classes and a powerful trade union. The combination of constructiveness and class struggle is a mixture that appealed to many Africans, particularly to intellectuals. Elements of socialism and collectivism, state- and public-owned enterprises that undertook to further the goals and serve the needs of the nation accompanied by efforts of private enterpreneurship and its keen initiative to enhance fast growth, were a unique and refreshing combination. The humanistic message of the kibbutz, the moshav and the cooperatives in Israel appealed to African leaders who were brought up in an atmosphere of struggle against the humiliation and suppression of man in a democratic way, without considering proletarian dictatorship as even a remote solution for their countries.

Nowhere in the world have African visitors, students or course participants had such an unlimited access to all sources of information and know-how as in Israel. The reason for this was not only the friendly relations between Israelis and their African guests. The more important reason was that the individual in Israel has regarded achievements in developing working processes and planning models more as a general and human asset than as his private property. Before the arrival of Chinese experts to African countries in recent years, there was hardly a direct human contact between local trainees and foreign expert personnel. The direct, simple, uninhibited and open approach of Israelis was new and encouraging in those years.

If there is another distinctive point to be emphasized, it is the abundance of features of Israeli collaboration. There is scarcely a field in the wide spectrum of socioeconomic aid in which Israel has not participated in one of the countries, from training women in social work to their training in poultry farming, from training the youth movement to training youngsters in settlements, from instructing adults in public management to instruction in building bridges and dams. The characteristic features of Israel's economic and trading activities in Africa can be summarized as follows:

1. Israel never approached a prestige project, neither in financing nor in constructing such projects—as many other countries did in order to show their ability and power. These prestige projects often caused great losses to African countries: high maintenance expenses, disappointment, social strains and economic damage. One can hardly find a showpiece in Africa

which was initiated, let alone financed or carried out by Israel or Israelis.

2. Israel never took part—maybe partly due to the tiny size of its own economy—in any huge plan concerning exploitation of raw materials, e.g. aluminum or electricity. The only unsuccessful project, of a limited order, was the timber project in Gabon, although the Israeli plywood industry was ready to absorb all its output. Israel never considered projects above its ability, neither had Israel any interest in being regarded as a neocolonial investor exploiting the natural resources and manpower of black countries. Consequently, Israel did not take part in any inter-African or regional project.

3. There is hardly a plant in Africa which Israel built on a turnkey basis, namely with local investors' full financing, without self-participation, only by selling of the process, know-how and construction. These projects are considered by Africans, not always justly, as projects from which promoters have derived more benefit than owners. Very few projects in Africa were accomplished by Israel without bidding to tender, without competition, or projects in whose planning and erection the financer had the main say. The Israeli ear was attentive to fears and suspicions (very often justified) of Africans concerning anything that had strings attached to it.

4. Most projects in which Israelis have participated were based on specific know-how or on exclusive specialization in Israel. Projects in the field of agriculture, such as poultry farms, citrus plantations, cotton, large-scale operation of agricultural equipment, lottery projects, plastic or pharmaceutic industry, irrigation—all these applied specific know-how or experience which Israel was willing to impart to others and of which Israel had the appropriate manpower potential to share with Africa.

5. In the field of trade Israel did not take advantage of its special status. Israeli loans were not given on the condition that only Israeli merchandise should be purchased, though many times those loans were directed toward utilization of Israeli know-how or inputs. Certainly, many Israeli experts engaged in various fields of activity often recommended the purchase of Israeli inputs best known to them like irrigation equipment, seeds, insecticides or pesticides, and even stamp printing. The overall percentage of Israeli exports to African countries does not prove an abuse of this advantage by Israeli firms. In several African countries, Israeli trade—as the result of Israel's geographic location—had a certain comparative advantage, which, like many others, have not been fully exploited.

6. It is not by mere chance that a considerable part of the economic and trading activity can, in one way or another, be related to assistance, training and cooperation. A great part of the Israeli aid was tied to social-educational fields which did not have any influence on economic contacts, except for military aid which quite often was accompanied, for obvious reasons, by orders of equipment.

TABLE 1 Israeli Exports: Total and African (In US $ Millions)

Year	Total Israeli Exports	Index	Israeli Exports to Africa	Index
1967	555	100.0	24.3	100.0
1968	639	115.2	27.1	111.5
1969	729	131.4	34.2	140.7
1970	779	140.3	41.6	171.2
1971	959	172.8	47.5	195.5
1972	1,149	207.0	45.1	185.6
1973	1,381	248.9	42.7	175.7

TABLE 2 Israeli Imports: Total and African (In US $ Millions)

Year	Total Israeli Imports	Index	Israeli Imports from Africa	Index
1967	715	100.0	27.0	100.0
1968	1,115	155.9	30.2	111.8
1969	1,331	186.2	31.3	115.9
1970	1,455	203.5	30.1	111.5
1971	1,833	256.4	25.0	92.5
1972	1,983	277.3	31.9	118.1
1973	2,943	411.6	57.1	211.5

7. Tables 1 and 2 represent total Israeli import-export growth in 1967-73, compared with the growth of Israeli imports from and exports to Africa. While total Israeli exports have increased during those years by 149 percent, exports to Africa have only increased by 76 percent. During those years, Israeli exports to Africa were approximately 4 percent of total Israeli exports, and only in 1968-70 had they reached the rate of 5 percent. This rate is very low considering the above-mentioned comparative advantages and the great Israeli effort invested in Africa. Israeli imports from Africa are not high either, as indicated in Table 2; and while Israel's total imports in 1967-73 have increased by 312 percent, imports from Africa have increased by only 111 percent. This percentage is misleading. Israel's major imports are equipment, inputs for industry, oil and grains—which are not available in Africa. In the above-mentioned period Israeli agricultural imports have increased by 49 percent. Major African goods imported by Israel are food commodities—oil seeds (Ethiopia), coffee (Uganda, Kenya, Ivory Coast, Tanzania), hides (Ethiopia, Zambia), cocoa (Ghana, Nigeria), peanuts

(Malawi); and for industry: timber from Gabon, Congo and Ivory Coast, and carbonates from Kenya. The increase in Israel's imports of these products was relatively small.

8. In order to present a clearer picture, we have included a table showing the last four years of trade in more detail (Table 3). When analyzing this table we should keep in mind that export to African countries is only 4-5 percent of total Israeli export, and that import of Israeli merchandise is usually a very small percentage of African countries' total import. Ethiopia has attained the maximum, its import from Israel is about 2.5 percent of its total import, and its export to Israel about 1.5 percent of its total. Ethiopia is the closest country to Israel, and Israel has the largest comparative advantage in trade with this country. The other East African countries, also geographically advantageous for Israel, import from Israel only about 1 percent of their total, while several other African countries like Ivory Coast, Zaire, Nigeria and Ghana, have desired less than 0.3 percent of their total import from Israel. Africa with 10 percent of the world population represents only 2 percent of total world trade, while Israel with only 0.1 percent of the world population represents approximately the same percentage (or more) of world trade. Because of this gap and the special relations between Africa and Israel, it could have been presumed that trade activity would be higher. There is a disproportion between Israel's vast activity in Africa and its achievements in the field of trade. From the dynamics of the trade of Israeli export (which in the last decade has increased at an average rate of 14 percent per year) nothing in the increase of trade with or export to Africa supports the opinion that Israel enjoyed a serious commercial advantage. On the contrary, the relatively large aid Israel gave its African friends was far larger than the economic advantages Israel enjoyed.

9. The composition of Israeli export to Africa is beyond our present scope. Its main characteristics are change in items parallel with development of home production, and steady increase in export of chemicals, agricultural equipment and building materials.

10. Clear, specific summaries concerning the activity of Israeli contractors are not available, especially in respect of Solel Boneh Overseas Ltd. and Water Resources Development Co. These activities had started in West Africa—in Ghana, Sierra Leone, Nigeria and Ivory Coast, and were widely extended in Ethiopia, Tanzania, Uganda, Zambia and Kenya. Israeli companies have built hotels in the Ivory Coast (Mayer Brothers), Nigeria, Tanzania, Kenya and Zambia; and housing schemes in the Ivory Coast, Kenya and Uganda. They constructed roads, dams, and erected numerous public buildings in various countries. The turnover of all these projects reached at its peak up to 12-15 million a year. Most projects were obtained by bidding for open tenders, and only a few on the basis of negotiated

TABLE 3 Israeli Trade with Africa (In US $ Thousands)

Country	Exports from Israel				Imports to Israel			
	1970	1971	1972	1973	1970	1971	1972	1973
Total: Africa	41,564	47,472	45,100	42,700	30,088	25,007	31,953	57,100
Total: Selected East African Countries	19,325	20,540	16,589	12,175	5,469	4,995	4,526	6,774
Ethiopia	4,364	3,537	3,964	4,007	1,973	2,090	2,366	4,514
Kenya	3,655	4,186	2,796	3,026	1,197	1,010	1,208	1,665
Uganda	5,613	7,958	3,095	—	2,136	1,321	283	—
Tanzania	1,905	1,401	1,317	1,267	127	196	354	379
Zambia	2,923	3,019	5,138	3,524	15	39	95	—
Malawi	217	166	36	140	18	326	208	216
Madagascar	171	20	58	73	3	13	12	—
Mauritius	477	253	185	138	—	—	—	—
Total: Selected West African Countries	9,914	11,606	10,767	14,595	5,219	2,426	4,247	4,069
Ghana	2,144	3,103	2,299	2,417	594	487	470	200
Nigeria	3,585	4,950	6,152	5,631	40	30	18	10
Ivory Coast	1,161	1,255	1,428	4,925	926	413	752	1,904
Gabon	1	166	37	281	1,640	837	2,008	1,896
Zaire	2,959	2,132	851	1,234	304	107	361	1
Congo-Brazzaville	64	—	—	107	1,715	192	638	58
Total: Other African Countries	12,325	15,326	17,744	15,930	19,400	17,586	15,836	46,257

contracts or on other contractors' finance basis. Very few projects were financed by Israeli government loans, some of them were carried out by joint Israeli-local companies. Large contracting companies, French, Belgian, English, Italian and Yugoslavian, were eager to undertake projects in African countries. Some of these companies have been in existence since the colonial period, and were financially very well-off with heavy equipment on the spot as well as good facilities and local connections. It has to be assumed that Israeli companies interested in penetrating the market (especially in 1964-67 during the recession in Israel, when there was a surplus of all kinds of professional workers, especially engineers, technicians, high-standard planners) had—in view of this strong competition—to quote highly competitive prices which did not leave impressive profits, even if we take into account foreign currency incomes from savings on salaries of a few hundred Israeli employees, during fifteen years of activity. As far as we know, Israeli companies have accomplished all projects on time and to the satisfaction of clients. Though some projects caused great losses due to impossibility of anticipating difficulties of execution at such a distance from home (not mentioning losses due to changes of governments, as in Uganda)—the economic balance as a whole is positive, especially because of the utilization of manpower, which at certain times would have been redundant at home, and which instead accomplished constructive work at a fair price. The other side of the coin should also be regarded, namely losses that the Israeli Foreign Trade Risks Insurance Company had to absorb. In several cases there were heavy losses, after having insured 95 percent of the political risk of projects carried out in these countries.

11. For many years no industrial plants or agricultural ventures have been initiated by Israel. Israel has tried very hard to attract investors from abroad, and therefore could not venture into overseas investment. Israel is very poor in foreign currency and keeps close control over it. Within the Ministry of Finance, there is a Committee for Overseas Projects and Investments composed of representatives of the Ministry of Finance, the Ministry of Commerce and Industry, the Ministry of Agriculture and the Ministry of Foreign Affairs. This committee examines very carefully any request concerning overseas investment, even a minor one. The committee does not approve overseas projects unless they are important to the furthering of Israeli foreign trade, and unless they are politically viable and favorable. Only few ventures have been approved and undertaken in the last years, most of them of a moderate size, adapted to Israeli possibilities, and mostly in cooperation with local factors and operating profitably. Koor Industries Ltd., the industrial conglomerate controlled by the Histadrut (general federation of labor), is the owner or initiator of most of these. Two pharmaceutic plants (in Zaire and Ethiopia) in partnership with Assia-Teva from Israel and local investors;

a cotton farm in Ethiopia; a skin-pickling plant in Ethiopia in partnership with local and American investors; a venture for growing maize seeds in Zambia; a plant for assembly of air conditioners; and a plant for aluminum door and window frames in Ghana—all these were founded by Israel in Africa in partnership with local authorities (there was a plastics plant and a plant for hydraulic-equipment production in Kenya, both in private hands). Most of these ventures were based upon Israeli technical or managerial know-how and some are being supplied with subassemblies or components from Israel.

Since the Yom Kippur war, when African countries severed diplomatic relations with Israel, trade has continued with most countries and has grown with some of them. Most countries, although put under heavy pressure by Arab oil-producing countries, were not happy to break economic ties with Israel. In the balance they may have lost, at least in the economic field, slightly more than Israel, and would probably only gain from renewing friendly relations with Israel. It may take some time before full normalization is achieved, and the real question is whether at least a part of the mutual enthusiasm can be regained in order to continue rendering a unique dimension to friendship and economic cooperation.

11

Shimeon Amir

ISRAEL'S DEVELOPMENT COOPERATION: YOUTH PROGRAMS*

Because of the continually accelerating rhythm of change in society, in both developed and developing countries, we are faced with an enormous challenge in the education of youth. Not only must such education help youth to accept basic social and national values, it must also ensure the identification and involvement of the younger generation in the development of ideals and policies. Youth education must assure the assimilation of changes brought about by accepted technological innovations. Unless these challenges are met satisfactorily, the danger of estrangement of youth and the growth of dissident cultures, destructive of existing national and social goals, looms large.

In developing countries two factors make the problem even more acute. The first is the very high proportion of young people in relation to the entire population, and the second is the more rapid and drastic character of changes that must be faced in the transition from patterns of traditional society to those of modern society. In 1971 the ratio of people under the age of twenty in developing countries was more than 50 percent, while in developed countries it was only 35 percent. In Africa the ratio was even higher, reaching 55 percent.

Youth in developing countries must face many conflicts, the chief of which is that of "two groups of bodies aspiring to centrality in the society."[1] The new political entity, the state, as a sovereign body with powers of enforcement, as opposed to the traditional tribe, village or region. The goal for those responsible for the education of youth is the development of young people's civic responsibility and active participation in the modern political

*Reprinted with permission from Praeger; originally appeared in *Israel's Development Cooperation with Africa, Asia, and Latin America* (New York: Praeger, 1974).

system; and, at the same time, the conservation of patterns of loyalty to the village, tribe and region, whenever such loyalties can be successfully established.

The function of that elementary social unit, the family, is also undergoing change. In this situation every available tool in addition to formal education must be used to channel the energies and aspirations of young people into creative outlets. Educational programs of various kinds play an important role, and youth movements and organizations have a prominent place among them. They can contribute greatly toward the creation of a useful youth culture that can help the young to become a socializing factor in a society that is changing rapidly. "Youth is the meeting point and the inter-generation point of transfer, and for this reason youth culture can serve as the principal meeting point for the longstanding aims of society on one hand, and inclinations and processes of social change on the other."[2] In Israel's history, youth movements played a prominent part. The several stages and patterns of these movements had a profound effect on the programs in which Israel's experts participated abroad.

Although Israeli youth movements had their roots in those of Europe of the late nineteenth, or early twentieth century, they were basically different in character. They were not merely protest movements in opposition to adult society, with a sizable dose of Rousseauism and despair of human society mixed with idealization of anarchistic patterns of individualism. Israeli youth movements were protests against existing patterns that limited Jewish life both in the diaspora and in Palestine. They combined recreational activities, such as scouting, indoor games and song fests, with ideological education in discussing and developing opinions on political issues and—more difficult—in laying the basis and strengthening the motivation for future self-realization of ideals in adult life. From their very beginnings each of these movements set a precise scale of values, differing in details but basically uniform in concentration on performance of pioneering functions in building the country, in defense, and in the establishment of a society inspired by ideals of social justice. The central normative concept was pioneerism; its concrete expression was a situation where young men and women left their middle-class homes, studies and patterns of existence in the diaspora to come to Israel and form collective settlements, to work on roads, or to do other hard, physically exhausting labor and to participate in defense organization. Among youth movements in Palestine, some were devoted to working youth, others to studying youth, and some included both. Although it might sound pretentious, those hundreds of thousands who belonged to youth movements, even if they did not join an agricultural settlement after they reached their majority, or spent only a short time there, shared for a time a justified belief that they actually participated in the process of nation-building and practicing one of its basic precepts of self-realization.

An institution in the history of Israel's educational process is the Youth Aliya—the Youth Immigration organization. Originally established in the early 1930s to save Jewish children from Nazi-dominated countries in Europe, it developed into an admirable organization that offered homes, mainly in agricultural collectives, cooperative settlements, or in special educational institutions, to tens of thousands of young people aged fourteen to eighteen who arrived in Israel without families or who were native Israelis who could not stay with their families. The organization developed a pattern of continuing work and studies in settlements, supervised and assisted by a body of professional teachers and social instructors. Many groups of graduates of Youth Aliya established new settlements or became otherwise involved in the development of the state. Undoubtedly membership in youth movements has had a lasting effect on the individuals in Israeli society.

In the years just preceding Israel's statehood, and during the early years of the state, two national youth organizations achieved prominence—Gadna and Nahal. Gadna (*Gedudey Noar*, youth formations), founded in 1940, engaged youth aged fourteen to sixteen (later up to eighteen) in physical and paramilitary training combined with scouting, education in civics, and fostering of social values. The program included weekly lessons and field days once a month, but the focus was on yearly national service camps and excursions and cross-country marches.

Nahal (*Noar Halutzi Lochem*, fighting pioneer youth) is an integral part of the army. It was formed shortly after the establishment of the state for graduates of youth movements who intended to join old settlements or establish new ones. According to a pattern established since then, they are able to enlist together in the army, alternating periods of military training with work in established agricultural settlements or in new border settlements. While enlisting was obligatory under the law of military service, joining the Nahal was voluntary. The special interest of Nahal members in becoming paratroopers accounts for their excelling not only in settlement and in agriculture but also in military functions. Upon completion of army service they are given four choices: (1) continuing as farmers, members of the kibbutz in which they worked; (2) forming or joining a new settlement; (3) taking up another occupation; or (4) starting university studies. Usually the choice is new settlements in border areas.

All countries that requested Israeli advice on youth programs had such programs, usually sponsored by the state, frequently by religious or professional groups, and sometimes by a voluntary service. Israeli advisors were inspired by their own diversified experience. They offered a selection of organizational and conceptual elements that combined youth culture and social ideals of youth movements with Youth Aliya's formal education and work; Gadna's physical training and national and civic education; and Nahal's pioneering civilian and military service. Each country faced its own needs, arising from differing backgrounds of youth programs, and adapted programs suggested by Israeli advisors that were most suited to their needs.

The professional agency that provided guidance for the above projects until 1971 was the Department of International Cooperation in the Ministry of Defense. The first requests for cooperation specified an interest in Gadna and Nahal types of activities, and Israeli expertise in this field was concentrated in the Ministry of Defense. Since there is no ministry for youth in the Israeli administration, and in order to avoid duplication, the Department of International Cooperation was charged with assisting all youth programs, although the majority were completely civilian in character. In 1972 a new independent center was created for directing international cooperation in youth programs, with no ties to the Ministry of Defense. It is one of the activities financed and coordinated by the Division for International Cooperation. Its director is assisted by a board of specialists drawn from ministries and university departments. The center is responsible for the coordination and pedagogical guidance of a variety of extracurricular and nonconventional modalities of youth activities, both urban and rural. It is expected that in the future it will be in a better position to offer for application abroad the cumulative experience of Israelis in diversified youth movement activities.

Of the nineteen projects abroad in 1971, thirteen were conducted in Africa and six in Latin America. In Asia, Israel participated in Singapore for several years and in 1970 received requests for advising on the organization of national youth programs in Thailand and the Philippines., Programs in Africa dealt mainly with rural populations. Those in towns were directed primarily to secondary-school students and concentrated on civic education and physical training for a number of hours weekly. A basic study, covering three African countries, classified organizational patterns of the programs according to the criteria of "the degree of control over the members' activities exercised by the movement and the center." [3] It lists three broad categories: (1) Activities in which the movement has "complete and intensive control." These include for the most part prolonged courses (six months to a year) at training farms and bases. The trainees acquire skills in agriculture, in trades (carpentry, mechanics, building), in education in civics, literacy, general knowledge, and in a few cases the elements of paramilitary training. (2) Activities in which the movement exercises only a limited amount of control, such as new villages or traditional adopted villages to which members of the movement return after leaving the training centers. (3) Activities with a very loose control by the movement. Here the functions of the movement are limited to a specific number of hours weekly. Members of the movement did not in the past have any opportunity to spend a prolonged period under the guidance of the movement. Two prototypes of this category might serve the rural clubs in the villages and the Gadna-type classes in secondary schools in towns. Both are engaged mainly in educational functions, with emphasis on literacy in rural clubs and on civics and national education in urban secondary schools.

The first category is the most likely to have a lasting effect on its graduates, but at the same time it is the most difficult for the state to carry out on a major scale because it requires a substantial budget to maintain trainees for a lengthy period. It also requires a great deal of qualified manpower during its formation, and this might oblige the state to lean heavily on foreign advisors. The idea of using the army in part for civilian, peaceful and constructive duties is very attractive. Apart from the better utilization of manpower, pioneer movements inspired by Nahal can have a far-reaching and educationally symbolic effect by spreading a prophetic ideal: "And they shall beat their swords into ploughshares."

Over a period of time there are several conclusions regarding use of the army for peaceful purposes. The stay in a training farm should not exceed one year. Past experience has shown that longer periods—some up to three years—created serious problems for ex-servicemen. Their stay in the army for longer periods, in an agricultural or other training depot, under conditions much superior to those in their villages, often made return to their homes very difficult; the majority did not return but drifted towards towns, often increasing unemployment. A relatively minor problem facing organizers was the question of fixed wages or pocket money.[4] Though sums are small, the use of money as an incentive in youth service is questionable. A most important preoccupation is obviously the manning of administrative and educational staffs. Sometimes teachers are used as instructors, but the experience is not always successful. Teachers tend to impart formal discipline and create a school atmosphere. Youth instructors should create a spirit of comradeship and use it as a medium for achieving the aims sought.

In all forms of youth activity elements of service, usefulness, and purposefulness of the organization must be incorporated. In Europe, cradle of the youth movement idea, decline came about because the movement did not develop into an instrument with a well-defined, purposeful activity. Sometimes it evolved into the youth section of a political party—usually the opposition party—or, in a dictatorial, one-party system it degenerated into the nationalistic, parade-happy offspring of the government party. The youth revolution movements, during the 1960s in Europe and in the United States, in their different varieties, bear witness to the complexity of the problem and to the inadequacy of relevant solutions in developed countries. All are perturbed by the generation gap and the lack of creative feedback between the scale values of the managing generation and those who follow.

The challenge facing all of us is similar. In developing countries it becomes even more complex. There the goal is "the development of civic responsibility, participatory political culture. The individual considers himself an active part of the political system and is oriented toward relating to all groups in the political system."[5] Groups, when able to achieve these goals, can assist meaningfully in the processes of building a "value and cultural infrastructure common to all members of the society as well as defining the feeling of belonging of the individual to the new collective, a feeling which goes beyond the formal contractual link, committing him as a citizen to the new state center."[6]

In projects with Israeli participation, efforts were made to find concrete expression for the identification of the youth movement with national and societal goals. Whenever possible, especially in greater national movements, members, upon completion of their regular service, were requested to return to their villages or to form new ones to help fulfill objectives of the movement. In cases where participants spent only a short time in camp, even when their activities were only extracurricular, some concrete function for fulfilling a real need of the community was identified.

In Lesotho the problem of land erosion is critical, and every year extended areas of arable land are destroyed. Lesotho's youth movement, active in farm training centers in rural areas, took part in programs combating erosion. In Chad members of the local *Jeunesse Pionière* participated in afforestation projects, undertaken on a large scale in conjunction with the Food and Agriculture Organization (FAO). In Costa Rica the national youth movement was active in rural areas in the form of voluntary clubhouses, and its activities included volunteer work camps. In each region the type of function assigned was determined by local needs.

At several international meetings the question was presented as to whether activities of "export" (or foreign) volunteers should be independent of or coordinated with ongoing development projects assisted by national and international agencies. It was always the opinion of Israeli delegates that to be effective, such activities must be fully coordinated with local development projects. Apart from concentration of efforts, because of tremendous and ever-growing needs in developing countries, coordination of volunteer projects with ongoing development programs would promote identification and participation of youth in the process of national and international development, and avoid estrangement or apathy.

The problems and challenges in youth programs are tremendous and constantly growing. The greatest problem is unemployment, which becomes particularly acute when accompanied by a rural exodus. This leads to pockets of poverty, misery, and marginal living conditions. Rehabilitation of youth in urban areas is much more difficult and costly than the outlay necessary to prevent or limit rural exodus.

Israel has only limited experience in urban youth activities abroad, apart from Gadna-type programs in secondary schools. Some successful projects were carried out in vocational training on a part-time basis in Tanzania. Two reasons for the success of this activity were the combination of employment in industry with theoretical training and previous participation in youth movements. Perhaps these two factors should serve as general guidelines for youth programs in urban areas. Isolated vocational training does not fill a real need and does not offer a concrete solution unless suitable employment is secured as a result. In the second place, employment by itself is not enough. Youth must be provided with proper motivation and adequate social and national value scales generated by youth movements. Perhaps the greatest challenge for the development community of the world today is to provide in each region, according to its needs, appropriate organizational and administrative conditions and the machinery required to create adequate employment opportunities for urban youth, while enabling it to enjoy sufficient time for supplementary vocational training and cultural and civic education. A type of urban Youth Aliya, along the lines mentioned above, would seem the answer to this challenge. The expenditure necessary for this type of activity would be considerable, but its success is only possible if governments are willing to give it the high priority it deserves.

NOTES

1. Quoted in R. Shapira and Y. Oren, *Contribution of Youth to Development of the State* (Jerusalem Division for International Cooperation, 1970), p. 3.

2. Quoted in ibid., p. 10.

3. R. Shapira *et al.*, *Israel Assistance to African Countries: Youth Programmes* (in Hebrew), quoted in ibid., p. 27.

4. P. Gonen, "Principles of Organization of National Services and Youth Movements" (manuscript, 1972, in Hebrew).

5. Shapira and Oren, *Contribution of Youth*, p. 4.

6. Ibid., p. 35.

III

POLITICAL AND

CULTURAL RELATIONS

12

Edy Kaufman

ISRAEL'S FOREIGN POLICY
IMPLEMENTATION
IN LATIN AMERICA

In considering the attitudes of policymakers of Latin America (LA) countries towards the Middle East conflict, it becomes necessary to analyze, on the one hand, the influence of domestic forces (local Jewish and Arab communities, political parties, the church, the military, trade unions, students, intellectuals, mass media, etc.); and, on the other hand, the impact produced by the external setting. Developments in the world system have affected those relations, as have the more direct action of the superpowers, the non-aligned countries, Cuba and the actors in the conflict itself—Israel and the Arab countries.

Although there has been a consistent trend during the early seventies for the Arabs to be more actively involved in a seriously planned drive in LA, in historical perspective, Israel, as a whole, maintained the initiative. In this study a brief analysis is attempted to evaluate the use of Israel's foreign policy instruments and their resulting effects.

The major aims of Israel's foreign policy are connected with strategic military issues submerged in its conflict with Arab countries. Israel's major goal is to secure sources of military supply and economic aid. It is not surprising that since the creation of the state, Israel has primarily been involved with the two superpowers, Russia and the United States, and with the secondary powers of the Western European subsystem. The two superpowers are also the homes of the two major Diaspora communities. Thus the developing world of Asia, Africa and LA has held a less important position on the priority scale of Israel's foreign policy. Israel's aims in the developing world have been more of a diplomatic character: attempts to win recognition, to establish permanent representation on a bilateral level, to gain votes at the

United Nations, to secure political support for its stand against terrorism, etc. With regard to certain adjacent African and Asian states, Israel has also sought common military and geopolitical goals. The presence of large Jewish communities in LA has played a part in the formulation of Israel's policy.

The position commanded by each of the three continents in Israel's foreign policy is difficult to determine, especially as the importance of each has fluctuated over the years. However, by checking the number of official policy statements related to Asia, Africa and LA respectively in *Israel's Government Year Book* from 1949-50 to 1967-68, it is possible to observe serious disproportions to the detriment of LA, particularly during the early sixties.

The prominence accorded to Asia and Africa (in particular) is confirmed by an analysis of the annual speeches delivered in the Knesset by foreign ministers when submitting the Ministry's budget. Golda Meir in the 1961-62 budget devoted the equivalent of 165 newspaper column lines to Africa, 86 to Asia, and 22 to LA, even though she said of LA that there were multiple opportunities available to Israel there for strengthening its ties.[1] That LA has received less attention than the other two continents is further confirmed by an analysis of Ben Gurion's foreign policy concerns: LA is ranked last, after the Arab countries, the four great powers, peripheral states, and Asia and Africa.[2] Many interviewed Israeli diplomats were critical of this disproportion, particularly as Israel had received greater political support from LA than from other developing areas.[3]

In the early stages of Israel's statehood, when relations with Asia were almost nonexistent and Africa was still under colonial rule, LA was given a high priority. The first large-scale, coordinated effort on LA was initiated by the prestate Jewish-Zionist leadership. Their aim was to enlist the support of the elites and general public of LA for Zionist aspirations in Palestine. Even while World War II was raging and the United Nations was not yet in existence, the Zionist leadership was actively preparing for the possibility that the Palestine question would be brought up before the international community. This was the primary reason for the establishment of the Pro-Palestine Committees of the mid-1940s in numerous LA countries, and for intensive lobbying engaged in by a handful of dedicated representatives of the semigovernmental Jewish Agency, in LA capitals and later at the United Nations. On the eve of Israel's birth and during its first years of statehood, LA countries constituted no less than one-third of the total UN membership. LA's importance in the international arena was also appreciated during the 1948 period since a special section which dealt with LA existed in the Israeli delegation to the United Nations, whereas " . . . no other geographic regions of the world merit[ed] separate and clearly defined sections or advisers within the Israel U.N. delegation.''[4]

After the creation of the State of Israel, the Foreign Service developed gradually, and even until the late fifties it was not represented by full embassies all over Europe. This was due to a policy wherein priorities had to be fixed according to limited budgets and limited personnel. Thus LA was left to the care of local honorary consuls. Most Foreign Ministry efforts were invested in more problematic areas, particularly Asia. The relationship with the continent where Israel was located was of the greatest importance to Foreign Minister Sharett.

The reasons for this and for the postponement of more intensified relations with LA until the early sixties include: first, Israel felt it imperative to overcome its isolation in Asia which was due to the following factors: a barrier of Arab countries; the existence in Asian countries of large Muslim populations; a general noncomprehension of the relationship of the Jewish people to the land of Israel and the Bible, due to totally different religious sources and the absence of local Jewish communities; and the feeling that Jewish settlement in Israel was a "white colonialist venture." Second, the trend of the Israeli government at that time was towards "neutralism," and it was therefore felt that there was a coincidence of Israeli and Asian views and thus Israel might be accepted as part of the Third World and its anticolonialist struggle.

The Asian drive continued over the fifties but after the Sinai War of 1956, rapprochement with Africa became Israel's major foreign policy venture in the developing world. This African trend was particularly strong under Golda Meir's administration, since that period coincided with the creation of a large number of new states whose development was extremely important and which held no "traditional positions" on the Middle East conflict. Israel thus had an opportunity to create a positive image by means of physical presence (technical assistance programs, etc.). The possibilities presented for increasing trade with Africa by opening the Straits of Tiran, as well as the permanent and powerful anti-Israeli element of North African Arab countries in African organizations, made the Israeli drive even more urgent. Until the late sixties, Israel devoted only sporadic diplomatic campaigns to LA, usually connected with UN debates; thus the content of Israeli-LA relations was limited and of a political, noneconomic nature.

Factors which contributed to the increase of Israeli attention to LA were the crisis in Israeli-Argentine relations precipitated by the Eichmann kidnapping of 1960, the Cuban Revolution under Fidel Castro in 1959 which signalled that in the future Latin American countries might not automatically follow US instructions—and the need to create concrete motives for LA's basic support of Israel. (By then, technical assistance was facilitated by the initial successes and experience accumulated on the other two continents, and was apparently enhanced by the new spirit of the Alliance for Progress then being launched in LA).

LA's importance received further attention for various reasons, including the Yom Kippur War of 1973. The war highlighted Israel's growing isolation, the rupture of Afro-Israeli relations, the pro-Arab policies of most West European countries in the wake of the oil crisis, and renewed Arab attempts to eliminate the Israeli presence from Asian gatherings.

Another influence in Israel's LA policy which must not be underestimated is the relations with LA Jewish communities. They are as important as Israel's desire for political support on the multilateral level. The "Jewish dimension" in the attitudinal prism of major Israeli leaders—already well studied by Brecher[5]—has perhaps not been stressed enough only because present relations with the communities are satisfactory. Sharett referred to Israel's relationship with LA as a "triangular harmony": "Israel's relations with Latin American governments; Latin American governments' relations with local Jewry; and Israel's relations with Latin American Jewry."[6] The interaction of these three actors is of great importance to Israel and the question is to what extent this interaction was and is adequately implemented. We shall therefore proceed to analyze the means of implementation: diplomatic, cultural, military, economic, technical, and informational.

ISRAEL'S FOREIGN POLICY INSTRUMENTS

Diplomatic Relations

Diplomatic relations that followed creation of the State of Israel found a solid and well developed basis in the intensive pro-Israel activity of local LA elements in its prestate period. In 1921, Rudesindo Martinez, Jr., in his book *The Hebrew People and Political Zionism*,[7] gave eloquent support to the Jewish struggle for a national homeland in Palestine and connected it with the Dreyfus case. When the British Mandate of Palestine was approved in San Remo, Argentina, Brazil and Uruguay supported the Balfour Declaration.

The atrocities committed by the Third Reich and the resultant problem of large numbers of unabsorbed Jewish refugees from Europe strengthened LA ruling circles in endorsing the claims for an independent Jewish state. For that purpose, LA representatives of the Zionist Federations met with those of the Jewish Agency. They were highly instrumental in establishing committees supporting a Hebrew Palestine in the years 1945-46, and continued to function until 1949 when Israel was accepted into the United Nations. The creation of such committees was attributed in most cases to the initiative of a few individuals, i.e., the envoy of the Jewish National Fund, Nathan

Bistritzki; Jewish Agency officials, Moshe Tov, Benno Wisser and Abraham Mibashan; and the coordinating efforts of Mrs. Yarden at the LA Department of the Jewish Agency in New York. A declaration of the Argentine Committee explains the motivations for the formation of such bodies:

> Contemporary history records, as one of the most shameful facts, that the anti-Semitic persecution was carried out with the premeditation and cruelty characteristic of regimes which destroy human dignity wherever they establish themselves or strike temporary roots. Our country, which harbors extensive settlements established by Jewish efforts and which counts in all fields of endeavor with Argentines coming from Jewish homes, has not been free from such objectionable movements. The policy which was carried out in the Third Reich and in the countries occupied by it, the most cruel extermination, has impelled the Jews to place an even greater stress in their demand for their historic land of Palestine where they may, within the British Commonwealth of Nations, establish a home for the Jews persecuted in other lands. The Balfour Declaration had solemnly promised such a homeland .... Convinced that the full implementation of the Balfour Declaration will contribute both to the welfare of the Jewish people and will remove the blot of persecution from civilized society, we invite all those who are inspired by the ideal of human solidarity to join the pro-Palestine Committee. Through this committee we shall add strength to the efforts of those who promote the creation of the Jewish Homeland in Palestine.[8]

Composed mostly of liberal elements (in some cases the same members had been involved in supporting the Spanish Republic, and belonged to anti-Fascist Committees during World War II, they joined the new "just" cause that appeared in the mid-forties: the establishment of the Jewish State.[9] The Society of Free Masons gave unrestricted support to the Jewish State, a fact leading to many of its active members enrolling in these committees, for example, in Uruguay.[10] In El Salvador and Chile, devoted Christians took active part in these bodies; and in many cases, outstanding political leaders headed the drive. In Chile, four previous and future presidents of state were to support Israel and the Zionist cause: Arturo Allessandri (conservative), Gabriel González Videla (radical, Center party) Salvador Allende (socialist) and Eduardo Frei (Christian Democrat). While in El Salvador the government was hostile to the Jewish cause until December 1949, a coup d'état on December 14 of that year brought in Reinaldo Galindo Pohl, one of the five members of the Junta, who was the Vice-President of the El Salvador pro-Palestine Committee. The president of that same Committee, Ruben H. Dimas, was to be appointed minister of culture.[11]

Although most of the daily work was carried out by local representatives of the Jewish Agency on the continent, some non-Jewish members were no less active in support of the cause. Gustavo Gutiérrez, a Cuban, was sent to several LA countries in 1946, and Gabriel González Videla represented LA in the World Committee for Palestine Congress of 1945 held in the United States. In the same year, a LA Zionist Congress took place in Uruguay and an impressive number of solidarity messages were extended by prominent political leaders and intellectuals from all over the continent. The Committees helped in bolstering public opinion, lobbying in Parliaments[12] and extracting statements of support from political personalities. However, its main task was to get "comments expressed in the form of instructions to the delegations of these countries to the United Nations Assembly."[13] The international arena is where most of the efforts were centered.

During the first years following Israel's independence, most of Israel's representation was carried out by an honorary consul; a local Jewish representative, who in most cases continued his prestate function as an officer of the Jewish Agency. Many of them were remarkable workers: Samuel Goren in Chile, Salvador Rosenthal in Colombia, Eric Heinemann in Guatemala, Benjamin Shapira in Paraguay, and Fastlich in Mexico. The first official Israeli diplomatic representative in LA was Jacob Tsur as minister in Uruguay. He presented his credentials in October 1948 in Montevideo and was registered in Israel's records as the fourth diplomatic nomination. He was later transferred to Buenos Aires where he presented his credentials to General Perón on August 1, 1949.[14] He was also accredited as nonresident minister in Chile and Paraguay in 1950. After President Vargas came to power in Brazil in 1951, an Israeli legation was opened in Rio de Janeiro. In 1953 a legation was established in Mexico. In all cases, the countries reciprocated and opened diplomatic missions in Israel. But most LA states had no permanent Israeli representative and the large part of the responsibility was carried by Moshe Tov, who in 1955 was appointed roving Ambassador to all twenty LA countries. He had to distribute his time among LA presidents, foreign ministers and LA delegates to the United Nations in New York.

Although most LA countries were willing to establish closer permanent relationships with Israel,[15] Israel chose to invest most of its energies in other continents. It was only more than a decade later that diplomatic representation was considerably enlarged, as shown by the following graph:[16]

By 1972 Israel had full diplomatic relations at the ambassadorial level with nineteen of the twenty LA countries. Until the severence of relations in

GRAPH 1   Growth of Israeli Permanent Diplomatic Representation
in Latin American Countries

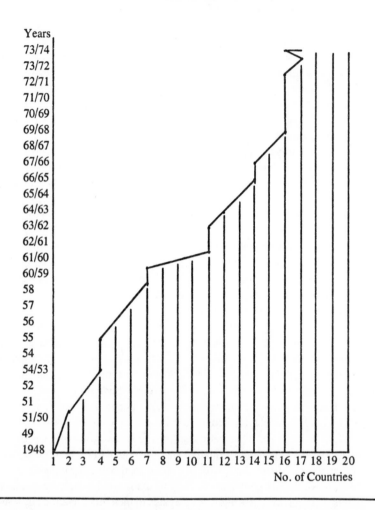

September 1973, Israel had a legation in Cuba. In seventeen countries there are permanent missions and in the remaining two, Honduras and Nicaragua, they had nonresident ambassadors living in neighboring countries. Israel is thus third, after France and Great Britain, in extracontinental representation. Most embassies were functioning in 1972 with a small staff: an ambassador, a first secretary and administrative personnel. Those in Argentina, Venezuela, Brazil, Chile and Mexico had a larger staff. Apart from permanent representations, Israeli diplomacy uses other means to further its aims.

There were frequent visits of leading political figures to the continent: Foreign Minister Sharett in 1953 and 1957; chairman of the Knesset Foreign Affairs Committee, Meir Argov in 1957; Foreign Minister Golda Meir in 1959; President Zalman Shazar in 1966; and Minister Abba Eban in 1960, 1964, 1970, 1972 and 1973.

While most of these visits were official in nature, many other ministers and members of parliament visited LA countries in connection with the Jewish communities, and particularly in electoral periods of the World Zionist Organizations, in order to raise support for their own political parties in the Diaspora. Mention should also be made of the special missions of Ambassadors Itzhak Harkaby and Jacob Tsur which covered nearly all LA countries, twice in June-July and October. 1967, in attempts to obtain backing for Israel's position in the international arena before, during, and after the Six-Day War. Israel has always sought to be represented at ceremonies of transference of presidential power or national anniversaries. Since the very beginning of the state, this aspect had been taken care of with great efficiency.[17]

It is difficult to make a general estimate regarding the quality of Israeli diplomatic service in LA. Some ambassadors have been active at all levels, while others have been more concerned with the Jewish communities. After the first years when leading Israeli figures represented Israel in LA, the quality of Israel's representatives declined. In recent years, more important people have gained ambassadorial positions. Most of those interviewed in LA, when comparing the quality of Israel's diplomats with those from Arab countries, were favorably impressed by Israeli representatives, though they also make clear distinctions between the highly successful and the average diplomats.

Cultural Relations

The role of intellectuals in forming public opinion in LA is very strong. The public has a distrust of politicians and a certain respect for writers, folk singers, artists and university teachers who willingly accept the challenge of becoming involved in political life. This aspect is particularly important for Israel's relations with LA. An experienced Israeli diplomat noted that Israeli and LA intellectuals have a mission to fulfill in bringing the two peoples closer.[18] The formation of images about Israel was a determining factor during the first years, when no tangible material or economic interests could explain LA support, and LA intellectuals were largely responsible for that image.

With Israel's independence, its diplomats and local honorary consuls undertook the duty of political representation; the Jewish Agency took responsibility for the strengthening of Zionism, and the pro-Palestine Committees were to become cultural institutions whose duty was to serve as an intellectual link with Israel.[19] The Instituto de Relaciones Culturales Mexico-Israel was formed in 1949, and in 1950 a similar one was formed in Chile. The same combination of judges, former active politicians, clergymen, university professors, journalists and artists continued to head these institutions. Most of them were non-Jewish and when some years later ex-honorary Isaeli consuls were replaced by permanent Israeli diplomats, they also became involved in the general cultural work. In 1956 the Central Institute of Cultural Israel-Ibero America, Spain and Portugal Relations was formed in Jerusalem. Its aim was to strengthen ties with the institutes in LA. At its peak it included eighteen institutes in LA and one in New York.[20] In 1972 there were twelve institutes functioning normally.[21] One of the reasons for the decrease was that in many cases the same people continued to run the institutes over a period of twenty years and were not always replaced when they passed away. Many of the younger intellectuals influenced by other developments became less sympathetic towards Israel. It was partially the desire to keep old friends in office that, in many countries like Uruguay and Chile prevented the efforts necessary to find a new generation to succeed them. In the aftermath of Israel's creation the only possibility of balancing political aid of LA with "normal" relationships of reciprocity was the cultural exchange program of which Israel was the active promoter. Another reason for the relative diminution of the cultural drive was Israel's ability later to reciprocate with technical assistance, a program started in the sixties.

In the beginning Israel was interested in projecting its common Spanish-Sephardic cultural background.[22] Soon after independence however, these relationships were superceded by a growing expression of reciprocal desire to know the other society. Such cultural ties allowed Israel to have relations with opposition circles and intellectuals in dictatorial countries, thus balancing the uncomfortable image of its close relations with some unpopular governments. Although most of the institute's activities are of a cultural nature, its members did not hesitate in moments of crisis to call for political solidarity with Israel. As stated by the late president of the Chilean Institute, Professor Vergara Bravo, in a message to his fellow members:

> We believe that the activities of Latin American-Israeli Institutes, no matter how modest, and reduced in some cases, constitute nevertheless, a significant contribution to the knowledge about Israel; no efforts are irrelevant for her [Israel's] definitive consolidation as a sovereign state, through a stable peace, with historical, natural and secure borders, free forever from the fear of a surprise attack or guerrilla warfare of armed groups, supported or at least tolerated and

acclaimed by the opponents, who give them refuge in their respective territories.[23]

The Institute's success in each LA country depended fundamentally on the people involved (and one cannot exaggerate the intensity of their work). The general cultural background is indeed much more favorable than in Asia and Africa. Figures given by the American Jewish Committee indicate that by 1970 there were 424 books published in Spanish and Portuguese on Jewish topics.[24] The existence of a Jewish community also encourages the creation and consumption of Hebrew literature, concerts and lectures, etc.

The variety of activities covers a large spectrum. Israel hosts visiting intellectuals, writers and artists—guests of the institute. The Israeli Institute also offers scholarships, lectures, seminars, special weeks devoted to the study of cultures of different countries, translations of LA literature into Hebrew, art exhibitions, concerts and radio programs. Streets, schools and forests have been named after LA heroes, personalities, or countries. Spanish-language teaching programs, introductions to Israel's life and landscape to LA diplomats,[25] awards to LA writers and devoted members of the institute make up Israel's contribution.

Similar activities take place in different LA countries. The Israeli Philharmonic Orchestra and the Batsheva ballet troupe attract large audiences. Football competitions between Israeli and LA teams and other sports activities have become quite regular. Exhibitions about modern Israel and special aspects of its society serve as a general way to cast light on this country.[26] Books about Israel, travelers' impressions, supplements in newspapers and magazines, biblical contests, and other activities are now common. The Israeli-American Institute in New York offers lectures by LA diplomats and politicians, as well as a stage for artists coming to New York from the South.

The Hebrew University and institutes of higher learning and research in Israel make important contributions. Associations of Friends of the Universities in most LA countries organize cultural programs; teachers and students take part in exchange programs and common research projects. The existence of a LA Studies Department at the Hebrew University facilitates direct contact with the academic community on the LA continent. Honorary degrees have been awarded to prominent LA figures, e.g. former Mexican President Miguel Alemán. Donations to the University Library by LA governments and universities and LA diplomats teaching at the university are further examples of these close reciprocal contacts. Although by now routine, these events and activities[27] have made an impact on Israeli-LA relations. At the moment there are bilateral cultural agreements between Israel and sixteen LA countries.

Military and Defense Programs

Israel has no identifiable strategic or military interests in LA vital to its own security. Nothing in LA even faintly resembles the strategic importance or geographic proximity of areas bordering on, or approaching Israel as the Arab countries. Nevertheless, in the course of the last decade, Israel developed an extensive program of cooperation which, until recently had been directed by a special department in its Ministry of Defense (the Department of International Relations and Cooperation).

Much of this program, called Special Assistance, has never been truly military. Rather, it consisted of civic action programs relating primarily to Nahal-type rural cooperative projects, based within a military framework, as well as the establishment and organization of Youth Movements. Despite the strongly nonmilitary character of the Special Assistance programs, these involved direct interaction between Israel's Ministry of Defense and Israeli military (and sometimes civilian) personnel on the one hand, and LA military establishments on the other. (In some cases the youth movements are civilian-controlled, e.g., Costa Rica.) In several cases these programs have constituted an important part of the total volume of bilateral relations between Israel and the LA nations.

The development of the Special Assistance program catered to mutual interests. For Israeli policy makers, conscious of the strategic political importance of the LA military, this was an effective and respectable way of maintaining their presence close to the location of political power.[28] Here, Israel was able to contribute from its unique experience both with Nahal and with Youth Movement organizations. For several LA military establishments the Israeli experience provided not only a relevant model for civic action and a way of tackling national problems, but was no less instrumental in building a positive and constructive image of the armed forces in their respective nations.[29] Nahal-type programs used by the army for agricultural and colonization tasks were adopted by Bolivia, Ecuador (1963-64), Peru, and much later (1971) by Colombia.

The National Youth Movement was another type of cooperative activity. Although this type of activity had also been directed by Israel's Defense Ministry as part of the Special Assistance program, it has mostly been done in cooperation with civilian authorities.[30] The first pilot experiment with National Youth Movement in LA was successfully conducted in Costa Rica with Israeli involvement and organizational aid during its first years, 1966 through 1969. The Costa Rican experience had a strong demonstrative effect and similar programs were started in Panama (1971), Venezuela (1973) and El Salvador (1972).[31]

In promoting the National Youth Movement in LA Israel was, during the first years, extremely careful not to copy indiscriminately its own Gadna paramilitary program, despite requests from several governments to do so.[32] The Costa Rican National Youth Movement (MNJ)—established in a country where the military had long been dissolved—aimed at purely civic targets. It promoted educational and cultural activities in youth centers; it organized pioneering activities and special operations to build up a sense of purpose and voluntary spirit among Costa Rican youth. Such activities included construction of school and community facilities, public health activities, fund raising for welfare purposes, tree planting, road paving, etc.[33]

The other facet of Israel's military relationships with LA centers around purely military themes—selling military equipment to LA countries. Because of the nature of this transaction, very little information is available. Nevertheless, even on the basis of few and scant references in the Israeli press, a certain trend can of late be discerned. The factors involved in preparing the stage for Israel becoming a significant arms supplier to LA are: first, LA wants alternative sources of military supply so as to reduce its dependence on one dominant source, as shown by the different political character of the buying regimes in LA. Second, Israel's credibility as a military power has engendered confidence in the equipment used by its armed forces. The previous factors would not be of much relevance unless we recognize a third. Since the late 1960s, Israel has become a producer of sophisticated and important military items.

With its new industrial-technological capabilities—largely a product of post-1967 developments—Israel's defense establishment has seen in the export of military hardware, an important end in itself.[34] Major Israeli firms engaged in the production of arms and military communications equipment have embarked upon an active sales policy.[35] Aircraft have been purchased by several LA countries, such as the recent sale to Bolivia for $5.5 million of six Arava planes.[36] Visits to Israel by numerous LA officers holding various ranks have resulted in their becoming familiarized with Israel's armed forces and defense industries, thus facilitating increased interaction and the establishment of joint projects between these countries. It would not be an exaggeration to state that by now the economic value of Israel's export of military equipment to LA has by far surpassed the other, more "conventional" items in trade relations.

Economic and Trade Relations

There have been several objective and subjective impediments to intensifying trade between Israel and LA. The distances between these countries are enormous and transport irregular, prolonged and expensive. In addition, high tariffs, protectionist policies and other restrictive measures on imports have been practiced by many LA countries. L.A. economic instability is almost "structural," manifested by high inflationary rates and frequent currency devaluations. Also, Israeli entrepreneurs are unfamiliar with LA market conditions. Furthermore, the development of alternative markets for LA exports have increased: during the latter period of "détente," the Soviet and Eastern European presence on the continent has been strongly felt and Japan's economic drive in some of the more developed LA countries has been impressive. Until the oil crisis, even Western Europe revealed an interest in renewing its economic links with LA. This accounts for Israel's hesitance in entering LA markets and the small trade volume, as well as the marginal, if not insignificant, place on the balance sheets of both sides. This state of affairs is reflected in Table 1.

Despite difficulties and present low trade level, officials of Israel's Ministry of Commerce and Industry see good prospects for expanding trade with LA. This evaluation is based on the actual record: the upward trend in commercial trade relations since 1967, dramatized by a 46 percent increase of Israeli exports in a single year (from 1970 to 1971); LA's desire to reduce economic dependence on the United States, thus intensifying relations with other countries; and the gradual increase of development projects, both agricultural and industrial, which increase possibilities for commerical opportunities (irrigation equipment for agricultural projects, etc.).[38] Commercial trade potential of LA for Israel is definitely undertapped at present, since LA seems only to be in its "discovery stage" for Israeli firms and enterprises.

Israel's major trading partners in LA are Argentina, Brazil, Peru, Venezuela and Mexico, which in 1971 accounted for 80 percent of its exports to the region.[39] On the import side, Argentina sold Israel $12.8 million worth of goods in 1971 ($15.5 million in 1970); Brazil, $9 million in 1971 ($4.6 million in 1970); Uruguay, $5.5 million in 1971 ($4.5 million in 1970); Peru $2.1 million in 1971 ($3.7 million in 1970); and Venezuela, $1.2 million in 1971 ($270,000 in 1970). In 1971 Israel exported $4.9 million to Peru ($2.2 million in 1970); $3.5 million to Brazil ($2.7 million in 1970); $2 million to Argentina ($1.3 million in 1970); $1.7 million to Mexico ($2.0 million in 1970); and $1 million to Venezuela ($1.5 million in 1970).[40]

Israel's main exports to the region are industrial products and chemicals. In 1971, 29 percent of Israel's exports were chemicals, 19 percent textile, garment and leather products; and 17 percent electric and electronic equipment.[41] The last group of items has been a rapidly expanding industry since 1967, representing the rising export potential of Israel's industrial (military) establishment. Israel's purchases in LA were made up primarily of basic food stuffs. In 1971, meat accounted for $18 million (from Argentina, Brazil

TABLE 1   Latin America's Share in Israeli's Foreign Trade[37] (millions of $ US)

Year	1960	1961	1962	1963	1964	1965	1966	1967	1968	1969	1970	1971
Total Israeli Imports	496	584	626	662	815	815	817	457	1,093	1,302	1,426	1,786
Total Imports from LA	3	3	8	7	11	15	22	16	22	26	32	32
Total Israeli Exports	211	584	271	338	352	406	477	517	602	689	734	915
Total Exports to LA	4	3	3	3	6	6	6	6	9	10	11	16

and Uruguay), and rice for $2.4 million(Uruguay, Argentina and Brazil). Other items accounted for relatively minor sums (wool, coffee, fishmeal, etc.).[42]

Within the growing web of economic relations with LA, Israeli companies offering technical services and know-how on a commercial basis occupy an important place. Several companies have been engaged—some more successfully than others—in construction work (Vered in road building in Peru and Central America, Solel Boneh in construction of housing projects in Buenos Aires); others have been selling planning services (most notable is TAHAL in the field of water resources and agricultural planning); or industrial and technological know-how (IPD, Israex, and more are entering the LA scene—like Israel Aircraft Industry, Tadiran, etc.).

Technical Assistance

Less than a decade after independence Israel was already offering technical assistance both to newer and older developing states. An Israeli official publication presents what are in their view the major advantages of its program: Israel's independence (post-World War II) allows it to offer help to nations who have only recently achieved independence, help in the transition from the colonial stage. Israel has accumulated a rich fund of agricultural development and vocational training know-how—two basic needs of developing countries; the climatic and ecological characteristics are similar to those of many other developing nations, while those of developed ones are not; nearly all Israelis speak western languages, making it possible to train cadres in their spoken tongues; Israel was never a colonialist power, has no common boundaries with, and no political aspirations in other developing countries; the democratic character of Israeli society projects the attractive concept that development and freedom can be combined; Israelis have no racial prejudices, a factor that frequently hampers experts from developed nations of East and West; Israeli experts are usually more devoted to their missions and lack the colonial "boss" qualities and participate, together with the local elements, in the simple tasks and the hard work; the influence of Zionist ideologies stresses the importance of manual labor and pioneering virtues; Israel's international cooperation, based mostly in the export of knowledge without large capital investments, does not create a psychological atmosphere resembling exploitation.[43]

Among other important features is Israel's mixed social structure which does not lend itself to the rather rigid definitions of its being either "capitalist" or "socialist." It presents a special model that can be considered by the developing states as a separate and applicable experience. Although the entire model may not be relevant, certain aspects of it are—the system of land ownership, agricultural cooperative settlements (moshav), labor insurance, etc.

As early as 1949 Panama expressed a special interest in oranges and suggested that it would finance the trip to Israel of a group of peasants, if Israel would cover the cost of a three to four-month training period in growing Jaffa oranges.[44] However, at that time Israel opted to start technical assistance programs in other continents, first in Burma and since 1956 in newly independent African countries which were the center of Israel's interest for its international cooperation. In the early 1960s Israel enlarged its foreign aid program to include LA.

In 1961, the Director General of the Ministry of Agriculture, Itzhak Levi, studied the possibilities of technical assistance to Brazil. Both countries signed the Recife Treaty for technical cooperation and Israel began with agricultural aid (special cornstalk and other projects). Since then, bilateral relations with other countries in this field developed rapidly. By 1967 most LA countries had signed specific treaties with Israel and by 1972 all countries, with the exception of Cuba,[45] had bilateral technical cooperation agreements with Israel. Many of the projects were encouraged by international and regional organizations, particularly with the help of the Organization of American States (OAS) and the Inter-American Development Bank (IDB). Thanks to the travel grants offered by OAS, Israel has become the extra continental country with the largest contingent of LA trainees. The first Israel-OAS Secretariat agreement was signed in 1962 and since then its scope has been enlarged several times. The IDB has also promoted research projects and study teams of Israeli experts in LA. Most Israeli activity has been in agricultural projects. Tables 2 and 3 show the exchange programs in the major fields of activity.[46]

TABLE 2 Technical Cooperation During the Last Eight Years: Israeli Experts Abroad (by Country and Profession), 1960-1968

Country	Total	Agriculture & Nutrition	Health	Education	Engineering	Cooperativism & Labor Matters	Others
Argentina	4	2	—	1	—	—	1
Bolivia	20	14	—	4	—	1	1
Brazil	31	23	—	—	1	—	7
Chile	23	17	—	2	2	—	2
Colombia	22	16	1	1	2	1	2
Costa Rica	14	1	—	9	—	—	3
Dominican R.	11	9	—	—	—	—	1
Ecuador	22	13	—	4	3	1	—
Guatemala	10	9	—	1	—	2	—
Guyana	1	1	—	—	—	—	—
Haiti	5	4	—	—	—	1	—
Honduras	2	1	—	—	—	1	—
Jamaica	3	2	—	—	—	—	1
Mexico	7	1	2	—	—	2	2
Nicaragua	3	2	—	—	1	—	—
Peru	31	19	—	—	1	3	8
Salvador	10	9	—	—	—	—	1
Trinidad	8	4	—	—	1	1	2
Venezuela	44*	34	6	—	1	1	2
Total	271	181	9	22	12	14	33

* Including the Central Israeli Team for Latin America

TABLE 3 Fellowships in Israel (by Country and Profession), 1960-1968

Country	Total	Agriculture	Cooperativism & Labor	Medicine & Health	Vocational Training	Comm. Devpt. Social Work	Academic Studies	Education	Youth	Various
Argentina	111	58	29	—	—	2	2	2	—	18
Barbados	1	—	1	—	—	—	—	—	—	—
Bolivia	96	22	17	—	—	—	—	18	24	15
Brazil	124	82	23	—	—	1	4	—	—	14
Chile	135	67	30	—	—	2	1	1	14	20
Colombia	155	67	35	—	—	2	1	1	26	23
Costa Rica	79	13	6	—	8	2	—	—	32	18
Dominican R.	46	23	12	—	—	1	1	—	5	4
Ecuador	117	53	16	—	—	1	3	—	29	15
Guatemala	66	18	17	—	—	1	—	10	11	9
Guyana	56	17	8	15	—	—	8	1	—	7
Haiti	23	9	12	—	—	2	—	—	—	—
Honduras	35	13	13	—	—	2	—	1	—	6
Jamaica	63	35	7	—	—	—	6	6	7	2
Mexico	199	136	31	—	—	1	1	—	16	14
Nicaragua	27	12	7	—	—	—	—	—	—	8
Panama	45	17	3	2	—	—	1	—	14	8
Paraguay	31	17	6	—	—	2	—	—	—	6
Peru	160	72	36	—	—	1	1	9	21	20
Puerto Rico	1	—	1	—	—	—	—	—	—	—
Salvador	46	20	9	—	—	2	1	—	7	7
Trinidad	11	7	4	—	—	—	—	—	—	—
Uruguay	95	30	24	—	—	4	2	—	14	21
Venezuela	196	115	25	—	—	4	7	—	18	27
Total	1,918	903	372	17	8	30	39	49	238	262

An important source of technical assistance is the Center of Studies on Labor and Cooperation for LA run by Histadrut. Since 1962 courses have been organized in Israel as well as in LA. The first course was given for LA trade union leaders and included training programs for trade union leadership, rural labor leaders, establishment and running of cooperatives, public housing, cooperative marketing, health services in rural areas, etc. The Research Center for Agricultural Settlement at Rehovot provides advanced studies in regional planning, and LA attendance at Rehovot's international congresses of statesmen and scientists of developing countries has been growing, with seventeen LA countries participating in 1973.

There has been a trend toward a more comprehensive form of aid in social, economic and cultural planning, and scientific cooperation, particularly with the more developed countries such as Mexico, Brazil and Argentina. Compared to Africa, LA shared until 1972 only a small part of Israel's technical assistance program. While figures appear to be rather similar to those for Asia, it is important to remember that only a few Asian countries maintain normal reciprocal diplomatic relations with Israel. While one could argue that the major cause of this unusual distribution has to do with the Israeli order of priorities,[47] there is evidence that some LA countries did not show great receptivness, delaying the execution of suggested projects.

The impact of technical assistance can be evaluated by the efficiency in furthering development of the recipient country and the political gains for the supplier. Without going into detail,[48] Israel's technical aid to LA has been successful in achieving its objectives.[49] The political implications for Israel are difficult to determine. There are no clear indications that these means have always contributed to getting LA countries to support Israel's policies. In the case of Haiti, Israel has received active support and it strengthened the already existing pro-Israeli attitude of the Dominican Republic. However, Chile—during the Allende regime, and Peru—whose attitude to Israel in international organizations has been critical—have also received large numbers of experts. Long-run expectations include the creation of a positive Israeli image in recipient countries, strengthening cooperation in the fields of trade, tourism, etc., and establishment of personal relations and friendship with important members in the political life and administration of LA. These activities serve indirectly to ameliorate the position of local Jewish communities, giving them a sense of pride of their coreligionists. In many cases, particularly in remote and isolated areas, the expert is seen by local Jewry as Israel's representative. Another interesting reward is the strengthening of Israel's position in Washington which acknowledges Israel's foreign aid contribution.[50] Last but not least, this activity is important for the Israeli self-image, the sense of "mission" inculcated by Ben Gurion.

PROPAGANDA

The *Los Angeles Times* has noted the importance of propaganda in LA both for Israel and the Arab countries: "What it costs, neither Israeli nor Arab diplomats will say. But the bill must be impressive, for the slick pamphlets and mimeographed broadsides flood the mails."[51] Zionist activists have always been aware of its importance. In 1948 the New York Bureau of the Jewish Agency for LA produced a review of the LA press on "Palestine."[52] News from Argentina pointed out the difficulties of placing articles in prestige newspapers such as *La Prensa* and *La Nación*, and suggested concentrating on other, less prestigious ones.[53] Three volumes of press cuttings from the Jewish and non-Jewish press of 1949 were collected in Argentina.[54] The Telegraphic News Agency, ANA, and, to a lesser extent, the Jewish Telegraphic Agency, were very instrumental during this period in facilitating immediate access to information about Hebrew Palestine.

Gradually many of the information functions were taken over by Israeli Embassies, but even today much of the written material is prepared and circulated by organized Jewish groups. The outstanding examples are publications geared in general to intellectuals and particularly to those on the Left: e.g., *Indice* (DAIA), Buenos Aires; *Raíces* (Argentine Zionist Organization), Buenos Aires; *Comentario*, Buenos Aires; *Claves*, Santiago de Chile; and different publications of the Institute of Human Relations in Montevideo, Caracas, etc.

Most Israeli missions do not have press attachés, and only the major countries such as Argentina, Mexico, Chile, Uruguay and Brazil being served by local press officers. Nonetheless, contacts with the press are generally very effective and good. Greater propaganda efforts have been invested in Argentina, Brazil and Chile, the assumption being that these countries are the most influential disseminators of information in LA.[55]

The means used by Israel are comprehensive: in 1960 there were eighteen publications in Spanish language issued by the Foreign Ministry (sometimes in cooperation with the Jewish Agency).[56] Since then the quantity of material issued has varied, with a considerable increase since 1970. Many booklets are reproductions of statements and writings of European left-wing intellectuals (Sartre, Mnacko) translated for LA by Israel. Only occasionally are specific articles written by Jewish or non-Jewish Latin Americans, adapted to national problems and mentality, also circulated with the assistance of the embassies.

According to Israeli sources fifty broadcasting stations in LA carry monthly half-hour programs prerecorded in Israel. Many local Jewish communities have their own Hebrew hours (in Spanish or Yiddish) whose audience is made up mostly of elder members of the Jewish community. The

Israeli Embassies offer photos and films to newspapers and television networks:[57] the information deals not only with the Middle East conflict but also with the positive aspects of Israeli society and its technological achievements. Israel has also been assisting in the preparation of special supplements for newspapers and journals about Israel and in publishing articles by local journalists.[58] Catholic festivals, such as Christmas, receive special attention, the emphasis being on religious tolerance.[59]

Groups of journalists and individuals have visited Israel. The results have often paid off in their reports published in L A dailies. All within a matter of a few days, the Israeli Embassy in Buenos Aires reported four articles in the traditional daily *La Nación*, some by visitors to Israel; four articles in the prestigious *La Prensa*; an interview with a returning visitor in *Clarín*; and an interview with General Rabin in the weekly *Confirmado*. At the same time, most newspapers cover Passover celebrations in Israel.[60] In most cases, Embassy staffers speak fluent Spanish and are happy to be interviewed by local radio and TV stations on topics about cultural, social and political matters. In some cases the Israeli ambassador thus becomes a well-known figure in national public life.[61]

An information center has been functioning in Buenos Aires and has provided general material on Israel. Israel's information is generally considered to be more effective than that of Arab diplomatic representatives, although objective handicaps, resulting from changes in the international political situation and Israel's security policy, have considerably undermined Israel's efforts since 1967. There has been a particular lag in communication with left-wing circles, a fact which has caused concern to Israeli commentators and many LA Jewish community leaders.[62] Arab interests in leading newspapers have increased considerably over the last years in some countries (Brazil, Argentina).

LATIN AMERICA'S RELATIONS WITH ISRAEL

Ignoring the Jewish dimension for a moment, the most prominent payoff that Israel expects from its foreign policy in LA is political support. Since the Middle East issue has so frequently been raised in international forums, where members are obliged to take a stand, Israel's efforts have been directed towards getting multilateral support. In practically all cases where Israel at its birth, eleven were LA.[64] LA nations can be divided into three ment's main objective in the continent was the assurance of a positive vote at the United Nations. Bilateral relations, such as representation, recognition of Jerusalem as Israel's capital, increased trade, arms deals, or air traffic are important, but still secondary.

The strong emphasis on the United Nations has historical reasons. LA votes assured partition in 1947. LA accounted for 40 percent of the ''yes'' votes at UNSCOP (United Nations Committee on Palestine)—a decision which was endorsed by the General Assembly on November 29 by thirty-three positive votes, thirteen of which came from LA. When Israel joined the United Nations on March 11, 1949, eighteen of the thirty-seven favorable countries were from LA. Since then LA nations have been well represented among the initiators of pro-Israeli resolutions tabled at the United Nations.[63]

Diplomatic Bilateral Relations

With the general deterioration of support from multilateral organizations, diplomatic bilateral relations have acquired great relevance for Israel. It is in this context that LA countries have shown a far more positive performance than other developed and developing states. At present, all but one country in LA maintain full and normal diplomatic relations with Israel—a level which has not even been achieved in Europe (no relations exist with Portugal and Spain). Of the twenty-two countries which immediately recognized Israel at its birth, eleven were LA.[64] LA nations can be divided into three groups according to when they recognized Israel. The first group to recognize Israel on its declaration of independence included Guatemala, Uruguay, Venezuela, Nicaragua, Panama and Costa Rica. The second group to recognize Israel after September 1948 included the Dominican Republic, El Salvador, Honduras and Paraguay. The last group did so in 1949 before, during, and after the debate on Israel's acceptance in the United Nations. These include Chile, Argentina, Brazil, Mexico, Bolivia, Ecuador, Colombia, Cuba, Haiti and Peru.

Argentina, always on a reciprocal basis, established the first LA legation in Israel in 1949, followed by Brazil, Uruguay and Guatemala. Until 1955 these four diplomatic missions were in Tel Aviv. Guatemala was the first to move its embassy to Jerusalem. By 1972 fourteen countries had permanent diplomatic representation in Israel, all at the ambassadorial level.[65] This number is impressive when compared with African representation in Israel at the beginning of 1972: seven African permanent representatives, with one representing three countries (before they all severed diplomatic relations with Israel in 1973); and four Asian permanent representations (Japan, Burma, Philippines and Turkey).

During the sixties, ten of the fourteen LA representations were moved or installed in Jerusalem. This gives LA diplomats an absolute majority among the eighteen head missions centered in Jerusalem, an important fact as it clearly imples the recognition of Jerusalem as the capital of Israel. (When the Dominican Republic moved its legation in 1965 from Tel Aviv and raised its rank to ambassadorial level, it announced that it recognized Jerusalem as the capital of Israel.)[66] In most cases, Israel's request for such transfer was met without much opposition. In a few cases where Arab circles attempted to prevent such transfer to Jerusalem, their efforts were fruitless, as is the case of Venezuela.[67] In other instances, even positive inducements did not bring about such transfer. Argentina refused to build a new embassy in Jerusalem even though the money for this had already been collected by Argentine Jewry.[68] Once again, it is symptomatic that the "big" three, Argentina, Mexico and Brazil have their embassies in Tel Aviv (as does Peru). At present the LA embassies in Jerusalem are: Guatemala, Chile, Panama, Haiti, Colombia, Venezuela, Ecuador, Costa Rica, Dominican Republic, Uruguay, Bolivia and El Salvador.

Another return from bilateral relations is the large number of important LA visitors and their subsequent declarations (foreign ministers, representatives to the United Nations and other high officials). During their visits to Israel, many of them expressed their open and unrestricted support. The value of such pro-Israeli statements must be measured not only by its implications to Israel's foreign policy and evidence of an existing solidarity with Israel, but it is also important for internal purposes. It allows Israel to project a more optimistic picture to its citizens and avoids the image of its isolation in the international community.

After visiting Israel many LA parliamentarians have returned to pronounce a pro-Israeli position, and in some cases have moved for adopting pro-Israeli resolutions in their parliaments. Such has been the case with Chile, Uruguay, and Costa Rica. LA parliamentary meetings of Montevideo (1967), and Bogota (1970) expressed solidarity with Soviet Jewry and criticized aspects of discrimination in the United Nations.

Ambassadors serving in Israel are often artists and intellectuals, as with Germán Arciniegas of Colombia, Rosario Castellanos from Mexico, J. Carcía Granados of Guatemala and Rev. Benjamín Núñez of Costa Rica. Argentina's and Brazil's diplomats have mainly been career diplomats, while Chilean, Uruguayan and other representatives have been political appointees. Still others send representatives who have a more personal relationship towards Israel. Argentina, and recently Chile, have, during different regimes, sent Jews active in local politics and identified with Israel, making the question of representation problematic. In general, LA ambassadors become greatly aware of Israel's problems and thus develop a friendship extending beyond their terms of office.

Another expression of close relationships are the treaties signed between LA countries and Israel. While bilateral treaties could be considered a formal instrument for strengthening relations between the two countries concerned, in most cases we analyzed the signature of such treaties was more a declaratory asset than an action-oriented commitment. Most treaties are associated with visits of ministers of special delegations. The first agreements were made in the early fifties; they were commercial and stipulated the terms of trade with Argentina, Brazil, and Uruguay. Later, cultural agreements were signed with these countries and eventually with others in accordance with the expansion of different relations in LA. Since 1961 agreements of technical cooperation have been signed with almost all LA countries. These are periodically renewed. Close bilateral relations with most LA countries is a possibility for Israel to consolidate its recognition and normalization in the international system and a means of overcoming its growing sense of political isolation.

CONCLUDING REMARKS

While this paper is only a preliminary attempt to describe Israel's presence in LA, some conclusions are in order: 1. Ignoring the influence of other intervening or interfering variables, an inverse relation seems to exist between the power level of a given LA state and its support for Israel. Most large Latin American countries wish to play an important role in international politics and to maintain more extensive contacts with the Arab states. Because of this general outlook on world politics, they have been reluctant to identify with either side in the Middle East conflict. This conclusion counters the present image of the continent as a monolithic bloc. Over a period of twenty-five years (1948-73) LA countries which ranked highest in capability (Argentina, Brazil, Mexico) supported Israel least. Medium capability nations (Chile, Colombia, Venezuela) showed more support, and small nations (Uruguay, Costa Rica, Guatemala, Dominican Republic and Paraguay) tended to provide Israel with the highest level of political support. Most LA countries show a high degree of consistency in their position vis-à-vis Israel, a fact that appears to be connected with the importance of precedent and the LA habit of continuing in adopted positions.

2. On a multilateral level, LA support for Israel has been diminishing, particularly after 1967. However, there has been no concurrent deterioration of bilateral relations. On the contrary, bilateral transactions and exchanges have intensified (trade, technical assistance, scientific and military cooperation, etc.). It is difficult to affirm that more intensive bilateral relationships are maintained with LA countries which give Israel the greatest multilateral support. The two largest Israeli missions were in Buenos Aires and Caracas, both capitals of countries that do not provide significant political support at the United Nations.

3. Positive attitudes in LA, reflected by support given Israel on the eve of independence and during its first years of statehood, together with the existence of more immediate problems engaging Israel in other regions of the world, made Israel a relative latecomer to the continent. During political

crises, such as the military conflict with its Arab neighbors (1956-67) and during important UN deliberations, Israel appealed for LA support. Since the beginning of the 1960s, there has been a tendency to develop a longer-range policy towards LA. This is reflected mainly in the technical assistance programs and the intensification and encouragement of visits by Latin Americans to Israel. Such developments were undoubtedly influenced by the growing capability of Israel to óperate a more varied foreign policy and to allocate larger resources for its application. The evolution of Israel's relations with LA shows a decline in political support for Israel concurrent with an increase in Israel's activities on the continent, but these trends are not necessarily related. Intervening factors, such as Israel's deteriorated position in the international community at large and a growing disagreement of political groups in Latin America with Israel's stand on the question of the acquisition of territories by force, may have diminished support for the Jewish state. Since the beginning of the seventies, Arab countries have initiated more vigorous and carefully planned activities in LA. LA leaders have often reacted by showing greater reluctance to take sides on Middle East issues. Although the balance has become more delicate, the deep rooted ties between LA and both Israel and the Jewish people remain strong.

NOTES

1. *Davar* (Tel Aviv), March 21, 1961.

2. *Middle East Background* (Jerusalem: Foreign Ministry, Information Division, May 28, 1973).

3. Michael Brecher, *The Foreign Policy System of Israel* (London: Oxford University Press, 1972), p. 283. Also interviews with Israeli diplomats, nos. 18, 19, 44, 45 (names withheld).

4. Edward B. Glick, *Latin America and the Palestine Problem* (New York: Theodore Herzl Foundation, 1958), p. 35.

5. Michael Brecher, *Foreign Policy*, pp. 229-50.

6. *Davar*, June 6, 1956.

7. Rudesindo Martínez (H), *El pueblo hebreo y el sionismo político* (Santa Fe, Argentina: Casa Editora La Unión, 1921).

8. *La Prensa* (daily), Buenos Aires, February 8, 1946.

9. Interview with former Uruguayan Blanco (White) party minister, Carlos Tejera.

10. Interview with Eduardo Correa Aguirre, Montevideo, October 1972.

11. Zionist Archives, Jerusalem, Z5/577, letter from Carlos E. Bernhard, secretary of the Zionist Organization of El Salvador to the Jewish Agency for Palestine, Latin American Dept., New York, December 23, 1948.

12. See the resolution passed by the Senate of Cuba in February 1949 saluting the establishment of the Constitutional Assembly of Israel. Zionist Archives, Jerusalem, Z5/556, letter from Senator Santiago G. Rey Perina to Sender M. Kaplan, political director of Unión Sionista de Cuba, February 15, 1949.

13. Zionist Archives, Z5/1087, letter from Nahum Goldman to A. Mibashan, July 31, 1946.

14. *New York Times*, August 2, 1949.

15. In a report about his visit to Paraguay, A. Mibashan, Keren Hayesod United Appeal representative to South America, stressed that Israel should establish normal diplomatic relations, arguing that the Paraguayan government was surprised that having been one of the countries that voted for partition and the seventeenth to recognize Israel, "considers it as a lack of consideration that till now there is no form of official representation of Israel in Paraguay and vice versa, in Tel Aviv." In this respect it adds that Bernardo Ocampos, minister of foreign relations, exhorts the following: "In my file on Israel there is only one document: a cable of Mr. Toff from New York thanking for the recognition; we have not even a cable directly from Tel Aviv." Zionist Archives, Z5/513, November 14, 1949.

16. Data from the *Israel Government Year Book* (in Hebrew) (Jerusalem: Hamadpis Hamemshalti, vol. 1948-1972/73).

17. See letters commending the positive role played by Eric Heinemann as Israeli representative in the nomination of presidents in Honduras and Costa Rica in 1949. Zionist Archives, Z5/547, letter from Israel Blumenfeld, representative of the Jewish Agency in Costa Rica on November 15, 1949, to Benno Weiser, New York.

18. Itzhak Harkabi, *The Israel-Economist Journal* (Spanish), Jerusalem, May 1968, p. 8.

19. Zionist Archives, Z5/513, letter from Mibashan to Weisser, December 19, 1949, Buenos Aires. The formation of the Mexican one was explained: When The Mexican Committee for Palestine that so efficiently defended the just cause of the Israelite people was dissolved, the idea of creating an institute for cultural relations between Mexico and the State of Israel emerged. Members are writers of continental fame, diplomats, journalists and commentators, university teachers, physicians and cultivated ladies. Zionist Archives, Jerusalem, Z5, Agencia Judía para Palestina, Mexico, December 14, 1949.

20. *Cronicas Israel–América Latina* (Jerusalem) 5, no. 48-49 (March-April 1965): 1.

21. Yosef Govrin, "Israel-Latin America in the Field of Cultural Relations" (Hebrew), *Gesher* (Israel) 17, no. 69-96 (December 3-4, 1971): 256.

22. An interesting example is Israel's support for the adoption of Spanish as an official language in the international organization. In a speech by Israel's ambassador Moshe Tov at the Budget Committee of the UN in 1952, he favored Spanish as a working language at ECOSOC (Economic and Social Council) and stressed the contribution of Sephardic Jews in the court of Alphonse the Wise for the enrichment of the Spanish language, the printing of the first Jewish dictionary in Spanish in 1552, and many other features that linked the Jewish people to the Spanish language. Israel, Brazil and Haiti were the only non-Spanish-speaking countries that favored the acceptance of this language. The text of his appeal was widely circulated in LA and he was effusively greeted in several countries. *Israel y el idioma español en las Naciones Unidas* (Guatemala City: Instituto de Relaciones Culturales Guatemala-Israel, 1970).

23. *Boletín de Actividades*, Instituto Central de Relationes Culturales Israel-Ibero America, September 1969, p. 1.

24. Yosef Govrin, "Israel-Latin America," p. 254.

25. Some of them distinguished writers such as Germán Arcinegas of Colombia, Vicente Gerbasi of Venezuela, Rosario Castellanos of Mexico and Carmen Naranjo of Costa Rica, have been writing extensively about Israel in books and articles published in their own countries.

26. Taking just one example: in Guatemala 20,000 people visited a 15-day exhibition on Israel. *La Hora Dominical* (Guatemala City), March 2, 1969, p. 17.

27. A full list of activities in Chile is provided in *Boletín Informativo Beni Israel* (Santiago de Chile), June 1966, p. 5.

28. An official of Israel's Ministry of Defense admitted that this was indeed a consideration taken into account.

29. See comment by Shlomo Erel in *El ejército como factor de desarrollo* (Tel Aviv: Estado de Israel, Ministerio de Defensa, June 1968), p. 86.

30. At the end of 1972 the nonmilitary functions of the veteran Department of International Relations and Cooperation of the Ministry of Defense were transferred to the Ministry of Foreign Affairs. See note in *Ma'ariv*, December 25, 1972.

31. Information provided by Department for International Cooperation of Israel's Ministry of Foreign Affairs.

32. Interview with Defense Ministry official, op. cit.

33. Detailed analysis of Costa Rica's MNJ was prepared for internal use of the relevant government agencies by Rina Shapira of Tel Aviv University.

34. See article by Yuval Elitzur in *Ma'ariv*, May 18, 1973, p. 18.

35. Ya'acov Ardon, "SOLTAM sells arms abroad," *Jerusalem Post*, May 11, 1973; Gil Keisary, "SHAFRIR and GAVRIEL in the SALON," *Ma'ariv* (Friday supplement, Yemim Velelot), May 25, 1973; Shmuel Segev, "Exports of Israeli Military Electronics: $40 Million," *Ma'ariv*, June 7, 1973; Rachel Primor, "Israel Aircraft Industry to participate in Brazilian Air Salon," *Ma'ariv*, July 8, 1973; Shmuel Segev, "Mexico unravels secrecy over cooperation with Israel in aircraft production," *Ma'ariv*, May 10, 1973.

36. *Ydiot Acharonot*, May 15, 1975.

37. Source: Halishka Hamerkazit Lestatistika, *Shnaton Statisti le'Israel*, (Israel's statistical yearbook) (Jerusalem, 1972).

38. See Moshe Pinsky, "Relaciones comerciales con América Latina," *The Israel Export and Trade Journal* (October 1972): 5.

39. Ibid., p. 5.

40. The export-import data for individual countries is taken from *Israel's Trade with Africa, Asia, Oceania and Latin America, 1970-1971*. Issued in Hebrew by Israel: Ministry of Commerce and Industry, unit for trade with Africa, Asia, Oceania and Latin America, June 1972, p. 48.

41. Ibid., p. 49.

42. Halishka Hamerkazit Lestatistika, *Shnaton Statisti le'Israel* (Jerusalem, 1972).

43. Sherutei Hasbara (Hebrew—What is the character of Israel's contribution to the developing world?), Sherut Hapirsumim, Prime Minister's Office, Misrad Rosh Hamemshala, March 1969. There is a measure of idealization in this presentation. For a deeper analysis of Israel's activities in this field, see Leopold Laufer, *Israel and the Developing Countries: New Approaches to Cooperation* (New York: Twentieth Century Fund, 1967).

44. Zionist Archives, Z5/611, M. Freudmann to Benno Weiser, director of Latin American Section, Jewish Agency, New York. Panama, December 2, 1949. In the same letter, Freudmann mentions that the president, Dr. Arias, born in Panama's citrus province, was looking for ventures that would allow Panama to recover from the inertia which had left its treasury penniless.

45. Until relations were broken, Israeli experts in citrus, irrigation, fishery and other fields served in Cuba, mainly through nongovernmental organizations such as the kibbutz movement.

46. *Israel and Latin America* (Jerusalem: Ministry of Foreign Affairs, International Cooperation Division, 1970).

47. *Shalom* (Magazine for alumni of Israeli training courses) (Jerusalem, 1973): 17.

48. The evaluation of Israeli projects in Brazil, Venezuela and the Dominican Republic has been studied in 1972 by Gideon Naor and Shaul Regev, from the Research Institute of Agricultural Settlement in Rehovot, 1972. Current research at the Hebrew University deals thoroughly with this aspect.

49. This conclusion is reaffirmed in the evaluation of La Joya regional scheme run by Israel in Peru. Erik Cohen, "Israeli Technical Aid to Peru: A Case Study of International Cooperation" (unpublished manuscript).

50. Mentioned in a lecture given by Netanel Lorch at the Hebrew University on March 4, 1973.

51. *Los Angeles Times* (daily), "Mideast Feud Rages in Latin America," May 20, 1969, pt. 1, p. 20.

52. "Ojeando la Prensa Latin Americana." Zionist Archives, Z5/548, letter from Enrique Weisleder to the LA Department of the Jewish Agency, N.Y., San Jose, Costa Rica, January 10, 1949. He also suggests including a pro-Israeli article published in the *Diario de Costa Rica*, which would satisfy the writer and the newspaper and will encourage them to continue publishing these sorts of articles.

53. Zionist Archives, Jerusalem, Z5/513, letter from Benno Weiser to A. Mibashan, n. p., November 10, 1949.

54. Ibid.

55. DI 11, Interview with Israeli diplomat (name withheld).

56. *Knesset Minutes*, 4th Knesset, Second Sitting, 203rd Sessions, January 2-4, 1961.

57. In one week (1965) in Uruguay, two photo articles appeared in a leading newspaper, four more in other important dailies (about the Israel National Museum, the celebration of African Liberation day in Jerusalem, two acts of sabotage in Kibbutz Ramat Hakovesh, Afula, and the Student Day Festivities in Jerusalem).

58. An extraordinary example: between May 14 and 17, 1967 in Montevideo, eight leading newspapers commemorated Israel's 19th anniversary with similar articles.

59. E.g. reports of Argentina's saint, the Virgin of Luján, painted in the Basilica of the Assumption in Nazareth, January 1968.

60. ID 30, Interview with Israeli diplomat, report of April 1969 (name withheld).

61. *Mundo Uruguayo* (Montevideo weekly) April 1, 1964, reports that Israel's ambassador has been the first to open a series of television programs of interviews to ambassadors.

62. See articles in *Ha'aretz* (Tel Aviv daily) December 26, 1969; and *Ma'ariv* (Tel Aviv daily) May 14, 1973.

63. The part of our project dealing with Israel-Latin America at the multilateral level is covered by our associate researcher Joel Barromi.

64. Lectures given by Netanel Lorch, former director of Latin American Dept. of Israeli Foreign Ministry, at the Hebrew University on "Israeli-Latin American Relations."

65. *Liste des Membres du Corps Diplomatique en Israel*, Ministère des Affaires Etrangères, January 1972.

66. DIA. 31 Interview with Latin American diplomat, March 1972, (name withheld). Statement made by Raid Cabral during his visit to Israel in 1965.

67. CJ 11 Interview with a Jewish community leader (name withheld).

68. *Ma'ariv*, May 18, 1960.

13

Yoram D. Shapira

EXTERNAL AND INTERNAL INFLUENCES IN THE PROCESS OF LATIN AMERICAN-ISRAELI RELATIONS

This chapter will analyze some of the major determinants in Latin America's relations with Israel. It is useful to treat the twenty Latin American (LA) republics collectively since they constitute a relatively cohesive regional subsystem. They display a historical uniformity far greater than that of other subsystems in the world. Spanish-Portuguese colonialism has left common traditions, ethics and cultural traits such as language and religion. There are common social structures and economic problems. The interaction of LA countries and "the rest of the world" is primarily governed by a common, geopolitical factor; that is, the region's presence on the periphery of a world superpower. As one observer has stated: "The countries of Latin America are now, and have always been, client states, members of a sub-hierarchical structure within the overall international hierarchy..."[1] Latin America is also unique in that it is the only region primarily composed of developing nations which has significant, resident Jewish and Arab communities as well.

These varied determinants may be viewed as inputs fed into the policy-making process engaging LA governments. They are divided into two groups. First, there are those which belong to the external setting: the two superpowers and Cuba, the neutralists, and the Arab countries. Second, are the internal or intrasystem determinants: the Jewish and Arab communities, labor unions, student bodies and intellectual groups, the military, the Catholic Church, political parties and movements, and public opinion and the press.[2]

There is another kind of input which is integral to an understanding of the complexities of the decision-making process: the psychological environment of the decision makers; their belief system and images. Although this element is beyond the scope of this chapter,[3] some general comment is necessary.

Most LA countries have had little direct political interest in the Middle East. For this reason relations with Israel have been influenced by images of that country and by the respective value systems of LA decision makers, as well as by political realities. The greater the absence of direct involvement, the greater the part played by images and the "attitudinal prism."[4]

From Israel's point of view, images may be either favorable or negative. They can also be divided into a number of distinct groups. The forum at which a statement is made will determine to a large extent the type of image presented. For instance, declarations made by LA personalities on a visit to Israel or an Arab country will differ from diplomatic statements made at the United Nations. The status of the individual making the statement—i.e., whether he is making it while acting in an official capacity or as a private citizen—will also have a bearing on the image.

LA perceptions of Israel are subject to change. Images that were prominent during the early days of Israel's existence (holocaust, humanitarian, anticolonial) were replaced in later years by others (dynamic, militaristic, imperialist, anticommunist, etc.). Images that reflected positive perceptions of Israel were later transferred to the Arab countries. (For example, radicalism and socialism, Israeli traits in earlier days, now apply to the "progressive" Arab regimes.) These changes were the result of a multifaceted process which affected Israel, the Arab countries, and the nations of Latin America.

Preceding the discussion of individual state actors within the external setting, some comment on the global system is necessary, for changes in the structure and character of the system have affected Latin America's relations with Israel. The establishment of the Jewish State in 1948 coincided with the initiation of the era of the "tight bipolar system." In 1948 support for the creation of Israel came from both the Soviet Union and the United States. It was thus demonstrated to Latin America that Israel was basically not a problem of the cold war (East/West), but was an example of an anticolonialist liberation struggle—in this case, against Great Britain. Israel's acceptance to the United Nations was further facilitated by Latin America's adherence to the basic principle of universalism embodied in the UN Charter.

1956-62 was the era of the loose bipolar system. The condemnation of

Anglo-French intervention at Suez and Israel's Sinai Campaign in 1956 by both superpowers represented their first attempt at cooperation in the framework of "peaceful coexistence." Latin America also united against Israel; in this case, Israel had joined the North in a North/South struggle, i.e., acted "in collusion" with developed countries against a developing one. The growing presence on the international scene of new, developing nations which adopted radical policies and were often supported by the Soviet Union, influenced Latin America to reassess its position and to regard the South position as one close to the East. Latin America consequently tended to identify with the Western block.[5] From 1962, the Middle East conflict was viewed in the cold war perspective, with the Arabs being supported by the communist countries and Israel by the West, which included Latin America.

In 1962, the year that ushered in the era of "multipolarity," Cuba's isolation was the first indication that Latin America was involved in the process of emancipating itself from its traditional paramount, the United States. Since then, there has been a slow but steady rapprochement between some LA countries and the nonaligned nations. Afro-Asians, identified mainly with the Arab cause, have influenced more LA nations to adopt either an equidistant or negative position vis-à-vis Israel. Over the last years, the relaxation of superpower interrelationship, and internal changes in Latin America, have encouraged the LA tendency towards nonalignment. The clearest expression of this has been in the multilateral and international framework rather than in the bilateral relations between Latin America and the Middle Eastern states.

THE EXTERNAL SETTING

The United States

Much discussion has been devoted to the amount of influence exercised by the United States on LA governments with regard to Israel. Edward B. Glick tackles this issue with particular reference to some of the resolutions with which the United Nations dealt between 1947 and 1952. He contends that "there are as many different opinions on the subject as there are people writing about it," and that conclusions are usually determined by each writer's personal biases. Nevertheless, Glick quotes an experienced LA delegate to the United Nations who, at the second session of the Palestine Partition deliberations, did not support partition. The delegate insisted that the United States "did not use very much pressure, if any at all. There was only a presentation of US views. Even this was not very strong." Glick also reproduces a statement, made by a member of the U.S. mission, which denies the use of threats, intimidation, or pressure tactics in order to secure votes for partition.[6] He quotes Thomas J. Hamilton, chief of the UN bureau of the *New York Times*: " . . . . . . it is an undisputed fact that the United States exerted its influence to the utmost to obtain acceptance of its proposals for the establishment of a Balkan Commission and the "Little Assembly." No such comparable influence was exerted on behalf of the partition plan."[7] Glick concludes: " . . . even if pressure was employed by the United States, there is no proof that it was effective." He cites examples of small, economically dependent LA countries which voted against partition (Cuba), or abstained (Honduras and El Salvador).

On several occasions some delegates, although representatives of small countries, were at odds with the United States on crucial issues related to the partition plan. These issues involved questions as important as Jewish independence in part of Palestine, and the inclusion of the Jewish parts of Jerusalem in the proposed state. Glick points out that García Granados, Guatemala's delegate, actively tried to prevent the adoption of a Palestine trusteeship plan, and that Uruguay's Rodríguez Fabregat was a staunch advocate of Jewish sovereignty over the Jewish part of Jerusalem.[8] These positions were definitely not congruent with U.S. ones at that stage of deliberations.

Subsequent issues of importance (to Israel, if not to the United States) strengthen the earlier observation that the United States—the hemispheric paramount—has not exerted pressure on LA countries. One such issue concerns the location of diplomatic missions. Israel considers Jerusalem its capital, and the location of a mission in Tel Aviv implies a reluctance to acknowledge this. The U.S. embassy is still in Tel Aviv, but most of the U.S.'s "clients" in Latin America have moved their embassies to Jerusalem. Significantly, the countries which have kept their missions in Tel Aviv are the larger and more independent ones: Argentina, Brazil, Mexico, Cuba (until the 1973 break) and Peru.

A rare instance of U.S.-prompted, pro-Israeli action occurred during the Fifth Emergency Special Session of the UN General Assembly, convened in the wake of the 1967 war. Eighteen LA nations supported a draft resolution that received fifty-seven votes in favor, forty-three votes in opposition and twenty abstentions. It thus fell short of the two-thirds majority required for passage. The resolution was more favorable to Israel than the counter, pro-Arab resolution, drafted by Yugoslavia.

Most significant was the composition of the work committee that shaped the resolution. It included Argentina, Brazil, Mexico and Trinidad-Tobago whose delegate, P.V.J. Solomon, was the acting chairman of the LA bloc. The participation of the three major LA nations strongly indicates U.S. encouragement; direct involvement in an issue concerning the Middle East conflict has never been characteristic of any of the three nations. Admittedly, Argentina and Brazil were members of the UN Security Council during the 1967 deliberations. But the "big three," compared to more pro-Israeli LA nations, have traditionally been neutral. Their activism would appear to have been the result of Washington's urging.[9]

Washington's interest in exerting pressure is explained by the nature of the June 1967 conflict and its aftermath. This was a dispute wherein the United States and the Soviet Union found themselves diametrically opposed, their respective Middle Eastern clients involved in bitter warfare. LA support for the United States and Israel during the emergency session triggered a fierce reaction from the Soviet ambassador to the United Nations. Louis B. Fleming of the *Los Angeles Times* reported: "At the end of the emergency assembly last summer, there was a bitter break between the Soviet Union and the Latins. Gromyko, in an angry speech of frustration after the failure of all the Soviet initiatives, said the Latins had been the victims of rude pressure and coercion by the United States. These charges brought a remarkably strong rejoinder from Dr. P.V.J. Solomon, ambassador from Trinidad-Tobago."[10] These few examples indicate that while U.S. pressure was exerted in a case of extreme importance, there was generally little or no pressure, and that on the question of Israel, Latin America has been fairly independent of its traditional paramount. That until 1968 LA countries tended to align with the U.S. suggests Latin America's general acceptance of the U.S. voting pattern rather than submission to specific pressures.

The Soviet Union and Cuba

Although the Soviet Union and Cuba, the two socialist-Marxist nations most active in Latin America, have sided with the Arabs in the Middle East conflict, they have held significantly different positions. Even the local allies of the Soviet Union, the various LA Communist parties, evidence different shades of opinion. Cuba, in its attempt to be a leader in the world "revolutionary camp" and among radical leftist forces, has initiated and hosted several international conferences which have often been the venue for verbal attacks on Israel. Usually such attacks were subsequently explained. And Cuba, resisting Soviet pressures, did not sever diplomatic relations with Israel until the nonaligned conference of Algiers in 1973.

The Tri-Continental Conference of Solidarity of Peoples, attended by delegates from African, Asian and LA liberation movements, in Havana (January 3-12, 1966), signalled the anti-Israeli stand of Latin America's radical Left. Spurred by Arab delegations, the conference adopted an extreme anti-Israeli resolution. This resolution condemned the Zionist movement and the existence of Israel "in occupied territory"; considered Zionism "an Imperialist movement by nature," whose methods are "racist and

fascist''; advocated combating Zionist infiltration and penetration; and called for the cancellation of all treaties with Israel, the immediate breaking off
of all political relations, the total economic and cultural ostracism of Israel,
and the expulsion of Israel from all international organizations. It expressed
full support for the Palestine Liberation Organization (PLO) in its "war of
liberation."[11] Some delegations did not subscribe to these extreme for-
mulae, and either abstained or were absent from the session. Among these
were the delegations of Uruguay, Chile and the Soviet Union.

Subsequently, high Cuban officials made it clear to Shlomo Levav,
Israel's diplomatic representative in Cuba, that the Cuban government did
not consider itself responsible for resolutions adopted at the Tri-Continental
Conference and was not committed to them. They stressed that the confer-
ence's participants were representatives of political parties and organiza-
tions, not governments.[12] In Cuban publications containing the text of the
Tri-Continental Conference, the resolution adopted against Zionism and the
State of Israel were systematically omitted.[13]

The Organization of Latin American Solidarity Conference (OLAS), first
held in Havana in August 1967, was another occasion on which the Arab-
Israeli conflict came to the fore. Here again, Cuba's independent posture
within the "communist camp" was made clear in a speech by Fidel Castro,
at the conference's closure. Castro began by condemning "Israeli aggression" and "U.S. Imperialism." But, in the same speech, he replied to
attacks levelled at Cuba—mainly by pro-Moscow LA Communist parties—
for its refusal to sever diplomatic relations with Israel after the Six-Day War,
as did all other communist countries except Rumania. He said: "And it is
worthwhile to speak about commercial relations, for some of the mafia—
... those who attack our revolution in such a slanderous and base fashion,
without any serious and powerful argument—have spoken of our not breaking off diplomatic relations with the state of Israel. Neither did our country
break off relations with Albania when a great number of countries from the
socialist camp did . . . . ''[14]

Vis-à-vis the same issue, Castro told K.S. Karol, correspondent for the
British New Statesman and the French Le Nouvel Observateur, that Cuba
condemned Israel unequivocally but did not question Israel's right to exist.
He said: "We have not broken off our diplomatic relations with Israel, and
certain comrades asked us about it . . . during the OLAS conference. We
have responded to them that the socialist countries never upheld the principle
of breaking relations with those who commit aggression. Had that been the
case, they would have broken relations a long time ago with the American
aggressors in Vietnam.''[15] Castro, according to Karol, was also critical of
the conduct of Arab countries before and after the 1967 war. Referring to
Arab propaganda on the eve of the war, Castro stated that true re-

volutionaries would never threaten a whole country with extermination. He also claimed that the United States was the "real instigator" of the war, and added that for Cuba the lesson of the Middle East crisis was clear: nobody can save a country if that country is unable to save itself.[16]

In January 1968, during yet another conference—the International Cultural Congress of Havana—Arab delegates threatened congress unity by insisting on a joint condemnation of American and Zionist imperialism. Non-Arab delegates did not agree completely with the strong, anti-Israeli resolution, and the Cubans had to mobilize Vietnamese and North Korean delegates to calm tempers and remove the Middle Eastern topic from the agenda.[17]

Cuba's diplomatic relations with Israel, on legation level, continued until September 1973. There was a mutual understanding that a "low profile" would be maintained, and agricultural experts from the Israeli Kibbutz movement and Israeli scientific personnel unofficially visited Cuba. Cuba did, however, provide Arab countries with verbal support. The Cuban press gave frequent coverage to pro-Arab announcements, which often took the form of joint communiqués issued after visits by Arab delegates to Cuba and vice versa.[18] Editorials sympathetic to the Palestinian cause were printed.[19]

While attending the fourth summit conference of nonaligned nations in Algiers, Castro suddenly announced his decision to sever diplomatic relations with Israel. Not only foreign ministry officials in Jerusalem were caught by surprise;[20] the Cuban minister in Israel also expressed astonishment.[21] Israeli observers explained the unprecedented move in Castroite diplomacy as a spontaneous attempt to placate the Arabs, particularly Libya's Qaddafi, who had been denying that Castro could legitimately attend a nonaligned conference.[22] The official Cuban rationale, as explained by the government organ *Granma*, was that such an act was in unison with Cuba's condemnation of Israel's "imperialistic aggression" and refusal to evacuate occupied Arab lands. The move, said *Granma*, was in response to the demands and sentiments of the nations represented at the Algiers conference.[23]

After October 1973 it also became apparent that the Cubans were ready to lend more than verbal support to the Arab-Palestinian cause. Prior to October 1973, references to actual Cuban involvement in the Middle East were limited to sporadic reports of Cuban military personnel assisting the Republic of Southern Yemen.[24] But in April of 1974, reports of Cuban military presence in Syria reached the press.[25] This presence signals not only a closer coordination of Castro's policy and that of the Arabs, but a synchronization of the policy of the once "independent" radical LA leader and that of the Soviet Union.

The Soviet Union possesses its own channels which are utilized for propaganda and political purposes in the Western Hemisphere. There are the local, pro-Moscow Communist parties which, with but a few exceptions, follow the general Soviet line on the Middle East (see reference to Communist parties below). Then, Moscow's radio broadcasts occasionally attack Israeli activity in Latin America. A case in point is a commentary by Aleksey Serov which focuses attention on Israel's program of international cooperation with LA countries. Some excerpts from that commentary indicate the types of appeals and sentiments the Soviets use in their propaganda, particularly their allegation that there is collusion between Israel and "Yankee imperialism":

> The training of youth under *Gadna* and *Nahal* schemes is also carried out systematically in Israel itself. In recent years dozens of young Latin Americans . . . have completed courses in which they were taught Zionist and anti-Soviet ideas . . . *Histadrut* finances courses and seminars on problems of labor and the labor movement organized by Israel for trade union officials of countries of the Third World, including Latin American countries [sic]. As can be imagined these problems are reduced to an apology for Israel's aggressive policy and defamation [sic] of the policy of the socialist countries, and primarily the Soviet Union. For these purposes *Histadrut* receives considerable sums of money from US trade union organizations, through which they get big grants from the CIA.
>
> The Israeli leaders are linked with the U.S. intelligence service through other unofficial channels. For example, for spreading its ideas Tel-Aviv tries to use the Zionists who are in the Peace Corps, which is controlled by the CIA.[26]

Anti-Israeli pamphlets are also circulated. In recent years these have been of a defensive nature, reflecting Moscow's uneasiness at public reactions to Soviet policy as regards Soviet Jewry. Typical are: *Soviet Jews: Myths and Reality; Testimonies of Those Deceived* (letters and declarations of, as well as interviews with, "disappointed" Russian Jews who emigrated to Israel); *We Cannot Remain Silent* (progovernment declarations obtained from Soviet rabbis); and *The Life of Soviet Jewry*.[27]

Other propaganda publications are more aggressive, attacking Israel and Zionism. Such a pamphlet is: *Anticommunism: The Occupation of the Zionists*, which includes sections devoted to "Fascists in blue shirts," Deir Yassin, and Meir Kahane.[28] A much larger publication, purporting to be "scientific," and with numerous footnotes, is Yuri Ivanov's "study": *Attention! Zionism*.[29]

Neutralists

Since the mid-fifties political support for the Arab states has been growing
steadily among "neutralist" Afro-Asian organizations. Their attitude has
probably influenced some LA countries, for these countries have taken to
practising a similar foreign policy, which includes voting against Israel.
Previously, nonalignment or a third position in foreign policy had not been
practised by many LA countries.[30] With the new wave of LA regimes trying
to develop foreign policies more independent of the United States than
before, this concept has important implications for Latin America and
therefore for Latin American-Israeli relations.

The old neutralist tendency gained new momentum with the rise of
radical-nationalist military regimes such as those of Peru and Panama in the
late 1960s, and with the ascendance of Allende's socialist-Marxist administration in 1970. Despite Allende's fall, this tendency is still present. It seems
to be expanding, either because such regimes have a demonstrative influence
on other governments in the hemisphere, or because of the 1973 comeback
of an old champion of nonalignment: Juan Domingo Perón of Argentina.[31]

"Neutralism" in Latin America's relations with Israel is felt much more
now than in previous years, and is working noticeably to Israel's detriment,
at least on the multilateral level. This is so because many elements combined
in the 1960s to provide Arab action and influence with new leverage in the
region: changes in the international system; the expansion and crystallization
of groups with overlapping memberships like the nonaligned, the developing nations, and the 77; growing Arab presence among such groups;
radicalization of at least some Arab regimes; and certain internal developments in Latin America. The need that some LA governments have to
occupy prominent positions within the developing or nonaligned community
has required moves toward rapprochement with the Arab countries which
constitute a large part of such groups; groups of which Israel is not even a
member.

This courting of the Arabs has already resulted in several diplomatic
setbacks for Israel. Arab delegations attending the Second Ministerial Meeting of the Group of the 77, hosted by Peru from October 25 to November 6,
1971, obtained approval for an anti-Israeli resolution. The resolution, presented to the meeting whose main concerns were economic, contained a thin
economic rationale, but made demands clearly of a political nature. Entitled
"Recommendation Concerning the Economic Consequences of the Closure
of the Suez Canal," the resolution stressed the vital importance of that
waterway for the development of international trade, and expressed "deep
concern" about the economic affects of its closure, especially effects on
developing nations. It included a statement associating the continued closure
of the canal with the "occupation of Arab territories by Israel," and it

expressed the conviction that "Israeli withdrawal from occupied territories is a requisite for reopening the Suez Canal and for its continued operation under peaceful and normal conditions."

The resolution ended with clauses expressing "firm support" for the United Nation's and the Organization of African Unity's efforts to open the Suez Canal in accordance with Resolution 242 of the UN Security Council. It also recommended that the topic (economic effects of the closure of the Suez Canal) be included on the agenda of the UN Conference for Trade and Development (UNCTAD) that was to convene in Santiago, Chile, in April-May of 1972.[32] The Third Session of UNCTAD took up the topic, and on April 13, 1972, the earlier resolution was adopted.

The two resolutions were only a prelude. A more severe blow was dealt in the UN Security Council vote of July 26, 1973. The two LA nations then serving on the Security Council were, by coincidence, Peru and Panama—the two "radical" military regimes with strong neutralist (and in the case of Panama, anti-U.S.) biases. The two joined six other "nonaligned" members to propose a draft resolution which censured Israel for its continued occupation of Arab territories, called for Israeli withdrawal, and demanded that any Middle East solution take into account the legitimate rights of the Palestinian people.[33] This anti-Israeli draft resolution, which threatened to undermine the delicately balanced and older Resolution 242 of the Security Council, was vetoed by the United States. Still, the position taken by Peru and Panama alarmed Israel's Ministry of Foreign Affairs.[34]

The amount of influence the "neutralists" can exert on Latin American-Israeli relations will be largely determined by the degree of cohesion such a subgroup can achieve in Latin America. Although some observers talk of the emergence of a "club" which would include Argentina, Peru, Panama and Cuba,[35] it is still far-fetched to visualize these nations formulating a joint policy on the Middle East. Bilateral relations between Israel and the radical military governments continue to be good and Israel's involvement in technical assistance programs (in Peru in agricultural areas, in Panama in the National Youth Movement) has ever grown.[36]

Arab States

During the last years of the British Mandate in Palestine there was more pro-Zionist than pro-Arab activity in Latin America. In 1948 there were only five permanent diplomatic missions from Arab countries in three LA countries: Brazil, Mexico and Argentina. Arab political activity was mostly centered in Argentina where the Arab community had developed close relations with Peronist leaders. Pro-Arab activities in Argentina increased with the arrival in 1947 of Lebanese Minister Gabriel Tueni. Local pro-Arab organizations[37] published leaflets and collected funds. In September 1947 an official delegation, representing the Arab states, visited Latin America to enlist the support of local Arab communities.

On the establishment of the State of Israel, Arab propaganda's main job was to contend that Israel was a fictitious state, doomed to failure. It claimed that Israel persecuted Christians. The Arabs also tried to influence public opinion on the subject of Arab refugees, and they disseminated attacks on Zionist and Jewish "imperialism" and "colonialism," especially among leftists.[38] Between 1947 and 1949 most Arab political activity was concentrated in New York, where pressure was brought to bear on LA delegates at the United Nations—with little success, as is demonstrated by the LA vote on partition. From then until the late fifties, Arab diplomatic activity in Latin America was fairly limited.

Available data on Arab diplomatic representation shows that not all Arab countries keep a network of diplomatic missions in Latin America, nor do they have representatives in every LA country. They give priority to the major LA countries, those with a substantial Arab community, and, lately, those with similar political beliefs. Of the Arab countries, Lebanon was the first to have representatives in several LA nations. Since the sixties, Egypt has taken a leading role, and is represented in thirteen countries, including all those which have other Arab missions. In the mid-sixties, Algeria made some diplomatic efforts to become a prototype radical Arab state in its relations with Latin America, but this only lasted until Ben Bella was overthrown.

LA representation in Arab countries has increased considerably over the last years. In 1971-72, fourteen of the twenty LA countries had forty-two permanent, diplomatic representatives in six Arab countries. Argentina had the biggest network with five missions, followed by Brazil, Venezuela, Chile and Cuba. In 1969-70, from a total of forty-five representatives in nine Arab countries, Argentina maintained seven, Brazil and Cuba five.[39]

Most LA embassies are concentrated in Lebanon and Egypt; similarly, these two countries have the greatest amount of representation in Latin America. There is a high degree of reciprocity on the permanent mission level, but twice the amount of LA nations are represented in Lebanon than Lebanon has missions in Latin America. To this list may be added Arab League representation that began in 1952 when Issa Nakhle, accredited as press attaché to the Egyptian Embassy and later a Syrian diplomat, opened an office in Buenos Aires. The office continues to function despite a crisis in 1964, caused by the relations of its representative Hussein Triki with right-wing circles. Today, the Arab League has offices in Chile and Brazil as well.

Besides permanent missions, special Arab delegations visit, particularly from Lebanon and Egypt. In 1973 Egypt's minister Hussein Zulfikar Zabri visited eight countries. Over the last years Palestinian organizations have sent special delegates, one of whom was the former mayor of Jerusalem Rauhi Al Khatib.[40] These Palestinian delegates have mostly contacted nongovernmental bodies such as trade unions,[41] universities, etc.

Most of the Arab diplomatic effort has been aimed at combating Israel. Cultural activity is not emphasized to the same extent that it is by Israel. Arab diplomacy has also made the LA Jewish community its target, hoping to disclose its "double loyalty" manifested by fund-raising, immigration and other Zionist activities. This type of diplomacy reached its zenith when Hussein Triki influenced Cornejo Linares, an Argentine congressman, to suggest that a Committee of Inquiry be set up to investigate the "Anti-Argentinian activities of the Zionist Organization," and to disseminate rumors of a Zionist plot to create a separate Jewish Republic in southern Argentina.[42] Arab activism generally takes the following forms:

Mobilization of local Arab communities: Much effort has been invested in uniting Arab organizations on a national and regional level. The June 1973 Congress of Arab Argentinian Organizations, the third in sixteen months, is a good example of this.[43] Communities from one Arab country are often unwilling to cooperate with ambassadors from other Arab countries—for example, Lebanese unwillingness to help representatives from radical, Muslim countries like Syria and Egypt. Tactics similar to those used by Israel are utilized by Arab representatives to create a sort of commonwealth which will provide financial, as well as political support. A recent example is the fund raising campaign for refugees displaced from the Golan Heights, publicized by the Syrian government in Brazil.

Mobilization of extreme right-wing and left-wing organizations: Arab groups find much to work on among extremist groups. Although they initially attempted to mobilize both fringes of the political spectrum together, a "division of labor" proved to be necessary. Conservative Arab countries will appeal to conservative groups, and "progressive" Arab countries to radical groups. A curious result of this policy took place at the United Nations in 1962: Ahmed Shukairy, then head of the Saudi Arabian delegation, openly praised the Argentine Nazi group Tacuara. The Argentine delegate expressed dismay that Saudi Arabia had saluted his country by praising a group of Nazis. Another example of cooperation with pro-Nazi groups is the Chilean publication *Cruz Gamada* (swastika), most of which is devoted to "Palestine, Arab land" and "communist-Jewish infiltration" or "capitalist-Jewish exploitation."[44] Another comic result of the collusion with anti-Semitic forces took place in Buenos Aires in 1964. At a public meeting called to express solidarity with the Arab states, the Arab League delegate was greeted with "expel the Jews to Israel" and the Nazi salute.

Establishment of economic links: From early on, economic pressures have been utilized by Arabs. Egypt's threat to cancel its order of Chilean nitrates in 1947 and 1948 succeeded in making Chile's pro-Israeli president abstain in the Partition vote, and Israel's recognition was thus delayed. To some extent Egypt also influenced Cuba's vote, by using sugar sales as a lever. Venezuela's neutral attitude on the Middle East is an expression of its oil interests, as a "partner" to Arab members of Oil Producing and Exporting Countries (OPEC). The military regime ruling Brazil has been influenced by that country's expanding economy to develop relations with Arab oil-producing countries for the purpose of seeking investment prospects: oil extraction in Saudi Arabia, the establishment of a cement factory in Algeria, and other enterprises.[45]

Furthering of personal relations: Arab embassies are involved in a wide range of social activities, diplomatic receptions, ceremonies, and in the establishment of personal contacts with the elite. Those who perform a service for the Arab cause are sometimes rewarded.

Utilization of press and propaganda: The Arab League publishes *Arabia* and *Nación Arabe*, both right-wing in character. The Algerian embassy in Argentina and the PLO produce material catering to left-wing organizations. Most of the leaflets distributed are against Israel rather than about the Arab countries, and are generally translations of European or Arab articles. From time to time, petitions and advertisements signed by the Arab League are published in traditional newspapers such as *Mercurio* in Chile or *La Prensa* in Argentina. Infrequently, communiqués are issued and published by some newspapers.

Besides this open activity, there are maneuvers aimed at getting control of some newspapers: the Brazilian *Tribuna* wrote that "the weekly *O'Cruzeiro* received substantial help in the form of capital from a group of Lebanese businessmen, in order to counteract the Jewish influence in the Brazilian Press."[46] Another source mentioned that for $2 million Arabs had acquired support from some newspapers in Brazil.[47] In 1967, the establishment of PIO, an Arab news service, was announced in Buenos Aires. This was to be for an exchange of information between the Arab world and Argentina, and was to be run with the cooperation of the Syrian News Agency, *Agence d'Edition Arabe* and Jordan's news agency.[48]

Invoking nationalist appeals: Since the late fifties arguments have been invoked pointing out the similarity of the Arab struggle and LA nationalist aspirations. For a time Nasserism was billed as a way to national liberation, and Nasser's book aroused great interest, particularly in army circles. In the mid-sixties, the Arabs concentrated on getting Castro's support for the Arab cause, for Cuba was playing a leading role in the Third World as a country which had found a way to national liberation.

Recently there was a drive to get General Perón involved in the Arab cause. Eight Arab ambassadors visited him in April 1973 in Spain in order to reaffirm "the friendship of the Arab world towards Argentina and to remain at the disposal of the former leader and the future government of the [Peronist] Justicialist Liberation Front."[49]

Opposition to the United States, nonalignment policies, and similar resolutions on the Middle East conflict are invoked to stress the common background of Latin American and Arab policies. A poster in Buenos Aires speaks of 1969 as "the year of Argentine-Arab fraternity. United for the same cause we shall fight for liberation and restitution of our usurped and occupied territories, Argentine Malvinas, the British Falkland Islands and Palestine and the Arab Territories."[50]

Violence: So far, Arab organizations have perpetrated less violence in Latin America than on other continents. During the UN General Assembly in 1972, the delegate from Costa Rica complained that he had been threatened by Arab delegates. No other cases were reported. Palestinian organizations planned terrorist activities, but only one operation was carried out—Edna Peer, secretary to the Israeli Embassy in Paraguay, was killed in May 1970. Also, the famous terrorist Leila Khaled and other terrorists have used Honduran passports when carrying out plane hijackings. A recent announcement that the PLO is planning to open an office in Buenos Aires provoked strong reaction from the Jewish community. Argentine community leaders have received threatening telephone calls more than once, and bombs have exploded in synagogues and shops; the community leaders fear that these activities have been Arab-inspired. The deterioration of Israel's position in the international arena after 1967 has assisted Arab diplomacy to make the gains it has of late in Latin America.

THE INTERNAL SETTING

Interest Groups

Jewish Communities

From the beginning of the present century, Jewish institutions have largely identified with Zionist ideals.[51] For the majority of the world's Jewish population, World War II only intensified the need for a Jewish state. There were Jewish anti-Zionists in the Communist parties of some LA countries (Argentina, Uruguay, Mexico) and assimilated Jews who were largely indifferent. But with the advent of the Six-Day War anti-Zionist groups split, Jewish social and cultural organizations once wary of identifying with Israel, identified actively, and of 207 people asked, 93 percent answered that "a Jew has to participate in the problems of the state of Israel."[52]

This feeling does not necessarily mean that every Jew is affiliated to a Zionist movement. Of 794,450 Jews, only 50,617 are members of Zionist organizations. (In Argentina, out of a Jewish population of 480,000, 19,660 are members of Zionist groups. In Brazil the numbers are 160,000 and 11,500 respectively.)[53] But in societies where assimilation is strong, the reaction of many Jews is to make Israel the main expression of their Judaism. This is understandable, for the cultural and religious background of most of the older generation is weak. Hence there is a close relationship between Israeli representatives and local communities. In many countries Jews regard the Israeli ambassador as their "spiritual leader."[54] He not only deals with the community's internal business, but often acts as its liason with non-Jewish institutions. The Jewish community is called "the colony" (of Israel). Some non-Zionist groups do everything possible to distinguish between "Israeli" and "Israelite," terms used indistinguishably by most Latin Americans.[55] In particularly critical situations, Israeli diplomats meet government authorities to discuss matters pertinent to the local community; recently, two Israeli officials met General Perón and discussed, among other things, the well-being of the Argentine Jewish community.[56]

Jewish communities' ties with Israel must often face a society generally hostile to dual loyalty; the melting pot concept is taken very literally in Latin America. One way Jews counter accusations is by showing concern for both their country of citizenship and Israel. They refer to their *patria* (homeland) and *madre patria* (motherland). Jewish communities have been active in voluntary associations and have contributed to national social welfare programs. Such efforts are usually acknowledged. Although not comparable to Jewish influence in the United States, LA Jewish leaders and Israeli diplomats agree that the presence of Jews in Latin America and their active involvement influences their governments positively. Their activism is expressed in the following ways:

Jewish vote: Due to the lack of democratic elections in many LA states and the relatively small number of Jews, Jewish electoral influence is not strong. In urban areas, where there is a strong concentration of Jewish voters, the election of an anti-Zionist or antisemitic candidate might be prevented. This happened in the case of the right-winger Marcelo Sánchez Sorondo, a Peronist who failed to get a majority in the elections of April 1973 in Buenos Aires, whereas everywhere else Peronists were winning outright. Jewish voting patterns which favor center democratic parties may influence some political parties to take pro-Israeli stands.

Economic power: Economic power can affect the attitudes of groups and decision-makers either by being actually used for that purpose or by evoking certain reactions towards those who possess it. Economic power may be a reality or a myth. For instance, a survey conducted in Argentina among non-Jews revealed that a substantial proportion believed that Jewish economic power was greater than American, British or Italian economic power.[57] Such beliefs lead to two sorts of behavior patterns. Either there will be those who try not to antagonize what they perceive to be an economically powerful community, or there will be those who are hostile—particularly leftist and trade union circles who will identify Jews with "capitalists" and "exploiters."

In some small LA nations (El Salvador) individual Jews have considerable influence deriving from personal wealth and social contacts. The use of economic power to support political parties and candidates is an atypical phenomenon. When it does occur it involves individual members of the community, never the Jewish community as a whole. Financial support was provided by individual Jews during the Chilean presidential elections in 1964 and in the last Venezuelan presidential elections.

Jewish political leaders: There are few cases of Jewish parliamentarians, the outstanding exception having been Chile. Unlike Jewish members of the legislature in Great Britain or the United States, these members do not consider themselves representatives of the Jewish communities. If they hold a positive stand vis-à-vis Israel, they tend to influence non-Jewish parliamentarians indirectly. The same applies to Jews involved in higher administrative and ministerial positions. In most cases, Jewish institutions do not regard active involvement in politics by their members favorably. These institutions prefer to remain officially neutral on national issues so as to avoid identification with a particular party, especially in countries with little political stability.

Jews as members of elite groups: Jews in Latin America are not members of traditional elite groups such as the military or the landed oligarchy. Few Jews have diplomatic careers and few hold politically outstanding positions. Sebrelli considers the oligarchy a closed circle into which Jews have not entered. In the few cases where Jews have married into traditional families and "have become part of the oligarchy, they have renounced their Judaism, severed all connections with the community, abandoned the tradition, and have accepted Catholicism, even if only nominally."[58]

In that economic development has forged connections between new interest groups and ruling elites, there is greater acceptance of Jewish entrepreneurs, technocrats, and those involved with the mass media. Only a minority of those accepted undertake to defend Israel's position overtly. Furthermore, while Jews are important in trade groups and the liberal professions, these sectors exercise a marginal influence on foreign policy unless it is directly related to their economic interests.

Organized Jewish communities: The most outspoken, active pro-Israeli elements have been the Jewish institutions representing the communities. For while such a role should logically be the function of the Zionist Federations, in the last decade it has been the Jewish communities which have undertaken such action. An anti-Israeli position held by a LA government might be indirectly anti-Jewish too, and Jewish activity might be explained thus. Nevertheless, it is impressive to consider the amount of political support given by Jewish organizations and communities to Israel.

Speaking on behalf of the large Jewish community of Argentina, DAIA resolved: "(1) to fully support Israel's efforts for direct negotiations with the Arab states; (2) to endorse unconditional support for the people of Israel in its just struggle in the defense of its integrity and security; (3) to ratify its full solidarity with the State of Israel, and to invest all its efforts in the cause of peace in the Near East."[59] The same organization reacted to events such as the 1968 fire damaging the Israeli exhibition,[60] the pro-Arab statements of some workers trade unions,[61] and the pro-Arab petition circulated by the Arab League. This last case brought DAIA into direct confrontation with the Arab League office in Buenos Aires.[62] Representatives of all Jewish communities met in Montevideo in 1968 and in Lima in 1972, and expressed full support for Israel.

Arab Communities

Arab communities in Latin America appear to be much more assimilated than the Jewish ones. General Perón's special emissary to Egypt, Feisal Alnefouri—himself an Argentine of Syrian descent—explained: "... with regard to the Arab colony [in Argentina], till now nobody took interest in this [ME] affair. This is due to the fact that Arabs tend to integrate totally in their new society and regard themselves as loyal citizens ... Perón tends to side with Arabs and not with other immigrants ... because the Arab immigrants have always proved their loyalty to Argentina...."[63] This statement explains the dilemma the Arab nations face in trying to get these communities to support them. The communities pride themselves on their being fully integrated, and this integration undermines political support for the Arab cause. In general their attachment to their country of origin is similar to that of any other immigrant group. But their descendents seldom visit the relatives "back home" and, even if they do, this does not necessarily lead to political engagement.

The total Arab population of the continent is estimated at 2.5 million, of which two-thirds is Christian, and the rest Muslim or Druse. The largest communities are in Argentina (500,000), Brazil (400,000) and Chile (100,000).[64] Most Arabs came to Latin America before 1948, the majority

from Lebanon and Syria. In El Salvador, Honduras and Chile, many Arabs
are of Palestinian origin. A considerable number in Venezuela, and 8,000 in
Brazil, are refugees of the 1948 War.[65] There are Arab communities in
nearly all LA countries. Many Arabs live in the countryside and in small
cities. Wherever there is a large Jewish community (Argentina, Brazil,
Uruguay, Chile), there is an even larger Arab one. Where there are only a
few Jewish families (Honduras, El Salvador), there is a larger Arab nucleus.
Although they outnumber the Jews, they are less involved in the Arab-Israeli
dispute; hence their influence is smaller. Most Arabs are economically well
off and in some cases very wealthy. Until the recent nationalization in Chile,
they controlled 85 percent of the textile industry. Many are actively involved
in national political life. However, many of the active Arabs prefer to stay
neutral vis-à-vis the Israeli-Arab conflict. There have even been cases where
LA Arab politicians have been vocally pro-Israeli. Senator Abdala of
Uruguay, a former member of the Council of State (Colegiado), visited
Israel with a peace plan. Senator Turbai of Colombia, president of the
Liberal party, has repeatedly made pro-Israeli statements. Others have been
outspokenly pro-Arab. Jorge Dager, a presidential candidate for the small
Venezuelan Fuerza Democrática Popular, has openly committed his party to
the Arab cause. Probably financed by the Arab governments, he appeals to
his constituents in Arabic.[66] On the whole, Arabs are not considered an
electoral force, despite their significant numbers. And yet in Argentina,
Perón's decision to remain neutral on the Arab-Israeli conflict, was
explained as a desire not to upset either of the two strong communities,
drawn up on opposing sides.

It has always been stressed that the personal relations between Arab and
Jewish communities are good, particularly as many of them are in similar
fields of trade and industry. Relations were also fair on the institutional level
before 1948, a period in which Jews were members of Lebanese and Syrian
social organizations. In Havana, the Zionist Federation had offices next to
the Arab center. After 1948, Arab-Jewish committees for Peace in the
Middle East were formed in Argentina and Paraguay.

The 1967 war produced a breach: the Jewish community identified
strongly with Israel, while the Arab community was urged to identify
actively with the Arab cause by representatives of the Arab countries. Many
of the small social, sports and cultural organizations, especially Christian
ones, tended to keep away from confrontation. But the representative bodies
openly supported the Arab League, just as the Jewish representative bodies
supported Israel. All the Arab newspapers and weeklies began pro-Arab
propaganda, sometimes of an anti-Semitic nature. In Argentina the *Diario
Sirio-Libanés* (closed after forty-five years for lack of funds), in Chile
Mundo Arabe, and in Brazil *El-Nafir el-Arabi* and *El Arz*, are no different in

their condemations of Zionism and Israel than the official publications of the Arab governments. Arab community members participate in public meetings,[67] formulate statements, distribute anonymous leaflets, print commemorative posters, etc. Since 1967, there has been a vigourous attempt to pull Arab communities out of the passivity of the last decades, and to enroll them in the Arab cause.

Unions, Students and Intellectuals

Before the creation of the state of Israel, and during its first years of statehood, the LA Trade Union Movement was pro-Israel. Vicente Lombardo Toledano, the then powerful president of the Confederation of LA Workers (CTAL), sent a cable stressing the right of the Jewish people to self determination and full independence.[68] This was also the position of some distinguished Communist trade unionists, such as Pedro Saad from Ecuador, whose efforts on behalf of Israel's Federation of Labor (Histadrut) at the ILO Conference at Philadelphia in 1945, were acknowledged with gratitude by Jewish Agency representatives.[69]

Since then, while some trade union leaders have followed the Soviet Union's hard line, the Populist and Christian Democrat leaders have been outspoken in support of the Jewish state. José Mercado, president of the Colombian Workers Federation, declared that "the 19 million members of South America's labor unions will not remain indifferent to the fate of Israel, and 'we are ready to defend you.'"[70]

This positive attitude is partly a product of the intensive work carried out by the Histadrut. From the early sixties it organized special courses in Israel for LA trade unions in the fields of leadership, cooperativism, etc. Histadrut delegations have repeatedly visited countries of Latin America, and have had some of its members appointed as labor attachés. A Histadrut representative based in Buenos Aires keeps in contact with workers organizations on the continent. The Centro de Estudios de Cooperativismo y Cuestiones de Trabajo en América Latina, founded by the Histadrut, also publishes specialized material and provides advisors and courses. These activities have been acknowledged in articles[71] and declarations by LA trade unionists. The Sindicato de Empleados de Comercio del Distrito Federal y el Estado Miranda of Venezuela (SIDEC) awarded the Israeli Embassy a diploma on May Day "for its role in the growing links and cooperation between Venezuela and Israel."[72]

Relations with the Peronist-controlled General Confederation of Labor (CGT) in Argentina have been hampered by that union's hostility towards Israel, reflected in statements. One such was issued by Andrés Framini, another by the Bahía Blanca branch which decried the fact that Argentina was being sold to international imperialists, among which are "international Zionists."[73] These relations were largely due to the Arab League whose representatives succeeded in influencing some CGT leaders. Still, at the special CGT Congress that took place in June 1973, the representatives of the Trade Union Organizations of Iraq, Egypt, Algeria and the International Confederation of Arab Workers Union (CISTA) walked out when the organizers, after consulting Peronist leaders, refused to ask the Histadrut representatives to leave.[74]

Relations with student bodies have deteriorated more acutely. Prestate support of Israel by left-wing student organizations was expressed in written statements[75] and posters put up by the Federation of University Students (FEU) in Cuba in 1948, in which they demanded that the government establish diplomatic relations with Israel.[76]

From then until the early sixties, the attitudes of student organizations were mostly positive. They strongly supported the participation of Israel in the pro-Soviet International Union of Students' Congress at Sofia in 1964. They similarly supported the participation of an Israeli Youth delegation at the International Youth Festival in Algiers, which failed to take place. During the 1967 war, pressured by the first news from the Middle East and by the concern of Jewish left-wing students, many student unions remained neutral and even expressed sympathy for Israel.[77] Since then, most leftist activist student groups have adopted a passive but strongly pro-Arab line; hence the joint communiqué signed by the Organización Continental Latinoamericana de Estudiantes (OCLAE) and the National Union of Students of Syria.[78] But although the feeling of organized students in Latin America is basically anti-Israeli, it is mild compared to the intense hostility of the European New Left.

Jewish involvement in left-wing organizations has had various effects. Those participating in Castroite and New Left organizations have not been actively hostile to Israel, while pro-Soviet Jewish militants have been consistently critical of Israel and Zionism. There are also Jewish anti-Zionist groups in "cultural" and "progressive" clubs in Uruguay, Argentina and Mexico. Pro-Zionist leftist groups do exist in major LA Jewish communities. Although isolated from national politics—since emigration to Israel is their ideology—they are nevertheless sympathetic to the struggle of university left-wing groups, trade unions and guerrillas. They have often been critical of Israeli policies,[79] but fulfill the opposite function at the universities, where they appear as supporters of the "progressive" Zionist sector of Israel.

Intellectuals—writers, artists, scientists—are an important group, for apart from those who follow the Soviet line, they have constantly and publicly supported Israel. In the mid-sixties, there was a break between pro-Israeli and pro-Arab intellectuals. The reaction to the anti-Israeli resolution adopted at the Tricontinental Conference in Havana in 1966, and the criticism aimed at those LA participants who did not oppose it, points to the new situation. Pro-Israeli intellectuals say that they want Israel's legitimacy to be recognized, a solution of the Arab refugee problem and the creation of a Palestinian state next to Israel.[80] These intellectuals are often organized into Peace Committees by left-wing Zionist groups, which are related to Mapam (Left-Wing Zionist United Workers party in Israel). Some of their many publications are: *Claves* in Montevideo and *Indices* and *Raíces* in Buenos Aires. In most cases, these committees have functioned for a short period of time.

The pro-Soviet Jewish Communists have sporadically tried to create Jewish-Arab Peace Committees as well,[81] with no real success. Other pro-Arab intellectual groups are organized in Special Committees of Solidarity with Palestine. In Argentina, the editor of a pro-Communist weekly *Política Internacional* has announced the establishment of a Latin American Committee for Palestine, that has published declarations in support of Palestinians.

The Military

The importance of the military in the LA political process cannot be overstated. Most LA nations are directly controlled by military governments. In other nations, the armed forces keep a sharp eye on civilian politicians and function as a veto group. Even in countries with strong civilian traditions, like Chile and Uruguay, the military have recently become directly involved in governmental affairs. Only in Mexico, which successfully curbed military intervention in politics decades ago, and in Costa Rica, which deliberately dismantled its military establishment, can one consider the military an insignificant political factor. The military's perception of political phenomena therefore assumes great importance in the policy-making process.

Influences that shape the military's attitude to Israel come from different sources. First, there is the "professional" point of view. There is little doubt that LA military men have been profoundly impressed by Israel's military capability as it has been demonstrated in four major wars and in innumerable military operations of a minor nature. The words of Ecuadorian General Gustavo Banderas are representative: " . . . for us small countries, Israel is an inspiring example of courage and faith, of ability and high moral standards."[82] Second, in addition to being a professional elite, several LA military establishments are unmistakably "modernizing elites." They therefore find Israel a source of inspiration as well as a guide for action.

Israel's experience with Nahal, where military training is combined with settlement and agricultural development, aroused much interest as a way of developing "civic action" by the armed forces.[83] This interest was dramatically expressed by an Ecuadorian military publication: "The State of Israel, through the Units of *Nahal*, shows us a new road in military organization and philosophy. It is showing us that the Armed Forces can widen the scope of their activities, for the benefit of the rural population, with a humanitarian mission ... and even more, it has demonstrated to us that the soldier-farmer is the one who defends his farm with greater eagerness and heroism, and while defending his land, his family ... he is defending his fatherland."[84]

LA officers have also been impressed by Israel's socioeconomic progress.[85] Those armed forces oriented towards civic action have found that the harnessing of the military *à la* Israel, offers advantages absent in the technical assistance programs which the big powers sponsor. Israel's assistance is also considered "disinterested," with no strings attached. Military establishments have always considered Israel's aid as effective as big power assistance, while at the same time it does not jeopardize the national sovereignty of their nations.[86]

Third, the LA military are a governing elite. Often characterized by anticommunist fervor,[87] the military—either in government or "close" to it—see Israel as a western outpost standing in the way of the Soviet Union and revolutionary leftist governments. This community of interest, be it real or imaginary, has become more pronounced since the Arabs moved Left, and since the 1960s when Cuba was busy fomenting revolutions in Latin America. Israel's triumph in the Six-Day War was seen by the more conservative and pro-Western establishments as a victory over a common enemy.[88]

The military factor as an independent variable seems to have worked toward the intensification of relations between Israel and several LA nations, primarily in the field of civic action technical assistance programs. The influence of this factor has been most noticeable in the case of the Andean republics—Ecuador, Peru and Bolivia, as well as Brazil and, to a certain extent, Panama—all developmental military regimes.

The Catholic Church

Latin America's population is predominantly Roman Catholic. While it is difficult to determine the precise impact that Catholicism has on prevailing attitudes and belief systems, it is possible to discern the role of the Roman Catholic Church acting in an attempt to influence foreign policy decisions. The one major issue which brought about direct and intensive intervention on the part of the Catholic Church in order to influence policy decisions of LA governments, concerned the political territorial status of Jerusalem. The

Jerusalem question was already the subject of hectic diplomatic debate during preindependence Palestine deliberations at the United Nations. And it was repeatedly on the General Assembly's agenda during that body's third, fourth and fifth sessions (September-December 1948, 1949, and 1950, respectively).

The Vatican believed that the best way to protect Roman Catholic interests was to set up an international enclave in Jerusalem (*corpus separatum*) under exclusive UN jurisdiction. The internationalization of Jerusalem was conceived of in the UNSCOP report and was recommended in the Partition Resolution of November 29th, 1947. The Jewish Agency's initial consent to this plan was motivated largely by the fear that refusal might endanger the passage of the entire Partition Resolution.[89] Acceptance of internationalization was quickly reversed once the Israeli-Arab war of 1948 broke out. Both Israel and Jordan were vehement about not relinquishing control of their respective parts of the Holy City.

The Vatican continued pressing for total internationalization of Jerusalem. In December 1949, an Australian resolution calling for full internationalization, and requesting the Trusteeship Council to prepare a draft, was passed in the General Assembly with thirty-eight votes for, fourteen against, and seven abstentions. While the United States opposed the resolution, thirteen LA states supported it, three (Costa Rica, Guatemala and Uruguay) opposed it, and four abstained. Edward Glick, who studied the Vatican's influence on Latin America's stand vis-à-vis the issue, observed: "There seems little doubt that the showing of the Latin American states in this ballot was in large measure the result of both the public and private efforts of the authorities of the Roman Catholic Church."[90] Glick considers the changes from opposition or abstention in a preliminary committee vote to support within a matter of days a proof of last-minute pressures by the Vatican. He also notes the uniqueness of the Uruguayan voting record on the Jerusalem issue: on five out of six occasions in the UN Jerusalem vote, Uruguay adopted a pro-Israeli stand. This fact might be explained by Uruguay's anticlerical tradition.[91]

Although the Australian resolution remained the official UN line on Jerusalem, the issue was, to all intents and purposes, forgotten. While the Vatican did not recognize Israel's sovereignty over the New City[92] and also refused diplomatic recognition of the Jewish state, most LA countries established embassies in Israeli Jerusalem.

An attempt to "resurrect" the International Jerusalem scheme was made when the entire city fell under Israeli control in 1967. Apparently the Vatican, by proxy, attempted to revive the idea of a *corpus separatum*. Thus, the abortive LA draft resolution submitted to the Fifth Emergency Special Session of the UN General Assembly on June 30th, 1967. The draft

contained a clause reaffirming earlier recommendations urging the establishment of "an international regime for the city of Jerusalem which should
be considered by the General Assembly at its 22nd session."[93]

An informed observer from Buenos Aires, commenting on the LA performance during that Special Session and on LA political attitudes during the
Middle East crisis, asserted that their position on Jerusalem was greatly
influenced by the Vatican. If the Vatican agrees to internationalization
restricted to the Holy Places proper, the Latin American nations will not
object to unification of Jerusalem under Israeli control."[94] The importance
of the Church may also be gleaned from the fact that both Israel and the Arab
countries appeal to Church personalities to support causes the two sides
consider of political consequence. This indicates the weight attributed by
both Israel and the Arab countries to public statements that come from
Church figures as a significant factor in LA public opinion. Thus we read of a
pro-Arab act in the form of a ceremony held at the main Cathedral of Buenos
Aires. The occasion was a mass conducted by Archbishop Antonio Cag-
giano "in memory of victims of a recent attack on Lebanese territory by
Israeli troops." The ceremony was attended by the Egyptian and Syrian
ambassadors, a Lebanese diplomat and the director of the Arab League
offices in Argentina.[95] Some of the leading members of the Third World
clergy have signed pro-Arab petitions.

There are instances of distinguished Church leaders lending support to
Jewish and Israeli causes. A major contemporary issue concerns the free-
doms of Soviet Jewry. Prominent LA figures such as Sergio Méndez Arceo,
Bishop of Cuernavaca and active in the World Christian Movement of
Fraternal Solidarity with the Jewish Community of the Soviet Union,[96] have
been involved in this issue. There have also been numerous statements from
LA ecclesiastic circles supporting the worldwide campaign for Soviet
Jewry.[97]

Political Parties

Within the LA political party spectrum there are discernibly different
attitudes to Israel which may affect the process of policy making. To be sure,
the position of an individual political leader is sometimes based on emotional
factors.[98] But the discussion here presented is limited to those differences
based on ideological-political considerations, which are more easily de-
tected.

Anti-Israeli attitudes are seen on the fringes of the political spectrum.
Extreme right-wing pro-Catholic conservative groups are often anti-Semitic
and anti-Israeli. Such are the cases of marginal but noisy Mexican groups:
the Unión Nacional Sinarquista (UNS), and the student group Movimiento

Universitario de Renovadora Orientación (MURO). In Argentina Tacuara is a similar group. The right-wing continually belabors Jewish double loyalty. In some cases, it has also taken to violence: bombs in synagogues and hooliganism against individual Jews. Such incidents increased markedly in certain periods such as the one following the kidnapping of Adolf Eichmann by Israeli security agents in 1960.[99] Rightist extremists argued that Argentine sovereignty was violated. The Tacuara and Guardia Restauradora Nacionalista talked of a "Jewish Fifth Column" and called for the severance of relations with Israel.[100] Anti-Semitic and anti-Israeli activities by militant right-wing organizations include small demonstrations against Jewish or Israeli institutions and public meetings. Rightist anti-Semitic publications do not appear regularly, but publications such as *Posadas* in Mexico or *Nuevo Orden* in Argentina have released original and translated anti-Semitic texts. Some of the "original" literature is reproduced in Arab publications like *Patria Arabe* in Argentina or *Mundo Arabe* in Chile. In such cases it is clear that representatives of the Arab governments and of the Arab League have encouraged it.

Gorups within the militant Left and the communist parties are also anti-Israeli each group having its own rationale. Support for Israel tends to come from Center and Center-Left parties, and in several cases from the moderate Right. Strongest support for Israel comes from Aprista or social democratic parties: the Peruvian APRA, Costa Rica's PLN, the Dominican Republic's PRD, etc.[101] Party identification is most pronounced in the case of Costa Rica's *Partido Liberación Nacional* (PLN). José Figueres, PLN leader and twice president of his country, said: "In the last four decades, Social Democratic Parties have placed the Scandinavian nations at the top of the world community, and have forged the state of Israel [sic]. Today, the two most distinguished Social Democratic leaders are Willy Brandt and Golda Meir."[102]

In an essay, Alberto Baeza Flores, one of the ideologues of LA social democracy, asserts that social democracy is allied with the LA democratic left in achieving its "great strategic objectives." In specifying social democratic allies, he cites the Socialist parties in Western Europe and the Israeli Labor Party (Mapai).[103]

Chile's political party system offered an example of party support for Israel, for Chile was, until recently, Latin America's best example of a multiparty system. The entire political range was represented, and from that range the Center and Center-Right parties were the most outspoken in support of Israel. On the occasion of Israel's twenty-third anniversary (1971), representatives of the Christian Democratic and the Radical party delivered most sympathetic statements in honor of Israel, at a special session held by the Chilean Chamber of Deputies.[104] The following year the Chilean

Senate commemorated Israel's twenty-fourth anniversary, and several senators from the Partido Radical and one from right-wing Partido Nacional expressed warm sympathy.[105] If Chilean Congressional speeches delivered on such occasions were an indication of changes in party attitudes toward Israel, then we note a marked attrition in the position of leftist parties (socialists, communists) during the 1960s, June 1967 being the turning point. By way of comparison, the declaratory support given by radical and liberal-conservative political figures remains more or less stable.[106]

There are important differences in attitudes toward Israel among socialist parties. The small Partido Socialista Uruguayo offers an example of the more hostile posture. In a joint communiqué issued at the end of a visit to Algeria, the PSU delegation "categorically condemned Zionism and Imperialism and reiterated its effective support for the Palestinian People's battle against Imperialism and Zionism for regaining its homeland."[107]

Much more benevolent and balanced expressions, from Israel's point of view, have come from what has been until recently the continent's most powerful socialist party in Chile. In a special hommage to the Histadrut at its fiftieth anniversary, Socialist representative Erich Schnake, addressing the Chilean Chamber of Deputies, praised "one of the world's most organized labor unions—an institution that represents, to a great extent, what the idea of labor organization is for a socialist." While giving much credit to various Histadrut achievements and enthusiastically extolling the kibbutz, the deputy was critical of Israel's policy towards its Arab neighbors. Schnake eulogized Israeli socialists, communists, and people of the Left who, according to him, live in a country where it is difficult to be a leftist and where the threat of war induces nationalism and chauvinism. Nevertheless, he continued, Israeli leftists have stood by bravely and with dedication, and they manifest class attitudes which will bring peace and tranquility to the Middle East.[108]

Many of Latin America's pro-Moscow Communist parties echo the anti-Israeli line, with the same propaganda appeals and rhetoric. Among the various Communist parties there are variations. On the extreme side are Peruvian Communists. In an article issued by the Lima-based Communist periodical *Unidad*, entitled "Zionism, Aggressor Against the Arabs, Makes a Call at Peru," the Sixth conference of LA Jewish Communities was virulently attacked: "We Peruvians shall not tolerate that foreign Jews (*hebreos*) come to realize acts of provocation in our homeland, and much less so when the CIA and other imperialist agencies are involved."[109] More moderate, though still very critical, have been statements by the large Chilean Communist party which, at the outbreak of the 1967 war, blamed the "rulers" of Israel for subordinating themselves to US policy in the Middle East. The party also said the war worked against the interests of both sides, and called for direct negotiations. Although "supporting resolutely" the fight of the Arab peoples for their liberation, the Chilean Communist party clearly asserted the "legitimate right of the State of Israel to exist."[110] It is worth noting what Volodia Teitelbaum, a senator of Jewish origin and a central figure in the Chilean Communist party, said in an interview with the Israeli Communist daily *Kol Ha'am* in May 1967. Teitelbaum not only expressed a conviction that Israel had a right to exist, but also condemned the "racist attitudes" of the Arabs who wish to erase Israel from the map. He even stated that the resolution made at the Tricontinental Conference in Havana was a grave mistake and seriously damaged the communist movement.[111]

Israel is not a serious issue for the significant guerrilla movements in Latin America, be they urban or rural. The Tupamaros have thus far refrained from making public statements on the Middle East conflict, and have denied any contact with Palestinian terrorist organizations. The militant Argentine Trotskyite guerrilla movement (ERP) condemned, and dissociated itself from the bombing attempt at the Hebrew Society in Rosario, stressing that the ERP "does not follow any discriminatory principle on racial or religious levels."[112] So far no actions whatsoever have been taken by local guerrilla organizations against Israeli diplomats. In the few cases where Jews were kidnapped, they were immediately released once a ransom was paid.

The importance of party orientation in shaping foreign policies in LA should be kept in its proper perspective. Free competition of political parties within a democratic context is more an exception than a rule in Latin America. The party factor may only assume importance where there are regular transfers of power between parties, or where there is an uninterrupted electoral process—for example, in Costa Rica, and, until recently, Chile and Uruguay. In some countries (Argentina, Venezuela) such transfers were possible between periods of military rule. Party differences are almost irrelevant in the case of Mexico where the ruling PRI party has been unchallenged, and make little sense in the majority of the LA countries governed directly by the military, or in countries under traditional autocratic rule.

Another reservation to be made is that within the party spectrum the forces at the political extremes, where much of anti-Israeli sentiment concentrates, have at best a marginal influence on the policy-making process. This is due either to their being alienated by hostile civilian or military elites (if, for example, they are the militant Left and most Communist parties) or because they are numerically weak political anachronisms (for example, the extreme Right). In certain situations, antigovernment criticism from opposition forces may alter the government's position on Israel. The political-economic situation prevailing in Uruguay during 1972 rendered the government ex-

tremely vulnerable to attacks by leftists and radical forces. Its support of
Israel in the United Nations, a traditional and almost uninterrupted support,
brought it under heavy fire from communists in parliament and from the
leftist press. At a meeting with leaders of the Uruguayan Jewish Community, a former minister of foreign affairs intimated that such attacks put the
Uruguayan government in an uncomfortable position and he pointed to the
growing difficulties of being the only champions of Israel on the continent.[113]

The final comment to be made about the party factor is that most parties
which assume actual power have to reconcile interparty affinity with wider
state interests. This usually works towards the neutralization, in varying
degrees, of the ideological proximity to Israel.

Public Opinion and the Press

Since the June 1967 war, the Middle East attracts more attention than any
other extracontinental issue. Perhaps this is due to the prolongation of the
dispute, and to the fact that both the Arab and Jewish communities have been
politically active in Latin America since the 1940s. Both immediately before
and after the 1967 war, a public opinion poll in Buenos Aires indicated that
the largest proportion of those interviewed had no opinion on, or knowledge
about, the Middle East situation. The ignorance of the general public
suggests that those active on the question were mostly organized groups and
public opinion makers. The attitude of the majority concerned with the
Middle East problem was moderately pro-Israeli.[114]

LA gentiles friendly to Israel have no inhibitions about airing their views
in letters to newspapers, in live broadcasts, etc. Before, during, and after the
Six-Day War, Israeli embassies received hundreds of letters of support and
sympathy. Some of those published showed a very strong commitment and
often expressed a readiness to fight for Israel.[115] In Venezuela, for example,
support came from the provinces and the capital, and from every stratum of
the population (though mainly from teachers, physicians, and Catholic and
Protestant priests). Support also came from associations such as the Spanish
Socialists, the Cuban Exiles, the Basque community, the Rotarians, and a
Cooperative of Services. Similar support of all kinds is mentioned in N.
Lorch's memoirs of his diplomatic service in Peru.[116]

To a large extent, the mass media mould general attitudes on the Middle
East conflict. In Cuba, the state-controlled press faithfully represents the
official government view,[117] but most LA countries are more flexible and
allow independent opinions on extracontinental issues. In the commercial
press, coverage on the Middle East is very intensive. Most of the news is
taken from Western agencies,[118] but many articles are contributed by local

journalists, politicians and visitors to Israel. Excluding left-wing newspapers, anti-Semitic leaflets and sensational weeklies, the attitude of the press is generally favorable to Israel and covers not only military developments, but Israel's social achievements as well.[119] Special supplements devoted to the latter subject have appeared thanks to the initiative taken by Israeli diplomats and local Jewish circles. Jews, employed in the mass media, account partially for the sympathetic attitude. Quite a few radio stations and newspapers, however, are owned by local Arabs—which partially accounts for pro-Arab reportage.

A survey of 683 press cuttings from sixteen LA countries (Cuba excluded) on the Middle East conflict and Israel,[120] from August 1971 to June 1972, showed the following: 76 percent favorable to Israel; 14 percent unfavorable; 6 percent took no stand; 4 percent opinion unknown. A content analysis of the same articles showed that 28 percent dealt with events in the Middle East; 24 percent with social progress in Israel; 13 percent with the persecution of Jews in the Soviet Union and in Arab countries; 10 percent with terrorists activities and the Palestinian problem; 9 percent with the status of Jerusalem, the occupied territories, and minorities in Israel; 7 percent with Israeli aid to Latin America, Asia and Africa; 6 percent with Nazism and anti-Semitism; 3 percent with public declarations of LA public opinion makers. The press has had a positive image-making role vis-à-vis Israel.

Concluding Comments

From Israel's point of view, the growing influence of the external setting has had an overall negative effect. This refers mainly to the important implications for Latin America of the general process of movement from a bipolar global system to a multipolar one. Concommitants of this process have been: a deterioration and loosening of relations with the hemispheric paramount, the United States; a greater freedom of action for the Soviet Union in Latin America (to a great extent due to U.S. permissiveness); and the growing influence of the nonaligned or neutralist countries on the foreign policies of LA nations. The final characteristic of this general trend, which has been to Israel's detriment, is the greater involvement of LA states in international relations.

Another factor with profound implications for the continent's relations with Israel is the process of social change and radicalization taking place: the Cuban revolution in 1959; the rise of radical nationalist military regimes in Peru and Panama in the late 1960s; and the rise (and fall) of Salvador Allende in Chile. These developments have influenced the behavior of other nations in the Western Hemisphere, and have affected—along with important changes in the Middle East—the real or perceived images of Israel and of the Arab countries.

Since the Six-Day War Israel has been moving closer to the United States. Israel's own economic development has eroded its image as a developing country. This, and its repeated military victories, have cost Israel a certain loss of support within progressive and radical circles in Latin America. The radicalization of some Arab regimes, on the other hand, has enhanced the "progressive" Arab image.

The combined effect of these developments has produced a change in the base of support for Israel. While in the first years of its existence Israel was supported by the more progressive elements in Latin America because it represented a radical force in a largely conservative, reactionary Middle East, support for the Jewish state now comes from the more conservative camp in Latin America.

Organized Jewish communities in Latin America have generally helped to acquire increased political support for Israel from their respective governments. Their effectiveness seems to be greater than that of the Arab communities which play a parallel role. The major reasons for this are a stronger organizational network and deep involvement with Israel. Although Arab countries have intensified their interest in LA Arab communities over the last years—often using the same patterns as Israel does with the Diaspora—there is still a gap between the effectiveness of the respective communities, mainly because of increased Jewish identification with Israel since the Six-Day War.

NOTES

1. Norman A. Bailey, *Latin America in World Politics* (New York: Walker and Company, 1967), p. 16.

2. Inputs contributed by Israel's foreign policy are not discussed here as they are dealt with in another article in this book.

3. A detailed analysis of the psychological environment is part of a research paper now under completion at the Hebrew University by Edy Kaufman, Joel Barromi and this author.

4. See Michael Brecher, *The Foreign Policy System of Israel* (New Haven: Yale University Press, 1972).

5. This process is well documented by Hayward Alker Jr., and Bruce Russett, *World Politics in the General Assembly* (New Haven: Yale University Press, 1965), pp. 124-39.

6. Edward B. Glick, *Latin America and the Palestine Problem* (New York: Theodor Herzl Foundation, 1958), pp. 106-7.

7. Ibid, p. 107.

8. Ibid, p. 164.

9. An Israeli diplomat who was present at the UN emergency special session confirmed this view to this author.

10. *Los Angeles Times*, September 21, 1967, part I, p. 24.

11. For text of draft resolution, see *Israel: UN tema para la izquierda* (2nd ed., rev. and enlarged) (Buenos Aires: Editorial Nueva Sión, 1968, pp. 218-19).

12. *Israel:UN tema*, p. 290.

13. Ibid.

14. Quoted from official Cuban government translation in Irving Louis Horowitz, Josué de Castro and John Gerassi, eds., *Latin American Radicalism* (New York: Vintage Books, 1969), p. 565.

15. *Israel:UN tema*, p. 291.

16. Ibid, p. 291.

17. K.S. Karol, *Guerrillas in Power* (London: Jonathan Cape, 1971), p. 400. See also Andrew Salkey, *Havana Journal*, (Baltimore: Penguin Books, 1971), p. 208.

18. See for example Syrian-Cuban communiqué issued while a Cuban delegation headed by Armando Hart visited Syria, July 1968. *Granma*, July 29, 1968.

19. See editorial by A. Zapata, *Granma* (Havana), June 5, 1969, on second anniversary of the Six-Day War. His closing sentence reads: "As long as the voice of the Palestinian combatants—carried in the fire of their AK-10s, bazookas and mortars—is not heeded and respected, there will be no solution in the Middle East."

20. Joseph Harif, *Maariv* (Israeli evening newspaper), September 10, 1973.

21. Dan Arkin, *Maariv*, September 10, 1973.

22. Joseph Harif, ibid.

23. *Granma*, as quoted in *Maariv*, September 12, 1973.

24. Israel Broadcasts (Hebrew news), March 10, 1973; *Maariv*, April 18, 1973.

25. See *Maariv*, April 1, 4, 1974; and *Haaretz* (Israeli daily), April 2, 1974.

26. Excerpts from commentary by Aleksey Serov, *Moscow [Radio] in Spanish for Mexico, Central America and the Caribbean*. 03.00GMT, June 27, 1971.

27. *Hebreos soviéticos: Mitos y la realidad* (Moscow: Editorial de la Agencia de Prensa Novosti, 1972); *Testimonios de engañados: Documentos sobre la situación de los inmigrantes en Israel* (2nd ed.) (Moscow: Agencia de Prensa Novosti, 1972; *No podemos callar* (documents of the conference of Jewish clergy and representatives of Jewish religious communities in the Soviet Union, Moscow, March 23, 1971) (Moscow: Editorial de la Agencia de Prensa Novosti, 1971); Solomon Rabinovich, *Cómo viven los hebreos soviéticos* (Moscow: Editorial Novosti, 1971).

28. V. Bolshakov, *El anticomunismo: Ocupación de los sionistas* Moscow: Editorial Novosti, 1972).

29. Yuri Ivanov, *Ojo con el sionismo: Notas sobre la ideología, organización y práctica del sionismo* (Mosco: Editorial Progreso, 1971).

30. The most notable attempts at "nonalignment" were the "first round" of Peronist administrations in Argentina during 1946-55, when an independent foreign policy was being developed. There was a short-lived Brazilian experience with neutralism under the Jânio Quadros and João Goulart administrations of 1961-64; and to some extent in Guatemala under Jacobo Arbenz, 1951-54.

31. Perón's comeback even by proxy through the Campora presidency aroused immediate hopes in Arab circles for a change in favor of the Arabs in Argentina's foreign policy. See news entitled "Perón to participate in nonaligned conference in Algeria," *Maariv*, June 26, 1973.

32. References to the Lima Resolution are based on the Spanish text: "Resoluciones Aprobadas por la Segunda Reunión Ministerial del Grupo de los 77, "MM/77/11/R.2/Add. 22, November 7, 1971.

33. For commentary on the vetoed resolution see article by Philip Ben, *Maariv*, July 27, 1973, p. 2.

34. *Jerusalem Post*, August 2, 1973.

35. See Mario Monteforte Toledo, "Sudamérica se divide en zonas de Influencia," in the Mexican weekly *Siempre*, no. 1042 (June 13, 1973) :40.

36. Internal report issued in late 1972 by the Center for International Agricultural Cooperation in Rehovot, which conducts much of Israel's agricultural assistance program, considered Peru as one of the four "best" countries in LA from the point of view of Israeli assistance. At the same time the report admitted "difficulties" in Israel's assistance program in Chile. Internal unpublished report, "Agricultural Assistance Activity of the Center" (Rehovot, late 1972).

37. The Syrian-Lebanese Club, Fatherland and Honor, The Central Arab Committee for Aid to Palestine, the Official delegation of the pro-Palestine Arab States, The Patriotic Lebanese Association, and the Arab Executive Committee for the Defense of Palestine.

38. See article by Natan Lerner, "Arab Anti-Jewish activities in Latin America," *Scope* 2, no. 2 (October 1964), :2

39. Data has been compiled from *The Middle East and North America: A Survey and Reference Book* (London: Europa Pub. Ltd., 1948, 1950, 1959, 1965-66, 1969-70, 1971-72).

40. *La Nación* (Buenos Aires daily), May 12, 1970.

41. A delegation of the International Confederation of Arab Workers visited in 1969 some Central American countries and in 1973 a special delegation walked out from the Congress of the Argentine CGT (General Confederation of Labor) because of the presence of a delegation of Israel's Histadrut.

42. See Juan Carlos Cornejo Linares, *El nuevo orden sionista en la Argentina* (Buenos Aires: Ediciones Tacuarí, 1964). Among other things he mentions the "separatist" character of Jewish education, the "Zionist military camps," the distortion of news, etc.

43. This congress took place in Mendoza in June 1973, with the participation of the Syrian and Egyptian ambassadors as well as the director of the Office of the Arab League in Buenos Aires. *OJI*, (Buenos Aires: Latin American Jewish Congress, June 27, 1973, no. 26/73 [175]).

44. *Cruz Gamada*, Partido Nacional-Socialista (Santiago de Chile) 6, no. 15 (December 1969).

45. *La Opinión* (Buenos Aires daily), May 25, 1973.

46. *Tribuna da Impresa* (Rio de Janeiro daily), June 20, 1973.

47. *Yediot Achronot* (Tel Aviv evening newspaper), June 20, 1973.

48. *El Mundo* (Buenos Aires daily), October 24, 1967.

49. *La Opinión*, April 7, 1973.

50. Signed by CASPA (Committee of Support and Solidarity with the Arab Peoples), *Boletín Informativo* (DAIA, Buenos Aires), no. 14.

51. One example: "The beginnings of the organized Jewish life in Uruguay, a strong Zionist movement has developed, composed of several groups and parties according to the political and social ideology that each immigrant had in the Zionist framework of old Europe. The majority of Jews from Europe and Russia were definitely Zionist." José Jerosalimsky, "Apuntes sobre la vida de los judíos en Uruguay," *Commentario* (Buenos Aires), no. 54 (May-June 1967) :83.

52. Norberto Litvinoff, "Estudio de actitudes en la comunidad judía argentina," *Indice* (DAIA, Buenos Aires) 2, no. 5 (April 1969):98.

53. *OJI* (Buenos Aires), no. 21/71 (38), September 1971.

54. Interview with Mexican Jewish community leader (CJ72).

55. At the time of the Eichmann trial, President Frondizi confused two words in a statement stressing that "hundreds of thousands of *Israelies* [italics mine] live in Argentina protected by democratic legislation." The reaction of the Argentine-Jewish Institute insisted on clarifying the difference stressing that only few *Israelites*

living in Argentina are of Israeli origin. *La Nación*, July 10, 1960.

56. Following a meeting held on June 12, 1973 in Madrid with Israeli diplomats Jacob Tsur and Joel Barromi, General Perón eloquently praised the contribution of Argentine Judaism to Argentina's progress: *OJI*, no. 25/73 (174), June 19, 1973. The Jewish organization of Argentina, DAIA, sent a message to Perón thanking him for the statements made during the meeting with the Israeli diplomats (*La Opinión*, June 16, 1973).

57. Survey by the Argentine Institute of Social Studies of 440 civilians and 60 army men on racial prejudice in Argentina reveals that 55 percent of the army men believe Jews have the greater economic power; 39 percent of them believe that North Americans do. Juan José Sebrelli, ed., *La cuestión judía en la Argentina* (Buenos Aires: Editorial Tiempo Contemporáneo, 1968), p. 174.

58. Juan José Sebrelli, *Cuestión judía*, p. 248.

59. *Boletín de Informaciones* (DAIA) 7, no. 19 (April 1970):21.

60. *La Nación*, September 26, 1968.

61. *Informativo DAIA*, no. 27 (September 15, 1971):10. DAIA rejects the terms of a resolution passed by the CGT branch in Bahía Blanca, Argentina.

62. The DAIA statement was published in *Clarín* (Buenos Aires daily), October 14, 1971, and the Arab Leagues' in *La Nación*, October 29, 1971.

63. *El Akhbar* (Cairo daily), May 10, 1973.

64. Estimates vary considerably according to the source. No objective information permits us to accurately determine the size of Arab communities. According to Arab sources there are 1 million persons of Arab descent in Argentina. See article on Arab-Argentine Congress, *Los Andes* (Mendoza, Argentina daily), June 23, 1973.

65. Information based on internal Israeli government document.

66. A similar (MEP) tactic was utilized by another party in Venezuela—the Movimiento Electoral del Pueblo, which enjoys communist support. *Tribuna Popular* (Venezuela daily), November 8, 1972.

67. The demonstrations often have a special character; the one that took place in Buenos Aires on the 6th anniversary of the Six-Day War, organized by the Arab Argentine Youth for the Liberation of Palestine and the Arab Peronist Youth, burned the flag of Israel. *OJI*, 24/73/73 CI, June 13, 1973.

68. "The Confederation of Workers of Latin America has been extending its support to the cause of the Jewish people and has explained to the peoples of the twenty sister nations of the Western Hemisphere what the persecution against the Jews represents and the significance of a homeland in Palestine for persecuted Jews from Europe and those who wish to settle there." Zionist Archives, Z5/856, July 15, 1946.

69. Zionist Archives, Z5/2418; letter from Mereminsky, Jewish Agency for Palestine to Pedro Saad, Federación de los Trabajadores del Ecuador, N.Y., January 12, 1945.

70. *Jerusalem Post* (daily), July 5, 1962.

71. Cf., e.g., Carlos Burr P., "Contributión de Israel al cooperativismo chileno," *Boletín Informativo-Sociedad Beni Isroel* (Santiago de Chile), June 1966.

72. *Boletín de Actividades*, Instituto de Relaciones Culturales Israel-Ibero América (Jerusalem), September 7, 1971, p. 11.

73. *Informativo DAIA* (Buenos Aires), no. 27 (September 15, 1971):10.

74. *OJI*, N24/73 (173), p. 4.

75. Zionist Archives, Z5/24218, see letter by president of University Student Union of Ecuador to Mrs. Rajel Sefaradi Yarden, May 12, 1944.

76. Zionist Archives, Z5/558, letter from M. Kaplan to Benno Weiser, Havana, December 23, 1948.

77. The Federation of University Students of Uruguay (FEUU) declared that it is unquestionable that the right of Israel to its sovereignty and its existence cannot be considered a threatening factor to the countries of the area. The actual war affects only the authentic and real interests of peace and national liberation of the Arab and Jewish peoples." June 10, 1967 in *Israel: Un tema para la izquierda*, p. 305.

78. "The undersigned delegations support the legitimate armed struggle of the Palestinian people as the only means to regain its national rights in its motherland occupied by Israeli colonialism and considers this battle to be a part of the movement of liberation of the world." *Juventud Rebelde* (Havana), August 2, 1968.

79. See article in *Maariv*, October 2, 1972 about the refusal of Zionist youth movement Hashomer Hatzair to relate to the Fatah organization as "terrorist."

80. Interview with Ernesto Sábato, *Fraie Schtime* (Buenos Aires bimonthly) 3, no. 16-17 (November-December 1969). See also another interview with the same writer in *Raíces* (Buenos Aires) (September 1969):24-26.

81. Efforts in this direction have been made by pro-Soviet International Movement for Peace Council in several countries. See Boletín de Informaciones, *DAIA* VIII, year 23 (April 1971):71, about such an attempt in the city of Tucumán.

82. *El Comercio* (Ecuador), May 26, 1970 (letters to Editor section).

83. General Romualdo Fajardo Alvarez, "Rápida Visión de Israel," *Revista del Ejército de Colombia* (February 1964):94.

84. "Conscripción Agraria Militar Ecuatoriana," *Ministerio de Defensa Nacional* (Quito: Ejército Ecuatoriano, CAME, January 12, 1970), p. 3.

85. Rodolfo G. Proaño (lieutenant coronel), "Israel: Estado del futuro," *Revista del Colegio Militar "Floy Alfaro"* (Quito), June 5, 1966, pp. 21-22.

Oscar Torres Llopsa (lieutenant coronel), "El ejército de defensa de Israel: Un caso de participación de la fuerza armada en el desarrollo" *Revista de la Escuela Superior de Guerra del Perú*, (December 1964).

87. John J. Johnson, "The Thinking of the Military on Major National Issues," in *Government and Politics in Latin America*, ed. Peter Snow (New York: Holt, Rinehart & Winston, 1967), p. 532.

88. On impact of Soviet ties with Arabs and Castro on Latin attitudes, see F. Lerner in *Davar*, August 6, 1967.

89. Glick, *Latin America*, p. 142.

90. Ibid, p. 147.

91. Ibid, pp. 148, 162.

92. In his visit to the Holy Land in January 1964, Pope John XXIII conspicuously avoided crossing the border from Jordan to Israel via Jerusalem.

93. "Latin Nations Bid Israel Withdraw." *New York Times*, July 1, 1967, p. 1.

94. F. Lerner, "Latin America Will Make Its Stand in Coordination with the Vatican," *Davar*, August 6, 1967

95. *OJI*, no. 42/72 (140), October 25, 1972.

96. *OJI*, no. 41/71 (86), October 13, 1971, p. 3.

97. See for instance support of Uruguayan Church leaders, *OJI*, no. 29/72 (126), July 19, 1972, p. 4.

98. One example is of a staunchly pro-Israeli president of Ecuador who explained his attitude toward the Jewish state in a letter to Israel's ambassador saying: "For me Israel is a metaphysical need for Humanity." Israeli diplomat interviewed, March 1972.

99. A detailed report of these anti-Jewish activities can be found in the Bulletins of the Representative Organizations of the Jewish Community in Argentina (DAIA) and in the regular Information Bulletins (OJI) of the Latin American Jewish Congress, Buenos Aires.

100. Sensationalist right-wing magazines have published headlines such as "In Israel There Are Less Jews Than in Our Country," and "The Espionage of the Most Racist Race, Via Zionist Organizations," *Propugnando Verdades* (Buenos Aires weekly), June 28, 1960.

101. This statement was confirmed by party activists from Acción Democrática, Partido Peruano (APRA), Partido Revolucionario (PRA), Febreristas from Paraguay and the Chilean Partido Radical interviewed during a seminar for the study of the Israeli experience in socialism, held in Beit Berl, Israel, May 10, 1972.

102. *Relaciones de Costa Rica con la Unión Soviética.* Respuesta del Sr. Presidente de la República Don José Figueres a una carta pública. (San José: Publicaciones del Ministerio de Gobernación, April 6, 1971), p. 3

103. *América Latina y el Socialismo Democrático* (San José: Centro de Estudios Democráticos de América Latina (CEDAL), Colección Seminarios y Documentos, 1970), p. 41.

104. See statements by Deputies Eduardo Sepúlveda Muñós of the PDC and Camilo Salvo of PR, *Diario de Sesiones*, República de Chile, Cámara de Diputados, Sesión 39a Extraordinaria, May 19, 1971.

105. *OJI*, Servicio de Información no. 18/72 (115), p. 3.

106. This observation is based on comparison of speeches delivered in the Chilean Congress in 1963, 1971 and 1972. The sources for 1971 and 1972 are cited in previous footnotes. The 1963 speeches were published by *El Mercurio* (Santiago de Chile), May 9, 1963.

107. *Agencia Noticiosa Judía del Congreso Judío Latinamericano*, *OJI*, Servicio de Información no. 8/72 (105) (February 23, 1972) :2.

108. *Diario de Sesiones*, República de Chile, Cámara de Diputados, Legislatura Extraordinaria, Sesión 22a, December 17, 1969.

109. *Agencia Noticiosa Judía del Congreso Judío Latinoamericano*, *OJI*, Servicio de Información no. 43/72 (141) (November 10, 1972).

110. *El Siglo* (official daily of the Chilean Communist party), June 6, 1967.

111. *Israel: Un tema para la izquierda*, pp. 304-5.

112. *Informativo DAIA*, no. 27 (September 15, 1971):10.

113. Interview with a Jewish community leader (JC 50).

114. *Boletín Interno*, Centro de Estudios Sociales, DAIA, July 24, 1967, p. 1. Results of a public opinion poll by the IPSA Institute, S.A., ordered by DAIA.

115. *Algunos extractos de prensa radio, mensajes, cartas y telegramas...* (Caracas: Embajada de Israel, Depto. de Prensa, July 5, 1967).

116. N. Lorch, *Hana'har Halochesh* (Maarachot, Israel/Hebrew), 1969, pp. 156-66.

117. Even in this case there is no preventative censorship. The wording of articles in official papers such as *Granma* follows the general government position, the terminology being left to the writer. There were cases in which friendly countries like Syria were criticized by journalists who were not entirely clear about the official line.

118. Such is the case in Mexico concerning all topics of foreign affairs. Modesto Seara Vázques, *La política exterior de México* (Mexico: Editorial Esfinge, 1969), p. 19.

119. See special issue of *Ercilla* (Santiago de Chile), "Israel: en la Tierra Prometida," January 21-27, 1970; *Extra* (Buenos Aires), "Los judíos sin miedo" (May 1969) and many others.

120. Source: *Foreign Ministry of Israel.* Report on the mass media. Monthly Bulletin, August 1971-June 1972. The compiled data might be slightly biased by the fact that press cuttings were sent by Israeli diplomats in LA.

14

Susan Aurelia Gitelson

ISRAEL'S AFRICAN SETBACK IN PERSPECTIVE

Israel's great success in Africa in the late fifties and early sixties made its setback at the beginning of the seventies all the more disappointing. To understand the changes in Israel's relations with Africa, it is important to view Israel's position in perspective and to distinguish between its relatively large attainments at the bilateral level with individual states and its continuing difficulties at the multilateral level within African and other international organizations.[1]

ISRAEL'S EARLY ACHIEVEMENTS IN AFRICA

Israel became actively involved in Africa after the Suez campaign of 1956, which resulted in the opening of the Gulf of Aqaba to Israeli shipping and the possibility of direct communication with African states. Israel was recovering from the shock of the 1955 Bandung conference of Asian and African states from which it had been excluded. That experience had indicated how imperative it was for Israel to rectify its mistaken policy in Asia, where it had not established diplomatic relations with new states upon their attaining independence.

Since Israel's leaders were primarily concerned at the political-diplomatic level with overcoming the isolation which the Arab states were trying to impose, they felt that it would be useful to maintain ties with newly independent African states. They also hoped to gain African votes in the United Nations. Establishing links with the second tier of states beyond Israel's Arab neighbors would provide political and strategic benefits, and support Israel's economic goal of expanded trade with other countries. On the ideological level, Israel could transmit its form of pragmatic socialism, strengthen its ties with Christian populations which felt spiritually connected to the Holy Land, and fulfill the humanitarian goal of helping the oppressed and being a "light unto the nations."[2]

182

To carry out these goals, Israelis made contacts with African trade union and political leaders even before decolonization. The outstanding example was Ghana, which in 1957 became the first black African state to gain independence. The advantages of Israeli technical assistance—the ability to improvise, utilization of small-scale, relatively inexpensive techniques, particularly in agriculture, and the willingness of Israelis to work manually (in contrast to many colonial officials)—impressed President Kwame Nkrumah, as it was later to please other Africans. Israel's relative prominence in Ghana was important for establishing contacts with other African leaders on the eve of independence, as for instance Foreign Minister Golda Meir was able to do during her visit to Accra in 1958 at the time of the All-African People's Conference.

ISRAEL'S POSITION IN AFRICA: IMAGE AND REALITY

The fact that Israel recognized the new African states and offered them useful aid when they were particularly eager to find alternative sources of support other than former colonial powers, created a friendly aura which Arab propaganda was unable to dispel. Israelis gained respect and a positive world image as a result of their activities in Africa. They were able to earn greater recognition in the West by offering advice on the modernization of African countries. The African programs, in turn, helped bolster Israel's self-confidence as a donor, and no longer just a recipient, of development assistance.

While Israel had humanitarian motivations in establishing relations with African states, it was also greatly concerned with countering Arab propaganda and boycotts. It thus decided to establish its presence through diplomatic representation and at least a few technical assistance projects in as many African states as possible, rather than consolidate its efforts in just a few of the larger or friendlier nations. As a result, Israel created one of the most extensive networks of diplomatic missions for outside states in Africa. In 1960 it had six missions; in 1961, twenty-three; and in early 1972, thirty-two missions.

To many Africans and Israelis, Israel appeared to be a major power in Africa, even though its global power position and its actual financial contributions to Africa were less than those of many other countries. This image was enhanced by stories in both the Israeli and African press about how much Israel was doing. While this reputation reassured the Israeli public about its great importance to Africa, it also created false expectations about Israel's actual power position.

The political realities were evident from the early sixties, particularly at the multilateral level. While the Arabs could not compete with technical assistance to individual countries, they could and did apply pressure on

Africans to condemn Israel in international forums. Arabs gained from their substantial membership in the radical African group established in Casablanca in 1961, the Nonaligned Conference held in Belgrade in 1961 (to which Israel was not invited), and the United Nations. The Soviets tended to support the Arabs, while the British and French were not terribly friendly to Israelis as they considered them potential competitors on the African continent. While it might have been anticipated that the large Muslim populations in a number of West African states would support the Arabs, in actuality most Muslim leaders, such as Hamani Diori of Niger and Daouda K. Jawara of Gambia, preferred to separate religion and politics. They also remembered past ignominies of Arab slave trade. Some African leaders, such as Nkrumah, preferred to protect their power base in Black Africa against Nasser's efforts to gain political influence.

Israel received its first great shock in January 1961 when Nkrumah, who had been so amicable to Israel, signed the Casablanca declaration of radical states condemning Israel. Nkrumah explained away the real importance of the pronouncement, but this event set a pattern for African behavior on subsequent UN resolutions. Even states with very good bilateral relations could not be counted upon to support Israel in the world forum, although the more moderate states tended to vote more sympathetically toward Israel, or at least to abstain or be absent so as not to lend their votes to the Arabs. The moderates consisted mainly of francophone states, such as the Ivory Coast and Gabon, which formed the Brazzaville group in December 1960. Membership was enlarged the following year at Monrovia, to include some English-speaking states such as Liberia and Nigeria.

Although the Brazzaville and Casablanca groups were officially dissolved once the Organization of African Unity (OAU) was established in 1963, moderate and radical tendencies continued to exist within the regional organization. During its early years, the emphasis of the OAU was to a great extent on the development of individual states and on a more moderate approach to continental and global policies, even though there were always some states, such as Guinea under Sékou Touré and Ghana under Nkrumah, which pressed for greater Pan-African activity against neocolonialism and racialism. The most that Arab members of the organization could secure in their attempts to gain backing for their Middle East position was nominal declaratory support for UN resolutions. The Africans preferred to maintain ties with both Israel and the Arabs.

Since the African states did not live up to Israeli expectations of support either, Israel did not feel secure on the multilateral political level. Nonetheless, this did not prevent the growth of mutually beneficial aid and trade relations during the sixties. Although Israel lacked substantial financial resources, it offered technical assistance in agriculture and education both by sending experts to the field and by organizing courses at the Afro-Asian Institute for Labour Studies and Cooperation established by the Histadrut in 1960 in Tel Aviv, at the Mount Carmel International Training Center for Community Service set up in 1962 in Haifa, and at the Hebrew University—Hadassah Medical School in Jerusalem. Useful information on science and technology was exchanged at the Rehovot conferences which were held biannually from 1960 at the Weizmann Institute.[3]

Meanwhile, Israel's growing industrialization led to expanded trade with Africa. Israel was able to offer food products, wearing apparel, medicine, agricultural machinery, electronic products and office supplies. Exports were promoted by Israeli personnel engaged in technical assistance on the continent, who understandably ordered those products with which they were most familiar. There was criticism in some countries that Israelis were selling their goods at unrealistic prices. In this they were only following the practices of some French, British, American and other commercial concerns, but since Israel is a small country which has many parastate firms directly identified with it, they were particularly vulnerable to criticism. In exchange Israel imported mainly primary products from Africa, including industrial diamonds from the Central African Republic and Zaire, uranium from Gabon and Zaire, and beef from Ethiopia and Kenya. The Africans were wont to complain that Israel did not import enough from them. In reply, the Israelis pointed out that many of the main commodities Africans offered, such as coffee and cocoa, were sold on world markets in Paris, London or elsewhere.

As Israel became more industrialized and consumer-oriented, it also began to lose favor with those concerned with revolutionary social change. Originally Israel's aid had been attractive to Ghana, Tanzania and other African countries because the country was a viable socialist model for developing states. Israeli institutions, such as the kibbutz (collective agricultural settlement) and Nahal (paramilitary agricultural youth group), were more appealing than parallel communist examples, and were more suited to small states than alternative programs from more affluent countries. When Israel began to act more like other developed countries, which were competing intently for external markets, its initial attraction began to wear off.

CHANGES FROM 1967 TO 1973

After the Six-Day War, Israel generally expanded its economic position in Africa, but at the same time encountered serious political problems, especially in multilateral forums. Israel continued its technical assistance programs at a fairly even level, maintaining about three hundred Israeli experts in Africa and receiving about seven hundred African trainees in Israel each

TABLE 1 Israel's Trade with Africa, 1967-1973 (in US $ millions)

Year	Black Africa		South Africa		Total	
	Export	Import	Export	Import	Export	Import
1967	20.4	23.8	4.0	3.3	24.4	27.1
1968	22.4	24.8	5.7	5.2	28.1	30.0
1969	26.1	25.4	8.2	5.8	34.3	31.2
1970	30.5	20.0	10.7	10.2	41.2	30.2
1971	38.0	17.1	9.4	8.1	47.4	25.2
1972	37.4	20.4	8.8	11.6	46.2	32.0
1973	30.2	24.6	11.9	32.4	42.1	57.0

Sources: Statistical Abstract of Israel (Jerusalem, 1970-73); and Ministry of Commerce and Industry (for 1973).

year. During this period Israel improved its trade relations so as to achieve a favorable balance of trade with Black Africa in 1969. Israel's single largest partner on the continent, however, has been South Africa. Table 1 reflects fluctuations in African trade from 1967 to 1973.

Israel also expanded its commercial activities in Africa through Solel Boneh, Vered, Mekorot and other parastate companies. These construction and development firms built roads, hotels, office buildings, dams and other medium-sized projects. They also maintained the pattern initiated in the fifties in Ghana of joint ventures with both Israeli and local capital and manpower, usually in small factories manufacturing pharmaceuticals, food products and other goods. Private Israeli investors, such as Mayer Brothers and Federmann, were active in constructing hotels and dwellings, especially in the Ivory Coast. In that country, as well, Israel encouraged mechanized agriculture through Motoragri, a parastatal Ivorian firm which became a prototype for similar ventures in Ghana, Liberia and elsewhere. Many projects, such as Motoragri, have been extremely successful in terms of both development and profits; others have been uneconomic and unsuited to the countries in which they were promoted. Contributing to the lack of success of certain projects was the desire of some unscrupulous Israelis to reap quick profits, or the attempt of some African government officials or businessmen to achieve personal gains at the expense of the overall possibilities for national development.

PROBLEMS AT THE BILATERAL LEVEL

Even during the period marked by the expansion of commercial relations and the continuing requests for technical assistance, Israel had to face increasing competition from other sources, as well as other negative pressures at the bilateral level. Israel was particularly criticized in East Africa for impeding traffic through the Suez Canal. Israel's position in the continent was made more difficult by: (1) decreasing political interest of the major powers in Africa, reflected in lessened financial assistance; (2) increasing flow of Arab oil money to Africa, especially to countries with significant Muslim populations; and (3) growing radicalization of various African leaders and countries, combined to make Israel's position on the continent more difficult.

(1) At a time when the problems of development have become more evident to Africans and when the need for external assistance, as well as for internal self-reliance, has become greater, the major powers have indicated less concern with the continent. This has been particularly evident with regard to France, which has the highest per capita aid record but has tended recently to level off or to reduce its financial and military assistance. The countervailing trend, which is healthy from an African viewpoint, is that developing nations have been searching for more diversifed sources of aid and political relations. This has led some states, such as Zaire, Nigeria and Ghana, to follow the Tanzanian example and establish or strengthen diplomatic and aid ties with other countries, particularly China.

(2) More funds are available from oil-rich Arab states in recent years. Saudi Arabia and Libya have shown greater interest in Black Africa, particularly in economic and religious areas. Both countries offered financial aid to poor states, such as Chad or Niger, which have been suffering from acute drought and have had great difficulties in financing their budgets. King Feisal of Saudi Arabia (in whose country the holy places of Mecca and Medina are located) and Colonel Muammar Qaddafi of Libya (who espouses a revolutionary view of Islam) have been competing in efforts to mobilize Muslim populations in African countries in support of the Arab cause. These efforts are aided by the growing Islamization of the continent, in part as a reaction to Western institutions and culture.

Money and rhetoric have reinforced political pressures, especially on the states contiguous to Arab countries. This has been particularly evident in Chad, where the Arabs had supported the National Liberation Front (Frolinat), the rebel Muslim group on the Libyan border, and in Ethiopia, where the Arabs have been aiding the Eritrean Liberation Front (ELF) and Somalia.

(3) Dissatisfaction of many Africans with the West and with domestic leadership, as well as their increasing concern about white-minority regimes of southern Africa, have led to an increased radicalization of political groups in Niger, Ethiopia and other countries, and of the national regimes in Uganda, Ghana, Dahomey and elsewhere. Since Israel is identified with the West, but is not needed as a main trading partner or major source of military or technical assistance, it is fairly easy to express radical policies by breaking

relations with Israel, while at the same time retaining ties with major western powers. This has been the policy followed by Mali, Congo (Brazzaville) and other states.

While such factors at the bilateral level help explain individual instances of African states breaking relations with Israel, starting with Uganda in the spring of 1972 and including several francophone countries in late 1972 and early 1973, they cannot account for the wholesale rupture of relations in the fall of 1973. This snowballing effect is explainable only in terms of events at the multilateral level.

PROBLEMS AT THE MULTILATERAL LEVEL

Small states, such as those in Africa, depend to a great extent on their ability to be united in international organizations in order to exert moral force on the major powers and thus safeguard their interests and promote their development. Under the circumstances, Arab countries, which can produce many votes in various international bodies, are more important to Africans than is Israel, which has only one vote—and then not in all world forums. Arabs have six member states in the OAU, for example, where Israel has no representation, and eighteen votes in the UN, where Israel has only one. Arabs' superior numerical position has given them greater influence than Israel in choosing chairmen and members of international committees and in gathering support for resolutions on southern Africa which are all-important to Black Africans. In turn, Arabs have pressured OAU members to take a united stand against Israel, especially on withdrawal from the territories and on the Palestinian question.

Since the United Nations has been such an important instrument of moral force for African states, which together comprise one-third of the General Assembly's membership, they are particularly concerned about the effectiveness of the United Nations. African states view compliance with Security Council Resolution 242 (1967) and 338 (1973) as enhancing the prestige of the world body. Support of these resolutions is also viewed as safeguarding the rule of international law, which is so important to small states. As long as Israelis are deemed to be flouting Resolution 242 by not withdrawing from occupied territories, they will continue to have difficulties with Africans.

Black African states attempted to keep clear of the Arab-Israeli conflict for as long as possible, despite continued Arab pressures to have them condemn Israel. After the Six-Day War in 1967 only Guinea broke diplomatic relations with Israel; the OAU merely encouraged implementation of Security Council Resolution 242. As time passed, direct and indirect African support for Israel in both the OAU and the UN began to wane. This was especially evident in the UN votes beginning with 1971.

The early seventies have seen the intertwining of several significant trends: growing radicalism of many Africans on the question of southern Africa, burgeoning Arab participation in African continental affairs, and increasing African activity and partiality in the Middle East conflict.

African leaders have been emphasizing the problem of southern Africa more intensely than in the past both in their speeches and in their readiness to give financial support to the African Liberation Committee (ALC). Arabs have been urging Africans to identify Israel with South Africa and Portugal, and the Palestinian Liberation Organization (PLO) with African freedom fighters. South Africa appears in the guise of a technologically superior Western society, which seeks to defend itself against overwhelming hordes of less-developed peoples.

Israel has followed an ambivalent course by trying to develop close ties with Black African countries, while maintaining positive relations with South Africa because of its strategic location at the Cape of Good Hope, its economic significance to Israel as the most developed country on the continent, and its power over the welfare of the South African Jewish community. The dilemma became most apparent in 1971 when Israel's contribution to the ALC was rejected as coming from a neocolonialist, imperialist state, while concurrently the South African government froze its Jewish citizens' financial contributions to Israel.

The Arab states have pointed to South Africa's desire to emulate Israeli techniques against terrorists infiltrators, as evidenced by the visit of C.P. Mulder, minister of the interior, to Israel in September 1973. Israel's efforts to have others distinguish between the apartheid system in South Africa and its own policy of administering the territories have not succeeded very well. In fact, the OAU with combined African and Arab support included Israel in the oil embargo they imposed on the imperialist states of South Africa and Portugal in November 1973.

In general Africans have shown greater willingness to support the Arab side of the Middle East conflict in return for Arab support of the liberation of southern Africa. There has been increased Arab participation in the OAU, especially since 1971. This became possible when the southern Sudanese imbroglio and the quarrel between Morocco and Mauritania subsided. Improved relations with Arab states also followed the accession in 1970 of President Anwar Sadat in Egypt, who appears to arouse fewer apprehensions than did Nasser about the possibilities of Arab subversion of the African continent. On the other hand, Qaddafi represents a new type of religious fanatic backed by surplus oil revenues, who presents a potential threat to Black Africans.

The six Arab members of the OAU—Algeria, Egypt, Libya, Morocco, the Sudan and Tunisia—contribute more than one-third of the organization's budget. They have also been increasingly active at the political level, as indicated by the election of Arabs, or of people sympathetic to their cause, to central positions. The chairman of the Assembly of Heads of State and Government in 1971 was Mohammed Ould Daddah of Mauritania, and in 1972 King Hassan II of Morocco, who also lent his capital, Rabat, for the OAU summit. In 1973 leadership passed to General Yakubu Gowon of Nigeria, who had enjoyed Egyptian and Soviet military support during his country's civil war. Although the 1973 summit was held in Addis Ababa, Colonel Qaddafi led a vociferous, though unsuccessful, campaign to move OAU headquarters from that city to Cairo or elsewhere. This would have reduced Ethiopian prestige and strengthened Arab influence.

Arabs have enjoyed a propaganda advantage with Black Africans because of African sensitivity to the problem of "territorial integrity," which is embedded into the OAU Charter (Article III, 3). African countries are continually threatened by secessionist movements and boundary disputes, and their concern with territories occupied by Israel has grown because some of them perceive the situation as a precedent for South Africa or Rhodesia encroaching on Zambia. Apprehension about territories taken by force has led African leaders in their most recent resolutions to demand that Israel withdraw from all occupied territories.

The general pattern at the OAU has been for Arabs or the OAU administrative secretary-general to bring up the Middle East questions at the end of a summit meeting and, even where disagreements exist, to stress the traditional African preference for consensus, which in this case means advocacy of the Arab position. It has been especially difficult to counter this strategy since votes usually are not taken and reservations are not recorded.

The OAU became more actively involved in the Middle East conflict when it appointed a committee at the 1971 summit to act as quasi-mediators in an attempt to reactivate the Jarring mission. Chairman Ould Daddah of Mauritania became head of the committee; the other nine member countries were considered friendly either to Arabs, to Israel, or to both. The actual group which visited Israel and Egypt in November 1971 was headed by President Leopold Senghor of Senegal and included Presidents Ahmed Ahidjo of Cameroon, Yakubu Gowon of Nigeria and Mobutu Sese Seko of Zaire. The original report made by the four "wise men" after observations in the area showed somewhat more sympathy to Israel's position and greater objectivity than contained in the OAU resolution of June 1971. It advocated the resumption of "indirect negotiations under the auspices of Dr. Jarring," an interim agreement for opening the Suez Canal, and free navigation in the Straits of Tiran. They were also concerned that "secure and recognized boundaries" be determined in the peace agreement; security be achieved through UN guarantees, demilitarized zones and international forces, including troops to be stationed at some strategic point; and withdrawal terms be embodied in the peace agreement.

Once African leaders who had participated in the OAU mission met in the UN and later at the OAU summit, where Arabs exercised stronger influence, most of them reverted to a position condemning Israel. Nonetheless President Senghor tried to take a more moderate position than most in order to salvage his position as a quasi-mediator.[4]

The OAU situation was summed up in an article printed in *West Africa*[5] during the Yom Kippur war. It indicated that Israel's relations would not improve with African countries even if it were to win the war, because it would refuse to withdraw from the 1967 cease-fire line, as had been "unanimously demanded" by the OAU resolution at the heads of state conference in May 1973. The article stated that " . . . Israel at the moment is not going to attach importance to resolutions." The Israelis "feel that their own army, rather than the UN votes they have in the past carefully cultivated, is their best defense." African support was directed to Egypt, " . . . an OAU member, [which] has the strongest armed forces in the continent. Five other OAU members are engaged in the fighting. So whatever other African states may say about the wisdom of the present Arab initiatives, there can be no doubt about OAU sympathy for them. General Gowon as Chairman of OAU has already emphasized this, as has Nzo Ekangaki, the Secretary-General. Even President Houphouët-Boigny of the Ivory Coast (long considered an advocate and friend of Israel) recently expressed unexpected sympathy with the Arab viewpoint."

For the OAU, "the balance seems to have tilted against Israel at the time of the failure of the 1971-72 OAU peace mission, in which several leaders not ill-disposed to Israel (Senghor, Gowon, Mobutu) were persuaded that the Arabs were being more reasonable about peace initiatives because of Israel's refusal to reactivate the UN mission of Dr. Jarring."

While good bilateral relations with Israel have had some effect on African leaders within the OAU, they have had a much weaker influence in other international forums where Arabs are more numerous and have greater support. This has been especially evident in the Nonaligned Conferences held in Lusaka, Zambia in September 1970, and in Algiers in September 1973. Even though Israel has no formal treaties with any of the major powers and thus is really more nonaligned than most members of the self-constituted movement, it has never been admitted to membership.

The Arab advantage was most apparent when the venue of the 1973 conference was established at Algiers. Heads of state from seventy-six nations assembled, including thirty-one from Africa and eleven from the Arab world. There were representatives from sixteen liberation movements, composed of fourteen from Africa, one from Latin America, and one from the PLO. Together the delegates agreed to draft a charter offering "a common plan of action all over the world in the political and military fields." The Arabs were thereby enabled to incorporate their cause among those advocated by the Africans. Algeria's foreign minister, Abdelaziz Bouteflika, told the delegates that it was "more than ever necessary to use all means to speed the victory of the African peoples . . ." but that, "in the same manner, the Palestinian people have a right to be able to rely on the resources of the nonaligned . . . . Furthermore, we must give equal support to Arab countries, victims of imperialist Zionist aggression who wish to recover their lost territories." [6]

Yasser Arafat, head of the PLO, and Hafez el-Assad, president of Syria, joined other Arabs in making a special plea for support of the Palestinian cause against Israel. A resolution against Zionism was passed at the final meeting by the customary consensus, without formal votes. Although the resolution condemned Israel, it "was understood to have been weakened far beyond what the Arab states would have liked. The Arabs would like diplomatic and economic pressure on Israel but many Latin Americans, Africans and Asians were either uninterested or opposed." [7] The Algiers meeting was also the site of behind-the-scenes planning by the Arabs for the October war, according to American intelligence sources. [8] It certainly indicated a hardening of the Arab offensive.

From Algiers many heads of state proceeded to New York for the opening of the UN General Assembly. Here attacks on Israel increased as African states began to announce their break with Israel. As President Mobutu of Zaire put it at the Assembly on October 4, 1973, continuing enmity between the Middle East protagonists had forced Africans to choose between a "friendly country—Israel—and a brother country—Egypt." For Mobutu, "the choice was clear." [9]

The Yom Kippur war, which began with an Arab attack on October 6, served as a catalyst for the actions of many other African leaders. They felt compelled to choose at last between the two sides whom they had wished to befriend simultaneously, even though heads of states elsewhere did not find the same need to sever relations with Israel.

The Africans apparently also found it difficult to maintain their ties with Israel when most of the major powers influential in Africa were partial toward the Arabs. The Soviet Union aided them substantially. The Chinese were overtly hostile to Israel and even refused to participate actively in UN measures for a cease-fire and for establishing an emergency force in the Middle East. Although France and Great Britain asserted their "neutrality," they in effect were aiding the Arabs. Nevertheless, none of the Western European countries had broken relations with Israel. In contrast, only the United States among the major powers sustained its vital material and diplomatic assistance to Israel. The most important additional sources of support came from, among others, Latin American states, Holland, South Africa and Portugal. The position of the southern African white-minority regimes on Israel has tended to strengthen African identification with the Arabs.

The new African-Arab solidarity was reinforced in November 1973 by the decisions of the OAU Council of Ministers in Addis Ababa and the Arab summit conference in Algiers to place an oil embargo on South Africa, Rhodesia and Portugal, as well as on Israel. The Arabs also announced the creation of a development bank to assist Africans with an initial capital of about $200 million.

AFRICA'S GREAT RUPTURE WITH ISRAEL

The cumulative impact of the OAU meeting in Addis Ababa in May 1973, the Nonaligned Conference in Algiers in early September, the UN General Assembly, which opened a week later, the Yom Kippur war itself from October 6, and finally the generally unsympathetic international environment, were to intensify pressures upon the African states to rupture diplomatic relations with Israel. It is noteworthy that most of them indicated that they would renew relations once Israel had withdrawn from the territories. Under existing international conditions, however, African states felt that they could not retain ties with Israel.

When Israel crossed the Suez Canal into Africa, OAU Administrative Secretary-General, Nzo Ekangaki, transmitted President Sadat's request to condemn Israel to all African heads of state. He urged them, in addition, "to examine the situation with the required attention and urgency within the framework of the solidarity which the OAU has never failed to express to Egypt, our sister state and founding member of our organization, and to our Arab brothers."[10]

Some African states immediately condemned Israel severely. Tanzania, for instance, declared that the war was "the direct result of the insolence and the deliberate and continuing aggression of Israel against the Arab people. Israel therefore is fully responsible for this dangerous development and Israel bears the blame. Israel has repeatedly and openly defied United Nations Resolutions demanding her to withdraw from the Arab territories which she occupied as a result of her own aggression of June 1967." As a result, the Tanzanian government stated that it "would like to reaffirm its unflinching support for the Arab countries in their just struggle to resist Israel aggression and to regain their lands which have been illegally occupied by Israel."[11]

Nigeria reacted in a similar vein, but with more moderate language, in stating: "The responsibility for the deterioration of the situation and the subsequent outbreak of war in the Middle East rests entirely on Israel which has stubbornly defied appeals by the Organization of African Unity, the Nonaligned Movement and the United Nations Organisation to withdraw from occupied Arab territories .... The Federal Military Government ... calls on Israel to withdraw immediately from all occupied Arab territories and to stop further aggression against Egypt and other countries in the area." [12]

The break came, according to *Ha'aretz*, because of the "brutal pressures of the Arab states in the economic and military spheres." [13] The Arabs had been applying various forms of direct and indirect pressure. According to one of the African ambassadors at the United Nations, the Egyptian approach was "soft, mild, courteous." They would persuade rather than bully. For instance, they might say, "We are all aware that a portion of Egypt is occupied by a foreign state, on part of your continent. We leave it to you to take appropriate action." On the other hand, Libyans tended to be "extreme, nasty, undiplomatic, extremely aggressive and bullying." In the division of labor among Arab states, Tunisians, who in the past had usually been "aloof and detached," were judged to be "more statesmanlike." They were "more sophisticated than the Libyans." [14]

Pressure was also applied directly or indirectly by the most important African states on weaker countries, through the OAU or through their influence within subregions. For instance, when a local power, such as Zaire in Central Africa, takes a decisive step like breaking diplomatic ties, this affects the views of smaller states in the area, such as Rwanda. On the other hand, even if a group of smaller states takes such an action, it may not necessarily influence the major country in the region. The Ivory Coast, for instance, did not feel called upon to follow immediately the pattern set by the four other members of the Conseil d'Entente in French-speaking West Africa.

Many African states did try to counteract these pressures by stressing their rights as sovereign states to decide their own foreign policies. Quite a few leaders were also desirous of containing the expansion of Arab influence within the OAU. As one African ambassador to the UN said in September 1973, "African states don't want their policies dictated by others. Each state is sovereign." [15] A short time later, nonetheless, his country's independent stand on Israel caved in.

Some of the states which had been especially friendly with Israel held off temporarily. For instance, President Jomo Kenyatta of Kenya declared on October 10, 1973: "One thing we should not poke our noses into is the conflicts of other peoples. I for one will not drag you into the conflicts of other peoples. We will remain friends of all and enemies of none. Our only enemy is the one who might dare to play about with our hard-won independence. Any habit of following one side today and the other side tomorrow will be tantamount to prostitution, and this is what we reject.''

A week later, an editorial appeared in the *Sunday Nation*, one of Kenya's major papers, indicating that the African break in diplomatic relations was ''national ingratitude and diplomatic ineffectiveness.'' The editors wrote that Israeli aid programs ''have been more successful than those of most of the major and richer nations.'' Therefore, it was ''national ingratitude that only one of the African countries thanked the Israelis for anything, choosing rather to dwell on the anti-Arab evils of the 2.5 million-people nation. Evil or not—and every nation has its share—the Israelis have put a great deal in this continent.'' [16]

By November 1, Kenya could hold out no longer. In the official notification of severance of relations, the Kenyan government maintained that ''Occupation of land by force of arms is not only against the United Nations Charter but also against the national principles of Kenya. Therefore, as long as Israel continues to occupy Arab lands taken by force of arms, Kenya has decided not to maintain diplomatic relations with Israel.''

Liberia, which has generally been considered very friendly to Israel, also managed to retain ties as long as possible. However, on November 2, 1973 the government indicated:

> Inasmuch as Liberia, a charter member of the OAU, has pledged its unwavering solidarity with the Arab Republic of Egypt, also a charter member, to regain its territory illegally occupied, and since Israel has persisted in its refusal to surrender Egyptian territory in contravention of Security Council resolutions, the Government of Liberia now considers that to maintain diplomatic relations with the State of Israel would not be in harmony with African unity and solidarity. Moreover, it is felt that this adamant behavior of the State of Israel, unless reversed without delay, might lead to another violent outbreak of hostilities in the Middle East, thereby threatening world peace and security.
>
> Therefore, the Government of Liberia hereby severs diplomatic relations with the Government of the State of Israel and this severance will continue as long as Israel illegally occupies Arab territories.

A very small number of states was able to withstand the enormous pressures. The Ivory Coast persisted as long as possible, despite the example of its neighbors and France's hostile attitude. At the other side of the continent, Malawi, Lesotho and Swaziland, all of which are located near South Africa, and the island of Mauritius have so far retained their ties with Israel, in keeping with their generally moderate foreign policies.

The extensive list of countries which did break relations with Israel before and during the war includes Nigeria and Zaire, two major countries which have enormous economic potential because of their natural resources, and which have been growing in importance in African affairs. The list includes Senegal and Cameroon as well, the other two states which were included in the visit of the "four wise men" to the Middle East, despite continuing efforts by Senegalese president Leopold Senghor to retain his role as a quasi-mediator. Some African states, such as Tanzania, had long indicated their identification with Egypt, but had attempted to maintain a "nonaligned" position in regard to the Middle East. Others, such as Ghana, had maintained friendly relations with Israel before the break. Ghanaians in Accra had even indicated that they had hoped to move their embassy from Tel Aviv to Jerusalem. Given this attitude, stress was on the territorial issue rather than on bilateral relations. Ghana indicated that it had broken relations "until such time as Israel withdrew from Arab lands." [17]

The biggest shock was Ethiopia's severance of relations, both because of its strategic importance as the only other non-Muslim state on the Red Sea and its location near the Bab al-Mandeb Straits, and because of cultural affinities dating back to the time of King Solomon and the Queen of Sheba. Ethiopia has also been one of the major recipients of Israeli technical assistance, including such vital areas as the military and police. Against these positive factors was balanced growing Arab pressure to move the OAU capital away from Addis Ababa, possibly to Cairo; Arab support for the ELF and the Somalis, two predominantly Muslim forces plaguing the Ethiopian empire; and pressure upon the government from the more radical, often younger officials to support the Arab side. Many radicals have been extremely critical of American and Israeli military aid to Emperor Haile Selassie. It has been easier to appease them under the circumstances by breaking relations with Israel than by severing ties with one of the superpowers. The emperor, moreover, stressed his concern with the occupied territories: "Since it was difficult to compel Italy to leave Ethiopia after it had acquired our land by force, our sympathies here are obviously with the states whose territories have been occupied by force." [18] These combined pressures, according to a well-situated Ethiopian, have enabled the Arabs to "break the backbone" of Israeli-African relations.

The emperor decided to give very high priority to maintaining his prestige in the OAU. That Haile Selassie placed African solidarity with Egypt above friendship with Israel was evident, for instance, in a keynote speech during the special meeting of the OAU Council of Ministers in Addis Ababa in November. He stated: "In demonstrating their solidarity with Egypt and the other states whose territorial integrity has been violated, OAU member states are committing themselves to uphold the fundamental principles of interstate relations without which there can be neither peace nor progress." At the same time the emperor indicated, as have other African leaders, that

African support for Egypt should bring renewed Arab efforts against the "colonialist and racist" regimes of Southern Africa.[19]

EVALUATION OF ISRAEL'S POSITION AND THE FUTURE

Africa's rupture with Israel was disturbing, but the latter could not have done much to avert the break without substantial change in its foreign policy, especially in regard to occupied territories. Israel could have modified little at the bilateral level, although it might have improved some of its programs or been more careful about the tarnishing of its image by some unscrupulous private entrepreneurs. Israel did attempt several alternative diplomatic strategies after Uganda broke relations. In some cases, it raised the level of representation (as in Rwanda); in others it lowered the status (as in Niger). The government first tried to be more selective about countries it assisted, and then returned to a policy of endeavoring to maintain its presence wherever possible. None of these alternative strategies made any substantial difference in the wake of the Arab diplomatic onslaught at the multilateral level.

Many Israeli officials and citizens have been dismayed by African "ingratitude." The people who have been most disturbed were those who had built up false expectations about Israel's major power position in Africa. The tendency to overestimate Israel's importance to Africa in the past led to an exaggerated sense of betrayal. Israeli reactions were evident in various local newspaper editorials. *Hatzofe*, the National Religious party paper, expressed the prevalent sense of dismay: "One of Israel's diplomatic errors was its great effort to establish close ties with the African states without first establishing whether these regimes were stable and mature enough to make the effort worthwhile. Careful consideration would have shown that the enormous sums spent in developing Africa would have been put to infinitely better use in absorbing immigrants and in reducing the social gap in Israel."[20] A letter from the prosperous suburb of Savyon also conveyed the Israeli sense of African ingratitude: "I think that [the] eventual desire of these states [to renew their links with Israel] should be met with complete indifference. More than that, we should refuse to renew the development assistance to any state which severed relations. The heavy burden of our taxation which most of us are willing to bear in order to repair the damages of this war would become intolerable if even a penny were spent to bolster the economy of those who let us down when the pinch came."[21]

Editorials in other newspapers were somewhat more balanced. *Ha'aretz*, which provides the widest coverage of international affairs, recognized that Israel's position in Black Africa, built up over many years, was practically destroyed. According to *Ha'aretz* "This fact should not be minimized." We have reason to respond with annoyance and even anger on this return for our kindness. But even at this time—it is better to recognize the truth. "We turned to the Black continent not as philanthropists, but after we failed to establish firm roots in Asia." Although the original desire was "to leap over the wall of Arab hatred and even to diminish it," experience proved that Israel could not gain the UN votes it had hoped for. At least African votes helped block hostile resolutions. "Later even this support disintegrated." Despite this situation, the editorial continued, one should not say that "all our work was in vain. For a considerable time our position in Africa enhanced our international prestige." Now pressures from Arabs, especially Libya and Saudi Arabia, and from the "nonaligned" states have over-whelmed us. Our declining position in Europe may also have contributed. This "mad rush to disown us does not reflect honor on the African states." Israel will not forget who broke relations with it during difficult times. When, after the war, African states attempt to restore relations with us, they should not assume that they will be high on our scale of priorities in the near future.[22]

The left-wing paper Al Hamishmar (Mapam) indicated that the main cause for the break in relations was Arab pressure. This possibility should have been anticipated and met by comprehensive and energetic political action to change the situation. Omer, representing the Histadrut viewpoint, looked to the future in calling for a broad political, diplomatic and propaganda offen-sive in Western Europe and Latin America. It also hoped to salvage whatever was possible in Asia and Africa.[23]

According to The Jerusalem Post, "There is no denying the political damage that Israel has suffered as a result of its growing isolation in Africa. If the cease-fire opens the path to a political settlement in the Middle East, no doubt many of the African states will seek to renew their links with Israel—and Israel will certainly be glad of it. But those links will never be the same again. The taste of betrayal at a time of crisis will remain."[24]

Practical concern continues to exist about major Israeli investments, especially in the Ivory Coast, as well as about future possibilities for trade. The commercial situation is particularly worrisome because of Arab efforts to have economic sanctions applied to Israel, as well as to South Africa and Portugal.

In retrospect, Israel's relations with Africa, which indicated great promise in the late fifties, reached their nadir in the early seventies. As a result of the blatant trend among many African states to side with the Arabs in the most difficult and costly war that Israel has ever fought, it is unlikely that relations will ever be the same again.

The future of Israeli-African relations depends mainly upon the resolution of the Middle East impasse. If a peace settlement is not reached soon, it will be difficult to repair Israel's relations with African states. If a settlement, including agreement on the territories, is accepted, it will be possible for

African states which broke relations under pressure to endeavor to renew ties with Israel. Generally, diplomatic practice permits the resumption of relations in the course of time. This has been evident, for instance, among African countries which have restored relations with the Soviet Union and China. By then, Israel will have reduced both its expectations of African states and the efforts it would be willing to expend on that continent. In the future Israel will probably be more selective in establishing diplomatic missions and sending technical assistance. Under such circumstances, Israel may look forward to correct and perhaps even cordial relations with many African states. It will also be able to expand trade possibilities once freedom of passage through the Suez Canal is again assured.

Just as war was the catalyst for breaking relations, peace can be the condition for their resumption. It will probably require a great effort on the part of Africans to overcome the disappointment left by their desertion of Israel in its time of crisis.

NOTES

1. Portions of this article originally published as *Jerusalem Papers on Peace Problems*, No. 6 (Jerusalem, 1974), first appeared in "Africa's Rupture with Israel," *Midstream* (January 1974). The author has also benefitted from discussions with Nehemia Levtzion and others.

2. For a full analysis of Israel's foreign policy goals, see Michael Brecher, *The Foreign Policy System of Israel* (London, 1972).

3. See Leopold Laufer, *Israel and the Developing Countries* (New York, 1967).

4. See Susan Aurelia Gitelson, "The OAU Mission and the Middle East Conflict," *International Organization* 27, no. 3 (Summer 1973): 413-19.

5. *West Africa*, October 15, 1973, p. 1443.

6. P. Enahoro, "Algiers Diary," *Africa*, no. 26 (October 1973): 19-20.

7. *New York Times*, September 9, 1973.

8. *Jerusalem Post*, November 4, 1973.

9. *Jerusalem Post*, October 5, 1973.

10. *Addis Ababa*, October 9, 1973.

11. Government communiqué, Dar es Salaam, 1973.

12. *Lagos*, October 12, 1973.

13. *Ha'aretz*, November 2, 1973.

14. Interview, United Nations, New York, September 5, 1973.

15. Interview, United Nations, New York, September 6, 1973.

16. Quoted in *Jerusalem Post*, October 29, 1973.

17. *Jerusalem Post*, October 29, 1973.

18. *Newsweek*, December 3, 1973.

19. *Jerusalem Post*, November 20, 1973.

20. Quoted in *Jerusalem Post*, November 5, 1973.

21. M. Jacobsen, *Jerusalem Post*, November 5, 1973.

22. *Ha'aretz*, November 2, 1973 (author's translation).

23. *Jerusalem Post*, November 4, 1973.

24. *Jerusalem Post*, October 26, 1973.

15

Meron Medzini

REFLECTIONS ON ISRAEL'S ASIAN POLICY

In the 1950s and early 1960s Israeli leaders often spoke of Israel as an Asian country. In 1956 Golda Meir observed: "It is natural that we view ourselves as an integral part of the Asian continent, and it is obvious that we shall endeavour to win our place among the peoples of Asia."[1] It is doubtful that Israel's people and leaders accepted this literally. In early 1967, in a speech made on the occasion of the establishment of the Israel-Asia Friendship League, Abba Eban repeated that Israel was an Asian country. In the same speech he also reminded his audience ironically that he had argued with similar enthusiasm a few days ealier that Israel had links with Europe so strong that European Common Market states must accept it as an associate member.[2] Israel has never been able to decide whether it is in fact a European country in spirit, tradition, political and economic ties, and an Asian country only because of geography. The Asian continent, on whose Western fringes Israel lies, was seen by Israeli leaders as a strange, incomprehensible entity, far away spiritually, religiously and politically. The common denominator between Israel and Asia—geography—was highly limited, the contrasts many and vast.

This negative image came out of the European or American background of Israel's leaders and diplomats, who were not at all familiar with Asia. The rare outstanding exceptions were David Ben-Gurion, who made an effort to study Buddhism, and Yigal Allon, who studied the history of modern India. But their studies were as limited as was their influence on Israel's Asian policy. The "European" view was common to Knesset members, editors and journalists as well as officials of Israel's Foreign Ministry. Most political parties in Israel demonstrated little interest in Asia, the exception being the former Achdut Ha'avodah whose leaders were interested in India, and Mapam which followed the evolution of Asian communist nations. These attitudes only strengthened after the first contact by representatives of the Palestinian Jewish community (the Yishuv) with Asian leaders in the 1930s

200

and on the eve of the establishment of Israel.[3] India's leaders, for example, opposed creation of the Jewish state. Under Nehru's instructions, India's delegates to the United Nations voted against partition. Other Asian delegations voted against or abstained in the crucial November 29, 1947 vote.[4]

Asian leaders made few visible efforts to welcome independent Israel. They were not versed in the Judeo-Christian tradition; some tended to equate Zionism with British imperialism and felt more akin to the Arabs. There was no anti-Semitism in Asia, but the absence of the "Jewish question" and of knowledge of the Nazi Holocaust also meant that Asian leaders failed to see the urgent need for a Jewish state in Palestine.[5] When Israel proclaimed its independence and sought to establish diplomatic, cultural and commercial relations, the majority of the then free Asian states rejected these attempts. A severe blow was dealt to Israel when it was not invited to take part in the 1955 Bandung Conference. This meant that Asia viewed Israel neither as an Asian state nor as one rightly belonging to the nonaligned group of new nations then in the process of formation.

This pattern of mutual misunderstanding soon reflected itself in Israel's Asian policy. Other weighty factors contributed their share. Israel's foreign policy has a number of central objectives; a brief discussion of them will show that Asia played a marginal role in their attainment.

The first objective is the preservation of Israel's security, territorial integrity and national identity. In the center of this lies the matter of defense. Since Israel's foreign policy is largely a function of its security needs, the purchase of arms is a major component. But Asia could not and has not contributed at all to this goal. In January 1957 Ben-Gurion declared: "From the point of view of our existence and security, the friendship of one European country is more valuable than the views of all the people of Asia."[6] Israel sought arms in Europe and America. There was never any feeling that Asia would be able or willing to supply weapons, although Israeli experts were later impressed with Japanese technology. Israel sought political support from Asians, mostly in the United Nations and other international forums, but was aware that it could not expect full and consistent Asian support in the international arenas because of national considerations of each Asian country. The aim was, later, at least to neutralize them. Soon it became evident that in spite of attitudes which ranged from neutral to hostile, it was possible to establish normal bilateral relations with some Asian countries irrespective of their UN stand.

Asia was not expected to contribute much to the strengthening of Israel's economy. Most countries on the continent were receivers, not donors, of foreign aid. Those which did extend aid—Japan, Taiwan and the People's Republic of China—did not direct it to Israel for political reasons. Israel received tremendous amounts of aid from the West, either from the Jewish people there or from various governments, particularly the United States. While it viewed the development of trade with Asia as an important goal, Israel never saw the Asian market as a major export target and preferred its traditional European and American markets. Shipping difficulties, the maritime blockade on the Straits of Tiran until 1956, the Suez Canal barring to Israeli ships, all hampered direct communications. Expensive Israeli products could not compete with cheaper Asian products. But Israel neglected this market for a long time, and it was only in the late 1960s and early 1970s that this error was being corrected.

Israel's information efforts also were directed to Europe and America. In none of Israel's ten diplomatic missions was there, until 1973, a press or cultural affairs attaché.[7] Hence the development of scientific and cultural ties with Asia also lagged. Members of Israeli institutions of higher education and research were naturally attracted more to America and Europe. Most of Israel's research grants came from American and European sources. Scientists from Israel doubted if they could learn much from Asian colleagues, save the Japanese. But Israeli universities began to train scores of Asian students and trainees and thus contribute to the growth of trained manpower on the continent.

Since there are only tiny Jewish communities in Asia east of Iran, Israel could not be helped by them politically or economically, or in the field of propaganda. Local Jews in Hong Kong, Bombay or Tokyo lacked political influence. This may have persuaded the Israeli Foreign Ministry to allocate funds for the establishment of diplomatic missions in places where large Jewish communities lived, to strengthen their ties with Israel and to sustain their Jewishness. In 1971 there were in Asia some 18,000 Jews, 14,500 of them in India.[8] These factors dictated low priority to Israeli activity there in the 1950s. In 1958 Abba Eban stated: "For many years our international relations were exclusively American or European."[9] The small returns anticipated from the enormous sums required to make Israel's presence felt in this vast continent deterred its leaders.

During the first years after independence, Israel's efforts in Asia were concentrated on obtaining a number of objectives, chief among them diplomatic recognition. Israel had hoped that recognition—especially by India—and ties with China would open the doors for political and economic activities in Asia. At the time there was much talk in Israel about its being a bridge between Europe, Asia and Africa.[10] Following recognition, Israel expected that establishment of diplomatic relations and Israeli presence in Asian capitals would enable it to combat growing political enmity and economic boycott practiced against it by Arab states. This was also part of a general Israeli drive to win universal recognition and break through the wall of hostility which Arab states attempted to erect around its borders. Israel even had hoped to win the friendship of a number of Muslim Asian states in order to lessen Arab pressure on it and blunt its impact, and also to create dents in the unified Arab stand. Although it was clear from 1947 that Pakistan and Afghanistan openly supported their fellow Arab states, there were hopes regarding Indonesia and, later, Malaysia.

Through Asian states, Israel wanted to join the growing bloc of nonaligned nations which had won independence in the 1945-55 decade. By this move Israel hoped to rid itself of charges levelled against it by Nehru and other Asian leaders that Zionism came to Palestine under the protection of British bayonets. Israel thought it could join this group because between 1948 and 1950 there was a marked preference among its leaders for pursuing a foreign policy independent of the two superpowers of the cold war. Because India and Burma espoused similar sentiments, Israel hoped to find common interest with them in this sphere.

Socialist Israeli leaders expected to find a common language with Asian socialist leaders such as Nehru and U Nu, and to open paths to them on the basis of their common socialist ideology. (In Asia only the governments of Israel, India and Burma were, at the time, led by socialists.) In the early 1950s the role of the Histadrut and Mapai was important in forging ties with Asian leaders. These were climaxed in 1953, during the first Asian Socialist Conference which met in Rangoon, and to which Israel was invited. Its delegation was led by Foreign Minister Moshe Sharett, who was also a noted Mapai leader. If this was a notable achievement, most of Israel's hopes and expectations were otherwise soon dashed.

India delayed recognition of Israel, and when it formally did so in September 1950, New Delhi refused to establish diplomatic relations and only permitted Israel to operate a consulate in Bombay. Nehru feared adverse Pakistani reaction; he bore in mind the presence of tens of millions of Muslims in India, and UN Arab votes that he needed during the many debates on Kashmir. He thought India's trade with the Arabs would suffer and saw little benefit in diplomatic ties with Israel. This was in contrast to what he was preaching in public at the time: peace and friendship among all nations.

Israel insisted on the principle of reciprocity on which Moshe Sharett was firm. At one stage India was prepared to discuss the opening of an Israeli diplomatic mission in New Delhi. Sharett thought that India should recipro-cate by establishing a mission in Israel. Nehru objected to this, first citing budgetary difficulties and later for political reasons. An opportunity was thus lost. India's attitude, veiled by constant moralizing and sermonizing on the part of its leaders and UN representatives, disappointed Israel. India's policy set the example to other Asian nations which were in no hurry to establish ties with Israel. Only four additional ones recognized it between

1949 and 1950: Nationalist China, Burma, Thailand and the Philippines. Others waited until they won their own freedom. Since that time it was Israel who had to grant them recognition, this presented less of a problem, although Israel delayed recognizing Laos, Cambodia, the two Koreas and the two Vietnams. In 1952 Israel established diplomatic relations with Japan, a year later with Burma and only in the late 1950s did it add Nepal, the Philippines, Thailand and Ceylon to those Asian nations where it was represented. A group of hostile Asian states remains to this very day: China, North Korea, North Vietnam, Indonesia, Pakistan, Afghanistan, Malaysia and Mongolia. These are either communist or Muslim states.

The second disappointment came when Israel was not invited to the Bandung Conference. Concurrently the Arab states became prominent members of the nonaligned bloc, and Nasser one of its outstanding leaders along with Nehru and Tito. Israel argued that its exclusion "has no validity from the point of view of international morality and the principle of equality and cooperation among peace loving nations, primarily those who only recently won their independence."[11] It should be recalled that Israel itself ended its short experiment with nonalignment when it supported the UN and U.S. actions in Korea in speeches and UN votes. This decision resulted from political, security and economic considerations, and also from the fact that the largest Jewish community resided in America. There was also a cooling off in relations with the Soviet Union and other Eastern European countries even before the Korean War. But arguments based on international morality had little meaning. The Israeli decision to support the West was realistic and correct, but from then on Israel could not appear before the new nations of Asia and Africa as a nonaligned country.

The third Israel disappointment stemmed from failure to establish ties with the People's Republic of China. Having recognized Peking in January 1950, Israel hoped for normal ties at the conclusion of the Korean War. Some Israelis still claim that in 1954 and 1955 it was the Israeli government that missed an opportunity to make meaningful contact with China, after the latter had on a number of occasions indicated interest in such ties.[12] It was argued that American pressure had led Sharett, then both premier and foreign minister, to hesitate at the crucial moment, before the decision was made in early 1955 to send to China a trade mission composed of middle-level officials who had no authority to negotiate the establishment of diplomatic relations.[13] Upon their return Sharett waited for a reciprocal visit by the Chinese before moving ahead. But by then it was too late. China had discovered the Arab states, and preferred to approach them rather than carry on talks with Israel. The end came at the Bandung Conference when Chou En-lai and Nasser met. Following this conference, China turned hostile and began to espouse the Arab cause openly, offering "volunteers" to Egypt during the 1956 Sinai war.

The only ray of light at the time was Burma. That country established diplomatic relations with Israel in 1953, and soon expressed interest in obtaining large-scale technical assistance in both military and civilian fields. U Nu was the first prime minister to make an official visit to Israel, in 1955. But even then many problems arose. Israel entered into undertakings it could not possibly implement; grandiose plans were prepared by Israelis with little regard to local conditions; lack of trained manpower was felt; Israeli goods failed to arrive on time; there were difficulties in transportation; excessive material demands by Israeli experts added to difficulties created by a strange language, culture, climate and Israel's general inexperience in the field of technical aid at the time—all this spelled mounting problems. In a way, Burma became Israel's training ground and mistakes committed there were not to be repeated elsewhere in the future.[14]

The Bandung Conference and the wave of Asian protests during and after the Sinai war demonstrated to Israel that in Asia at least, its achievements were meager. By 1956 it was represented only in Tokyo, Rangoon and Bombay. Burmese and Japanese legations were established in Tel Aviv. The volume of trade, because of the maritime blockade, was small. Israeli exports to all of Asia amounted to $5 million in 1956 (compared with $52 million in 1967 and $171 million in 1972). There was a feeling of frustration and gloom among those Israelis charged with dealing with Asia at the time.

Israel's military victory in the Sinai campaign improved things somewhat. It ironically served to raise its prestige in Asia more than any other factor. In spite of waves of protest from Asian capitals and UN delegations, Asian leaders were impressed. This was an example of how a small and poor country was able to train and maintain a large, powerful, mostly reserve army. Israel defended its borders with military and semimilitary settlements, developed its military industries, encouraged research in this field and diverted much of its limited resources to the defense effort. It was also able to maintain normal life in spite of the permanent state of siege, and devote itself to other national tasks, such as absorbing immigrants and developing the arts and sciences. As for Israel, the Sinai war had ended the immediate threat to its existence and, with pressure eased, it could now devote more thought and energy to other goals besides that of defense. A new look was taken at the world beyond the Middle East. This was the period of bold leaps over the ring of Arab states that ensured in the development of strong links with Turkey and Iran. It was the beginning of the Israeli effort in Africa. There was now more time and peace of mind for Asia. The maritime blockade over the Straits of Tiran was lifted thus ensuring direct communications with Asia. In 1957-62 diplomatic relations were established with Thailand, Ceylon, Nepal, Cambodia, Laos, the Philippines and South Korea. Budgetary reasons postponed the opening of the Israeli Embassy in Pnom Penh until 1967, that in Seoul until 1969, and a Consulate General in Hong Kong until

1973. There was a feeling of renewed drive, although at this time the main effort was directed to Africa, where it was easier to work than in Asia.

Timing was an important factor in Israel's success in Africa. African leaders, like their Asian counterparts, became aware of Israel after the Sinai war; most of them were facing Israel for the first time. They found a stronger, more confident Israel than had Asian leaders who met Israel before the Sinai war, when it was a more hesitant, less experienced country. Unlike in Asia, Israel began to work in Africa before many of its states became free and thus had assured itself an important role in their future development. The size and population of many African states were far smaller than those of Asia, and Israel could respond more easily to their initial requests. Even had it responded in Asia, results would have hardly been felt. In Africa there was no tradition of hostility to Israel and even a number of Muslim states were willing to establish relations with it. Africa was the scene of large-scale Israeli technical and military aid: the establishment of flying schools in Ghana and Uganda, training of Kenyan and other policemen, training of paratroopers from the Congo and establishment of paramilitary youth organizations and movements in a number of countries.[15] Above all, African states did not want to become involved in the Arab-Israeli conflict, and if they often voted against Israel in the United Nations, bilateral cooperation was maintained at a very high level. African leaders visited Israel and Arab states, and they realized that it was possible to maintain relations with both sides without being hurt by the Arabs.

Israel's expanding work in Africa attracted attention in Asia, where a number of leaders began to display more than a passing interest in obtaining military aid and instruction from Israel. As early as 1954, Burma had purchased a number of piston-engined fighter planes, and Israeli air force personnel was sent there to maintain them and to instruct Burmese pilots. Ceylon bought two warships from Israel in 1959. Israeli officers trained Nepalese paratroopers, Israeli advisers were instrumental in building the armed forces of Singapore. Military missions from Southeast and East Asia visited Israel to study the organization, structure and systems of the Israeli army. A number of Israeli chiefs of staff, among then Generals Dayan, Tsur and Rabin, visited Asia in the course of their service. Israel was reported to have sold ammunition to India during the Sino-Indian war of 1962.[16]

At this time there was also an expansion in Israel's technical aid program. Besides building and managing model farms in Thailand, Nepal and Cambodia between 1958 and 1966, 180 Israeli experts worked in ten Asian countries. They were also engaged in water and irrigation planning and regional development projects; they advised in public health, industry and the cooperative movement and conducted short-term courses in Asian states. The number of Asian trainees in Israel reached 410 in 1966, about one-fourth the total number of trainees in that year.[17]

The major setback occurred in Burma and was caused by the decision of the new leader, General Ne Win (who visited Israel twice) to freeze operations of all foreign countries. Israel was particularly affected, since its friends in Burma were identified with the deposed U Nu regime. As their influence waned, so did Israel's. Another setback took place in Japan. The Arab economic boycott was able to impress itself upon Japan, a country that gets some 90 percent of its oil from Middle Eastern sources. The Japanese government, unwilling to endanger the flow of oil so vital to its economy, decided not to fight the boycott and acquiesced in the decision of a number of major firms not to trade with Israel. Israel's attempts to show that it bought more from Japan than many Arab states put together did not impress Japanese businessmen and Israel had to turn to American Jewry for help. There were a number of exceptions when Japanese firms formed joint partnerships with Israeli companies, but on the whole the Arabs were successful in their efforts.

Asian reactions to the Israeli victory in the Six-Day War were far less angry than those eleven years earlier, but they were widespread. The UN voting record of the Asian states revealed that when it came to the international organization, anti-Israel feelings prevailed. None of the Asian states supported Israel openly, condemned Arab aggression, decreed UN impotence or criticized the Soviet Union for its role in the crisis.[18] It was evident again that in the eyes of some Asian leaders, Israel was still a nuisance and deserved only limited and marginal interest.

India and China, the largest Asian states, were successful in influencing the rest of Asia to take an anti-Israel stand, or at best to adopt a neutral position in the Arab-Israeli conflict. Privately, Asian leaders and UN delegates told Israelis not to take their votes or statements too seriously and said that the fruitful cooperation between them would continue. But Israel wanted an open endorsement in the United Nations to satisfy its people and to reap some benefits from its aid. Israel was able to persuade some Asian governments that ties with it and the Arabs would not harm them, but others were not convinced and preferred to speak against Israel—knowing that it would not retaliate—rather than speak against the Arabs. One exception was a pro-Israel declaration made by South Korea's President Park in 1969. But his country was not a UN member and there were few Arab embassies in Seoul.

On the credit side, although Israel's aid to Asia was small compared with that given by others (and small in comparison with Israel's own aid to Africa and Latin America), Israel did give it some advantages over the Arabs who did not extend any technical assistance at all to developing countries. But there were a number of setbacks in the period since the Six-Day War. In 1970 Ceylon broke off diplomatic relations with Israel. This was the result of an election promise given by the prime minister to a pro-Arab minority. Israel protested but had to withdraw its representative from Colombo. China continued to support the Arabs, and since 1965 has given political, material and military aid to the various Palestinian terrorist organizations. In 1965 Peking recognized the Palestine Liberation Organization, accorded its representative there diplomatic status and began to send it a small quantity of weapons. A number of Palestinians were also trained in China. Similar positions were taken by North Vietnam and North Korea which on many occasions denounced Israel.[19] China's admission to the United Nations in 1971 added another state, hostile to Israel, to the General Assembly and the Security Council, and speeches made by its delegates were bellicose and at times far more vicious than those made by the Soviet Union.

There was, however, an improvement in the picture of Israel's representation in Asia. In 1973 Israel established an embassy in Saigon and a Consulate General in Hong Kong. Cambodia opened an embassy in Jerusalem and South Vietnam was due to follow. The Philippines had opened an embassy in Tel Aviv in the early 1960s. The other Asian nations are represented by nonresident diplomats who reside in Paris or Rome.

In the early 1970s it appeared as though there would be a crack in the Arab boycott in Japan. Mounting pressure by a number of Jewish organizations in the United States, particularly the Anti-Defamation League of B'nai B'rith, led to promises by car manufacturers who boycotted Israel for years to appoint a distributor for Israel; Japan Airlines held talks with El Al for mutual landing rights and Israel negotiated successfully the sale of citrus to Japan. But otherwise there was no change. Japan Airlines still refused to fly to Israel, while major firms are as adamant as ever in having open trade contacts with Israel. Israel hoped that Japan realized it was possible to trade with both Israel and the Arabs, the Arab boycott having in any case been weakened by Israel's trading with a number of Arab states across the open bridges on the river Jordan. But as the Arab states were openly threatening to use oil as a political weapon, Japan recoiled and announced a strict neutrality in the Arab-Israeli conflict, which was seen by Israelis as an effort to placate the Arabs. But there has been a steady growth in Israeli-Japanese trade whose volume in the early 1970s exceeded $100 million. Israel feels that it has not yet fully exploited the Asian market. One of the problems is the absence of special Israeli products that can successfully compete in Asian markets, with the exception of polished diamonds and phosphates sold to Japan. Israel's sophisticated products are still intended for Europe and America, and in any case cannot compete with goods made in Japan, Taiwan, Hong Kong and Singapore. But it is in Asia that Israeli trade missions are now trying to develop new markets.

After twenty-five years of ties with Asia, there is still a tendency in Israel to give this continent a somewhat low priority after North America, Europe, Africa and Latin America. This tendency is expressed in low budgets and in small diplomatic missions. Israel is represented in Japan, a world power of over 100 million people, by five diplomats, compared with fifteen in London and Paris—not to mention the large missions in the United States. There has been little change in the image of Asia among Israeli leaders. Israel is still very closely tied to the United States and Western Europe, where major Jewish communities reside. It is in that direction that Israel's prime minister and other personalities head annually. On the other hand, a number of Israeli leaders have travelled to Asia: Foreign Minister Sharett to Burma in 1953, President Shazar to Nepal in 1966, President Ben Zvi to Burma in 1959, Prime Minister Ben-Gurion to Burma in 1961. Foreign Minister Golda Meir visited a number of Asian countries in 1962; Abba Eban followed in 1967. Israeli leaders regularly meet their Asian counterparts at UN sessions, and it is there that contacts are maintained even with representatives whose countries have no formal ties with Israel.

The number of Israelis interested in Asia, small in the early 1950s, has grown to a few hundred, mostly experts, diplomats who had served in Asia, scholars and students. However, the Asian continent has not yet entered into the consciousness of the average Israeli. School curriculum in history and geography practically ignores Asia and concentrates almost exclusively on Europe and the United States. Only recently were Asian studies introduced at Israeli universities. The Hebrew University of Jerusalem pioneered this, and it is now being followed by other institutions of higher education. The relatively high number of interested students surprised the small numbers of trained scholars, but even this breakthrough has not yet cleared the fog, the lack of interest, the prejudices, knowledge and awareness of Asia in Israel. Newspapers, radio and television have permanent correspondents in the United States and European capitals, but none in Asia, hence the inadequacy of reporting on that continent in Israel's media.

Since Asia was never at the center of Israel's interests, it was not the subject of intensive foreign policy debates, like those witnessed over relations with Germany, France, the United States and the Soviet Union. The Israeli public dealt with its government's Asian policy on rare occasions, such as the decision to support the United States on the Korean War, or the question of establishment of diplomatic relations with China, or, later, the problem of recognizing and assisting South Vietnam. In the absence of public debate on Asian policy, there was little pressure on those who made that policy. In those cases where a decision to establish ties with China or South Vietnam could have been made without much debate, the Israeli government preferred to postpone it because of external pressures, elections at home or coalition considerations. Budgetary reasons also played a role in the decision to open missions in Asia. Routine and red tape seems to have won out in a number of cases.[20] Israel did not react sharply when Calcutta police permitted Arab demonstrations to come close to President Shazar, who was on his way to Nepal. India refused to let him rest overnight in New Delhi and sent no official to greet him at the airport when his airplane stopped for refueling.

In a number of Asian states the press consistently supports Israel. This is evident primarily in India and has come about as a result of Israel's information effort in that country and the many invitations extended to public opinion moulders to visit Israel. For others as well, Israel is a subject on which the government can be challenged. In many Asian countries, public opinion as expressed in a free press has little or no influence on government policy. Yet in countries such as India, Japan and Singapore, the free press carries much weight. In the past Israel was identified with a number of leaders or political parties that had fallen into disfavor, among them U Nu of Burma and Premier B.P. Koirala of Nepal. But Israel has been able to overcome these connections; in 1973 it has extended its network of contacts to many figures, parties and trade unions and is no longer tied to a few individuals or groups in power. Israel is no longer saddled with the old slogans and approaches once characterizing its approach to Asia, which can be summed in the old Ben-Gurion dictum of "light unto the nations." Israel now talks a different language, has good ties with both military dictatorships and with freely elected governments. Socialism, once the basis for contacts with a number of Asian leaders, has given way to pure political, military and economic factors, often devoid of ideology save that of national interest.

It is not certain that Israel is prepared to deal with the vast transformation now taking place in various parts of Asia. Emotionally and psychologically, Israel is not yet prepared to face the new Asia. Organizationally, the answer is also negative. True, Asia does not devote much thought to Israel, but this does not mean that Israel has to react similarly. It has important interests in Asia which should be developed. One of the problems is that Israel has never defined exactly what these interests are, what are its goals and the order of priority for their attainment. In the absence of long-range political thinking, it has often been difficult to formulate a well-defined and devised policy. Israel has relied more on improvisation, on personal contacts and on expectations which did not always materialize. Perhaps this can serve more immediate needs, but it is doubtful if such a policy can solve the serious problems that have arisen as a result of events such as China's reentry into the international arena with growing interest in the Middle East, or Japan's transformation into a major economic, political and soon military power, or the possibility of changes in India. (When Bangladesh was created in the wake of the 1971 Indo-Pakistani war, it took Israel some six weeks before it recognized this new nation.) It cannot and should not be assumed that the policy of Asian states regarding Israel will remain inert forever. Various options, among them even the establishment of ties with China, should be considered. But much will depend on Israeli action.

It makes little difference whether Israel is geographically a part of Asia or not. It must act in that continent in the context of an overall foreign policy. A more sober approach based on knowledge and understanding of Asia's needs and moods is needed. There now exist many tools in Israel for achieving this knowledge and helping in its evaluation. Those responsible for policy have failed, so far, to make much use of them and have in the process encountered at times unpleasant and unexpected surprises.

NOTES

The original version of this article appeared in *Midstream* 18, no. 6 (June-July 1972): 25-35.

1. *Jerusalem Post*, July 3, 1956.
2. *Jerusalem Post*, January 24, 1967.
3. See for example David Hacohen, *Twenty Days in India* (Tel Aviv, 1948).
4. Of the Asian nations, UN members Afghanistan, Pakistan and India voted against partition, China abstained, the Philippines voted for and Thailand was absent from the vote.
5. See Walter Eytan, *The First Ten Years* (London, 1958), chap. 8.
6. Quoted in Nerzl Berger, "Separatism and Nationalism," *New Outlook* (Tel Aviv) 1, no. 3 (1957).
7. Israel's first press and cultural affairs attaché was appointed in Tokyo in early 1973.
8. *American Jewish Yearbook* (New York, 1973), p. 598.
9. Abba Eban, *Israel Among the Nations* (London, 1958), p. 10.
10. This idea was expressed as early as 1860 by Napoleon III's secretary, who wrote that Jews in Palestine could serve as a bridge between Europe and Asia. See Ernest Laharanne, *The New Eastern Question* (Paris, 1860). In 1965 Ben-Gurion said: "Our future is in Asia, even if our way of life is European, two-thirds of the human race lives in Asia and Israel lies at its gates." *The Guardian* (London, November 1965).
11. Statement by Moshe Sharett to the Knesset, March 16, 1955.
12. Meron Medzini, "Israel and China: A Missed Opportunity," *Wiener Library Bulletin* (London), no. 20-21 (October 1971): 32-40.
13. See David Hacohen, *Burma Diary* (Tel Aviv, 1963), pp. 376-418.
14. See Leo Laufer, *Israel and the Developing Countries* (New York, 1967), pp. 21-25.
15. Ibid., pp. 170-72.
16. Neville Maxwell, *India's China War* (London, 1970), p. 385.
17. Israeli Foreign Ministry, budget speech (Jerusalem, February 1967), p. 7.
18. See Arthur Lall, *The UN and the Middle East Crisis* (New York, 1968).
19. Meron Medzini, "China and the Palestinians," *New Middle East*, no. 32 (May 1971).
20. The Israeli Foreign Office had until recently only one Chinese-speaking ambassador :in Singapore). There are no Japanese, Hindi, Tagalog or Urdu-speaking Israeli diplomats.

16

Yaacov Shimoni

ISRAEL AND THE
PEOPLE'S REPUBLIC OF CHINA

The People's Republic of China was proclaimed on October 1, 1949. The last strongholds of retreating Nationalists fell later in the year (Canton in October, Chungking in November, Chengtu in December), and in December the remnants of Chiang Kai-shek's armies embarked for Taiwan (Formosa). As it became evident that the new, communist rulers were in control of the Chinese mainland, foreign countries began recognizing the new regime. The Soviet Union, followed by its allies, had recognized the People's Republic immediately, on the morrow of its proclamation. The first noncommunist country to do so was Burma (on December 17); India followed on December 30; Pakistan, Ceylon, Great Britain and Norway—early in January 1950. When Israel recognized the People's Republic of China, on January 9, 1950, it was among the first seven noncommunist countries to do so, the only one in the Middle East, in fact the only one all the way from England to the Indian subcontinent.

Israel had been recognized by Nationalist China in March 1949, but no relations had been established. Israel's motives in extending so prompt a recognition to Communist China were neither ideological nor utilitarian. Israel had no particular sympathy for communist regimes or doctrines and it could not expect any tangible, immediate profit from its act of recognition—which could be expected to displease, even antagonize, the United States, Israel's strongest and most important ally and supporter. Israel's motives were mainly reasons of international principle: recognition should be accorded to any state existing in fact, any regime firmly in control of its territory and population. Beyond the application of this principle—which was of major significance for Israel's own struggle for international recognition—Israel was hoping for the development, in a not too distant future, of close and friendly relations with a great nation (whose significance as a potential major power and a people of nearly unlimited energy and great

212

talent was clearly recognized at least by some of Israel's leaders, such as David Ben-Gurion). Recognition implied a decision in principle to establish relations, and the government of Israel spelled out that implication by its unpublicized decision in 1950 to proceed to the establishment of relations with China whenever such a step would be deemed propitious.

Israel could not follow up its act of recognition by the immediate establishment of diplomatic relations. Communist China had gratefully accepted and acknowledged Israel's recognition—in a cable signed by Prime Minister and Foreign Minister Chou En-lai[1]—and expressed its hope that friendly relations be established between the two countries. For Israel, this was a matter of the future. Its network of diplomatic representation was in its beginnings—with no post yet in the whole of Asia and Africa, and with many countries of Europe and most of Latin America covered nonresidentially by an ambassador responsible for several countries simultaneously. Immediate establishment of full relations with Peking was not deemed possible for weighty political reasons. The mere recognition of Communist China had displeased and antagonized the United States, on whose support and aid Israel was depending in its critical first years; the establishment of full relations might well be considered by the United States as going too far, as a hostile act, and would thus have dire consequences. In mid-1950 China became involved in the Korean War, fighting against UN forces, and early in 1951 it was branded as an aggressor by an overwhelming majority of the United Nations. It seemed inconceivable to provoke the whole world by establishing relations at that juncture.

These obstacles began disappearing in 1953-54. The Korean armistice of July 1953 removed the stigma of acute Chinese aggression against the United States. More countries had in the meantime established relations with China. Israel had set up its own first permanent missions in Asia—in Burma and Japan. The establishment of normal relations with China now seemed feasible and desirable. First contacts were established in 1953-54 in Rangoon, where the two countries' ambassadors maintained close and friendly relations. Both countries intended to set up full diplomatic relations—in Israel, a decision to that effect, though not publicly announced, crystallized in 1954, and China publicly stated its intention in September 1954.[2] Both countries preferred to go slowly, and it was decided to exchange trade and goodwill missions first. This procrastination is considered by many Israeli observers to have been a mistake which may well have prevented the establishment of full, normal relations in 1954—an opinion which remains in the realm of speculation.

An Israeli economic and goodwill mission headed by the Israeli minister to Burma, David Hacohen, visited China in February 1955. Its reception in China was polite, but somewhat cool, and its contacts were kept to a medium-to-low level. The mission agreed with its hosts that a similar Chinese delegation would soon visit Israel, and that the establishment of official relations would actively be considered; methods of liaison were determined.[3] In April 1955, Israel proposed to China the establishment of diplomatic relations forthwith. That proposal received but a hesitant, ambiguous reply; repeat messages through Israel's ambassador to Moscow elicited an indication that, although China still hoped for good relations, the time was not propitious for the establishment of full diplomatic relations.

What had happened between China's public announcement of imminent establishment of relations with Israel in September 1954, and the deferment and ultimate rejection of Israel's offer, from spring 1955 onwards? Chinese spokesman have never given a clear and honest explanation, and the interpretation of the sudden change in China's position can only be inferred. Communist China had discovered, early in 1955, prospects for establishment of relations with Arab countries, openings for penetration of the Middle East through positions to be built up in Arab countries; and it preferred these prospects to those of closer relations with Israel—afraid, like some other, noncommunist countries and economic enterprises, that close relations with Israel might harm those Arab Middle Eastern prospects.

High-level Sino-Arab contacts took place during the Asian Bandung Conference of April 1955, where Chou En-lai met Nasser and other Arab top leaders. Israel was excluded from that conference—despite the efforts of some of its chief convenors, such as Nehru of India and U Nu of Burma, who both gave in to Arab pressure and threats of boycott. This fact of Israel's exclusion, this success of Arab pressure tactics, may well have added its weight to China's decision to accord Arab relations priority over contacts with Israel. The Bandung Conference coincided with, and was partly instrumental in, a general turn to the Left in Arab, and particularly Egyptian, international policies. Chinese contacts with Arab states were now further cultivated. They soon resulted in the recognition of Communist China by Egypt, Syria and (royal, prerevolutionary) Yemen, in 1956; other Arab states followed after their respective coups and revolutions—such as Iraq and Sudan in 1958. China recognized the Algerian rebel government as early as 1958—the first non-Arab country to do so. The Sinai War of 1956 further cemented the incipient Sino-Arab alliance and hardened China's antagonism to an Israel now pilloried as an ally and collaborator of the imperialists.

When China first decided to renounce relations with Israel for the sake of an easier penetration of Arab countries, its motivation had been a calculation of political expediency rather than reasons of doctrine or ideological principle. Once Israel was written off, this situation was cloaked with an ever-thickening coat of ideological justification: Israel was the running dog of imperialism, an imperialist power itself, a reactionary aggressor, while

Arabs—and particularly Arab left-wing movements and guerrillas—were victims of aggression, the paragons of progress and revolutionary virtue, supported with all their heart and might by the Chinese people and government. This became one of the major topics of Chinese propaganda, incessantly repeated.

As to practical support, economic, financial or military aid, China has remained a minor, marginal factor in the Middle Eastern power game. China is not in a position to accord foreign nations very extensive economic aid, and among the clients of its modest aid network Arab states do not rank high on the list of priorities (in striking contrast to the priority list of the Soviet Union). As to military aid, China is not limitrophe with the Middle East, and is therefore unable to intervene physically and militarily. As it does not possess a strong navy, there is no Chinese naval presence in the area, and it has hardly any military experts or instructors to offer in the field of modern technological warfare. Chinese aid to guerrilla groups—Palestinian, and in the area of South Arabia and the Persian Gulf—is not extensive; consignments of arms and equipment—very restricted in quantity and nature—can reach those guerrillas only as long as the Arab states permit them to land and pass. Iraq permits the passage of such consignments; but the only Arab state in relations of complete mutual support and confidence with China is Yemen—itself marginal to the area and of minor significance.

Israel is still interested in the establishment of normal relations with China—and thinks such relations should not depend on China's views on Middle Eastern political issues such as the Arab-Israeli conflict (or Israel's views on Far Eastern issues and Chinese policies). Israel would like China to take a more balanced attitude and show more understanding; but normal relations, it holds, can be maintained even by countries divided by deep political differences.

Israel's voting record on the admission of China to the United Nations is considered by some observers as a significant element in the determination of China's attitude. Israel's vote changed with shifts in the parliamentary and political situation and nuances of the precise resolutions debated. In 1950 it voted against motions to seat Communist China in the form they were postpone a debate; in 1953 it abstained on similar proposals; and from 1954 to 1963 it voted for them. When the substance of China's admission was debated—always coupled with a de facto expulsion of Taiwan—Israel abstained. In 1961-63 Israel voted for an effort to admit the People's Republic without expelling Taiwan, and explained that it would vote for China's admission if such a formula could be agreed upon. In 1965-70 Israel voted against motions to seat communist China in the form they were presented; it always voted for the recognition of the issue as an "important question" requiring a two-thirds majority. In the decisive vote of October

1971, Israel voted without reservations for the admission of Communist China. Yet, China does not seem to have paid much attention to Israel's voting record—the positive votes of the early years, the abstentions and the negative ones later, and the favorable vote at the decisive hour. Israel maintains, in any case, that normal relations between nations should not be—and are not usually—made dependent on voting patterns at the United Nations.

There does not seem to be at present any chink in China's armor of complete support for the Arabs and rigid hostility towards Israel—up to an often repeated refusal to "recognize" Israel or have any relations with it, and sometimes implying a denial of Israel's very right to exist. It cannot be easy for China to maintain so rigid a position, and gradual changes may be expected. China will find out that it cannot at one and the same time support three incompatible forces within the Arab world—main stream moderately leftist countries like Egypt, Syria and Sudan; extremist revolutionary regimes like Iraq, Algeria and Yemen; and guerrilla groups aspiring to a complete upheaval and the elimination of all existing regimes. On the Arab-Israeli issue, UN membership may carry with it a certain moderation and the acceptance of more balanced responsibilities. China has not explicitly accepted Security Council Resolution 242 of November 1967 and its underlying principle of a peaceful settlement between the Arab states and an independent Israel within secure borders; but neither has it explicitly rejected it. When its spokesmen talk of the need for an evacuation of Israeli forces, a recognition of the rights of Palestinian Arabs etc., they carefully evade any commitment to "details": evacuation of what and withdrawal where, and what are the rights of Palestinians to be recognized—they leave their options wide open.

In its vital struggle with the Soviet Union, China is tempted to strike superextremist poses so as to embarrass the Soviet Union and drive a wedge between it and the most extremist revolutionary elements in the Middle East; a wildly extremist position on the Arab-Israeli conflict might come in handy. Yet China's new responsibilities as a member of the United Nations and particularly the Security Council, a better understanding of Middle Eastern realities, and a Chinese-U.S. rapprochement that may open flexible options in a new world situation no longer based on the bipolarity of two superpowers, may well propel China towards more moderate policies. Such a realistically calculated moderation would fit in with deeply rooted Chinese political traditions: introvert and averse to foreign adventures and conquest; and skeptically pragmatic. While for the moment there is not much that Israel could do to induce China to respond to its offer of friendly, normal relations—beyond clearly indicating that such an offer is being made and kept standing—the time for such relations may come as soon as Peking opts for global policies of realistic moderation.

NOTES

A shortened version of this chapter was published in the *Jerusalem Post*, February 18, 1973.

1. Information Services of the State of Israel, Foreign Press Division, Press Release, January 18, 1950.

2. Chou En-lai, *Report on the Work of the Government*, made at the first session of the First National People's Congress of the People's Republic of China, September 23, 1954 (Peking: Foreign Languages Press, 1954), p. 43. The statement was also quoted in the press; see Survey of China Mainland Press, U.S. Consulate-General, Hong Kong, no. 895, p. 6; and a release by the New China News Agency of September 23, 1954.

3. Hacohen published extensive notes on his mission to China in his book *Yoman Burma* (Hebrew, Burma Diary) (1963), pp. 375-422.

17

Michael Brecher

ISRAEL AND CHINA:
A Historic "Missed Opportunity"

ISRAEL'S QUEST FOR LEGITIMACY IN ASIA

Images and Realities

Asia brings to mind many images. To some, it is merely a geographical expression. To others, Asia is the home of the great religions, whose teachings have withstood the ravages of time and men. A third symbol evokes colonial rule and underdeveloped economics. A fourth is race or color. Finally, the term *Asia* suggests political and economic change of such dimensions as to transform the classic system of international relations.

Whatever image is selected, Israel clearly falls within the meaning of *Asia*. The Jewish state is part of the Asian continent. Judaism took root in Asian soil, flourished there, and exerted a profound influence on West Asia, both directly, and later through absorption of many of its ideas by Islam.

Israelis share with other Asians the fruit of a lengthy, and at times bitter, struggle for national self-determination. Like Indians and Indonesians, they have known the meaning of foreign rule. Nor was it mere chance that Israel achieved independence in 1948, for this was part of a sweeping historical process and the ferment of national consciousness throughout Asia. During the past ninety-five years an Israeli nation has been forged in the fires of struggle no different from that of nations all over Asia.

Israel is not economically underdeveloped in the same sense as are most Asian and African states; using indices of per capita income, per acre productivity, capital (or labor)-intensive industry, employment skills, and public health, Israel resembles a European state. However, its paucity of resources, the large number of unskilled immigrants, and the desert character of much of its land compels the same kind of massive economic effort imposed by shortage of capital and skills elsewhere in Asia. Nor does the flow of economic aid from the West ipso facto make Israel a Western state.

In racial composition, too, Israel is Afro-Asian almost as much as it is Western. Originally an overwhelmingly white European community, about 55 per cent of its 3 million people are today of Asian and African extraction; like everything else in Israel, the demographic picture was basically altered by the great "ingathering of the exiles" during the 1950s. As for the awakening of Asian peoples, few compare in pace and depth with the change wrought by a segment of Jewry returned to its ancient homeland.

The impact of the anticolonial revolution on the structure of international politics does not merit elaborate treatment here. Suffice it to note that a European-centered system gave way to a bipolar world political system and, after 1962, an increasingly multipower system, in which the new states of Asia are subjects rather than mere objects of political behavior. Of Israel's importance as an Asian state on the stage of world politics, attention need be drawn merely to the events of 1956 and the aftermath of the Suez War, and the May 1967 crisis culminating in the Six-Day War.

Israel may fit these images, but its reception in Asia was decidedly cool. At the time of the UN General Assembly's Partition Resolution in November 1947 there were eight Asian members of the world body, apart from the Arab states. Only one, the Philippines, supported the creation of a Jewish state. Five were opposed: Afghanistan, Iran, Pakistan and Turkey—all Muslim states—and India, which has a large Muslim minority. Nationalist China abstained, and Thailand was absent.

Initial hostility gave way to a slow and as yet incomplete acceptance by the Asian community. In the first two years of statehood six Asian states recognized Israel: Turkey, Nationalist China, the Philippines, Ceylon, Burma and Thailand. Only one, Turkey, took the next step of establishing diplomatic relations at once. Until 1952 there were no full-fledged Israeli diplomatic missions east of Ankara and, as late as 1957, only two (in Tokyo and Rangoon). In part, this unusual state of affairs was due to the absence of tangible Israeli interests in Asia during the early years and the dearth of Jewish communities there. But there were more basic reasons for what was at best Asia's indifferent tolerance of Israel; these reasons point up counter-vailing images of Israel in Asia which persist in some measure to the present.

The Old Testament is an integral part of the Judeo-Christian heritage. Almost everyone in the West is aware of the ancient Jewish Common-wealths, of the Jewish faith, and of the powerful emotional ties of Jewry to the Holy Land through the centuries. Some Christians may question the justice or viability of the state of Israel, but few would ask of Jewry, "What is your claim to the Holy Land?" The Bible and spiritual kinship of Jews and Christians maintain a continuous knowledge of the Jewish connection with Zion.

Herzl did not succeed in his efforts to enlist diplomatic support for Zionist aspirations, but Christian leaders did not question the propriety of his actions or doubt the unique Jewish link to Palestine. This Christian predisposition to view the Jewish claim favorably is also revealed in Weizmann's account of his first meeting with Arthur Balfour in 1906. Balfour asked why Zionists insisted on Palestine as the Jewish national home; the Uganda offer was then to the fore. Weizmann spoke at length on the meaning of Zionism and then conveyed the essence of the Jewish claim: "'Mr. Balfour, supposing I were to offer you Paris instead of London, would you take it?' He sat up, looked at me, and answered: 'But Dr. Weizmann, we have London.' 'That is true,' I said. 'But we had Jerusalem when London was a marsh.' Balfour was moved and asked: 'Are there many Jews who think like you?' When Weizmann answered, 'I believe I speak the mind of millions of Jews,' Balfour commented, 'If that is so, you will one day be a force.'" Although Balfour did not become an immediate convert, Weizmann became convinced "that if someone had been found to present the case of Palestine [as against Uganda] to the British authorities, it would not have been difficult to enlist their sympathies and perhaps, in certain circumstances, their active support."

Such sympathy, let alone active support, was unthinkable among Asian leaders, because historic Israel, Jewry, and Judaism are little known east of the Arab world. The small Jewish communities in India and Iran were unable to provide a link with the peoples of Asia. The Bible, so rich in Jewish history and tradition, is as alien to the cultures of South and East Asia as are the Vedas to the West.

A spiritual leader like Gandhi might include the Bible among the great religious books, but he could not absorb the Zionist idea of an indissoluble link between the Jewish people and the Holy Land. A sophisticated and highly Westernized Asian leader like Nehru was aware of the tie but at the purely rational level. As a student of world history, he also knew of the ancient Jewish Kingdom. But that was long ago and, for him, paled into insignificance when set alongside the visible fact of an Arab community living in Palestine. Nehru commented on the Balfour Declaration of 1917: "But there was one little drawback, one not unimportant fact seems to have been overlooked. Palestine was not a wilderness, or an empty, uninhabited place. It was already somebody else's home." Many Westernized Asian intellectuals of the past half century subscribed to this view. Lack of knowledge about the Jewish connection with Palestine depreciated the Jewish claim in the Asian view. More than that, it tended to create the image of Jews as interlopers, aliens to Asian soil attempting to expel the indigenous people of Palestine.

Lack of knowledge provided the basis of another, even more damaging image, namely the identification of Zionism with British imperialism. To many Asian intellects, the Jewish link with Palestine began with the Balfour Declaration. And that declaration was a symbol of British imperialism planting "alien" Jews on Asian soil. For staunch anticolonialists, this tarred Zionism with the hateful brush of imperialism.

In some respects this was unavoidable. Britain had been given the mandate; creation of a Jewish national home depended on the leading imperialist power of the age. This meant the need to concentrate Zionist diplomatic efforts in London and Geneva. Only one Asian delegate ever sat on the Permanent Mandates Commission of the League of Nations. World Jewry was and is still predominantly Western; funds for resettlement came from Western Jews, as did potential immigrants at that stage. There was little inducement or opportunity to explain the Zionist case to Asia and much evidence of a link with the feared imperial power. To quote Nehru again: "The Arabs tried to gain their [the Jews'] co-operation in the struggle for national freedom and democratic government, but they rejected these advances. They have preferred to take sides with the foreign ruling Power...."

The image of Jews as alien to Asia was strengthened by the fact that creation of a Jewish national home required a large influx of Jews from Europe. As a small minority in Palestine in 1917, and still a minority in 1947, Jewish claim to national self-determination seemed questionable to many Asians. Asian nationalists did not view the Jewish struggle for statehood as part of the general Asian struggle for national self-determination. In Palestine, that place was reserved for Arabs.

Zionist leaders are partly to blame for this image, for they avoided an identification with anticolonial nationalist movements. No Zionist spokesman was to be found at the various antiimperialist conferences during the twenties and thirties. There were no public pronouncements allying Zionist goals with those of Asian nationalists. There were severe limits to freedom of action imposed by the nature of the mandate. Yet there was nothing to prevent left-wing Zionist leaders from championing the cause of anticolonialism. In failing to do so, they showed a remarkable lack of foresight, for which the State of Israel was to pay dearly. That isolation from the mainstream of Asian nationalism, now in the form of neutralism, continues.

The negative image of Zionist aspirations was powerfully influenced by the race factor. The vast majority of Jewish immigrants to Palestine until 1947 were white. How then could they be considered Asian? The fact that the racial composition of the people of Israel has changed sharply in the past quarter century has not altered the image. Israel was alien then because it was white, among other things; it is still white to most Asian intellectuals.

Another factor contributed to the hostility or at least nonsupport of Jewish claim to Israel. Anti-Semitism is not a part of Asian cultures, perhaps partly because there are few Jews in Asia. There was no concern about "the Jewish problem," nor any appreciation of the need for a Jewish state. Lack of knowledge about the Jewish link with Palestine led Asians to discount the Jewish claim; the lack of anti-Semitism led them to discount the need; and the fact of a majority Arab community led them to depreciate the justice of the Jewish case. This was true not only of non-Arab Muslims but also of non-Muslim and secularist Asian intellectuals. It was this powerful countervailing image with which the new State of Israel had to contend.

Partial Fulfillment

Israel's early quest for Asian acceptance centered on New Delhi. India was the rising star of the East, with China in the throes of civil war and Japan temporarily removed from the ranks of the great powers. India was the emerging leader of neutralism, and Israel was then in its "nonidentification" phase. Gandhi and Nehru were held in great respect among the Jews of Palestine. Nehru, in particular, appealed to the predominantly socialist leadership, for his was the voice of rationalism, modernity, progress and Westernization; a measure of the attachment was a Hebrew translation of his *Autobiography* in the thirties, before Nehru had achieved world renown and when the Hebrew-reading public was very small. Some Israeli officials hoped that the Indian leader, non-Muslim but highly respected by Arabs, would be willing and able to moderate Arab hostility provide a bridge between Israelis and Arabs. They had ceased to hope by the mid-1950s.

From the outset Delhi was unsympathetic. It had opposed the Partition Resolution of the UN General Assembly. When Israel was proclaimed in May 1948, India was not impressed. Whereas the United States and the Soviet Union granted recognition within a day, India waited. Even after the Rhodes Armistice Agreements (February-July 1949) strongly suggested that Israel was a fact, India waited. Finally, in September 1950, it granted de jure recognition. There the matter rests, for India has effectively, but at times uncomfortably, resisted all advances for an exchange of diplomatic missions. The only (tenuous) link is an Israeli Consulate in Bombay, eight hundred miles from the capital.

Israeli attitudes have run the gamut from expectation to hope to disappointment to dismay to anger and finally to indifference. The Israeli mood has been most forcefully expressed by ex-Prime Minister Ben-Gurion. On one occasion he remarked that Nehru claimed to be a disciple of Gandhi, but "I cannot understand how Mr. Nehru fits his behaviour to Israel with Gandhi's philosophy of universal friendship. Mr. Nehru gave definite promises to the Director-General of our Foreign Ministry eight years ago that he would soon establish normal diplomatic relations with Israel, but so far he has not kept his word.'' In a comprehensive survey of Israel's position in world politics three years after the Sinai Campaign, Ben-Gurion went further: "Nehru too claims allegiance to neutrality. . . . He is not even neutral in regard to Israel and the Arabs, for he has close ties and normal relations with the Arab countries—but he has stubbornly refused to establish diplomatic relations with Israel, and in his frequent visits to the Middle East he has on every occasion—and not by accident—overlooked Israel.''

By 1952 India's posture was unmistakable. Israel turned elsewhere with vigor. In that same year it pierced the diplomatic barrier in Asia by establishing a legation in Tokyo. For some time this was of little practical value—because of the Suez and Akaba blockades—but the symbolic benefit was considerable. More important was the forging of close ties with Burma. An inconspicuous visit by a Burmese delegation in 1952 marked the beginning of Israel's first diplomatic success in Asia. The following year, Foreign Minister Moshe Sharett represented Mapai (the Israeli labor party) at the first Asian Socialist Conference in Rangoon. This was a turning point, for Sharett put Israel on the map of Asia in his persuasive and charming manner. Diplomatic relations with Burma were established in 1953, and soon after, the experimental phase of Israel's technical assistance program got under way. Medical personnel, engineers, conservation specialists, and several technicians in various fields went to Burma.

Friendship blossomed in the spring of 1955 when U Nu visited Israel. Apparently the Burmese prime minister had also accepted an invitation from Egypt and proposed to visit the two countries in succession. Cairo attempted to put pressure on Rangoon by indicating that he would not be welcome if he visited Israel. U Nu responded by cancelling his trip to Egypt. That diplomatic triumph occurred almost simultaneously with a major and, in perspective, irrevocable setback for Israel in its embryonic relations with China.

ISRAEL AND CHINA

Israel made four important decisions concerning the People's Republic of China between 1950 and 1955: Two were of the tactical type, in terms of a foreign policy system, and two were at the strategic level: (1) on January 9, 1950 Israel's cabinet decided to accord de jure recognition to the People's Republic of China, which had been proclaimed in Peking the preceding October; (2) on May 25, 1954, the Ministerial Committee on Foreign Affairs and Defense decided against active pursuit of diplomatic relations with Peking until after the Geneva Conference on Indo-China; (3) on November 14, 1954 the government of Israel approved the dispatch of an official trade delegation to China; and (4) on March 28, 1955 Israel's Prime Minister/

Foreign Minister decided to decline Peking's overtures for diplomatic relations at that time. It is primarily with the last of those decisions that this paper
is concerned, for it symbolized an historic missed opportunity in the first
decade of Israel's foreign policy.

Moshe Sharett, then prime minister and foreign minister of Israel, was the
principal decision maker on the issue of relations with Peking. Many who
worked closely with Sharett during that period affirmed that he favored
formal ties with Communist China—among them Walter Eytan, Director-
General of the Foreign Ministry, David Hacohen (one of the principal
figures as Israel's minister to Burma), Daniel Lewin (head of the Foreign
Ministry's Asian Department), and Ze'ev Shek (Sharett's Political Secretary).[1]

Yet Sharett's image of China was one of insensitivity to its global
importance. He was neither hostile nor sympathetic—but remote. It was not
that he was oblivious of Asia. More than a year before independence Sharett
declared: "The next item and the principal one is Asia . . . . We are facing a
wall there; they see us as a sword the West is thrusting into the East. There is
a natural emotional tendency to identify with the Arab Movement. There
will be need of a great effort which may not succeed, but which may blaze a
path to the hearts of many people . . . . Our starting point is that we exist in
Asia, we are part of it, part of the renewed Asia and part of ancient Asia,
whether we like it or not.[2]

Sharett's focus was on India and its National Movement, not on China.
Like many Israeli leaders, he had long been mesmerized by the Gandhi-
Nehru Indian National Movement symbols. More generally, for Sharett as
for the entire Israeli high policy-making elite, China was peripheral to a
Euro-America-centered world view. By contrast, he was acutely conscious
of the possible impact on Israel's relations with the United States, the vital
source of economic assistance, diplomatic support—and, it was to be
hoped—arms. In his perception no foreign policy step that could undermine
America's patron role should be undertaken by Israel.

Sharett's U.S. orientation was strengthened by his most striking personality trait—caution, especially in the face of a venture into the unknown.[3] This
was emphasized in the form of a nuance revelation about another aspect of
Israel's East Asian policy. "Sharett was personally rather hesitant [about
China],' wrote a knowledgeable Foreign Ministry official. "I recall, for
example, that I had a difficult time persuading him that we should establish
relations with Japan, as he still regarded [the Japanese] as Fascist war
criminals on the same line as Germany: if memory serves me right, we got
[Ben-Gurion's] approval for relations with Japan while Sharett was on
vacation."[4]

Among Sharett's colleagues the perceptual imbalance between the United

States and China was even more glaring. The four general Zionist ministers were programmatically committed to a policy of alignment with "the free world" and, especially, with the United States. China was not only geographically and psychologically remote; it was also communist. The religious party ministers normally followed Mapai's lead and, in any event, felt no less an ideological affinity with America.

Among the Mapai ministers the two most influential and vigorous participants were Defense Minister Lavon and Minister without Portfolio Aranne. Their general view, shared passively or actively by many colleagues, is easily summarized: the United States was vital to Israel's survival and progress; it would be irresponsible to yield to Hacohen's pressure on something so remote as China. More specifically, their image was shaped by developments at the turn of 1954-55: Washington's courting of Nasser; the coming to fruition of the Baghdad Pact; delicate negotiations on U.S. arms aid; and the Eric Johnston Jordan Water Plan. With that perception, Lavon and Aranne strenuously urged Sharett not to proceed along the path to diplomatic relations with Peking.

Israel was among the earliest, in fact, the seventh of all noncommunist states to recognize the People's Republic of China, but was hesitant about normalizing relations. The issue was evaded in the weeks following recognition—on January 9, 1950. Then, suddenly, on June 20, the Chinese chargé d'affaires in Moscow visited Arye Levavi, Israel's chargé. Levavi reported to the Foreign Office the same day as follows: "He asked me, on instructions of his government, whether Israel was planning to send them a diplomatic mission. I replied . . . that the problem was only financial, and that we are highly desirous of maintaining close contacts with People's China. He said that this was understandable." At the end of June the Foreign Office informed Levavi: "The Government has decided in principle to establish diplomatic relations with People's China. However, nothing will be done in this direction until the situation in the Far East clears up. This is for you only, and you are to do nothing until you hear further from here."[5]

Israel's decision was taken at a meeting on June 28, following a recommendation by the Foreign Ministry Directorate (taken three days earlier) that Israel's minister to the Soviet Union be appointed, concurrently, as nonresident minister to China. That belated decision was stillborn: like the basic principle of nonidentification of which it was a part, it became a casualty of the Korean War. It was also Israel's first missed opportunity to normalize relations with Peking.[6]

After a lapse of almost four years another opportunity arose to establish diplomatic relations with the People's Republic of China. The principal setting was Burma, where Israel had opened its first Asian diplomatic mission towards the end of 1953. The initial approach was surprising, as

David Hacohen, Israel's first ambassador to Rangoon, reported in his diary.[7]

Two views competed for authoritative sanction among Israel's decision-makers. The most forceful advocate of a positive response to Peking was the pragmatic and unconventional Hacohen. From Rangoon China seemed not only massive in size and population; it was also another, and even more important window to the non-Western world. Unlike India, Pakistan, Indonesia, etc., it had neither a Muslim majority, nor a pro-Arab tradition—nor vital interest. This assessment was strongly supported within the Foreign Ministry by Eytan, the director-general, and Lewin.

At the other extreme stood Israel's ambassador to the United States, Reuven Shiloah. His contention was simple and direct: relations with Peking would bring no tangible benefits to Israel and would almost certainly offend the U.S. government, at a time when vital negotiations were taking place for arms and economic assistance. The resurgence of border violence and heightened tension in the Near East core made it even more imperative to retain Washington's friendship. That advocacy was staunchly supported—at first—by Ambassador Eban and Teddy Kollek, then director-general of the prime minister's office.

Among the high policy decision-makers, Sharett was favorably disposed but hesitant. To Hacohen's urging that he be authorized to conclude diplomatic relations, he reportedly said: "I am prepared to go along but I am not prepared to rush and, certainly, not to gallop."[8]

At the time both prime minister and foreign minister, Sharett was acutely conscious of the "American factor." Thus he sought the reaction of Israel's Washington embassy throughout and, at the outset, the U.S. government's attitude as well.[9]

Dire forebodings from Washington had a profound continuing effect upon Sharett's thinking and behavior. Soon after the Chinese demarche in December 1953, he had decided to recommend to his cabinet colleagues that the government actively pursue diplomatic relations with Peking. "You can certainly say that we are at the brink of this decision," said Sharett to a Foreign Ministry aide. The official was called to Sharett's home on Saturday evening, February 27, 1954: the recommendation was to be considered at the government meeting the next day. "I cannot swear on it under oath; but my recollection is that it was an incoming cable from Shiloah in Washington marked 'Top Top Secret.' It arrived Saturday night, just before the cabinet meeting where the proposal was to be discussed. "This item must be deleted from the agenda," said the prime minister/foreign minister pointing to "Diplomatic Relations with China." The "something" was the pressure from Israel's embassy in the United States.[10] Eban, too, confirmed that Sharett's decision not to seek cabinet approval at that stage to proceed towards diplomatic relations was taken on the basis of his advice.[11]

To the most senior Foreign Ministry official at the time, the role of Israel's United States embassy was decisive. Eytan, who was involved at every stage of the process, vividly recalled the cables from Washington and their impact upon the China decisions: "Sharett and I wanted to instruct the proposed delegation [to China] to negotiate diplomatic relations, I pressed extremely strongly, and Sharett was one hundred percent in support. Then came the powerful, repeated and persistent opposition from Eban. He pressed his opposition ferociously. His argument was that diplomatic relations with Peking would cause incalculable harm to Israel's relations with the United States. Sharett was not persuaded; he had not changed his opinion. However, his Cabinet colleagues decided against him. [And he added] We [Sharett and I] felt the time was ripe. Here was a golden opportunity.[12]

Eban remarked that Sharett's method of soliciting American reaction indicated uncertainty about the right course of action. "We should either have taken a decision to establish relations and then explained our action to Washington or not raised it at all with the State Department; to do it as Sharett suggested could only lead to a negative reply." And he was convinced, in 1954 as in 1965, that, "had we proceeded we could have explained it to Washington and avoided adverse effects."[13]

Peking does not seem to have been aware of the complex Israeli decision-making process in January-February 1954—which, in any event, was concealed by Hacohen's indication of Israel's wish to send a trade mission to China. Four months later, on June 29, Hacohen met Chou En-lai who was passing through Rangoon en route to Geneva for the conference on Indo-China. The Chinese prime minister "said he hoped I would pay a visit [to Peking] and that, following his return home, he would find time to deal with the visit of the Israeli delegation. He hoped to meet me there.[14] The formal invitation came in mid-September.

One week later Israel inadvertently took a sharp turn to the Right in its public posture towards China: on September 21, Eban voted in favor of the United States moratorium resolution, that is, not to consider the question of China's representation at the current (ninth) Session of the General Assembly. The reason for the abrupt change was simply the "American factor." "Eban was instructed not to oppose; but he took it upon himself to vote against Peking," asserted the head of the Asian Department at the time.[15]

The Chinese were piqued but seemed determined not to be swerved from their path. Two days after the UN vote Chou En-lai informed the first session of the first National People's Congress during a major foreign policy address: "Contacts are being made for establishing normal relations between China and Afghanistan, as well as between China and Israel."[16]

Peking's invitation to send a mission to China to discuss "all issues affecting 'two friendly states'" and Chou En-lai's statement about "normal relations'' posed a fresh challenge and created an opportunity for Israel's decision makers. The upshot was a compromise government decision—on November 14—on the appointment of a middle-ranking Trade Delegation without broad negotiating authority but with diplomats in the group to sound out Peking's "real" intentions.

The formal outcome was a five-point protocol signed on February 18, 1955, at the end of the delegation's four-week tour of China: (1) both sides desired trade relations on the basis of equality and mutual benefit; (2) both sides presented the foreign trade problems of their countries, studied the lists of commodities available for foreign trade, and examined other questions relating to commerce; (3) both sides agreed that mutual talks and exchange of information had laid the foundation for the development of closer commercial ties between the two countries; (4) both sides agreed to present reports to their governments on the atmosphere prevailing during the Peking talks, and to continue, through existing channels and others to be formed in the future, to develop commercial ties between the two countries; (5) on behalf of the government of Israel, the Israeli delegation expressed the hope that the government of the People's Republic of China would send a trade delegation to visit Israel as the official guests of the Israeli government.[17]

The Chinese parried that request to commit themselves to send a reciprocal mission to Israel. However, during informal talks they did not conceal their interest in diplomatic relations. Hacohen and Lewin sought and were granted meetings, respectively, with the deputy foreign minister and the head of the Asian Department in the Chinese Foreign Office. Both left without any doubt that Chinese officials desired to establish relations—and believed the presence of Israel's delegation symbolized its interest in normal ties as well.[18]

Sharett's attitude during that crucial phase was typical. He refused to be stampeded. Furthermore, he invoked the sacred principle of mutuality. On March 28, 1955 Lewin informed Hacohen of Sharett's decision: "The foreign minister, before bringing the matter of diplomatic relations to a decision, emphasizes that the Chinese delegation which was invited by us must first come to Israel." This was to be the test of China's real interest— "only if, and only after, it takes place" would Israel decide upon the issue of diplomatic relations. Hacohen was appalled by Sharett's decision on reciprocity as a precondition to any further Israeli action. The game was lost, for the decision on an immediate Israeli initiative for diplomatic relations remained negative until it was too late. The acceptance of Peking's overtures, when it did come, was belated and grudging.

As reports filtered in about the probability of Arab success in securing an anti-Israel resolution at the Bandung Conference, which began on April 17, Sharett sought Lewin's advice on how this could be offset. Lewin again emphasized the cardinal importance of diplomatic relations with China for Israel's relations with the Third World. Sharett continued to procrastinate. Hacohen reported to Lewin on April 22 that Chou En-lai had identified China with the pro-Arab resolution at Bandung. At that point—and only in the context of Bandung defeat—Sharett finally authorized Lewin to inform Kang that the government of Israel "desires to establish full diplomatic relations with the Government of the People's Republic of China at the earliest convenient moment." The letter was dated April 29. The reply was polite but noncommittal: on May 21, 1955 Kang wrote that he had already reported the proposal to his government.[19] There was no further word from Peking.

Sharett's act was belated. By then the Sino-Arab link had been forged at Bandung: there, Chou En-lai had invited all Arab states to send missions to Peking. They were soon to comply. Caution had triumphed—and Israeli diplomacy had blundered.

Post-Bandung Developments

Contacts between Israeli and Chinese officials—as well as unofficial links—on the issue of diplomatic relations have taken place spasmodically since Sharett's crucial decision and attempted reversal in the spring of 1955.

On May 23, 1955 China's ambassador to Burma explained—in a friendly and apologetic spirit—Chou's behavior at Bandung. In Hacohen's words, he said that "China wanted true friendship and relations of mutual respect with Israel. Relations between China and Israel had not been harmed in any way. Chou En-lai wanted to avoid saying anything on the Arab-Israeli problem but the prevailing sentiment at Bandung was in favor of issuing a joint declaration on all issues on the agenda."[20]

In July 1955 Israel's ambassador to Moscow, Avidar, visited Peking. The Chinese deputy foreign minister told him that the then-existing situation was unfavorable for diplomatic relations but he hoped that mutual interest and friendship between the two countries would continue to develop. He avoided reacting to a hinted inquiry about the invited Chinese delegation to Israel.

Between July and October 1955 Mordekhai Gazit, Israel's chargé d'affaires ad interim in Rangoon spoke with China's ambassador to Burma several times. At his first meeting, in July, he transmitted Lewin's reminder to his opposite number in Peking, who had not written after his acknowledgement of Lewin's early letters—on May 21, 1955 he had asked whether China was prepared to enter diplomatic relations. The reply was: "The People's Republic of China wishes to have relations with all countries which follow a policy of peace." Gazit persisted: "Does that include Israel?" The ambassador repeated, "The People's Republic of China wishes . . . ." This was reported to Jerusalem without any formal recommendation as to what Israel should do next.

Gazit saw the ambassador again in August and, once more, in October 1955. He inquired afresh if Peking was ready for diplomatic ties. The reply was evasive—that China's leadership was preoccupied with an impending session of the National People's Congress and could not take a decision at that time. He also reiterated, "The People's Republic of China . . . ."

Gazit surmised then and later that Israel could have "shot its way into Peking" even at that date; that is, it could have taken the initiative, interpreting the formula, "all countries which follow a policy of peace," as including Israel—he noted that Israel was not explicitly excluded—and sent an envoy to Peking with the goal of establishing a mission. "I could have got a visa to China right then," he added, and "Israel would have succeeded in forming normal diplomatic ties." [21]

On August 26, 1956 the Chinese ambassador to Budapest said to an Israeli diplomat: "It is a pity there are no regular diplomatic relations between our two countries, but your region boasts such unrest that, firstly, you must settle your differences with the Arabs." [22]

In December 1961 Israel's ambassador to the Soviet Union, Arye Harel, made a semiprivate visit to China; nothing came of his discussions. There were other contacts. As a Foreign Office summary-memo observed: "Israeli diplomats in various capitals persevered on instructions from their government, in their attempts to cultivate relations with their Chinese colleagues, but no results of substance emerged."

A notable instance of intergovernmental contact occurred in August 1963, when Chou En-lai addressed a letter to all heads of government concerning the nuclear test ban treaty, about to be signed, and urged a total ban on nuclear weapons, as well as the destruction of existing stockpiles. The letter arrived in Israel by ordinary mail. Prime Minister Eshkol replied in a friendly tone and again conveyed Israel's interest in relations. He also pledged "unreserved readiness to go along with every effort at disarmament in respect whether of atomic or of conventional weapons"; he hoped that disputes between states, among them the dispute in the region where Israel belonged would be solved by peaceful means and parleying. The letter was personally transmitted by a senior Israeli official to the Chinese Embassy in Stockholm. The Chinese ambassador listened politely to his suggestion for resumption of contacts. Peking did not respond. [23]

Israeli inquiries about trade were all rebuffed. In one case a private request for a Chinese visa received the following response: "When you can show us your Egyptian, Syrian or Iraqi visa, you can come back for your Chinese one." [24] Yet in March 1971 Israeli Transport Minister Peres noted that Israeli ships were carrying oranges between China and the Soviet Union. [25]

In July 1971 rumors of a telephone link between Israel and China via London were denied by Peking officially, with the reaffirmation of a "firm and unshakeable stand" against any contact with "Israeli Zionists."

Towards the end of July 1971 it was divulged that Mapam's representative in Paris, Eli Ben-Gal, had held conversations with members of China's embassy in Paris during the preceding three years. The Chinese desired the contact, he said, but. . . . The Israeli and Chinese governments denied the story, but Ben-Gal insisted on its accuracy.[26]

There were also several press reports at the same time about alleged Chinese interest in diplomatic relations with Israel, communicated by Romania's deputy foreign minister to Prime Minister Meir, during his first visit to Israel. On July 27 a Foreign Ministry spokesman in Jerusalem declared that China had not been a subject of the Meir-Macovesco talks. China, too, denied the alleged contacts concerning diplomatic relations with Israel. According to the *People's Daily*, "rumor-mongering can deceive nobody" about "the fabrication that contacts were under way" between Israel and China: "the efforts of these rumor-mongers are futile."[27]

In September 1971 the Beirut newspaper *Al Shaab* wrote that Chinese and Israeli representatives were meeting in Berne; further, that they had agreed Israel would support Peking in the approaching UN vote in return for Chinese pressure on the Arabs.[28]

On October 28, 1971 China's prime minister, Chou En-lai, declared that Peking was not planning to establish normal relations with Israel. Yet his remarks were not conspicuously hostile: "Among the countries which voted for the Albanian Resolution, of course, there were some countries which cannot have official governmental relations with China although their peoples are friendly with the Chinese people. One example is Israel. This does not mean that we cannot become friendly with the Jewish people. Israel started an aggressive war in the Middle East [1967] and has not yet resolved this problem. As a result Israel voted for China but it cannot establish diplomatic relations with China. This is a major problem but there must be no ambiguity in outlining one's position and drawing the line."[29]

This question arose following Israel's voting behavior on the issue of China's representation at the United Nations. There were four resolutions: (1) to postpone all voting from October 25 to 26, 1971 (53 for, 56 against, 19 abstentions)—Israel abstained; (2) to vote first on a United States proposal to require a two-thirds majority to expel the (Nationalist) Republic of China (61 for, 53 against, 15 abstentions)—Israel was for; (3) to require a two-thirds vote to expel the Nationalist regime, i.e., the first substantive resolution (55 for, 59 against, 15 abstentions)—Israel was for; and (4) to expel nationalist China and to seat communist China (76 for, 35 against, 17 abstentions)—Israel was for.

Foreign Minister Eban's cable of congratulations to his opposite number in Peking on October 29 was returned by China's postal authorities with the remark: "We have no relations with your office; therefore we do not deliver it."[30]

NOTES

Reprinted in abbreviated form and with additions, from this author's *Israel, the Korean War and China* (Jerusalem: Jerusalem Academic Press, 1974).

1. Interviews in Israel, 1966 and 1971.

2. To the Jewish Agency executive, March 18, 1947 (Jerusalem: Zionist Archives, File S25 1621).

3. For an analysis of Sharett's personality see Michael Brecher, *The Foreign Policy System of Israel* (New Haven: Yale University Press, 1972), pp. 247-49, 253-57.

4. A private communication to this author.

5. M. Namir, *Shlihut BeMoskva* (mission in Moscow) (Tel Aviv: Am Oved, 1971), pp. 147-49. Levavi related the June 1950 approach to him by China's chargé in Moscow five years before that episode was published (Levavi interview, 1966).

6. All other (13) noncommunist states which recognized China during the first wave (1949-50) established diplomatic relations with Peking, though some European countries did not do so until 1954-55, when Israeli diplomacy recorded another, more significant, missed opportunity.

7. For details see David Hacohen, *Yoman Burma* (Burma diary) (Tel Aviv: Am Oved, 1963), pp. 34, 61-62, 63, 91—diary entries of December 26, 1953, January 18-19 and February 17, 1954.

8. Hacohen interview, 1966.

9. For an illuminating exchange of cables between Sharett and Shiloah see Michael Brecher, *Israel, the Korean War and China* (Jerusalem: Academic Press, 1974), pp. 59-67.

10. Private communication to this author.

11. Eban interview, 1965. Others concurred.

12. Interview, 1971.

13. Eban Interview, 1965.

14. Hacohen, *Yoman Burma*, pp. 244-45, entry June 30, 1954.

15. Lewin interview, 1965.

16. English text, as reported by the New China News Agency, Peking, September 23, 1954.

17. The text is in Hacohen, *Yoman Burma*, p. 416, entry February 19, 1955. The mission to China is discussed in ibid., pp. 378-420.

18. Interview, 1971 and 1966 respectively.

19. Foreign Ministry source.

20. Hacohen, *Yoman Burma*, pp. 479-80, entry May 23, 1955. For further disclosures by Hacohen, almost twenty years later, of details of his discussions with Sharett in an effort to achieve diplomatic relations with Peking, see his memoirs, *Et L'Saper (Time to Tell)* (Tel Aviv: Am Oved, 1974), pp. 253-62. He also quotes an extract from a letter to him by Kissinger, then assistant to the president for national security: "Your efforts to persuade the Government of Israel to establish diplomatic relations with People's China and your comprehensive analysis is even more impres-

sive, considering the fact that during the fifties the awareness of China was insignificant'' (p. 262).

21. Gazit interview, 1966.

22. Foreign Ministry source.

23. *Ma'ariv* (Tel Aviv), July 12, 1964.

24. Private communication to this author.

25. Speech to the Haifa Chamber of Commerce, reported by Agence France Press, March 25, 1971.

26. This episode was widely reported in the Israeli press, at first in *Ma'ariv* (July 26, 1971), then in *Jerusalem Post, Ha'aretz* and *Al Ha-mishmar* on July 27, ff., as well as in *Kol Yisrael* on July 27.

27. *Statesman* (New Delhi), August 14, 1971.

28. *Jerusalem Post*, September 17, 1971.

29. Interview in Tokyo with Asahi Shinbun journalist, in *Asahi Evening News* (Tokyo), November 6, 1971; also reported in *Shiddurei Yisrael* radio news the same day.

30. Foreign Ministry source.

18

Shimeon Amir

CHALLENGE AND RESPONSE: ISRAEL'S DEVELOPMENT COOPERATION—1974-75

DEVELOPMENT ASSISTANCE COMMITTEE REPORT —THE CHALLENGE

The Development Assistance Committee of the Organization for Economic Cooperation and Development (OECD)[1] presents a dismal picture of present and future prospects of developing countries. In the wake of traumatic changes in the world economy—ubiquitous inflation, spasms in the monetary system, and above all, a fourfold increase in the price of oil,—countries of the developing world face truly tragic alternatives, ranging, at best, from substantial declines in growth to complete standstill and, at worst, to regression involving malnutrition and mass hunger. Especially affected are countries with a per capita income of one hundred dollars or less which depend on oil as their main source of energy, with oil imports often constituting some 25 percent of total imports. Globally, the increased price of oil in developing countries—some $9 billion—is the equivalent of the sum total of official development assistance extended by the Western world.[2]

The report leaves no doubt that, if present trends continue, the world is heading for a catastrophe which will first and foremost affect the already poorest, most suffering and most underprivileged members of humanity— some 500 million of them are already suffering from hunger and severe malnutrition now.

The report contains an optimistic note: technological and economic means to avert this disastrous course are available; what is required is the will to use them to achieve results. Above all, quantity and quality of development assistance must be substantially increased. Although couched in prudent terms, the report leaves no doubt that the onus for increased provision of

234

resources rests equally on the developed and the oil producing countries. The latter "owe" developing countries one-tenth—or $9 billion—of their additional 1974 income from oil.

Of particular interest to Israel are those comments and recommendations of the report which are relevant to Israel's own efforts and policies in development cooperation. The report indicates the rising component of technical cooperation[3] (28 percent, bilateral and multilateral) within total official development assistance. In 1973, bilateral technical cooperation constituted 24 percent of total official assistance—of OECD dimensions—as compared to 22 percent in 1970, and only 17 percent in 1965. Israel's main efforts in international cooperation have been in the field of technical assistance, and Israel has continually stressed the need of diverting increased means to the training and development of human resources.

As to the sectorial distribution of resources, the report takes a critical view of past performance of both donors and recipients, because of their relative neglect of agriculture and rural society.[4] Past policy of focusing on industry caused an accelerated mass rural exodus and rapid and disorderly urbanization, growth of slums and the creation of vast areas of human misery, a decline in the potential for food production, and an overall deterioration of conditions in rural areas. Therefore the report recommends an increase in efforts aimed at rural development, with two-fold benefits: (1) slowing down the rural exodus; and (2) increasing food production. In this respect, the report strikes an unexpectedly optimistic note:[5]

> If the leaders of the developing countries accept this objective, they will need to make a maximum effort to mobilize domestic resources in the form of increased savings and allocation of trained manpower. Rather, what is called for are bold programmes for accelerating administrative and institutional reforms necessary to bring about rural development involving the education, co-operation and participation of all sections of the population. Plans should be strengthened for agricultural research, rural education, expanded credit facilities and delivery of agricultural prerequisites.
>
> Of course the developing countries will want to call for—and they will need—assistance in the preparation and financing of these stepped-up programmes for broad agricultural development.
>
> Oil producer and DAC countries should work co-operatively in responding to needs of developing countries for major new investments in agriculture and rural development. New programmes as they are formulated by the developing countries to increase food production and reduce mass hunger should receive the most sympathetic consideration in allocation of additional development assistance on concessional terms.

ISRAEL'S RESPONSE

Ever since its beginning in the early 1950s, Israel's development cooperation has concentrated primarily on agriculture and rural society, and this
approach remained in evidence in 1974. Trends and policies of Israel's
development cooperation were conditioned in 1974—perhaps more so than
before—by political constraints. In the past, efforts had been made to
eliminate as much as possible political considerations from the decision-
making process in determining the geography of Israel's development cooperation. Projects were initiated, examined, negotiated and agreed upon—as
far possible—in terms of their merits, availability of means and the reciprocal will to mount the requisite efforts for successful implementation. Often
Israel was ready to participate in projects in spite of an adverse political
attitude of a given country. The only demarcation line between participation
and cessation of a cooperation project was the continued maintenance of
diplomatic relations: "Cessation of diplomatic relations led to cessation of
projects of technical cooperation."[6]

The process started in Africa in 1972, when Israel's relations with Uganda
were abruptly, terminated by President Idi Amin following his visit to Libya.
Already before the start of the Yom Kippur War (October 1973), some eight
countries in Africa had yielded to Arab pressure and severed relations with
Israel. After the war, Arab pressure increased tremendously—invoking
threats of economic boycott and embargo, insurgence, even threats to the
personal safety of leaders—coupled with promises of substantial aid which
in most cases have remained largely unfulfilled to date.

During the war, or shortly afterwards, most African countries severed
diplomatic relations with Israel. At the same time, most of them manifested a
lively interest in the continued, uninterrupted maintenance of trade relations,
including the services of Israeli technicians, engineers and contractors. The
leaders of several countries expressed a desire for the continuation of
ongoing projects of technical cooperation with Israel. After prolonged
deliberations, Israel decided to adhere to its traditional policy, and in most
cases, barring only very few exceptions, decided to discontinue bilateral
programs with countries which had broken relations with Israel.

This decison was not always easy, for it often meant putting a stop, for the
time being, to participation in cooperation projects of importance and
national impact. Those responsible for projects in the countries affected
often—if privately—expressed deep regret because of the political developments and acknowledged the existence of broad popular opposition to the
severance of relations with Israel. The consequences of ruptured diplomatic
relations inevitably gathered momentum as time went on, and when, at a
later stage, some mutual interest was evinced in renewed official develop-

ment cooperation, it had already become difficult to overcome the negative impact of severed relations, both in diplomacy and in official development cooperation.

In retrospect, it might be said that the government of Israel had no choice but to withdraw its experts once African countries broke off relations, both because of its established policy, and also because of public opinion in Israel prevalent during and following the war. As yesterday's friends yielded one by one to Arab pressure, it did not seem conceivable to the Israeli public that Israel's bilateral development cooperation could continue unchanged.

No limitation was placed on multilateral activities: Israeli experts recruited by international organizations continued to operate in African countries, where they were welcome, while Africans continued to arrive in Israel throughout 1974 to participate in courses and individual studies under the auspices of international organizations, as well as under commercial and private auspices.

The geographic breakdown of cooperation projects in 1974 (according to provisional figures of the International Cooperation Division) reflects, as expected, a marked decrease of Israeli operations in Africa. For the first time since Israel's international cooperation Israel assumed substantial porportions, Africa as a continent did not rank first in the number of long-term missions abroad. Tables 1, 2 and 3 show a breakdown of the total number of exports on long and short-term missions and trainees in 1974 as compared with 1973. (For trainees, Africa had ceased occupying first place even before 1974.)

There are a number of reasons for preponderance of cooperation projects with Latin America. This continent has a long-standing tradition of friendly ties with Israel, dating back to the prestatehood era, when Pro-Palestine Committees were centers for rallying political support for a Jewish state in Palestine; a fact which is hard to realize in 1975, when the word *Palestine* has degenerated and acquired a connotation of enmity to the Jewish people and their state.

The political background apart, there remains the fact that many of Israel's concepts in comprehensive development, in rural integrated planning and in many related institutions, found fervent acceptance and following in Latin America and were enthusiastically studied. As early as 1962 Israel initiated institutional ties with the Organization of American States (OAS),[7] and later also with the Inter-American Development Bank (IDB). This made possible the establishment of joint, long-term projects, linking technical capital assistance projects and concentrating on major development issues of high national priority.

Practically all development projects in Latin America, as well as most training programs for its nationals in Israel, are related to agriculture and

TABLE 1 Israeli Short-Term Experts on Long-Term International Cooperation Missions: 1974 and 1973

	Number		Percentages	
	1974	1973	1974	1973
Africa	49	138	25	50
Asia, Oceana and				
Mediterranean Area	551	47	26	17
Latin America	97	90	49	33
Total	197	275	100	100

TABLE 2 Israeli Experts on Short-Term International Cooperation Missions: 1974 and 1973

	Number		Percentages	
	1974	1973	1974	1973
Africa	24	150	9	36
Asia and Eastern				
Mediterranean	71	68	26	16
Latin America	176	199	65	48
Total	271	417	100	100

TABLE 3 Trainees in International Cooperation Projects by Israel: 1974 and 1973

Courses	Number in Israel		No. in Local	
	1974	1973	1974	1973
Africa	88	340	88	520
Asia and Eastern				
Mediterranean	424	426	330	233
Latin America	385	434	716	696
Total	897	1,200	1,134	1,449

rural society. The large number of short-term missions of Israeli experts to Latin America referred to above indicates the relative sophistication of the projects and the need to lend long-term "generalist" experts the support of highly qualified specialists, usually connected with a particular research institute. Whereas in the early years Israeli experts mainly served on single-purpose production campaigns, emphasis has shifted to postharvesting problems (such as storage and marketing) or rural institutions and their problems (such as supervised credit, formation of rural centers, training institutions), and research projects of an urgent character such as those involving irrigation, pest control or introduction of new, high-yield varieties of seed.

In 1974, the total number of multipurpose projects or single-purpose activities including local courses, in twenty-three countries of Latin America, came to about seventy-six. The figures refer only to official, government-sponsored activities. In their majority, they formed part of long-term projects, often in cooperation with some international agency, in addition to the particular government concerned. Mentioning some of the projects will suggest their general characteristics and trends.

In Brazil a group of experts continued their advisory services in the Northeast, mainly in rural planning, formation of an institute for the research of arid zones, and training experts in comprehensive rural planning. In Mexico, within the framework of an agreement with CONACYT (National Council for Science and Technology), a major interdisciplinary seminar on water utilization was held, with the participation of ten experts from Israel. An agreement was reached with the United Nations Development Program (UNDP) to establish research institutes for arid zones in Argentina, Chile and Peru.[8] Preparations were made for an integral development project in Guatemala, financed by IDB. The project will combine settlement, production and marketing.

Noting the success of the Bas-Boen project in Haiti, the Haitian government requested the introduction of similar methods in other parts of the country, where it plans to establish cores of development. This request was presented during the visit of Haiti's minister of foreign affairs to Israel in the spring of 1974. Courses for Latin Americans offered in Israel in 1974 included one on Budgeting for Development and Urban Financing. A group of Christian students of theology participated in a study tour to observe rural development. A workship on nonmetric data analysis in education was also held in Israel at the express request of the OAS, because of Israel's unique expertise in this sophisticated new methodology.[9] Plans for courses in 1975 and 1976 include Social Medicine in Rural Areas in conjunction with the Pan-American Health Organization; and Agrometeorology, in conjunction with the World Meteorological Organization.

Israel's development cooperation was also extended through other channels. TAHAL (Water Planning for Israel), an independent corporation operating in several Latin American countries, continued serving as a contractor for the IDB, executive agent for UNDP on a major comparative study of irrigation projects in five Latin American countries. The Israeli government decided to join the IDB as a nonarea member, hoping that such a step would enhance the competitiveness of Israeli firms in tendering the sale of their products and services. Similar motives underlay the decision to appoint a resident representative in Venezuela, taken by the Institute for Planning and Development (IPD), a joint venture of the Association of Architects and Engineers and of the government, which aims at promoting the sale of planning and consulting services abroad. Israel in 1974 continued to maintain cooperation projects in South Asia and Southeast Asia, as well as in the Pacific.

Growing interest in Israeli experience was evinced in 1974 by the Economic and Social Commission for Asia and the Pacific (ESCAP), previously known as Economic Commission for Asia and the Far East (ECAFE). The tremendous challenges of growing population, chronic lack of food, malnutrition, and increasing awareness of the fact that large-scale engineering works in themselves are no substitute for continuous efforts to modernize the rural milieu at the level of the individual farmer—all these led to several projects of cooperation with Israel. A study tour on Comprehensive Regional Planning and Development held in Rehovot in April and May 1974, enabled its particpants to observe Israel's approach to comprehensive regional planning at the substate or district level. Its purpose was to bring about a more equitable distribution of resources, both human and physical, among different strata of population, and to reduce or eliminate income gaps between urban and rural populations, as well as between industry and agriculture. Israeli experts participated in professional meetings of the commission, and negotiations were held to introduce regular courses on Israeli methods in relevant ESCAP institutions.

Another field of interest was a Water Resources Management course, held in Bangkok in 1973 and discussed at the Thirtieth ECAFE session (March-April 1974) in Colombo, Sri Lanka. The Bangkok course was organized by ECAFE, with the financial and technical support of The Netherlands and of Israel. The purpose of the seminar was to study methods and techniques likely to lead to the solution of problems encountered in the planning and operational phases of water resources management. The crucial importance of the role of water resources in the area was stressed by the executive secretary of ECAFE, who in his statement welcoming the participants, mentioned the staggering figure of $3 billion which would have to be invested in water resource development before the end of the decade, if its economic targets were to be met.[10]

The seminar followed an earlier related event, a comprehensive study tour on water resources which had been held in Israel. Its participants had a chance to observe Israel's thorough interest in various aspects of hydrology prompted by the limited quantum of this vital resource and the very nearly total of the country's available water supply, in addition to observing the physical and economic management existing resources. Participants also became acquainted with projects for flood-water interception, sewage reclamation, desalination and new water-saving methods such as drip irrigation.

At the request of ECAFE, an Israeli company carried out in 1974 a major study on the possibilities for growing fish in ponds in Thailand, Vietnam and Laos. The request was based on the assumption that while these countries possess considerable facilities for maritime and river fishing, commercial breeding of fish in ponds could be of great importance in many regions, where it could considerably increase the protein component of the local diet. Israel has had much experience—some of it pioneering—with pond-based pisciculture.

In its cooperation with the Mekong Committee, Israel expanded a number of its projects, mainly in the field of rural development and training. Thus, in the Nam-Pong area of Thailand, the combined center for training and rural services and inputs constitutes an important factor for modernizing adjoining villages. A plan has been presented for a new settlement region—Huay-Luang—which might become a model for the settlement of extensive regions, offering new homes and farms for farmers forced to leave areas affected by the vast engineering works of the Mekong project.

A seminar on the Transfer of Technology in a Developing Country took place in Israel in the Spring of 1974. It was successful because its subject was not only analyzed and discussed in the classroom, but also observed in the field, in the presence of people involved in the process. The participants from ECAFE countries and from Israel undertook visits, discussions and studies in selected subjects in four sectors: agriculture, land development, industry and science. They studied the vertical development of industries and services, from the initial stages of acquisition (or the local development of technology), through the different stages of trial and error, up to advanced grades of production for domestic use and export. In addition to learning about such subjects as flower growing, the seminar participants also studied Israel's approach to services (e.g. tourism) and such highly sophisticated topics as science-based industries.

Individual Israelis were also active in international institutions and specialized agencies in Asia. One Israeli expert was engaged in Rajasthan (India), on behalf of the IBRD, where he introduced new methods to increase cultivated areas and to raise agricultural yields through improved extension services. So promising were the results, that a request was subsequently made for the introduction of similar methods to other parts of India.

In Africa, an Israeli company has been engaged for years in several countries, introducing the use of heavy machinery for deforestation and agricultural development, and its work continued also after the October war. In 1974, in one of the countries in which the company concerned works, a plan for a modern settlement of—initially—one-thousand families was prepared, providing for expansion at a later stage. Characteristically, the plan incorporated model economic and social features and envisaged improvements in both agricultural and human conditions, in a manner typical of Israel's approach in such matters.

What are the prospects and projects for Israel's development cooperation in 1975 and 1976? At the end of 1974, some thirty senior experts of various UN bodies gathered in Israel to discuss the optimal use of water resources in a conference presided over by Israel's Water Commission. Simultaneously, a course on utilization of ground water was inaugurated at the Hebrew University, and another at the Volcani Agriculture Research Institute in Beit Dagon, for irrigation engineers from Iran. An international symposium on the use of brackish water for agriculture took place in Beersheva, organized by the National Council for Research and Development at the Ben-Gurion University of the Negev.

This coincidence of various events of study and training illustrates Israel's involvement in, preoccupation with, and expertise on, problems of water. This sphere seems destined to remain for many years to come a field of continued demand for Israel's cooperation and expertise. Other fields include: agriculture; rural society; cooperatives, trade unions and other institutions of the Histadrut (Workers' Federation of Israel); marketing extension services; and special programs for youth and for the involvement of women in national development. All of these elements are involved in Israel's integrated approach to development. Consequently, Israel's own development is likely to continue to be of great interest to others.

Some thirty scientific professional institutes serve as contractors for the implementation of special cooperation projects at home and abroad; among them are some ten institutes created (and functioning) exclusively for that purpose. They have gathered considerable experience, which they are seeking to adapt to changing needs. One of them—the Settlement Study Centre in Rehovot—is to become a department of Haifa University. Similarly, the Mount Carmel Centre for Community Development will be recognized in 1975 by Haifa University so that its future graduates will receive a university degree.

One major shift might well prove to be necessary in Israel's future cooperation plans. The sharp distinction between "developed" and "developing" countries which was already questionable in the past, is today becoming obsolete. For example Israel discovered that it was lagging behind in important fields of national endeavor such as the productivity of its labor force. Social tensions and income gaps are much more intensive today than Israelis had expected them to be some years ago. A growing number of visitors and students who arrive in Israel from "developing" countries reflect the very high levels of their own national educational institutions. In view of these facts, it would be desirable to change the orientation and designation of the various training institutes, and instead of seeing in them institutes for cooperation with developing countries, to regard them rather as development institutes in a certain field for participants from all over the world.

The future of Israel's development cooperation will continue to depend on political developments, both in the region and in the world as a whole. Politicization of development issues is regrettable and painful but is a fact nonetheless. Most African countries severed relations with Israel in 1973, although the Yom Kippur War affected them no more than did the Six-Day War of 1967. Sri Lanka broke off relations with Israel in 1970, three years before the 1973 war, the main development casualty being a promising project in Uda Walawe, conducted by the Settlement Study Centre in Rehovot and assisted by members of the OECD Development Centre. A major Asian country recently transposed its political animosity towards Israel even to such a minor area as a sports field. What the world needs today more than ever is to mobilize its resources and efforts for development. To the extent that reason will be allowed to prevail and development strategy—such as that outlined in the DAC report mentioned at the beginning of this chapter—will be universally accepted, Israel may continue to play a modest but not insignificant role in those fields where its own expertise and the needs of many other countries converge.

NOTES

1. 1974 Review, Report by Maurice Williams, Chairman of the Development Assistance Committee, Development Cooperation—Efforts and Policies of the Members of the DAC (Paris: OECD, 1974).

2. Ibid., p. 18.

3. Ibid., p. 119.

4. Ibid., p. 23.

5. Ibid., p. 32.

6. Shimeon Amir, *Israel's Development Cooperation* (New York: Praeger, 1974), p. 74.

7. Walter J. Sedwitz, "Technical Cooperation and the OAS," *KIDMA*, no. 5 (1974): 21.

8. See *KIDMA*, no. 5 (1975): 45, for details.

9. See *KIDMA*, no. 5 (1974): 45-46.

10. Report of the Seminar on Water Resources Management (ECAFE, Thirteenth Session, E/CN. 11/L.381, October 11, 1973).

IV

THIRD WORLD ATTITUDES

19

Ran Kochan

ISRAEL IN THIRD WORLD FORUMS

No other state of the size and population of Israel has established so wide a network of diplomatic legations throughout the globe.[1] There is at present no other state whose creation has aroused such a degree of protracted international controversy and whose existence, both as a state and a society, is still frequently disputed and threatened. The two phenomena are interlinked. In order to acquire diplomatic support and international legitimacy, Israel strove from the outset to link itself, diplomatically and otherwise, with as many countries and to as many international forums as possible. The Arabs' extension of their war against Israel into all spheres of international activity, necessitated, from Israel's point of view, retaliatatory action, not only along its borders, but also in foreign capitals and international gatherings. One of the guiding principles of Israel's foreign policy became known as the "presence policy." This meant, according to one Israeli diplomat, that "wherever an Arab flag fluttered in the breeze, an Israeli presence had to be established."[2]

This applied also—or perhaps particularly—to the various gatherings of the Third World. In no other segment of its international diplomatic activity was Israel confronted with such expressed collective reluctance either to admit it into the ranks of Third World states or, alternatively, to treat the Mid-East problem impartially. Although Israel managed to establish a wide network of bilateral links with many African, Asian and Latin American states in regard to its inclusion in, or treatment at multilateral meetings of Third World countries, Israel was considered somewhat of an 'untouchable.' The aim of this paper is to illustrate the range of difficulties that faced Israel when approaching these forums. Subsequently it will survey the approaches of some Third World forums to the Middle East problem in general, and to Israel in particular. The various geopolitical changes which have occurred in the Middle East—particularly since 1967—and their impact upon statements and expressions of collective Third World gatherings will also be analyzed and conclusions will be drawn.

This account is a short study of limited options in international politics, as exemplified by Israel's increasingly unsuccessful attempts to combat Arab efforts in multilateral Third World Forums. One of the most noticeable features of Israel's relations with Third World countries has been the discrepancy existing between attitudes and expressions at multilateral gatherings and those manifest in bilateral ties. Although leading to a great deal of displeasure, Israel preferred to ignore the former in favor of cultivating the latter. This discrepancy was somewhat reduced when most African states decided to sever diplomatic ties with Israel during 1972-73. It still exists in regard to those states which maintain friendly diplomatic ties with Israel on the one hand, and lend their vote to extreme anti-Israel resolutions adopted at multilateral meetings on the other. As in the past, Israel's ability to alter this course of events seems highly doubtful.

EARLY ILLUSIONS AND FIRST SETBACKS

It is pertinent to recall a conference, often overlooked, which took place in New Delhi in March 1947. This conference, known as the Asian Relations Conference (ARC) was the first Afro-Asian gathering and was attended by national leaders from twenty-eight countries (not all as yet independent). It was the first official opportunity for Jewish leaders from Palestine to meet their Asian colleagues, most of whom were also on the threshold of independence.

Initially, invitations to attend the conference were sent to the Hebrew University of Jerusalem, but, after consulting the Vaad Leumi (the General Council of the Jewish Community in Palestine), the president of the University cabled New Delhi that a university delegation could not represent the Jewish community as a whole. He therefore suggested that invitations be sent directly to the recognized representative of the Yishuv (Jewish Community in Palestine). On December 16, 1946, the Vaad Leumi received a formal invitation to attend the ARC.[3] A similar invitation was sent to the Arab countries and also to the Arab community in Palestine. With the exception of Egypt, no Arab representatives accepted the invitation. This mass absence was generally interpreted as a demonstration of sympathy with, and support for, the Indian Muslim League which had outspokenly boycotted the conference.

Inasmuch as the Jewish delegation was concerned, the meeting had a great impact, probably far greater than it deserved. The very invitation was interpreted as the first official recognition of the status of the Jewish nation in Palestine as a legitimate member of the Asian family of nations.[4] The naiveté and rashness of this conclusion became apparent one year later, for in January 1949, the second ARC was held in New Delhi to discuss Dutch policies in Indonesia ("'Police Actions,'' July-December, 1948). Israel, the newest of all states in Asia, was not invited. The Arab countries which had boycotted the first ARC were fully represented. The powerful threat of boycott was employed against Israel for the first time in New Delhi. As will be seen later, it was not the last time such a threat was voiced.

ENTRY UNDER THE BANNER OF SOCIALISM

The first, and perhaps the only successful attempt to associate the State of Israel with a Third World forum came in 1953 when Mapai, Israel's ruling party, was invited to attend the first Asian Socialist Conference to be held in Burma (Rangoon, January 1953). The conference, the first of its kind in Asian history, was well attended by delegates from socialist parties in Japan (Right and Left), Indonesia, Malaya, Burma, Pakistan, India, Lebanon, Egypt, and Israel. Two more Middle East countries, Iraq and Syria were invited but did not attend. In spite of the objections of some delegates, Israel's invitation was finally secured, mostly due to Burmese efforts.[5] From the outset it became blatantly clear that, apart from Burma (the host country), Israel was the only other Asian state that sent a delegation representing both a party and a government and thus could be instrumental in implementing conference resolutions.

The friendly atmosphere of the conference was somewhat disrupted when the Egyptian delegate refused to sit at the same table as the Israeli delegate and finally left the room. He was followed by the Lebanese delegate. This meant that the only remaining delegation from the Middle East was the Israeli one. It also meant that no resolution on the Arab-Israeli conflict could be endorsed without its prior consent. This was well demonstrated during the Second Asian Socialist Conference (ASC), held in Bombay (November 1956) under the shadow of war in the Middle East (Suez crisis, 1956). Again, as in 1952, there were no Arab delegations at this gathering. Kamal Djumblatt, the Lebanese socialist leader, was expected but did not arrive, and the one Arabic-speaking delegate was an Algerian who came from Indonesia where the National Liberation Front (NLF) had a center.

The final resolution expressed the conference's strong disapproval of the "encroachment and occupation by Israeli troops of Egyptian territory" and appealed ".. to the Israeli government to withdraw its troops within its borders."[6] Earlier efforts to introduce a strongly-worded condemnation against Israel were rejected and the clause expressing sympathy for Egypt was deleted under pressure from Israel's Mapai delegation. A later attempt to pass a resolution which would state that Israel's membership in the ASC was a bar to Arab socialist parties joining the organization was dismissed, as it implied Israel's expulsion from the ASC.[7]

The moderation of the resolution was in sharp contrast to the mood of most Asian governments which looked upon the Anglo-French-Israeli collusion with utter dismay and mistrust. The fact that no Arab delegates were present at the conference left the field open for Israelis to present their point of view. The fact that Israel, a member of the inner circle of the Asian socialist movement, was involved in the crisis stimulated the other members to seek a formula which would not antagonize the former too much. S. Rose, in his book *Socialism in South-East Asia*, claims that the whole matter "was particularly delicate because the ASC had come to lean quite heavily on the Israeli party. There seemed no way of avoiding condemnation of Israel's action, yet most of the delegations had no desire to drive the Israeli party out of the ASC."[8]

In spite of Israel's keen, but not always persistent, interest in keeping the Asian socialist movement alive, it gradually diminished in importance and finally, towards the end of the fifties, lost significance and relevance. Throughout its existence, it was mainly comprised of socialist parties which were in opposition in their respective countries, and as such had little—if any—influence upon governments in power. The statement by Moshe Sharett, Israel's foreign minister, at the first ASC in Rangoon (January 1952) that "we rejoice at having been admitted into the fraternity of Asian peoples assembled here under the banner of socialism" had little echo beyond the confines of the uninfluential socialist organization.[9] It has helped strengthen the bonds between Israel and Burma on the bilateral level; but it had no effect whatsoever on the Afro-Asian multilateral governmental level. This was most vividly demonstrated at the Bandung Conference of April 1955.

BANDUNG: THE GATE IS DOWN

The first Third World governmental forum to express a collective opinion on the Middle East was the Colombo meeting (Ceylon, April 1954). This forum, which was attended by five Asian prime ministers, paved the way, and in some respects was a rehearsal for Bandung.[10] Almost from the outset the Pakistani prime minister forced the meeting to discuss an issue which was not originally included on the conference's agenda. He proposed a resolution stating that the creation of Israel was a violation of the rights of the Arab people. He took the opportunity to condemn Israel's aggressive designs towards the Arabs, demonstrated by its refusal to allow Arab refugees to return to their homes within the territory that "it now held."[11] The Indian prime minister, Nehru, whose country recognized Israel in 1950, and U Nu, the Burmese premier whose country established close relations with Israel, made it obvious that they would not support the resolution. In the face of such opposition, the Pakistani premier agreed to omit the first paragraph of his draft, and said instead that he would be satisfied if the meeting merely condemned Israeli aggression in Palestine and expressed sympathy for the victims of this aggression, namely the refugees. This modified resolution was still unacceptable to both Nehru and U Nu. They pointed out that blame for aggression could not be attributed to just one party and that "according to new reports," aggression was committed by both sides. It was also argued that condemnation could only impede the United Nation's efforts to bring about a settlement. The final communiqué of that meeting was very different from the original Pakistani proposal. It merely expressed the prime minister's concern for the sufferings of Arab refugees in Palestine and called for their rehabilitation in their original homes. It contained no direct condemnation of Israel, nor did it specifically refer to it by name.[12]

When the five prime ministers met again in Bogor (Indonesia, December 1954) to work out an agenda and to determine the list of countries to be invited for the proposed all Afro-Asian conference, the Middle East question was raised again. From the outset of this meeting it became evident that the question of Israel's invitation would raise difficulties. First dissensions on what was to become a crucial issue on the Bogor meeting's agenda came from the Arab League Council at its meeting in Cairo on December 11, 1954. One of the recommendations of that meeting advised that all efforts should be directed toward getting Arab affairs put on the proposed conference's agenda. The Palestine problem headed this list. The Arab Council also requested its secretary-general to submit a note to the five premiers meeting at Bogor. A paragraph from the text of the note reads: "It is known that this conference will be a regional one. It has been the policy of the Arab states not to participate in any regional conference where *Israel is represented*. The Arab states do not have any doubt that Israel will not be invited to this conference and will not participate therein."[13]

The League's letter left no room for compromise. It stated in brief and precise terms that the meeting in Bogor—as indeed any future meetings of Third World countries—would be faced with a clear-cut choice: to include either Israel or the Arab states. As it was, Israel was excluded from Bandung. This fact may have violated the sponsors' principle, which required the universality of issuing invitations to every independent state within the Asian and African continents, yet it was clear to the organizers that if Israel were invited, all Arab countries would boycott the assembly. It was decided to abandon the principle rather than the conference. Nehru explained his attitude to his four colleagues in a letter which he sent a few days before the opening of the Bogor talks: "In the final analysis, I think it is better not to include Israel, if that is likely to lead to the Arab countries keeping away."[14] U Nu's last-minute efforts to secure Israel an invitation, which went as far as hinting that if it was not asked, Burma might not attend the conference, also failed when he found himself fighting a lost cause.[15] The conference summed up its decision in a final communiqué stating that all countries were to be invited "with minor variations and modifications." The "minor modifications" included North and South Korea, Formosa and Israel.

Official response in Israel to the Bogor decision was summed up by Foreign Minister Sharett: "The government of Israel regards this resolution as totally lacking in validity from any standpoint of international morality and principles of equality and cooperation between peace-loving nations, especially those who recently achieved their independence. We are determined to persist in the struggle for the recognition of Israel's status and rightful place at the conference."[16] Despite Sharett's determination to "struggle for Israel's rightful place," there was little hope. Israel had to wait and weather the storm yet to come.

The much-hailed Bandung conference, the first mass gathering of independent African and Asian states, met in Indonesia in April 1955.[17] From the outset it appeared inevitable that the Nehru-U Nu formula reached after Bogor, to the effect that issues which were the subject of specific controversy between two or more countries would be excluded from Bandung's agenda, had no chance to survive. The Arabs were determined to raise the Palestine question and President Nasser, on his way to the conference, made it clear that Palestine and North Africa were his main concerns at Bandung.[18] Both Nasser and Arab delegates from other Middle East countries devoted almost their entire speeches to attacks on Israel and Zionism. This massive verbal onslaught was designed to set the scene for adopting resolutions reflecting the Arab point of view. Premier U Nu's objections to the style and tone of the debate on the grounds that it was not "chivalrous to discuss the question when Israel was not present" fell on deaf ears.[19] The Palestine issue had snowballed and gained such momentum that no single voice, not even Nehru's, could stop it. Yet in spite of Arab solicitation, a Pakistani draft-resolution condemning the very creation of the State of Israel failed to gain sufficient support and was dropped. Instead, a somewhat milder draft calling upon conference members to declare their "support for the rights of the Arab peoples of Palestine" and calling for "the implementation of UN resolutions on Palestine" became a basis for all further discussion at Bandung. This formula was finally endorsed only after U Nu's clause calling for the "peaceful implementation of UN resolutions" was inserted into the resolution.[20] It took the Political Committee three solid days to agree on the insertion of the above clause. The Arabs, supported by the Chinese delegate and by other Muslim states in Asia, were determined to ignore Nehru's advice that "whether you are enemies or not or whether you have fought a war, there must be negotiations ... there is always some kind of settlement . . . you cannot end any controversy without some kind of talks or negotiations.''[21] It was only after realizing that the voting procedure required a unanimous agreement that the Arabs agreed on a compromise resolution. Had the conference adopted the procedure of a majority vote, the Arabs and their supporters could have moved any resolution they wished.

Nevertheless, Arab delegates at the conference were pleased with the outcome. Bandung was a new platform for exposing their views and unlike the United Nations at that period, also potentially a more favorable one. Halek Hassuna, acting secretary-general of the Arab League, summed it up: "All Arab delegates to the conference were unanimously agreed that the conference had been a success . . . Israel was forced into a situation compelling her to accept the U.N. resolution and to concede the rights of Palestine Arabs after her aggressive and imperialistic relations had been exposed to the world."[22] More realistically, Nasser made the following comment: "It is just a resolution. However, it has some moral value."[23]

In Israel, unofficial opinion regarded the conference as a serious political defeat. The overall impression was that Israel had been isolated from an important segment of the international community. One paper commenting on the conference said, "It remains a melancholy fact that the troublesome Palestine question has been allowed to contaminate one more international pot of ointment."[24] Official comment was more reserved. In view of Israel's exclusion at Bogor and the Arab mass presence at Bandung, the final outcome was regarded more with relief than disappointment. It was also realized that as long as the Arab-Israeli conflict remained unresolved, Israel would be forced to stay outside the newly formed groups of Afro-Asian states. This prediction has fully materialized.

The first precedent for Palestinian participation at a Third World gathering was established at Bandung. The Grand Mufti of Jerusalem arrived uninvited and unexpected, insisting on taking part in the Political Committee's proceedings. At first this was refused on the grounds that he did not represent any country. When the Yemenite delegation offered to include him as a delegate of that country, he was allowed to deliver his speech. This opportunity was fully exploited to describe "Israel's territorial designs" which were aimed, according to the Mufti, at annexing all Arab lands from the Nile to the Euphrates, including northern Hajaz as well as the Holy City of Medina. The Grand Mufti then appealed to Afro-Asian leaders to stop these territorial crimes which were particularly perpetuated in Palestine.[25]

It is worthwhile to mention another Third World gathering which met in April 1955, shortly before the opening of the Bandung conference. This was the first meeting of the Afro-Asian People's Solidarity Movement (AAPSM), a communist-inspired-and-sponsored organization which was chiefly designed to ease Soviet and Chinese efforts to gain a foothold in the new developing countries. Originally, two left-wing Israeli parties, Mapam and Achdut Ha-Avoda, were invited to attend the Preparatory Committee which was held in New Delhi in February 1955. But as in Bogor, the Arab delegates agreed to participate in the conference only if Israel was excluded. Accordingly, the Israeli parties were informed not to send any delegates to the conference. In return, the Arabs sent delegates from left-wing parties in Lebanon, Syria, Jordan, Egypt and the Sudan. In Israel's absence, the Arab group was able to pass a strongly-worded anti-Israel resolution condemning "the aggressive policy of the ruling circles of Israel" and sympathizing with "the plight of the Arab refugees" and their right to return to Palestine.[26]

Since the AAPSM's proceedings were overwhelmed by the Bandung conference held in the same month, it failed to leave a substantial mark in its original form. The movement acquired new momentum in 1957 when its headquarters were moved to Cairo, where it enjoyed the official grace and financial support of the Egyptian government. The reason for Egypt's support for this unofficial organization is explained by G. Jansen in his book, *Afro-Asia and Non-Alignment*: "On balance, Egypt and the Arabs generally, have drawn political benefits from the movement [AAPSM-RK]. It helped to strengthen the Arab link with Africa and it has, on its own popular level, isolated Israel from Afro-Asia. There has never been any question of Israel's becoming a member or being invited to any conference; quite the other way, innumerable resolutions from a variety of solidarity meetings and demonstrations have supported the Arab case on Palestine and denounced Israel."[27]

THE NONALIGNED AND THE MIDDLE EAST CONFLICT

Six years elapsed between Bandung and the next grand meeting of a Third World forum. When a group of twenty-five heads of state met in Belgrade in September 1961, they convened under a new banner and, on the whole, represented a more selective choice of states. No longer based merely on territorial criteria (Afro-Asia) but rather on a common ideological base, the new nonaligned movement appeared on the international stage with an ambitious goal, namely, to reduce tensions existing between the two superpowers. This highly inspired ambition could barely disguise the simple fact that for many participating states, this new forum offered yet another convenient opportunity to promote their individual interests. This was particularly true in regard to the Arab states whose main concerns revolved around the Middle East conflict rather than on a new world order.[28]

The fact that President Nasser of Egypt was one of the convenors of the conference was sufficient indication that Israel would be excluded. It also meant the inclusion of the Middle East conflict on the agenda, despite India's suggestion that local and bilateral conflicts be eliminated from the conference's agenda. It was Egypt, on behalf of the other Arab participants, which proposed a draft-resolution strongly condemning the creation of the State of Israel. This may not have been in line with the general aim of the conference of "contributing more effectively to world peace and security and peaceful cooperation among peoples," but then the Arabs had their own concerns.[29]

It was again U Nu, the Burmese prime minister, who rose against the motion and threatened to "publicly dissociate himself from the conference should such a resolution be passed." He added, "I came here because I believe my presence will help to lessen international tension, but not to increase the tension in the Middle East." Because Burma's stand was supported by some other states, the original draft-resolution failed to attract any wide support. Instead, a milder Burmese-Yugoslav draft was proposed and eventually passed.[30]

In comparison with the tone and length of the Middle East resolution which was adopted twelve years later in Rabat by the Fourth Summit of Nonaligned States, the Belgrade 1961 text was short, modest, and in retrospect, undemanding. It merely expressed "support for the full restoration of all the rights of the Arab people in Palestine in conformity with the Charter and resolutions of the U.N." Israel was neither mentioned by name nor indirectly condemned.[31]

By the time the Second Nonaligned Summit took place in Cairo in October 1964, U Nu was no longer in power. The absence of the Burmese prime minister was offset, from an Israeli point of view, by the membership of newly-independent African states, many of which had already had close bilateral relations with Israel. This may well account for the fact that President Nasser, the host, together with Arab delegates from other countries, were once more unable to seize the opportunity to pass a strongly worded resolution which would be to their liking. In spite of persistent efforts by the Arabs, the conference eventually adopted a largely watered-down version which, on the whole, resembled the mild Belgrade text. The only noticeable addition to the Cairo manifesto was the reference to "the inalienable right to self-determination" in regard to Palestinians, and support for "the Arab people of Palestine in their struggle for liberation from colonialism and racism."[32] It was anybody's guess who should be the objects of this struggle. Nevertheless, Nasser's arduous efforts throughout the summit to insert Israel's name into the resolution were frustrated.

After the 1964 Cairo summit, the Nonaligned movement lost a great deal of its initial impetus. While only three years separated Belgrade from Cairo, six years would elapse before the convening of the next summit in Lusaka, Zambia in September 1970. Although in 1968 President Tito of Yugoslavia proposed a summit conference to discuss the aftermath of the Arab-Israel war in June 1967, this was abandoned after the Soviet invasion of Czechoslovakia in August 1968. In July 1969, following yet another Yugoslav initiative, a consultative meeting attended by forty-six countries met in Belgrade and called for a summit meeting to be held the following year. Regarding the Middle East conflict, the meeting reaffirmed the 1964 Cairo resolution with some modifications. First, the "full restoration of the [Palestinians'] rights" directly alluded to "their usurped homeland." Second, and in response to the new status quo which emerged after the 1967 war, the meeting also called for "the withdrawal of foreign troops from all the Arab territories occupied since June 1967," in accordance with Resolution 242 of the UN Security Council on November 22, 1967, which specifically conditioned withdrawal upon ending the state of war between Israel and its Arab neighbors.[33]

The Belgrade meeting sparked off new initiatives. In April 1970 representatives of fifty-two states attended the Dar es Salaam (Tanzania) preparatory meeting which was supposed to finalize arrangements towards a summit conference. Among a host of subjects discussed, it was expected that the Middle East would also appear on the agenda. When the final resolution was released, it opened a new era in the attitude of nonaligned forums toward the Palestinian issue. Here, for the first time, the meeting pledged its readiness to grant all necessary aid to the people of Palestine in their struggle against "racialism and imperialism." Although Israel was not specifically mentioned in this part of the resolution, it was referred to in its earlier parts and the implication was clear.[34] Some states, Liberia in particular, protested against the tone of the text, but being in a minority at the drafting committee, hesitated to put their objection to a vote. As a result, the resolution passed uncontested and unprotested.

The Lusaka summit (Zambia, September 1970) which followed the preparatory meeting extended the ranks of the movement to sixty-four members (although seventy-four were invited). It also intensified the tone of its resolutions, particularly on the Middle East conflict. It stated that continued Israeli presence in the occupied territories (Sinai, the West Bank, and the Golan Heights), "the territories of three non-aligned countries, constitutes a violation of U.N. principles, a challenge to the aims on nonalignment, and a grave threat to peace." It blamed Israel for adopting a policy of "flagrant use of force," demanded immediate withdrawal from occupied territories, and pledged support for Palestinians in their struggle to regain their "usurped homeland." The conference, under the firm influence of both Muslim and radical Third World states, deplored Israel's obstruction of "efforts aimed at establishing peace" in the Middle East. It recommended to the United Nations that it "take adequate measures against Israel if it continues to disregard UN efforts."[35] This was correctly construed as a suggestion to impose sanctions upon Israel. In later years, such vague language became

rare and was abandoned in favor of unequivocal demands for sanctions.
sanctions.

Although the Lusaka conference highlighted the frustrations and limitations of nonaligned states in world politics, the period since then has been marked by much greater activity than the nine years following the first meeting in Belgrade. The Middle East issue became an often discussed item on the agenda, while the only noticeable changes were reflected in the growing harshness and severity with which Israel was treated. The Conference of Foreign Ministers of nonaligned countries which met in Georgetown, Guyana, on August 8-12, 1972, again deplored "Israel's negative obstructive attitude which has prevented the bringing about of peace based on justice." If this one-sided apportioning of blame may have sounded somewhat repetitious, the Guyana statement also revealed originality. First, it extended full support to Egypt, Jordan, and Syria "in their legitimate struggle to recover entirely and *by every means* their territorial integrity." Second, it declared its intention to intensify its initiatives "for the immediate and unconditional" withdrawal from Arab territories which stood in contradiction to the spirit and content of Resolution 242. Third, it urged all UN members to refrain "from supplying Israel with any weapons, military equipment or other material support likely to enable it to strengthen its military potential and perpetuate its occupation of Arab territories." Finally, it declared any change that Israel made in "the demographic, ethnic or political structure of the occupied areas: should be considered invalid."[36]
At a later stage, an Israeli retaliatory action against Lebanon, or the unfortunate incident of the shooting down of a Libyan airliner, both early in 1973, to name but two incidents, elicited prompt reactions by representatives of nonaligned states at the United Nations. In both cases, solidarity was expressed with "the victims of Israeli aggression"; and the international community was asked "to put an end to the permanent aggressive policy of Israel."[37]

The fourth conference of heads of state of nonaligned countries which met in Algiers on September 5-9, 1973, marked the culmination of Arab efforts up to that point in this Third World forum. The nine-point, two-page resolution "on the Middle East situation and the Palestine issue," went far beyond any text previously presented to any of the many gatherings of nonaligned states. It is worthwhile to condense this resolution with the aim of identifying its essential components, as well as to illustrate the extent to which this forum followed the Arab line:

> The Fourth Conference of . . . non-aligned countries . . . reaffirming the legitimacy of the struggle of the Palestinian people against colonialism, Zionism and racism . . . deeply concerned by Israel's

policy of aggression and expansion . . . denouncing Israel's persistent recourse, since its creation, to methods of violence and terrorism . . . demands the immediate and unconditional evacuation of all Arab territories occupied since June 1967 . . . reaffirms its total and effective support to Egypt, Syria and Jordan . . . to regain, by all means, all their occupied territories . . . calls upon the non-aligned countries to pledge their support for the people of Palestine in their struggle against Zionist, racist and colonialist settlements . . . declares its recognition of the PLO as the legitimate representative of the Palestinian people and of their just struggle . . . demands that all states forbid emigration to Palestine . . . condemns Israel's violation of human rights in the occupied Arab territories . . . welcomes the decision of certain member-countries to break off relations with Israel, and requests the other member-countries to take steps to boycott Israel diplomatically, economically, militarily and culturally, as well as in the field of sea, and air transport. [38]

The explicitly provocative tone of this text has since become routine in other Third World forums. It leaves no room for a compromise formula nor does it contain any positive inducements for a constructive dialogue between Israel and its Arab neighbors. The largest caucus of Third World states has since 1970 made no attempt to disguise its partiality and bias. The 1973 Algiers resolution reconfirmed this impression and strengthened this trend. One could hardly have been surprised when four days after the Egyptians and Syrians had jointly attacked Israel in October 1973, representatives of nonaligned states met at UN headquarters to discuss some "recent developments in the Middle East" and passed a resolution condemning "Israel's aggression against Egypt and Syria." In their rush to back the Arabs at any cost, these representatives were even willing to ignore the fact that both Egypt and Syria made no bones of their initiatives in attacking Israel first.

THE OAU AND THE MIDDLE EAST CONFLICT

Sub-Saharan Africa was envisioned by President Nasser as an obvious area of political activity and within Egypt's immediate sphere of interest (see the African circle in his *Philosophy of the Revolution*). The fact that Egypt itself was an African state facilitated its political entry into the newly independent continent. There was also an added incentive for the Egyptian drive: to frustrate Israel's remarkable progress in black Africa in the late fifties and early sixties. Beyond Egypt's grand designs in that continent stood a very concrete goal: to minimize Israel's prestige in Africa and cut off its presence altogether. Efforts in these directions were made at all levels of

Arab state interactions with sub-Saharan states. The multilateral gatherings of African states were no exception. It was there that the Arabs made their biggest advance, although it took some time before their intensive efforts bore fruit. Ultimately, Israel's presence in the continent was severely curtailed and its prestige suffered a considerable blow. While it is outside the confines of this essay to analyze the reasons which led to Israel's expulsion from Africa, it is useful to follow the gradual shift of the main African forum, the Organization of African Unity (OAU).

From the beginning, the Middle East conflict intruded into the gatherings of African states, seeking at times to disrupt the unity of the new emerging continent. The very first Conference of Independent African States (CIAS) held in Accra in April 1958 was drawn into a discussion of the Israeli-Arab dispute. An Egyptian resolution had provided that Israel, together with South Africa, Rhodesia and Portugal, be listed as a racist and imperialist power. This failed to muster enough support, for the conference refused to commit itself and merely urged "a just solution to the Palestinian problem."[40] Israel was neither specifically mentioned nor directly attacked. The fact that the host country as well as some other independent African states had already developed cordial bilateral relations with Israel, including schemes of mutual cooperation, prompted them to dissuade the conference from supporting the proposed Egyptian draft-resolution.

A second attempt to introduce the Middle East conflict to an African forum came three years later when five heads of state (King Mohammed V of Morocco, Presidents Nasser of the UAR, Kwame Nkrumah of Ghana, Sékou Touré of Guinea, and Modibo Keita of Mali) met for their Casablanca Conference. Unlike CIAS of 1958, the Arabs were successful in enlisting the conference's support for their cause. This meeting condemned Israel as "on the imperialist side in any important African issues, and as instrument of imperialism and neo-colonialism, not only in the Middle East but also in Africa." This resolution was the outcome of a quid pro quo arrangement, whereby the Arabs agreed to back the three sub-Saharan states in their support for the Lumumbist government in the Congo in return for the latter's support on the Arab-Israeli conflict.[41]

These expressions of collective support remained isolated incidents for some years, since most of the newly emerging states on that continent were reluctant to be drawn into what they regarded at that time as a non-African affair. The trend to exclude the intricate problems of the Middle East from African councils was particularly noticeable during the meeting which established the OAU in Addis Ababa in May-June, 1963. President Nasser and the rest of his Arab colleagues appeared to sense this reluctance when they agreed neither to raise the Palestinian problem, nor to seek sub-Saharan support in their war against Israel. President Nasser said at the opening session of the conference: "Even the problem which we consider to be one of our most serious problems, namely that of Israel . . . we shall not submit . . . for discussion at this meeting." [42] Although efforts were made in later years, the unofficial OAU stand remained unchanged until the Middle East War of 1967.

The June 1967 war added new dimensions to Arab efforts in Africa aimed at winning the OAU's collective support. Whereas in the period preceding the war the Middle East conflict had been mostly described in terms of the plight of Palestinians, afterwards the issue at stake revolved mainly around the territories which Israel had occupied. [43] Egypt, a founding member of the OAU, decided to make the most out of this new situation, having lost part of its territory, the Sinai peninsula. Nevertheless, the OAU was slow to condemn, and on the whole, tried to refrain from taking sides. Guinea's and Somalia's efforts shortly after the end of the Middle East hostilities, calling for an urgent meeting of the OAU to discuss the "Israeli aggression," failed to gain the required two-thirds majority and was turned down on the grounds that the matter was being dealt with by the United Nations. [44] The Arabs, slightly disheartened by the lukewarm support, resumed their efforts at the fourth OAU meeting of heads of state at Kinshasa, in September 1967. Although the issue was not officially on the agenda, Egypt succeeded in passing a last minute resolution which "reaffirmed the principle of territorial integrity" and "expressed concern at the grave situation that prevails in the UAR." The meeting expressed its sympathy for the UAR, yet again referred the whole question to the U.N. [45] This was the first time in the OAU's short history that a resolution was passed dealing specifically with the conflict.

Having established a precedent, a future course of action seemed clear. Following behind-the-scenes Arab solicitation, the Sixth Council of OAU's ministers at Addis Ababa in February 1968 agreed to condemn Israel as an aggressor and called upon it to execute an immediate and unconditional withdrawal from occupied territories. The fact that this resolution was adopted by acclamation rather than by vote, as set out by the OAU's "Rules of Procedure," was overlooked. [46] In contrast to the ministers' meeting in Addis Ababa, the heads of state gathering (Fifth Assembly, Algiers, September 1968) was less extreme in tone. An Algerian effort to enforce strong condemnation of Israel failed to gain wide support. The final resolution concerning the Middle East, although "reaffirming support for the UAR" neither mentioned Israel nor did it demand unconditional withdrawal. Instead, it called for withdrawal "in accordance with Security Council resolution 242." [47] The temporary African consensus regarding the relation between Israeli withdrawal and lasting peace was well summed up by Arsene Usher, foreign minister of the Ivory Coast: "The Algiers resolution was adopted unanimously because it was based on the Security Council resolu-

tion 242, which links total withdrawal from occupied territories with cessation of belligerence, recognition of sovereignty, territorial integrity, political independence of all states in the region, and the right to live behind secure
and recognized boundaries.''[48] Yet, as will be shown later, this line, which
at one time united both moderate and radical Africans, was finally abandoned in favor of stands which were diametrically opposed to the spirit of the
above statement.

Now that the Arab-Israeli conflict became a permanent item on OAU
agendas, the Arabs used any pretext to bring up the issue. Thus the Sixth
Assembly of Heads of State (Addis Ababa, September 1969) was asked to
condemn an Israeli retaliatory raid in Egypt (in reprisal for the latter's
declared war of attrition). The meeting condemned Israel's ''further aggression against *another part* of the national territory of the UAR,'' an African
sister state. On the wider issue of the consequences of the 1967 war, the
assembly resolved ''to use their [OAU's members] influence to ensure strict
implementation of previous OAU resolutions.''[49] Again, this was endorsed
by acclamation.

Nearly six months passed before the Middle East came up again, this time
before the fourteenth meeting of OAU's Council of Ministers (Addis Ababa,
February 1970). An Arab attempt to brand Israel as racist, quoting its ties
with South Africa (a sensitive issue in African politics) did not gain much
support and was strongly rejected by most moderate states. But Arab
delegates refused to be beaten; during a discussion on African liberation
movements, they pointed out that some Palestinian guerrillas were fighting
for the liberation of Sinai. As Sinai was part of an African state (Egypt),
these guerrillas were to be classified among African liberation movements,
and hence entitled to moral and financial support of the OAU. This new
argument also failed to persuade the delegates, for neither recognition of
those unknown ''guerrillas,'' nor denunciation of Israel were mentioned in
any of the resolutions passed.[50]

Whereas up to this point all discussions on the Middle East came under a
variety of clauses and items on the agenda, it was only at the Seventh
Assembly of OAU Heads of State (Addis Ababa, September 1970) that the
Arabs decided to try their luck and for the first time to include a specific item
under the title ''The Continuing Occupation of Part of the Territories of the
UAR by Foreign Forces.'' For some time they had been pushing the OAU
toward this discussion and now felt the time to be ripe, having a series of
resolutions on the Middle East already behind them. It was Senegal which
undertook the drafting of a resolution in order to make it acceptable to OAU
members of all camps. The resolution only expressed concern over ''the
occupation of a part of a sister-state,'' and asked that Resolution 242 be
applied in its totality and not ''conditionally or partially.''[51] Although the

Arab delegates were somewhat unhappy because of a resolution which reflected Israel's declared stand, they nevertheless supported its adoption. They decided to forego their displeasure in the knowledge that they had achieved yet another precedent by securing on the agenda a full discussion of Israel's occupation of Arab lands.

No time was wasted. In spite of looming problems within African polities (the overthrow of Milton Obote in Uganda, the Ivory Coast's proposal to hold a "dialogue" with South Africa, etc.), the Arabs insisted on the inclusion of a separate item on the agenda of the Eighth OAU Summit (Addis Ababa, June 1971) entitled "The Continued Aggression Against the UAR." The hasty procedure through which a draft-resolution was proposed aroused much criticism by conference delegates. But they were cut short by the Emperor Haile Selassie of Ethiopia who, in a volatile outpouring, begged the assembly to demonstrate its unity and solidarity, and to avoid bickering among its members which could only lead the entire OAU into disarray. This dramatic appeal finally led to the endorsement of a resolution calling upon Israel to withdraw its forces from all Arab territories "to the lines of June 5, 1967." Most significant was the fact that this resolution marked a distinct departure from previous OAU stands in regard to the conflict, for it was the first time that the collective body of African states had conceded openly that "the continued Israeli occupation constitutes a serious threat to the regional peace of Africa" and thus was the direct concern of OAU states. This was an important turning point which led eventually to a complete switch in the African states' attitude towards the conflict, and most particularly—toward Israel. It also marked the culmination of Arab efforts within the OAU to associate the Middle East conflict with African affairs.[52]

An interesting by-product of this resolution was the setting up of the Ten-Man Committee and the Four-Man Peace Mission to the Middle East. According to Arab interpretation, the mission's task was to "re-emphasize the African will to repel aggression committed against African soil." The mission was entrusted only to enlist maximum African support for the Arab point of view, particularly for their unequivocal demand that Israel withdraw from all occupied territories prior to any peace negotiations. The fact that President Senghor of Senegal, the driving force behind the African Peace Mission, assumed a wider term of reference, aiming at initiating a double dialogue between Cairo and Jerusalem, finally determined the failure of that whole ambitious venture. According to Egypt, the mission went too far beyond its original terms of reference and thus lost its relevance and usefulness. Yet it was Israel, according to President Senghor, which was blamed for its rigid attitudes and for jeopardizing the mission's peace efforts.[53]

The blatant one-sided attitude which the OAU assumed after 1971 was reflected in the resolutions adopted at both the Ninth and Tenth Summit meetings of African Heads of State. In the Ninth Summit (Rabat, June 1972), the participants took an emphatically nonconcilliatory stand by apportioning all blame for the Middle East impasse on Israel. The tone and language became even harsher at the Tenth Summit (Addis Ababa, May 1973). On this occasion the meeting deplored "the systematic obstruction by Israel of all efforts exerted to reach a peaceful solution" and declared that "the attitude of Israel might might lead OAU member-states to take, at the African level, individually or collectively, political and economic measures against it."[54] This threat almost fully materialized only a few months later, when the vast majority of African states severed diplomatic ties with Israel. It was also a forerunner of the extremely hostile resolution adopted at the nonaligned summit three weeks later (Algiers, September 1973).

Ten years of Arab perseverance at the OAU eventually paid off. The African states, in the name of continental solidarity, yielded to Arab will and strategy and voluntarily abandoned the principle of objectivity. When this process finally found expression at the bilateral level, Arab victory was virtually complete.

ISLAMIC FORUMS AND THE MIDDLE EAST CONFLICT

The Middle East conflict slowly but steadily intruded into the councils of a variety of Third World forums. These forums offered a convenient rostrum from which the Arabs could amplify their viewpoints and seek support for their struggle against Israel. These forums were not confined solely to the conflict, and on the whole, dealt with a variety of issues concerning the life and problems of the Third World. In contrast, the institutionalization of the Islamic factor through summit conferences and regular meetings of foreign ministers from Islam-dominated states was a direct response to the Arab-Israeli conflict. By initiating assemblies under the banner of a common creed, the Arabs hoped to achieve a variety of aims, most immediately to employ yet another forum in the Third World which would completely and unreservedly support their stands. The use of such gatherings to embarrass some predominantly Muslim countries both in Asia and Africa which maintained friendly relations with Israel, must also be considered in this context. A second aim was to extend the area of conflict beyond the immediate battle grounds of the Middle East into the entire Islamic subsystem, thus turning the conflict into one between Israel and the Muslim world, and not merely between the former and the Arab states. A third, and perhaps most speculative aim was to challenge Zionist organizations by a parallel Islamic organization aimed at counteracting the so-called worldwide influence of the former.

The Islamic conference in Kuala Lampur, Malaysia, in April 1969 set the

direction for future conferences based on this religious common denominator. The participants, mostly Arabs, but also non-Arab representatives from Pakistan, Afghanistan, India, Iran, Turkey, Indonesia, Malaysia,
Singapore, Thailand and the Philippines, devoted most of their time to
discussing the continued occupation of Arab lands, and particularly the
Israeli presence in and control of Islamic holy places. The fact that three
Palestine Liberation Organization (PLO) delegates took active part in deliberations can well account for the tone and content of resolutions unanimously adopted by the conference.

Although the 1969 Kuala Lampur meeting set a precedent, it lacked a
concrete and inspiring motivation for action. This deficiency quickly disap-
peared when the Al Aksa Mosque in Jerusalem was damaged (August 21,
1969) as a result of arson committed by a mentally disturbed Australian
citizen. The fact that he was neither Israeli nor Jewish was completely
ignored by those who seized the convenient—and loaded—opportunity to
call for the first Islamic Summit Conference (Rabat, September 1969). The
participants, "convinced that their common creed constitutes a powerful
factor bringing their peoples closer together" and "determined to strengthen
the fraternal and spiritual bonds existing between their peoples and to
safeguard their freedom and their heritage" found no difficulty in agreeing
on a common line of thought. They declared that "the continued threat upon
the sacred shrines of Islam is a result of the occupation of this City by the
Israeli forces" and thus "require that the Holy City should be restored to its
status, previous to June 1967." They also called upon the major powers to
intensify their efforts "to secure the speedy withdrawal of Israeli military
forces from all territories occupied as a result of the war of June 1967." No
reference was made to Resolution 242 or to the purpose it meant to achieve in
return for territories. It was only to be expected from such a convention that
its participants, "moved by the tragedy of Palestine," would affirm their
"full support to the Palestinian people for the restitution of their rights which
were usurped and in their struggle for national liberation." To ensure wide
circulation of the resolution, the meeting requested the UN Secretary General to distribute the text as an official document of the General Assembly
and of the Security Council.[55] This resolution was an indication of two clear
patterns which were to emerge in future drafts of such meetings: first,
repeated emphasis that the Arab struggle against Israel is closely associated
with the concerns and interests of the entire Muslim world; second, emphasis
upon the sacrilege which Israel is alleged to have performed by virtue of
controlling the Holy Places of Islam in Jerusalem. The second point in
particular, a highly charged issue in the Muslim world, was supposed to
provide the raison d'être for a common stand and, most desirable, a common
action.

The Rabat Summit has encouraged further activity under the Islamic half crescent. In February 1971, the Secretariat of the International Muslim Organizations (incorporating five organizations: World Muslim Congress, Pakistan; International Islamic Organization, Indonesia; Supreme Council of Islamic Affairs, Cairo; General Islamic Conference of Jerusalem, Jordan; and Moslem World League, Saudi Arabia) met in Mecca, Saudi Arabia, to discuss the "Judaization of Jerusalem." Calling upon the United Nations to halt "the continuance of the inhuman Zionist aggression in Jerusalem" and to "save the Holy City from Judaization" and its Arab citizens "from becoming refugees," this meeting also pledged its "fullest support to the commandos [PLO, RK]." In order to achieve all these aims, the meeting chose to evoke the "Islamic spirit of struggle and sacrifices" to achieve victory "as even did their forefathers." This too was distributed as an official document of the General Assembly and the Security Council.[56]

The Third Islamic Conference of Foreign Ministers (Jedda, February 1972), as its two predecessors in Jedda in March 1970 and in Karachi in December 1970, devoted most of its time to discussing the "situation in the Middle East." The conference's presupposition that the backing of "the sister Arab states striving to recover their lands and the lawful national rights of the Palestinians" were of "a responsibility and duty imposed by Moslem solidarity" set the stage for the resolutions adopted. The meeting resolved that "Member states should strive by an appropriate means to contribute to the liquidation of Israeli aggression... including political and economic retortion against Israel."[57] In their next meeting (Libya, March 1973) the foreign ministers went one stage further and called for the opening of offices in all Muslim states at which volunteers would be enlisted for a Jihad (Holy War) against Israel.[58]

By the time the second Islamic summit was held (Lehore, Pakistan, February 1974) it became apparent that the initial setup went far beyond its original confines. The Arab-Israeli conflict was still the backbone and the central theme around which Arab states wished to solidify support and initiate action, but on the whole, the summit assumed patronage over Islamic affairs throughout the world. Following discussions on the Middle East, the meeting resolved to grant full and effective support to Arab states to recover—by all possible means—their occupied territories. The Arab oil embargo which was imposed after the 1973 October war was hailed by participants as a successful method to increase pressure upon Israel and thus weaken it politically, diplomatically and militarily.[59] While politics and religion now became completely blended, the Islamic Organization had also developed an independent momentum of its own and as such added a new element of religious fanaticism into the already intricate politics of the conflict.

SUMMARY

The various forums described in this study were not the only ones to express collective attitudes vis-à-vis the Middle East conflict. There were others, some sporadic, some more permanent, which voiced their views and publicized their stands. The reason for their exclusion was mainly due to lack of space, but also to their relatively insignificant role in Third World affairs. Almost all those forums, mostly comprised of radical and left-wing movements, supported the Arab point of view while permanently denouncing that of Israel.

In regard to the focal bodies of the Third World, one should note the following: first, that the bulk of Arab effort has considerably intensified after the 1967 June war. Second, in the course of time, the tone and content of resolutions passed at these forums became vociferously more hostile and more condemning. Inasmuch as the first point is concerned, Israeli occupation of Arab lands was never condoned by any Third World country and the general consensus was that these lands must in the end be returned to their original owners. There were some disagreements about the terms of withdrawal, but on the whole—at least until the beginning of the seventies—there was widespread agreement that withdrawal would be carried out simultaneously with arrangements towards peace and in accordance with stipulations of Security Council resolution 242. Such conciliatory stands were unacceptable to the Arab states whose main aims were not only to secure withdrawal prior to any peace agreements, but also—and perhaps mainly—to isolate Israel from the international scene and force it to eventually yield to world public opinion. In order to secure these aims, the Arabs and their supporters were determined to drive Third World countries into a clear-cut choice even if this involved complete disregard for UN decisions which these states helped pass. For this purpose, the Arabs were willing to use any method of persuasion, including pressure and intimidation. The results, from their point of view, were quite rewarding: Israel was depicted as an aggressor and usurper of Arab lands and of the "legitimate rights of the Palestinian people." Israel was also forced to limit bilateral ties with many African and Asian states (this has not yet occurred with the larger community of Latin American countries). Finally, Israel found itself unwillingly clashing not only with the Arabs, but with the larger developing world.

It might be argued that the sole purpose of the above-mentioned forums was to pass resolutions, none of which could affect or alter immediate events of the Arab-Israeli conflict. This may be true in the narrowest interpretation of the issues involved. This argument is totally irrelevant if one considers the international scope of the Arab-Israeli confrontation. It disregards some recent developments, which have taken place as the outcome of efforts the Arabs invested in those forums. One should recall the resolutions passed both at the 1974 UN General Assembly and some of the UN affiliated agencies (UNESCO is perhaps the most recent and most extreme example). Admission of the PLO to the United Nations (with "observer" status) and the standing ovation given its leader, Yassir Arafat, could not have come about had the ground not been previously prepared at various Third World forums. The impact upon Israel's bilateral relations with many Third World states has already been mentioned. Decline on this front was also a function of Arab ability to mobilize various Third World forums in the service of their undisguised goals. Finally, the ever-increasing support which the Arabs gained from these forums may have boosted their confidence leading them to harden their bargaining positions vis-à-vis Israel, and indirectly influenced the Egyptian and Syrian decisions to attack Israel in October 1973.

NOTES

The author is grateful to Ophra Ben-Eliyahu for her research assistance.

1. In 1967 (prior to the June war) Israel had diplomatic delegations—mostly resident but also some nonresident—in over one hundred countries. In 1974 this number declined to seventy-one, due to the cutting off of diplomatic relations with most African states (1972-73) and with the communist bloc (1967).

2. Y. Shimoni, a senior official in the Israeli Foreign Ministry, in an interview with this author, August 1969.

3. *Ha'Aretz* (Tel Aviv), December 17, 1946.

4. See Kedem, *Eretz Israel Council for Friendly Relations with Asian Nations* (Hebrew) (Jerusalem, 1947).

5. This came following a visit to Israel by a Burmese socialist delegation, December 1952. It was the personal account of the head of the delegation of Israel's socialist movement and its achievements that finally secured Israel the invitation.

6. For a detailed account of the second ASC, see S. Rose, *Socialism in South East Asia* (London, 1959). For the text of the resolution, see p. 249.

7. *Dawn* (Karachi), November 7, 1956.

8. See Rose, *Socialism*, p. 248.

9. *India and Israel* (Bombay) 5, no. 8 (February 1052):20.

10. These were Mohammed Ali from Pakistan, J. Nehru from India, U Nu from Burma, J. Kotelawala from Ceylon, and Ali Sastroamidjojo from Indonesia.

11. The Pakistani draft also expressed anxiety over "current acts of violence committed by Israel against the Arabs." See *Dawn* (Karachi), May 1, 1954.

12. See G. Jansen, *Afro-Asia and Non-alignment* (London, 1966), esp. chap. 7, "The First Colombo Conference," pp. 143-68.

13. Halek Hassuna, *The African-Asian Conference: Bandung 1955* (Cairo: League of Arab States, 1955), pp. 21-22.

14. For Nehru's letter, see Jansen, *Afro-Asia*, p. 172.

15. David Hacohen *Burmese Diary: 1953-55* (Hebrew) (Tel Aviv, 1963), p. 356.

16. *Jerusalem Post*, March 17, 1955.

17. For a detailed account of Bandung, see George M. Kahin, *The Asian-African Conference: Bandung, Indonesia, April 1955* (New York, 1956).

18. *Egyptian Gazette* (Cairo), April 8, 1955.

19. *Jerusalem Post*, April 21, 1955.

20. For the full text of the conference's resolutions see "Final Communiqué of the

Asian-African Conference" (Djakarta, May 1955).

21. See Jansen, *Afro-Asia*, p. 200.

22. Hassuna, *African-Asian Conference*, pp. 143-44.

23. Nasser's statement was made in Calcutta on his way home from the conference. See *The Hindu* (Madras), April 28, 1955.

24. *Jerusalem Post*, April 25, 1955.

25. *Dawn* (Karachi), April 26, 1955.

26. See *The Hindu*, February 2, 1955.

27. Jansen, *Afro-Asia*, p. 263.

28. On the origins, development and ideology of the nonaligned movement, see
Jansen, *Afro-Asia*. See also Leo Mates, *Nonalignment Theory and Current Policy*
(Belgrade, 1972).

29. See the "Declaration of the Heads of State or Government of Non-aligned
Countries," in Mates, *Nonalignment Theory*, pp. 336-94.

30. See *The Nation* (Rangoon), September 15, 1961. Also, A. Ben-Asher,
"From Belgrade to Oran," *New Outlook* (Tel Aviv) 4, no. 8 (October 1961):14.

31. See "The Declaration," in Mates, *Nonalignment Theory*.

32. For the full text see *Keesing's Contemporary Archives* (London), November
28-December 5, 1964, p. 20,434. See also Mates, *Nonalignment Theory*, pp.
432-50.

33. *Keesing's Contemporary Archives, 1969-70*, p. 23663. Although not yet
enjoying formal status at the meeting, a PLO delegation attended the conference
upon the invitation of the organizers.

34. For text of resolution, see *The Preparatory Meeting of Nonaligned Countries*,
(Dar es Salaam, Tanzania).

35. See "Lusaka Declaration on Peace, Independence, Development, Cooperation and Democratization of International Relations," Nonaligned Conference,
Resolution I, Lusaka, September 8-10, 1970. It is interesting to compare the change
of attitude at the OAU (described in subsequent pages) which followed the Lusaka
summit of 1970.

36. In January 1971, President Tito again proposed a meeting of heads of state to
discuss the Middle East problem, but due to lack of general support, the idea was
abandoned. See *al-Ahram* (Cairo), February 21, 1971. For the Georgetown text, see
Conference of Foreign Ministers of Nonaligned Countries, NAC/FM/Conf. 1/Res.
3, August 16, 1972.

37. See General Assembly Resolution A/9049 (XXVII), February 26, 1973.

38. For the text see "Resolution on the Middle East Situation and the Palestine
Issue," NAC/ALG/Conf. 4/P/Res. 2, Algiers, September 9, 1973.

39. This meeting was held on October 10, 1973. See UNGA, A/9218 and UN
Sec. Coun. S/11019, October 10, 1973.

40. Jon Woronoff, *Organizing African Unity* (Metuchen, N.J.: 1970), p. 34.

46. Ibid., p. 51. In spite of this strongly worded resolution, no change of attitude
was recorded on the part of the three black African states which sought to increase
their bilateral ties with Israel. Unlike the Casablanca group in the years prior to the
establishment of the OAU, the rival "Brazzaville bloc" had made no attempt to
include the Middle East problem at either of its meetings in Monrovia (May 1961) or
Lagos (January 1962).

42. Ibid., p. 138.

43. President Habib Bourgiba of Tunisia called upon the OAU summit in Cairo
(July, 1964) to demonstrate its solidarity with the Palestinians who had lost their

territory. Yet this call evoked no positive reaction from the meeting. See *Pan Africanism* (London: British Information Service, August 1965), p. 34.

44. The meeting was proposed in a letter from the OAU secretariat which was circulated to all its members. Information from OAU sources.

45. This resolution was passed in spite of many delegates' protests to the hasty procedure in which it was adopted. See *Le Monde* (Paris), September 17, 1967.

46. Again, the Middle East item was not on the agenda, and was discussed under "miscellaneous." See *Ethiopian Herald* (Addis Ababa), March 1, 1963.

47. This formula resembled the one endorsed at the Kinshasa summit (September 1967). For text of this resolution, see AHG/Res. 53 (V), Algiers, September 1968.

48. See *Fraternité Matin* (Abidjan), September 29, 1968 (author's translation).

49. For the first text see "Resolution on the Aggression of the Israeli Forces Against UAR," AHG/Res. 56 (VI). For the second resolution, see AHG/Res. 57 (VI).

50. Information obtained from OAU sources in Addis Ababa.

51. The latter part of the resolution was inserted under the pressure of some moderate states headed by the Ivory Coast. For text of resolution, see AHG/Res. 62 (VII), Addis Ababa, September 4, 1970.

52. See "Resolution on the Continued Aggression Against UAR," AHG/Res. (VIII), Addis Ababa, June 21-23, 1971.

53. For the Egyptian interpretation, see *Al-Ahram* (Cairo), July 1, 1971. For a detailed account of the African Peace Mission to the Middle East and events which preceded that mission, see Ran Kochan, "The One-Man Initiative of President Senghor," *African Affairs* (London) 72, no. 287 (April 1973):186-96. See also Susan A. Gitelson, "The OAU Mission and the Middle East Conflict," *International Organization* 28, no. 3 (Summer 1973):413-19.

54. For the Rabat text, see *Jerusalem Post*, June 14, 1972. A Soviet reaction to the resolution suggested that it was "justly regarded as the beginning of Israel's isolation in the African continent," Tass (Moscow), June 19, 1972.

55. The non-Arab countries which attended the summit were: Afghanistan, Indonesia, Iran, Malaysia, Pakistan, Turkey, Chad, Guinea, Mali, Niger, and the Muslim community in India. States such as Cameroon, Ivory Coast, Sierra Leone, Zambia, Tanzania, Nigeria and Maldive Islands, were invited but turned down invitations. For text of the resolution, see UN Security Council, S/9460, October 2, 1969.

56. See UN Sec. Council S/10152, March 9, 1971.

57. See UN Sec. Council Gen. Assembly S/10665 and A/8686, May 26, 1972. Iraq and Southern Yemen refused to participate on the grounds that some states attending the conference also maintained friendly relations with Israel.

58. Information was still unavailable as to the implementation of this resolution or the numbers of volunteers who registered.

59. Radio Cairo, February 25, 1974.

20

Joel Barromi

LATIN AMERICAN STATES' CONDUCT AT THE UN GENERAL ASSEMBLY ON ISSUES AFFECTING ISRAEL

The foundation of the United Nations conferred on Latin American states unprecedented power and enlarged their foreign policy scope well beyond the familiar grounds of the Western Hemisphere and the European continent. Since then they have continued to be active, but have evolved changing positions on major issues such as the Middle East conflict. At the opening meeting of the first UN General Assembly, held in London on January 10, 1946, delegates of twenty Latin American republics constituted 39 percent out of a total of fifty-one member states. By the weight of their number and their common approach to global questions, they immediately became an influential caucus within the new world organization, called to take a stand on a wide range of international affairs. One year later they were confronted with the question of Palestine. In April 1947, at the request of the Mandatory Power, the United Kingdom, the first special session of the General Assembly was convened to make recommendations on the future government of Palestine. At the beginning of the deliberations, Latin American states supported the Jewish demand that the representative body of the Zionist movement, the Jewish Agency for Palestine, be authorized to participate in the debate. Uruguay, in particular, aroused the vigorous opposition of the Arab states, by arguing that the Jewish Agency should take part in the plenary meetings of the General Assembly with full rights by virtue of the

270

legal status originally granted to it by the League of Nations' mandate. Procedural discussions ended in a compromise; representatives of both the Jewish Agency and the Arab Higher Committee were invited to participate in the first committee's meetings.

The special session refrained from passing judgement on the substance of the problem of Palestine and decided instead to set up a UN Special Committee on Palestine (UNSCOP). The last stage of deliberations turned on the Special Committee's terms of reference. Latin American states showed their interest in two questions: the protection of universal religious interests, advocated principally by El Salvador and Chile; and the request that the Special Committee visit the camps of Jewish war refugees in Europe and ascertain their wishes—pleaded by Uruguay, Guatemala, and the Dominican Republic. Both points were incorporated in the terms of reference.

Among the eleven delegates appointed by the special session as members of UNSCOP, three were Latin American: Guatemala, Peru and Uruguay. Guatemala and Uruguay were active in drafting the Partition Plan—by which Palestine would be divided into a Jewish and an Arab state, with a special international regime for the city of Jerusalem—and in securing its adoption by UNSCOP. Eventually, Peru joined them in the affirmative vote. On August 31, 1947 UNSCOP transmitted the Partition Plan to the UN Secretary General together with a minority plan supported by three members which would have provided for the establishment of a federal state in Palestine, with Arab and Jewish regions. The report of UNSCOP was inscribed in the agenda of the second regular session of the General Assembly.

The first special session (and UNSCOP) can be considered for the purpose of our study, as a prologue. Most Latin American states had not yet committed themselves to any specific course of action, and their contribution had consisted mainly in prompting the General Assembly to give a fair hearing to the Jewish viewpoint. The lines of the Arab-Jewish conflict and of the great power involvement with it, took shape only in the second General Assembly. Before the votes can be analyzed, it will be useful to consider the methodology used.

METHODOLOGY: VOTING AND CONTENT ANALYSIS

Any general overview of the functioning of the United Nations as a whole must confine itself to broad outlines, thus offering little insight into the complexities and contradictions of specific situations.[1] In this respect, the studies on the conduct of regional groups at the UN General Assembly is often more rewarding. We followed the regional approach, but limited the scope of our research still further, focusing on a reduced number of UN items, connected with the Arab-Israeli conflict. This enabled us to scrutinize in depth all pertinent debates and votings and to examine in detail the different patterns of behavior and their underlying motivations. The groundwork of our analysis[2] was the compilation of a list of all significant votes cast on Israeli issues. Votes were considered significant only and whenever they fulfilled certain requirements. In particular, we included in our list only votes on proposals characterized by a clear pro- or anti-Israel connotation (and not simply votes in which Israel and the Arab states took a different stand). The hazards of a more or less arbitrary roster of "selected issues" were thus avoided.

The political value of votes was measured by the intensity scale, which takes into account the effort required to take a certain action or stand in determined circumstances.[3] The highest scores of 10 and 9 were reserved for cases of intensely pro-Israel behavior: sponsorship of pro-Israel proposals; votes cast in conditions of isolation or minority in favor of a pro-Israel proposal or against an anti-Israel one. The lowest scores of 1 and 2 were reserved for similarly intense anti-Israel behavior. Scores from 8 to 3 recorded the more common in-between positions. Markings showing the lowest intensity are 6 for abstention on a pro-Israel proposal and 5 for abstention on a pro-Israel proposal. Between them runs the 5.5 median line.

The intensity scale is an indispensable instrument for analysis of individual states. We made use of it particularly in the study of the different attitudes taken in a given country by subsequent regimes. The shortcoming of this scale is that it magnifies shifts and fluctuations to a somewhat larger-than-life size. For this reason it is unsuitable for analysis of bloc behavior. By the intensity scale a state or a small group of states taking an unpopular position can sometimes receive a higher cumulative score than those of a larger group of states, which voted closer to the median line. To avoid such distortions we introduced, for bloc analysis and for comparison of different states within a bloc, the compact scale, which views the objective fact of the vote. The compact scale is based on four positions: (1) pro-Israel vote (affirmative or negative); (2) abstention on an anti-Israel proposal; (3) abstention on a pro-Israel proposal; (4) anti-Israel vote. The scores are 8, 6, 5 and 3 respectively; the median line is located, as in the intensity scale, at 5.5.

Each country's conduct may be reduced to a single figure, the mean score, obtained through division of the sum total of scores by the number of votes. Uruguay ranks first with 7.2, Chile, Bolivia, Argentina and Cuba rate 6.0, 5.4 and 3.8, respectively.

We complemented the voting analysis by the content analysis of statements made by Latin American delegates: at the 1948 third regular session of the General Assembly, during the first Arab-Israeli war; at the 1956 first

TABLE 1 Content Analysis of Latin American Delegates' Statements at UN General Assembly

Item No	Contents	Incidence of Positive Pronouncement
1.	UN role, supranationalism, conciliation, UN mediation	370
2.	Respect for international law	117
3.	Promotion of international peace & security upholding of existing agreements	197
4.	Existence of war, danger of war, obligation to prevent it	115
5.	Justice morality	32
6.	Right of Israel to existence, independence & territorial integrity, validity of resolution 181 (II)	166
7.	Right of Israel to security, secure borders, freedom of navigation, prevention of or retaliation to Arab raids, Arab belligerence	96
8.	Negotiations, dialogue, agreed solution, negotiated peace treaties	128
9.	Jewish communities abroad, Jewish culture and history	32
10.	Relations with Israel, achievements of Israel, and its contribution to the world	17
11.	Arab belligerence, threats, use of force, aggression, intransigence, non-compliance with legal undertakings	68
12.	Palestinian rights, refugee problem, refugees' plight	97
13.	Arab states' right to security, territorial integrity, self defense	65
14.	Inadmissibility of conquest of territorial expansion, annexation, military occupation, withdrawal from occupied territory	113
15.	Arab communities abroad, Arab culture, history	26
16.	Relations with Arab states	9
17.	Israeli's use of force, aggression, threats, intransigence, noncompliance with legal undertakings and treaties, necessity of condemnation of Israel, of measures against Israel	158
18.	Protection of religious interests and holy places, internationalization of Jerusalem	151
19.	Small states' rights	49
20.	Great powers' intervention, role, duties	32
	Total	2,038

TABLE 2 Content Analysis of Twelve Latin American States*

	1948		1956		1967	
	Pro-Israeli	Anti-Israeli	Pro-Israeli	Anti-Israeli	Pro-Israeli	Anti-Israeli
Bolivia	0	3	27	44	2	5
Brazil	10	10	0	1	31	25
Colombia	23	13	16	21	52	50
Costa Rica	—	—	10	5	57	37
Cuba	3	25	0	3	—	—
Ecuador	—	—	25	40	53	84
El Salvador	2	27	0	16	—	—
Guatemala	59	1	—	—	—	—
Honduras	—	—	—	—	7	54
Peru	—	—	0	2	26	39
Venezuela	6	1	—	—	8	23
Uruguay	47	10	40	31	3	14

* Those states which took a more active part in some or all of the debates of 1948, 1956 and 1967.

special emergency session, convened after the Sinai campaign; and at the 1967 fifth special emergency session, held after the Six-Day War. The statements were classified into twenty items, listed in Table 1. The items can be grouped in four categories: (1) support of UN law and justice (items 1-5); (2) pro-Israel (items 6-11); (3) anti-Israel (items 12-18); (4) small states versus great powers (items 19-20).

Among the pro-Israel items, item 6 (Israel's right to existence, independence and territorial integrity) ranks first with a score of 166, followed by item 8 (negotiations) with 128. Among the anti-Israel items, item 17 (Israel's use of force, aggression) ranks first with 158, followed by item 18 (protection of religious interest, holy places, internationalization of Jerusalem) with 151 and by item 14 (inadmissibility of conquest) with 113. Item 18, which refers to religious concerns is different from purely pro-Israel/anti-Israel items. The attitude of most Latin American states on this issue was often influenced by other factors such as the Holy See's encyclicals and the Vatican's diplomatic activity. Yet the item is not unrelated to the Arab-Israel conflict. The Arab states had an obvious political interest to exploit Israel's vulnerability to international criticism and hostility, because of the emotional nature of the Jerusalem issue. The other states, including Latin Americans, were fully aware of the political implications and consequences of their stand. Table 2 gives the breakdown of pro- and anti-Israel positive and negative pronouncements.[4] In 1948 the pro-Israel scores rated higher, while in 1956 and 1967 the situation was reversed.[5]

In the following pages we will evaluate the conduct of Latin American states with the help of our computations. We shall do so with extreme

TABLE 3 State by State Mean Score Scale

	Period A	Period B	Total
Old Latin Americans			
1. Uruguay	7.3	7.1	7.2
2. Nicaragua	6.3	7.1	6.8
3. Costa Rica	6.2	7.1	6.7
4. Guatemala	7.2	6.2	6.6
5. Dominican Rep.	5.6	7.2	6.5
6. Paraguay	5.0	6.8	6.4
7. Panama	6.4	6.3	6.3
8. Ecuador	5.6	6.7	6.1
9. Chile	5.1	6.5	6.0
10. Haiti	5.1	6.9	5.9
11. Colombia	5.0	6.5	5.8
12. Bolivia	4.3	6.6	5.6
13. Honduras	5.3	6.0	5.6
14. Venezuela	5.6	5.5	5.5
15. Argentina	4.9	5.6	5.4
16. Brazil	4.5	6.0	5.4
17. Peru	4.5	6.1	5.4
18. Mexico	5.2	5.3	5.3
19. El Salvador	3.3	6.8	5.2
20. Cuba	4.9	3.0	3.8
Caribbeans			
1. Barbados			7.2
2. Jamaica			6.9
3. Trinidad & Tobago			6.3
4. Guyana			5.2

caution, knowing that quantitative measurements are always imperfect research tools.[6] Our conclusions will be drawn on the basis of a broad historical analysis of Latin American and Middle Eastern developments, against the background of the changing world environment.

BREAKDOWN INTO PERIODS

In the second General Assembly Latin American states were called for the first time to take a stand on the question of Palestine. They supported resolution 181 (II) of November 29, 1947, based on the recommendation of UNSCOP. They did so over the bitter opposition of Arab countries which emphatically rejected the Partition Plan and the very notion of the establishment of a Jewish state. The Latin American mean score for resolution 181 (II) was a high 6.85. Latin American mean scores remained generally high in 1948, but decreased in subsequent years. In 1956, after the Sinai campaign and the Suez war, Latin American states followed the lead of the United

States and solidly voted for Israel's unconditional withdrawal from the Sinai peninsula. Their mean score for vote 13 was 3.20.

Table 3 shows at this point a deep cleavage, followed by higher scores in later years. This split suggests the opportunity of dividing the first twenty years into periods: Period A from 1947 to 1956; and Period B from 1957 to 1968 after the Six-Day War. From the perspective of the present time we found it advisable to break down the epoch following the Six-Day War into two additional periods: Period C from 1968 to 1973, that is until the Yom Kippur War; and Period D from the Yom Kippur War to 1974. The span of time covered by Period D is brief; but the emergency of new factors (such as the oil embargo, the energy crisis, intervention by the two superpowers) justifies its definition as a separate unit.

The four periods relate to events which took place in the Middle East and which were debated and voted upon in the General Assembly. UN records on those issues provide all the data required for examining the behavior of Latin American states regarding Israel and the Arab-Jewish conflict. There is not a corresponding set of data for a parallel study of Israel's behavior in respect to Latin American problems and specific Latin American states. Few Latin American crises of international import occurred during the same period and some of them were deliberately kept out of the General Assembly agenda by entrusting their handling to the regional agency, the United States-led Organization of American States (OAS).

Between 1947 and 1974 there were no cases of direct Israeli-Latin American controversy, the only exception being the Argentine-Israeli dispute over the kidnapping in Argentine soil of the Nazi war criminal Adolph Eichmann (1960) and his subsequent trial and execution in Israel (1962). The Argentine complaint on this subject was dealt with by the Security Council in July 1960 and was never debated in the General Assembly. It can be surmised that Argentina's attitude towards issues concerning Israel was affected for a time by the Eichmann affair. This is therefore one example of feedback between Israel's actions and Latin American states' conduct. It was an exceptional case. On the whole, the aims of Israel's foreign policy towards Latin American states, at the United Nations and at the bilateral level can be considered as a constant. Israel's purpose was always to strengthen and expand its relations with Latin American countries and to obtain their support at the United Nations and in other international organizations. Yet there were changes and innovations in policies adopted by Israel to achieve this end. At a later stage, they had a considerable impact, as will be outlined below.

Period A: 1947-57

Most Latin American states supported Resolution 181((II) of November 29, 1948 which recommended the partition of Palestine into independent

Jewish and Arab states and an international regime for the city of Jerusalem. The Latin American tally was: thirteen states in favor, only one (Cuba) against and six abstentions. The Latin American mean score was 6.85, the highest among the different regional groups, well above the 5.5 median line. The November 1947 voting gave rise to the common notion of solid Latin American backing of Israel at its birth, gradually diminishing over the years. It should be recalled that the partition resolution, though upheld by the Jewish side and opposed by Arab states, could be viewed as a reasonable compromise between conflicting claims, including those arising from the religious interests of third parties.

When a year later, in 1948, Syria tabled a proposal requesting the opinion of the International Court of Justice on the validity of the Partition Resolution, the majority of Latin American states voted in favor and the mean score was a much lower 5.36. Traditional Latin American high regard for juridical principles and supranationalism had in this case the upper hand. Six months afterwards in May 1949, the Latin American group scored 7.55 on Israel's admission to the United Nations. In December 1949 the Latin American mean score fell to 4.64 in the voting on the internationalization of Jerusalem. These ups and downs point to the existence of specific attitudes held by the majority of Latin American states on specific issues. The outstanding example is the question of Jerusalem. Through the years Latin American states, with the exception of a few liberal and/or anticlerical countries, consistently favored the internationalization of the city.

The breakdown of votes by issues is an indispensable step for a correct assessment. But focusing on issues alone would overemphasise the rigidity of certain attitudes. In practice, every state keeps pragmatic balance between its different votes on issues of Israel's concern, determined by its broad political approach. In certain cases a vote adverse to Israel on the question of Jerusalem may be compensated by a more favorable vote on a different issue such as negotiations in order to achieve the required political effect.

The Latin American mean score for the whole of Period A is a rather low 5.38, below the median line, lower than the 5.80 Western bloc mean score, though higher than the 5.20 UN mean score. Content analysis figures show a pro-Israel ratio (100 to 79) in 1948 changing into an anti-Israel one (100 to 153) in 1956.

For an overall understanding of these elements it is essential to remember that the creation of Israel represented a violent disruption of existing world order, and consequently a cause of concern for conservative regimes such as those prevailing in Latin America. At the beginning of Period A, Israel was still struggling for survival, recognition and legitimacy. In the initial stage it enjoyed the diplomatic and military backing of the Soviet Union. United States support was less pronounced, while Britain, which had opposed the demand for Jewish statehood at the time of its Mandate on Palestine, remained hostile and exerted an influence in that direction on other Western European countries. Israel's image at its emergence was of a liberal-socialist new nation. Its foreign policy was based on nonidentification with the two world blocs, the Western and the Soviet. After the Korean War, Israel moved towards the United States and its relationship with the Soviet Union deteriorated, leading in 1953 to the temporary breaking off of diplomatic relations.

The Arab states at the same epoch were ruled by conservative, mainly monarchical, basically pro-Western regimes. The situation changed in Egypt with the 1952 revolution, the rise to power of Gamal Abd-el-Nasser and the 1955 Egyptian-Czech pact which inaugurated an era of close military and economic Soviet-Egyptian cooperation.

Attitudes of Latin American states toward Israel and the Arab-Israeli conflict were affected to a large extent by each country's internal situation and international orientation. Most Latin American states had joined late and sometimes reluctantly the military alliance against the Axis Powers, which at the end of World War II became the United Nations Organization. During the initial stages of UN activities Latin American members were eager to prove the sincerity of their attachment to the democratic coalition. Many of them saw fit, in this context, to help the Jewish people, the principal victim of Nazi Germany and the Jewish state, born out of the ashes of the holocaust. This was particularly true and genuine in the case of liberal and left-of-center postwar regimes, such as those of Uruguay and Guatemala, which rose to power on the wave of the defeat of Fascism and of socioeconomic changes brought about by the war. These political parties and governments, supported by the middle class and by labor unions, later became part of a broad and influential trend known as the "democratic Left." Striking examples of pro-Israeli conduct are the voting records of the Colorado government in Uruguay with a score of 8.50 and of the Arévalo government in Guatemala (1944-51) with a score of 7.75. Arévalo's successor, Jacobo Arbenz, established a radical leftist regime. Its scores on Israeli issues remained comparatively high (5.80).

Large areas of Latin America continued to be, in Period A, traditional societies, ruled by old established elites, landowners, the Church and the army. This applies to the personalist dictatorships of certain small states and to the conservative democratic regimes of larger countries such as Colombia or Brazil. In foreign policy these states were militantly anti-Soviet and anticommunist and solidly tied to the United States. Israel, as a potentially revolutionary element in the Middle East, aroused their misgivings. Their mean score in Period A is 4.87.

A special mention has to be made of populist regimes, also a by-product of the war, steeped in extreme nationalist ideologies and characterized by the charismatic contact between leader and masses. Their scores on Israeli issues tend to be low. Cuba, for instance, under the populist-nationalist-leftist regime of Grau San Martín (1944-48) rated 4.00. Perón's Argentina followed at the United Nations a fairly neutral line on the Arab-Israeli conflict (scoring 5.25) accompanied by friendly gestures to the Arab states and Israel at the bilateral level. (Argentina under Perón opened the first Latin American embassy in Israel.)

In the global environment, Period A is marked by the Cold War, the Korean War and the Indochina War. At the end of the period, the contradictions inside the Soviet camp erupted in the Hungarian revolt, while growing discord within the Western camp, especially over colonial issues, culminated in the 1956-57 Suez crisis. The United States ranged itself against Britain, France and Israel, with the nearly unanimous support of the Latin American states.

Period B: 1957-67

In period B Israel endeavored to develop substantial bilateral ties with Latin American states. In the 1960s the Israeli diplomatic network in Latin American grew to fifteen embassies and legations, while fourteen Latin American missions operated in Israel. Nine Latin American embassies were located in Jerusalem, notwithstanding the continued adherence of their countries to the principle of the internationalization of the city. Trade increased slowly, but mutual relations acquired a new dimension through the institution of Israeli technical assistance programs.

In international affairs, Israel and Latin America adopted converging orientations. Israel took a firm pro-American and pro-Western stand on major East-West issues. On colonial issues it supported Africa's emancipation and extended help to new African states, earning in return, considerable African support at the United Nations. Latin America remained pro-United States. A brief period of uncertainty in the aftermath of the 1959 Cuban Revolution, characterized by the emergence of short-lived left-wing regimes and radical political parties, was followed by reaction and stabilization, leading to the establishment of anticommunist and in many cases military regimes. The dynamic and interventionist policies of the Kennedy and Johnson administrations (Alliance for Progress—1960; the Dominican crisis—1965) reinforced United States dominance. On colonial issues Latin American states gradually moved to full support of decolonization and to close cooperation at the United Nations with the Afro-Asian group.

Israel's image in Latin America improved, due to its military exploits, economic achievements and stable democratic regime. While Israel moved in its internal structure from the Left toward the Center, many Latin American governments, including military and conservative regimes, showed a greater awareness of social and economic problems. Their approach was by now development oriented, irrespectively of their political setup and tenets. Israel's "economic miracle" and progressive social structure was studied with interest as a possible model of socioeconomic advancement, and a desirable alternative to Cuban-inspired revolution.

In Period B, the Arab states went through much violence and turmoil. Left-wing regimes were installed in Iraq (1958), Syria (1958) and Algeria (1962). In the international arena, most Arab states moved close to the Soviet orbit. The Arab image, which was vague in Period A, now acquired an unfavorable connotation. Latin American governments and large sectors of public opinion viewed with apprehension the close relationship between Castro's Cuba and the more radical Arab states as well as the ideological and organizational ties between the Castro regime and various Arab parties and movements, formally institutionalized in the 1966 Havana Tricontinental Conference.

In the global environment Period B brought the first East-West thaw and the beginning of a multipolar system in which China and Western Europe began to play independent roles. Both the Latin American and the Middle East subsystems remained basically bipolar. With the Cuban missile crisis Latin America became one of the focal points of world tension. Other major developments were the Vietnam War and the Six-Day War. In spite of difficulties, the United States retained its vigor and resilience, evidenced by its victory in the space race.

The interplay of factors is reflected in the voting picture. In Period B Latin American support reached its peak. The Latin American mean score rose to 6.15, surpassing the Western bloc mean score of 6.05. In spite of the pro-Soviet trend in the Arab world and the pro-Western stand of Israel, the Arab-Israeli conflict never became, in Latin American eyes, a straight East-West issue. On pure East-West issues like the question of Korea and of China's representation, the Latin American states continued to vote solidly with the United States, with scores of 7.97 and 8.00, much higher[7] than those on Israeli issues.

The breakdown by internal situations shows that in Period B rightist and military regimes produced higher mean voting scores on Israeli issues, rating 7.09 and 6.14. They apparently viewed Israel as instrumental in stemming hostile forces (Soviet penetration, international terrorism). Liberal regimes retained their marked pro-Israeli position with a mean score of 6.39. The few populist regimes remained cool (5.35), and the lonely communist state, Cuba, took a consistently anti-Israeli line (3.67).

An adverse development from the standpoint of Latin American attitudes toward Israel was the change in the balance of power within the UN system, due to the admission of an increasing number of new African and Asian countries. In Period A the average UN membership was 6.3. It jumped to an average of 111 in Period B. UN membership continued to grow in later years reaching 126 in 1968 and 135 in 1973.

The Latin American bloc, too, was enlarged by the addition of four Caribbean states between 1962 and 1966. Percentagewise, it decreased from 35.1 percent in 1947 to 18.2 percent in 1967. In political terms, it was further weakened by de facto recognition of Cuba. The Latin American bloc was dwarfed by the spectacular rise of the Afro-Asian bloc, which at the end of Period B reached the absolute majority of UN members. Within the Afro-Asian bloc, Arab states became a central factor due to their numerical growth (from five in 1947 to thirteen in 1967 and to eighteen in 1973) and to their influence on a larger group of Muslim Arab-oriented states like Mauritania and Somalia and, to a lesser extent, Pakistan and Malaysia. The new less influential Latin American bloc was drawn by the dynamics of the General Assembly to a working relationship with the Afro-Asian bloc and with the Arab group. Their support, in particular, became indispensable for election to UN bodies.

The last event of Period B was the Six-Day War. The fifth special emergency session saw the two superpowers facing each other in antagonistic positions. East-West confrontation overlapped the Arab-Israeli conflict. Latin American countries followed U.S. leadership and contributed to blocking the Soviet and Arab attempt aimed at achieving, through international pressure, as in 1956, Israel's compulsory withdrawal from occupied territories. The struggle centered on two proposals: one sponsored by eighteen nonaligned countries, demanding immediate and unconditional withdrawal of Israeli forces to the positions they held prior to June 5, 1967; the other, introduced by twenty Latin American states, linked Israeli withdrawal to the end of belligerence by the parties to the conflict. The last paragraph of the Latin American text reaffirmed earlier recommendations on the "desirability of establishing an international regime for the city of Jerusalem." The General Assembly found itself evenly split in two camps, with Latin American, Western and pro-Western countries ranged in favor of the Latin American proposal and against that of nonaligned countries, and the Arab states, most African states and the Soviet bloc taking the opposite position. Both resolutions obtained a plurality of votes, but were not carried for lack of the required two-third majority. Eventually the Security Council resumed consideration of the question and adopted a compromise resolution—Resolution 242 of November 22, 1967—based, like the Latin American draft resolution in the assembly, on the linking of Israel's withdrawal to other elements, such as the establishment of secure and recognized borders.

The Latin American mean score in the vote on the Latin American draft resolution and on the nonaligned countries' draft resolution was 7.80, the highest in Period B. The total mean score for the whole fifth special emergency session is lower (6.40), due to low scores in the votes on the question of Jerusalem.

A reflection of the changes in UN membership, structure and political climate was the Latin American states' unwillingness to enter into direct verbal clashes and arguments with the Arab states. At the fifth special emergency session Latin American states acted and voted against the Arab states' requests, but were extremely cautious and considerate in the choice of their language. Content analysis for this session shows that anti-Israel scores outnumbered pro-Israel scores by a ratio of 143 percent.

Table 4 indicates the difference between the Latin American voting pattern on Israeli issues and that on other sets of issues. On Israeli issues the rate of divergence is higher. Tables 5 and 6 show the voting patterns on Israeli issues of other geographical groups and of selected countries. The levels of support for Israel by Latin American states and by Western states are often similar, but never identical.

Period C: 1968-73

The Middle East temporarily receded from the center of world attention at the beginning of Period C, while developments connected with other geographical areas produced far-reaching changes in the global environment. The United States, entangled in the Vietnam War, lost part of its grip on world affairs. The American-Chinese rapprochement of 1971 restored to the United States its maneuvering capability facilitating pursuance of the détente with the Soviet Union as well as the inauguration of a new policy toward Southeast Asia.

The short-term price of abrupt abandonment of the long-held, uncompromising opposition to the People's Republic of China was a credibility crisis among the United States' most faithful followers, particularly in Latin America. A grave repercussion was the failure of the United States attempt to achieve the continuance of Nationalist China's UN membership. The US strategy was to secure, as in previous years, the adoption of a draft resolution cosponsored by the United States and by a number of Latin American states and other countries, requesting that the question of China's representation in the United Nations be decided by a two-thirds majority. While the bulk of the Latin American bloc, led by Costa Rica, cooperated with the United States, other Latin American countries proved reluctant or hostile. Some of them (Argentina and Mexico) were brought into line at a later stage; others (Chile, Ecuador, Guyana and Peru) remained impervious and voted together with Cuba against the proposal, contributing to its defeat. The tradition of nearly unanimous Latin American backing of the United States on crucial East-West issues was dramatically broken. The US setback on the Chinese

TABLE 4 Latin American Voting on Israeli, East-West and North-South Issues (Compact Scale)

	Israel Issues	East-West Issues Korea (Unifi- cation)	China (Represen- tation)	North- South Issues South Africa (Radical Policies)
Period A*	5.38	7.97	8.00	7.11
Period B*	6.12	7.77	7.68	8.00
Total	5.81	7.88	7.85	7.27

TABLE 5 Latin American, Western and Sub-Saharan African Voting on Israeli Issues

	Latin American Bloc	Western Bloc	Sub-Saharan African States
Period A	5.38	5.80	4.40
Period B	6.12	6.03	5.40
Total	5.81	6.00	5.00

TABLE 6 Five Case-Study Countries' Voting Scores

Latin American Mean Score	U.S.	Nether- lands	Belgium	Liberia	Philip- pines
5.38	7.0	6.7	4.6	5.3	5.2
6.12	6.7	7.8	7.7	6.4	5.4
5.81	6.8	7.3	6.4	5.9	5.3

question revealed that the United States was no longer able to muster a majority at the United Nations and that the General Assembly could be easily controlled by a coalition between the nonaligned countries and the Soviet bloc.

China's reentry into the world's political life gave a new impulse to global multipolarity. Other manifestations of it were Gaullist France's nationalist and generally anti-American policies and Germany's *Ostpolitik*. The apparent decline of American power was felt in Latin America and its effects were accentuated by the policy of benign neglect toward Latin American states introduced by the Nixon administration.

The feeling of political vacuum in the Western Hemisphere reinforced the ingrained Latin American tendency to seek in international bodies a source of power and a remedy for its own political and economic vulnerability. The OAS, which had been effective in the 1960s during the Cuban and Dominican crises, was the expression of US ascendency; as such it was of no avail in the new situation. Latin American states became actively involved with the so-called group of the 77, the Southern economic front set up for obtaining economic concessions and better terms of trade from Northern developed states. At the beginning of the 1970s the group counted about one hundred African, Asian and Latin American countries. Some Latin American states also joined the radical and anti-US group of the nonaligned countries, either as full members (Peru, Chile, Guyana, Trinidad and Tobago, and Jamaica) or in the capacity of observers. Important milestones of this political process were the 1971 Lima Conference of the Group of Seventy-Seven; the April 1972 Santiago UN Conference on Trade and Development (UNCTAD); and the August 1972 Georgetown (Guyana) Conference of the Nonaligned Countries. The choice of Latin American capitals as venue for these meetings was intended to show appreciation for the new international role fulfilled by Latin America. In practice, the Southern and politically anti-Western international alignments continued to be dominated by Afro-Asian countries, led by smaller groups or committees of politically active countries, within which Arab states were always prominent. One of the consequences of the Lima, Santiago and Georgetown conferences was to bring Latin American countries under growing Arab influence.

The militantly radical stand of certain Latin American states originated in changes of regimes. Such was the case of Peru, where a leftist military junta seized power in 1968. In Chile, the 1969 electoral victory of Salvador Allende's Popular Union Front brought to power a coalition of left-wing groups led by the Socialist and Communist parties. In Bolivia, successive leftist juntas maintained a precarious hold during 1969-71. Disputes with the United States on economic matters (expropriation of American oil companies in Peru and of American-owned copper mines in Chile) soon embittered relations between the new leftist regimes and Washington. Conversely, territorial and economic conflicts between the United States and Latin American states prompted these countries to assume an anti-American posture in international affairs. An example of this was the US-Panama dispute over the Canal Zone, which affected Panama's stand in the United Nations and UN-related bodies, particularly since the 1969 nationalist-leftist coup of Colonel Omar Torrijos. Similarly the US-Ecuador dispute over fishing rights and territorial waters, drew Ecuador, under the presidency of José María Velasco Ibarra (1968-72) to an anti-US position.

Other changes in the Latin American political map were: in 1972, the collapse of the parliamentary system in Uruguay—one of the remaining centers of the democratic Left—and its replacement by indirect military rule; and in 1973, the triumph of Peronism in Argentina. In foreign affairs the first moves of the Peronist regime were the reestablishment of diplomatic relations with Cuba and the participation as full member in the Conference of Heads of State of Nonaligned countries, held in Algiers in September 1973. A separate process of radicalization, particularly in the field of foreign policy, took place, in the meantime, in English-speaking and Africa-oriented Caribbean countries. Guyana, beset by racial tensions at home and by a border dispute with Venezuela, sought a way out in militant international activism and set an example for other Caribbean states. In 1973 the four Caribbean states established diplomatic relations with Cuba.

By 1973, the Latin American system presented a structure very different from that of 1968. One of its main features was the existence of a large group of Latin American states affiliated with the nonaligned countries. For the first time in Latin American history these countries were committed to full or partial allegiance to an international body, centered outside the Western Hemisphere and openly opposed to the United States. At the United Nations this situation deprived the Latin American bloc of much of its value as a political forum.

Israel entered Period C with a heightened international standing, by virtue of its stunning military victory and accelerated economic development. Its position was gradually debilitated by the continuance of intermittent warfare in the Middle East, the growing danger of full-scale war and the lack of any advance towards a political settlement.[8] Israel's negative reaction to the proposal submitted by the UN secretary general's special representative, Gunnar Jarring, in his memorandum of February 8, 1971, met with criticism, particularly on the part of Western European states. Egypt under the presidency of Anwar Sadat acquired an aura of moderation and reasonableness. Its relations with the Western world were further improved after the dismissal of Soviet military advisers in July 1971.

Israel's image, after the initial postwar upsurge, underwent gradual decline. In Latin America, Israel became the target of a sustained offensive launched by the extreme Left and often supported by the extreme Right, focusing on charges of expansionism and militarism. The Arab image benefited from the natural sympathy for the physical and moral sufferings of the losing side and from a new awareness of the Palestinian problem. The reputation of Arab states and organizations was tarnished by Arab terrorists' murder operations. Public opinion in the world at large and in Latin America strongly manifested its reprobation for crimes like the massacre of the Israeli team to the 1972 Munich Olympics. In many Latin American countries the abhorrence was reinforced by the existence of serious local problems posed by guerrilla units and terrorist groups.

At the bilateral Israeli-Latin American level, Period C is marked by enhanced Israeli activity in the fields of technical assistance. A new area of cooperation was that of scientific exchanges. Agreements on these subjects were signed with Mexico in 1972 and with Brazil in 1973. In 1972 Israel was invited to the OAS as permanent observer. The only country outside the Western Hemisphere upon which this capacity was conferred was Spain, the motherland of Ibero-America. Bilateral contacts also encompassed military cooperation, ranging from technical assistance for the establishment in several Latin American countries of army (or ex-servicemen) agricultural villages, to the sale of military equipment, offered by the burgeoning Israeli military industry.

In UN terms, the overall result of these efforts was Israel's surprising capability of rallying a considerable amount of Latin American support, notwithstanding unfavorable international conditions and changes taking place inside Latin America. At the 1971 twenty-sixth session, for instance, Latin American states achieved a mean score of 6.4 in the voting on a draft resolution introduced by Costa Rica and cosponsored by the Dominican Republic, Haiti and Uruguay, calling for the reaffirmation of the principle of a negotiated peace—a principle upheld by Israel and rejected by the Arab states. While the pro-Israel Costa Rican proposal was defeated by a wide margin, the assembly carried, with Western support, a mildly anti-Israeli resolution, criticising Israel's attitude toward the Jarring memorandum. The Latin American bloc was split in this voting and the mean score dropped to 5.25. Proposals hostile to Israel, such as those concerning the inalienable rights of the Palestinian people or the violations of human rights in occupied territories met with Latin American opposition. The mean scores on these votings were 6.64 and 6.74, the highest in Period C and similar to those recorded on analogous issues in Period B.

Period D: From October 1973 to 1974

After the Yom Kippur War new events occurred, the full impact of which cannot yet be gauged: the energy crisis, the sudden rise in Arab wealth and political influence, the rupture of diplomatic relations with Israel by African states. Cuba broke diplomatic relations with Israel shortly before the war, during the Algiers Conference of Heads of State, in September 1973. Guyana took the same step in March 1974. In the global environment the Yom Kippur War sparked a new trend towards bipolarity. The two super-powers' intervention proved decisive in stopping hostilities and in subsequent negotiations. The main feature was the resurgence of American prestige and influence.

Grave political convulsions occurred in Latin America: the violent over-throw of the Allende government in Chile in September 1973; Perón's return to the presidency of Argentina in October 1973 and his death in July 1974; the bitter strife between rightist and leftist factions inside the Peronist regime. The overall picture was of a reduced strength of the radical Left and of a broad shift to the Right.

The repercussion of world events in the United Nations was a further tilt towards the Arabs and against Israel, with Western European countries joining the anti-Israel camp on certain issues. Latin American states were affected by the general climate. The Latin American mean scores at the twenty-eighth session on inalienable Palestinian rights and on violation of human rights in occupied territories dropped to 5.05 and 5.19 respectively. Latin American states took a clear pro-Israel position when suddenly faced at the end of the session with a new particularly injurious anti-Israel proposal: an amendment to a draft resolution on apartheid equating Zionism with colonialism and apartheid. The Latin American tally was on that occasion two in favor, nine against, nine abstentions and five absent; and the Latin American mean score rose to 6.60. The difference between the figures shows a considerable fluidity in present Latin American attitudes. New factors are at work, such as fast expansion of relations between several Latin American states and oil-producing Arab states; the attempt on the part of some of the largest Latin American states (Argentina and Brazil) to attract large-scale Arab investment and financial support; efforts made by Arab states and organizations to transform the large Arab diaspora in Latin America into a political force; the capability of Jewish communities—which up to now did not play a significant role in the field of Latin American states' foreign policy—to counteract this pressure. Future conduct of Latin American states toward Israel and Israeli issues at the United Nations will be shaped by interaction of existing and developing forces at the global, Latin American and bilateral levels.

NOTES

1. The best comprehensive study of the UN General Assembly is still the now classic work of Hayward R. Alker, Jr. and Bruce M. Russet, *World Politics in the General Assembly*, (New Haven: Yale Univ. Press, 1965), based on a skillfull use of factor analysis. For limitations of factor analysis technique see "Factor Analysis: A Cautionary Note," in *Approaches to Measurement in International Relations: A Non Evangelical Survey*, ed. John E. Mueller (New York, 1969), App. B, pp. 309-11.

2. This analysis has been summarized in Joel Barromi and Carlos Feldman, "Latin American Voting on Israeli Issues at the U.N. General Assembly: 1947-1968," *Jewish Social Studies* (April-July 1974). The study is part of a research project on Israeli-Latin American relations carried out at the Hebrew University (Jerusalem) by Edy Kaufman, Yoram Shapiro and Joel Barromi.

3. For a similar methodological approach see John F. Clark, Michael K. O'Leary and Eugene R. Wittkopf, "National Attitudes Associated with Dimension of Support for the United Nations" *International Organization* 25 (1971):4.

4. Positive pronouncements are passages which refer to or support a given concept: for example Israel's right to existence. Negative pronouncements deny the validity of that concept. The pro-Israel total of 522, given in Table 2, includes 15 negative pronouncements, that is negation of anti-Israel concepts. The anti-Israel total of 655 includes 36 negative pronouncements, that is negation of pro-Israel concepts.

5. The pro-Israel ratio of 1948 corresponds to a pro-Israel voting score (see votes 2-7 in Chart 1); the anti-Israel ratio of 1956 corresponds to an anti-Israel voting score (see vote 13 in Chart 1). In 1967 Latin American states took in the voting a clear pro-Israel stand, which apparently contradicts the anti-Israel pronouncement ratio. The explanation lays in the new political climate of the General Assembly, due to changes in UN membership and other developments. In the prevailing circumstances a pro-Israel vote was unpopular and required greater effort than in previous times. Most Latin American states preferred to avoid further unpopularity that would arise from pro-Israel or anti-Arab pronouncements.

6. For problems of content analysis see R.L. Friedheim and J.B. Kadane, "Quantitative Content Analysis of the United Nations Seabed Debate," *International Organization* 24 (1970):486-89.

7. For comparative purposes pro-Western votes were computed as producing high scores and pro-Eastern votes as producing low scores.

8. Content analysis of Latin American statements show a high score for the item on war and danger of war.

21

Ran Kochan, Susan Aurelia Gitelson

and Ephraim Dubek

BLACK AFRICAN VOTING BEHAVIOR IN THE UNITED NATIONS ON THE MIDDLE EAST CONFLICT: 1967-1972

Regional conflicts, such as the one between Israel and the Arabs in the Middle East, often have international ramifications since they tend to attract the concern of major powers. How do small states, which are members of other subordinate state systems, relate to such conflicts, particularly when these involve vital security issues for members within the conflict area?[1] One way to analyze such a situation would be to consider bilateral relations between each of the conflicting members within one subsystem and individual members within another region.[2] Such an approach cannot offer a comprehensive picture of the combined attitudes of all members in one subsystem toward the protagonists in another. This shortcoming may be partially overcome by examining a different level of interaction, where bloc cohesion or intrasystemic differences can be distinguished and measured. One possible focus for such an analysis is the United Nations, where international conflicts are often discussed and where participating adversaries continually vie to gain support for their respective positions.

The purpose of this research is to analyze the voting behavior at the United Nations of members of one subordinate state system in relation to a conflict within a different subsystem. Several preliminary conditions had to be met prior to such a study. First, the conflict had to last long enough to check possible changes over time in the attitudes of regional members. Second, issues stemming from the conflict had to be on the UN agenda at fairly regular intervals. Third, the proposed subsystem had to sustain its interest in the conflict within the other subsystem.

These conditions were all present when the Middle East was taken as the conflict area and sub-Saharan Africa as the reference subsystem.[3] Black Africa appeared to be a relevant choice by virtue of its territorial proximity. The African group at the United Nations, through comprising one-third of total UN membership, could be largely influential in securing a majority on any issue placed on the agenda. A third reason for this choice was that black Africa's main involvement in the Middle East has been through its activities at the United Nations.[4] Since it has lacked resources to offer military and financial aid to the Middle East protagonists, its ability to exert any influence outside the United Nations has so far been limited.

This study will try to discern sub-Saharan African voting behavior at the United Nations on the Middle East conflict. The time span for the research extends from the Six-Day War of June 1967 through the Yom Kippur War of October 1973. This period is distinguished by the effect of Israel's acquisition of Arab territory in 1967, which introduced into the United Nations a multitude of issues and problems totally different from those it had previously considered.[5] This study is based on draft resolutions debated and voted upon in the UN General Assembly (UNGA) from the Fifth Emergency Meeting beginning in July 1967 to the twenty-seventh UNGA Meeting of December 1972.[6] Votes which took place either at committees or other UN agencies were excluded. Their inclusion would have led to duplication, since most crucial subjects were debated simultaneously at various UN forums. In the period under discussion, the UNGA usually became the central organ in which main multilateral diplomatic confrontation on the Middle East conflict took place.

This research will look upon the voting behavior of thirty-three sub-Saharan black African states.[7] The response of the latter to issues brought before the UNGA will be tested by scrutinizing thirty-four draft resolutions counted during the suggested period. These resolutions included fifty-four separate articles upon which General Assembly members were asked to vote. Fifteen of these roll call votes shared a purely humanitarian focus and received a universal voting consensus of UN members, including both Israel and Egypt.[8] Since these votes had no conflicting aspects, they were excluded from the discussion. The other thirty-nine roll call votes included all other areas under debate in which the two chief adversaries in the Middle East conflict were opposed to each other and voted dissimilarly (hereafter "conflict issues").

This research hopes to integrate quantitative and substantive evidence by testing three different dimensions. First, votes will be analyzed on the basis of their operational significance to indicate the main voting trends among black African states on the Middle East issue during 1967-72. Second, the contents of the thirty-nine conflict-issue draft resolutions will be scrutinized to isolate specific components which increased subsystemic consensus or, conversely, affected regional diffusion. Third, the above findings will be tested against explanatory factors with the aim of verifying some of the findings arrived at while discussing the above two dimensions. These factors hopefully will highlight some trends at the subsystemic level which were either latent or else were the outcome of dynamic changes in the contemporary political map of Africa and which had a direct, although not always immediate, impact upon black African voting behavior at the United Nations.

VOTING CONSISTENCY

In order to explore the extent of cohesion within the African group at the United Nations, it was decided first to measure the voting consistency of each single African state. The two aims of this effort were: (1) establish a numerical record of how sub-Saharan African states (SAS) voted on conflict issues; and (2) determine the meaning of these votes in terms of their operational significance. This refers to whether a vote was considered by either Israel or Egypt to be favorable or unfavorable to its respective expectations at the United Nations.[9] The operational significance of the votes is important since it goes beyond the simplified reference to whether a state is in favor or against stands taken by either one or the other adversary. Thus the thirty-nine voting rolls were relisted according to the following criteria:

X vote: when the SAS voted similarly to Egypt and opposed Israel's designation (hereafter operationally favorable to Egypt);

Y vote: when the SAS voted similarly to Israel and opposed Egypt's designation, or else voted differently from Egypt (hereafter operationally favorable to Israel);

Z vote: when the SAS abstained or was absent.[10]

Table 1 suggests the distribution of X, Y and Z votes for each SAS. It is only partially revealing, since it is based on mere voting consistency in accordance with the above criteria. While the simplified reference to Z votes as symbolizing only abstentions or absence may be technically correct, it

TABLE 1 Operational Significance of the Aggregated Roll Call Votes at the UN General Assembly (1967-1972)

Vote	X Votes No. of		Y Votes No. of		Z Votes No. of	
State	Votes	%	Votes	%	Votes	%
1. Botswana	3	7.6	18	46.2	18	46.2
2. Burundi	31	79.5	1	2.6	7	17.9
3. Cameroun	20	51.3	3	7.7	16	41.0
4. Cent. Afr. Rep.	0	0.0	2	5.1	37	95.0
5. Chad	15	38.5	3	7.7	21	53.8
6. Congo (B)	31	79.5	0	0.0	8	20.5
7. Dahomey	3	7.7	18	46.2	18	46.2
8. Eq. Guinea*	19	70.3	2	7.4	6	22.3
9. Ethiopia	14	35.9	4	10.3	22	53.8
10. Gabon	5	12.8	8	20.5	26	66.7
11. Gambia	8	20.5	15	38.5	16	41.0
12. Ghana	6	15.4	11	28.2	22	56.4
13. Guinea	37	94.9	0	0.0	2	5.1
14. Iv. Coast	3	7.7	14	35.9	22	56.4
15. Kenya	11	28.2	4	10.3	24	61.5
16. Lesotho	6	15.4	22	56.4	11	28.2
17. Liberia	5	12.8	27	69.2	7	18.0
18. Madagascar	9	23.1	21	53.8	9	23.1
19. Malawi	0	0.0	27	69.2	12	30.8
20. Mali	37	94.9	0	0	2	5.1
21. Mauritius*	9	33.3	2	7.4	16	59.3
22. Niger	16	41.0	2	5.1	21	53.8
23. Nigeria	26	66.7	2	5.1	11	28.2
24. Rwanda	5	12.8	16	41.0	18	46.2
25. Senegal	26	66.7	3	7.7	10	25.6
26. Sierra Leone	9	23.1	11	28.2	19	48.7
27. Swaziland*	4	14.8	8	29.6	15	55.6
28. Tanzania	36	92.3	0	0.0	3	7.7
29. Togo	12	30.8	13	33.3	14	35.9
30. Uganda	26	66.7	3	7.7	10	25.6
31. Upper Volta	9	23.1	10	25.6	20	51.3
32. Zaire	4	10.3	7	17.9	28	71.8
33. Zambia	35	89.7	0	0.0	4	10.3

*Three states, Equatorial Guinea, Mauritius and Swaziland, began to particpate in UN sessions only from 1968 and continued thereafter. They could take part, therefore, in only 27 roll call votes, although the other states participated in 39 votes.

appears to be substantially misleading. Since African states may vote Z, Y and Z interchangeably, they must have a reason for voting Z. Although it would be interesting to study the exact motives behind each decision to vote Z, it would be only marginally relevant to this stage of the research. Much more crucial is the operational significance of such votes, that is, the extent of satisfaction drawn by either Israel or Egypt when the SAS votes a certain way on any conflict issue. In the attempt to determine such significance, two alternatives emerge, both of which have to be understood in the context of the Israeli-Arab conflict within the UN environment: (1) a Z vote means a stand operationally favorable to Egypt, without the SAS explicitly voting X; or (2) a Z vote means a stand operationally favorable to Israel, without the SAS explicitly voting Y.

The political constellation at the United Nations enables Egypt to muster sufficient direct support (X votes) to pass most resolutions it initiates or supports in the General Assembly.[11] In order to increase Israel's isolation at the United Nations, Egypt has to attain a maximum of X votes. Any vote lacking such force fails to advance this goal. For the same reason, Israel's diplomatic efforts at the United Nations—while hoping to maximize Y votes—must be content when the number of Z votes increases. From Israel's point of view, the main value of such votes is that they diffuse voting patterns and thus deny Egypt the opportunity to emphasize Israel's isolation in the world organization.

Black African states have demonstrated in numerous multilateral forums (OAU gatherings, Third World meetings, the Group of Seventy-Seven, etc.) positions favorable to Egypt on the Middle East conflict.[12] It can be safely assumed that any UN vote which differed from unanimous stands adopted at such multilateral gatherings must have disappointed Egypt. Israel could only welcome such deviations from intrasystemic group consensus when the SAS did not explicitly vote X.

The above analysis of the political environment suggests that (1) Z votes have a distinct operational significance, analogous to both X and Y votes; and (2) as such, they are favorable to Israel. It has become possible, therefore, to rearrange the data of Table 1 in accordance with the operational significance of each SAS's vote.[13] This effort has also facilitated the grouping of African states into clusters which demonstrated similarity in voting behavior. To ensure clear limits between each cluster, a reliable margin of 60 percent and above of voting consistency has been introduced. The following subdivisions emerged (at least for 1967-72):

Cluster A: includes SAS whose 2X score exceeded 60 percent of the total votes;

Cluster B: includes SAS whose 2Y + Z score exceeded 60 percent of the total votes;

TABLE 2 Clustering African States in Accordance with the Operational Significance of their Roll Call Votes (1967-1972)

Cluster and No. State	Score of 2X+ Votes	%	Score of 2Y+ Votes	%
Cluster A				
1. Burundi	62	79.5	99	11.5
2. Congo (B)	62	79.5	8	10.3
3. Eq. Guinea*	38	70.4	10	18.5
4. Guinea	74	94.9	2	2.6
5. Mali	74	94.9	2	2.6
6. Nigeria	52	66.7	15	19.2
7. Senegal	52	66.7	16	20.5
8. Tanzania	72	92.3	3	3.8
9. Uganda	52	66.7	16	20.5
10. Zambia	70	89.7	4	5.1
Cluster B				
11. Botswana	6	7.7	54	69.2
12. Dahomey	6	7.7	54	69.2
13. Iv. Coast	6	7.7	50	64.1
14. Lesotho	12	15.4	55	70.5
15. Liberia	10	12.8	61	78.2
16. Malawi	0	0.0	66	84.6
17. Rwanda	10	12.8	50	64.1
18. Madagascar	18	23.1	51	65.4
Cluster C				
19. Cameroun	40	51.3	22	28.2
20. Cen. Afr. Rep.	0	0.0	41	52.5
21. Chad	30	38.5	27	34.6
22. Ethiopia	28	35.9	30	38.5
23. Gabon	10	12.8	42	53.8
24. Gambia	16	20.5	46	59.0
25. Ghana	12	15.4	44	56.4
26. Kenya	22	28.2	32	41.0
27. Mauritius*	18	33.3	20	37.0
28. Niger	32	41.0	25	32.1
29. Sierra Leone	18	23.1	41	52.6
30. Swaziland*	8	14.8	31	57.4
31. Togo	24	30.8	40	51.3
32. Upper Volta	18	23.1	40	51.3
33. Zaire	8	10.3	42	53.8

*Maximum score = 78. Eq. Guinea, Mauritius and Swaziland could take part only in 27 roll
call votes and hence their maximum score could reach only 54. Also, see note in Table 1.

TABLE 3 Redistribution of Cluster C Ratio Between X Direct Votes and Y Direct Votes in Percentages (Roll Call Votes During 1967-72)

State	X	Y
Cluster Cx		
Cameroun	87.0	13.0
Chad	83.3	16.7
Ethiopia	77.8	22.2
Kenya	73.3	26.7
Mauritius	81.8	18.2
Niger	88.9	11.1
Cluster Cy		
Swaziland	33.3	66.7
Gabon	38.5	61.5
Gambia	34.8	65.2
Ghana	35.3	64.7
Cluster Cz		
Sierra Leone	45.0	55.0
Togo	48.0	52.0
Upper Volta	47.4	52.6
Cent. Afr. Rep.*	—	—
Zaire*	—	—

*Both Zaire and the Central African Republic have each demonstrated a very high record of Z votes (over 70%). Testing ratios between X and Y votes is therefore irrelevant.

Cluster C: includes all other SAS whose 2X or 2Y + Z scores fell short of the proposed 60 percent limit.

Table 2 indicates the arrangement of these clusters.

While the most salient characteristic of Cluster C is the overall tendency toward Z votes, the record of such votes was only rarely absolute. In most cases, even though the tendency existed, the SAS also voted X and Y. It is therefore possible to refine this cluster by testing the ratio of X to Y votes for each SAS in order to expose the a priori leanings of black African states toward contending parties in the Middle East. The results of this test have led to the subdivisions within this cluster shown in Table 3.

Cluster Cx: includes SASs which revealed a general tendency toward Z votes, but on occasions when they expressed direct support, cast more than 60 percent of such votes as X (operationally favorable to Egypt);

Cluster Cy: includes SASs which revealed a general tendency toward Z votes, but on occasions when they expressed direct support, cast more than 60 percent of such votes as Y (operationally favorable to Israel);

Cluster Cz: includes SASs whose record of Z votes was impressively high (over 70 percent) or SASs which preferred to balance their direct votes between X and Y.[14]

Z votes have been interpreted as favorable to Israel, regardless of motives behind the SASs' vote. The ratio exercise has helped establish the de facto leanings òf states in Cluster C, which for various reasons refused or were unable to identify themselves during various stages of the discussed period with either Clusters A or B.

To sum up this section of the research, it has become apparent that during 1967-72 black African states voted quite differently on Middle East conflict issues considered by the UN General Assembly. Egypt's membership, along with other Arab states in the OAU, coupled with the consensus on conflict issues which Egypt secured at regional meetings (mainly the OAU), adds special significance to the above findings. The possible causes which led to such divisions remain to be probed. The first effort in this direction has been to look at the content of draft resolutions in order to establish the impact of these texts—if any—on black African states' UN voting behavior.

TEXTUAL COMPONENTS

In order to test the possible impact of the content of resolutions on the voting behavior of SASs, the thirty-nine conflict issues here carefully examined and broken down into the various components which form the central themes of these resolutions. In doing so, common components appeared which permitted their classification into four different categories. They are arranged in descending order according to the severity of their expected condemnation of Israel.

Category 1: One-Sided Demands

This category includes a variety of condemnations aimed at Israel's "aggressive acts" against the Arabs; requests for Israel's "immediate withdrawal from occupied territories" without prior conditions; demands that Israel pay compensation for the damage it caused to Arab property; and requests for unilateral enforcement of General Assembly resolutions by the Security Council, according to relevant articles of the UN Charter. The central common denominators in this category are: (1) a one-sided condemnation of Israel or a demand for a one-sided action such as "immediate withdrawal"; (2) the lack of insistence that a political settlement be conditional for the implementation of the above-mentioned demands.[15]

Category 2: Back to the Status Quo Ante

The central theme in this category revolves around the demand that Israel return to the territorial and demographic status quo existing before the June

1967 war, in return for a political settlement of all the controversies existing between Israel and the Arabs. These resolutions contain a generally-worded request that Israel withdraw from the territories it occupied during that war. But sometimes they take a more specific form, including demands to invalidate Israel's annexationist moves in Jerusalem, to return the 1967 refugees to their original homes, or to invalidate the physical and demographic changes made by Israel in specific parts of the occupied territories, such as Gaza, the West Bank, etc. The common denominators in this category are: (1) opposition to Israel's gains through the use of force; (2) the use of balanced phrasing with complementary effects. There is a noticeable tendency to weld together demands for Israeli action on the one hand, with settling the Middle East conflict and bringing about a lasting peace on the other; (3) the lack of one-sided denunciations of any sort or threats of imposing sanctions against Israel.[16]

Category 3: Self-Determination

In this category, the central common denominator is the demand for recognition of the legitimate rights of Palestinians to self-determination. The decision to isolate draft resolutions containing such components was made because of the special emotions which exist in Africa about self-determination questions.[17]

Category 4: Tactical Considerations

The main controversy at the General Assembly on components in this category is usually not about the substance of the resolutions, but rather about procedural or tactical considerations which on occasion reflect the different strategies of both Israel and Egypt. A few examples will illustrate the significance of this category: (1) an Egyptian-backed attempt to incorporate into an essentially humanitarian draft resolution (which evokes general acceptance) a paragraph of a one-sided condemnation (Category 1) to ensure the safe passage of the entire resolution;[18] (2) an Egyptian-backed attempt to alter established procedures at the United Nations, such as a motion calling for a simple majority vote on a substantive issue which requires a two-thirds majority;[19] (3) an Israeli-backed attempt to introduce a draft resolution with the deliberate intention to counteract another proposed draft resolution. The aim here is to divert votes from the draft resolution which is most likely to be adopted and thus to split "loyalties." The Latin American draft resolution in 1967, for instance, was expected to stand against the majority-backed Yugoslav draft (favored by Egypt), in order to frustrate its adoption by a unanimous vote.[20]

TABLE 4 Distribution of Votes in Categories According to Textual Contents

	Category 1				Category 2				Category 3				Category 4			
	Res. No. and Year	No. of Votes			Res. No. and Year	No. of votes			Res. No. and Year	No. of votes			Res. No. and Year	No. of votes		
		X	Y	Z		X	Y	Z		X	Y	Z		X	Y	Z
1	519A/67	6	13	11	2253/67	22	0	8	2672C/70	7	4	22	523/67	8	17	5
2	519B/67	7	10	13	2254/67	22	0	8	2787/70	7	4	22	2256/67	6	16	8
3	519C/67	3	13	14	2452/68	17	0	16	2792D/71	8	4	21	522/67	12	8	10
4	519D/67	5	12	13	2628/70	22	2	9	2963E/72	18	2	13	2443/68	11	3	9
5	521/67	0	16	14	2672D/70	23	0	10					584/69	10	12	11
6	524/67	4	19	7	2792C/71	14	0	19					2546/69	11	9	13
7	525/67	0	19	11	2792E/71	16	0	17					604/70	15	10	8
8	2535B/69	8	8	17	2799/71	18	0	15					619/70	9	11	13
9					2949/72	24	0	9					2727/70	13	7	13
10					2963C/72	24	0	9					2649/70	9	8	16
11					2963D/72	23	0	10					652/71	13	7	13
12													656/71	13	7	13
13													656/71	13	6	14
14													657/71	12	9	12
15													2851/71	11	7	15
16													3005/72	16	7	15

The following picture emerges as a result of having demarcated the various dominant components of all thirty-nine conflict issues and having grouped them: eight conflict issues were found to be in Category 1; eleven in Category 2; four in Category 3; and sixteen in Category 4. Table 4 indicates the distribution of votes within each of these conflict issues, based on the roll call votes of the thirty-three black African states.

Toward a Continental Pattern

A first glance at Table 4 indicates that within each category there is a definite pattern of African voting which is dissimilar to patterns emerging from other categories. This phenomenon is related to the decreasing degree of condemnation implied in each group.

Category 1 reveals a clear tendency to limit X votes (under one third), while simultaneously increasing both Y and Z votes. It also suggests a high degree of agreement—though not total—about African states' refusal during 1967-72 to endorse one-sided (i.e. anti-Israeli) condemnations, or a rejection of the principle of unilateral moves by one party without reciprocal conciliatory moves by the other. The fact that Egypt voted "For" and Israel "Against" indicated that draft resolutions of this sort were welcomed by the former. The voting pattern exhibited in this category was essentially "favorable" to Israel inasmuch as it frustrated Egypt's efforts to compel Israel to act unilaterally (such as withdrawing from occupied territories prior to a peace agreement). With one exception, all other votes in this category took place in 1967, shortly after the June war. The rejection of the principle embodied in drafts classified in this category might have had weight in Egypt's reluctance after 1967 and until 1972 to introduce drafts of this nature. However, a resurgence of components hitherto embodied in this category could be noticed in some of the resolutions presented to the General Assembly in the winter of 1973.[21]

Category 2 shows a substantial increase in the number of X votes (two-thirds or more out of the total). Similarly Y votes were reduced to zero, while Z votes reached an average of about one-third of the total. On the whole, it is possible to qualify this pattern as being favorable to Egypt because of the very high rate of X votes. Egypt itself consistently encouraged draft resolutions from Category 2 for that reason. Nonetheless, this category also suggests that a wide degree of agreement existed among black African states in regard to the components included. This agreement reached near consensus by 1972 and was total in 1973. (See Table 8.)

Category 3 shows an overall tendency toward Z votes (over two-thirds) at the expense of Y and X votes. It seems that mass abstention in this category was perceived by many black African states as a convenient outlet for two contradictory stands. On the one hand, African states acclaimed the principle of self-determination. On the other hand, they seem to disapprove the use of the principle directly at Israel's expense, or the branding of the latter as a colonialist entity, alien to the Middle East region. While draft resolutions of this kind met with Egypt's approval, the overall voting pattern until 1972 could be seen as "favorable" to Israel inasmuch as it did not endorse the Arab interpretation of the Palestinian problem. The 1972 voting pattern indicated a shift in the African approach vis-à-vis this problem, which was reinforced in the 1973 votes.[22]

Category 4 indicates that while the fluctuation within each voting designation was rather high, when compared with previous categories the overall tendency was toward an almost equal distribution among the three possible forms of voting behavior: X, Y and Z. This category suggests that when tactical, rather than substantive, considerations were dominant, the distribution of votes exposed black African states' sympathies or antipathies toward the two rival parties in the Middle East. (Note the resemblance to the distribution of clusters illustrated in Table 3). In the general context of this discussion, Category 4 can be viewed as being "favorable" to Israel because of the low number of X votes (less than one third), compared with the combined number of Y and Z votes (two thirds). The 1972 voting results indicated a marked shift in this category toward a pattern which was usually apparent in Category 2 (operationally favorable to Egypt).

Voting Clusters and Textual Components Combined

While the previous section depicted the aggregated African voting behavior in each of the four listed categories, it has not yet explained the attitude of single African states in relation to these categories. While this can be done without much difficulty, a greater challenge would be to test how each state within the five clusters proposed in Table 3 reacts vis-à-vis each of the four categories in Table 4. This test would be relevant for examining whether during the discussed period the contents of the draft resolutions were powerful enough to offset existing attitudes (tacit or explicit) of single African states toward the two Middle East protagonists. In other words, did the African states classified within the same cluster vote similarly or dissimilarly on components which were itemized in each category. Table 5 will facilitate this task.

A reading of the above table indicates that a distinct correlation exists between the SAS's location in any one of the five clusters, on the one hand, and its behavior in regard to each category, on the other. Each of the five clusters of states tends to demonstrate a rather consistent voting pattern within each category. In addition to this observation, the table enables us to define the voting pattern for the SAS as well as the cluster. This can be done in the following way:

SAS in Cluster A

The dominant feature of this cluster was the almost comprehensive X voting, which suggests overwhelming support for stands favored by Egypt. Apart from a few instances, the SAS in this group avoided direct votes favorable to Israel (Y votes). Only in Category 1 (one-sided demands), did some states move toward abstention (Z votes), thus indirectly expressing reservations over the content of some of the proposed draft resolutions. Looking at the total score, it can be seen clearly that this cluster formed the African backbone of Arab support at the United Nations.

SAS in Cluster B

Unlike the previous cluster where votes favorable to Egypt were clearly dominant in each category, the overall tendency in this cluster was favorable to Israel (when Y and Z votes are seen in combination). The exception here is noticeable in Category 1, where agreement with intrasystemic consensus (OAU) found expression in either direct X or indirect Z votes.

SAS in Cluster Cx

Here the SAS only rarely voted in a manner directly favorable to Israel. In Category 2 it voted X in most instances, whereas in Categories 1 and 3, the tendency was toward Z votes. In Category 4, the SAS tended to divide votes between those directly favorable to Egypt (X votes) and indirectly favorable to Israel (Z votes). The overall tendency of the SAS in this cluster, however, was toward abstention, but when it voted directly, it did so in a manner favorable to Egypt.

SAS in Cluster Cy

The SAS in this cluster often refrained from voting favorably toward Egypt (X votes). Only in Category 2 did it cast a few X votes, but it still preferred to exercise its right by voting mostly Z. In Category 1 most of the SAS's votes were directly favorable to Israel. In Category 3, Z votes predominated, while in Category 4 the general tendency was either directly favorable to Israel or else indirectly so (Y or Z votes). As in the previous category, the balance was in favor of Z votes, but when a SAS voted directly, it did so in a manner favorable to Israel.

SAS in Cluster Cz

In this cluster, two subgroups could be discerned: (a) the persistent abstainer; (b) the balancer between direct X and direct Y votes, when the SAS did not abstain. In regard to the latter, the balancing behavior was not necessarily

TABLE 5 Voting Clusters According to Categories

No. of Votes in Each Category

Cluster & State	8 Votes Cat. 1			11 Votes Cat. 2			4 Votes Cat. 3			16 Votes Cat. 4			39 Votes Total		
	X	Y	Z	X	Y	Z	X	Y	Z	X	Y	Z	X	Y	Z
Cluster A															
1 Burundi	5	0	3	11	0	0	1	0	3	14	1	1	31	1	7
2 Congo (B)	3	0	5	9	0	2	3	0	1	16	0	0	31	0	8
3 Eq. Guinea	0	0	1	7	0	2	3	1	0	9	1	3	19	2	6
4 Guinea	6	0	2	11	0	0	4	0	0	16	0	0	37	0	2
5 Mali	6	0	2	11	0	0	4	0	0	16	0	0	37	0	2
6 Nigeria	1	2	5	10	0	1	1	0	3	13	0	2	25	2	11
7 Senegal	1	0	7	10	0	1	4	0	0	11	3	2	26	3	10
8 Tanzania	5	0	3	11	0	0	4	0	0	16	0	0	36	0	3
9 Uganda	1	3	4	9	0	2	2	0	2	14	0	2	26	3	10
10 Zambia	5	0	3	11	0	0	3	0	1	16	0	0	35	0	4
Cluster B															
11 Botswana	0	8	0	3	0	8	0	1	3	0	9	7	3	18	18
12 Dahomey	0	6	2	3	1	7	0	0	4	0	11	5	3	18	18
13 Iv. Coast	0	6	2	3	0	8	0	0	4	0	8	8	3	14	22
14 Lesotho	0	7	1	6	0	5	0	1	3	0	14	2	6	22	11
15 Liberia	0	8	0	5	0	6	0	3	1	0	16	0	5	27	7
16 Madagascar	0	5	3	8	0	3	1	2	1	0	14	2	9	21	9
17 Malawi	0	8	0	0	1	10	0	3	1	0	15	1	0	27	12
18 Rwanda	0	8	0	5	0	6	0	1	3	0	7	9	5	16	18

Cluster Cx														
19 Cameroun	16	3	20	7	1	8	2	0	2	1	0	10	6	2	0
20 Chad	29	3	15	9	2	5	3	0	1	2	0	9	7	1	0
21 Ethiopia	21	4	14	11	2	3	4	0	0	0	0	11	6	2	0
22 Kenya	24	4	11	9	2	5	3	0	1	6	0	5	6	2	0
23 Mauritius	16	2	9	8	1	4	3	0	1	4	1	4	1	0	0
24 Niger	21	2	16	13	1	2	1	0	3	0	0	11	7	1	0
Cluster Cy														
25 Gabon	26	8	5	9	6	1	3	1	0	7	0	4	7	1	0
26 Gambia	16	15	8	6	7	3	4	0	0	6	0	5	0	8	0
27 Ghana	22	11	6	11	4	1	4	0	0	6	0	5	1	7	0
28 Swaziland	15	8	4	8	5	0	1	2	1	6	0	3	0	1	0
Cluster Cz														
29 Cent. Afr. Rep.	37	2	0	14	2	0	4	0	0	11	0	0	8	0	0
30 Sierra Leone	19	11	9	11	4	1	3	0	1	4	0	7	1	7	0
31 Togo	14	13	12	5	6	5	4	0	0	4	0	7	1	7	0
32 Up. Volta	20	10	9	11	3	2	4	0	0	9	0	7	1	7	0
33 Zaire	28	7	4	10	4	2	4	0	0		0	2	5	3	0

only within each category, but was also apparent between them. More specifically, whereas in Category 2 most votes were favorable to Egypt, in Category 1 most of the votes were directly favorable to Israel. In Category 3, the SAS's Z vote was apparent all along; and in Category 4, while the tendency toward Z votes was markedly high, the SAS divided its actual votes almost equally between being directly favorable to Egypt or Israel.

Intervening War: Intensified Trends

The above set of patterns should have become a key for predicting SASs' voting behavior at the United Nations when draft-resolutions with similar textual components, such as those already proposed, were to have been discussed and voted upon in subsequent General Assembly sessions. The intention to verify these patterns against the 1973 resolutions and roll call votes was largely frustrated by the unexpected October 1973 war, which almost led to the complete collapse of Israel's diplomatic presence in Africa. The method used in this research was helpful when observing trends which became apparent in the period preceding the war. More specifically, the gradual increase in the number of states voting favorably for Egypt (X votes) became more noticeable, particularly in Categories 2, 3 and 4.[23] Similarly, the number of African states moving from direct Y votes to Z votes (see Table 4) increased.

EXPLANATORY FACTORS

The analysis of textual components has indicated that they can influence UN voting behavior by leading various clusters of countries to adopt distinct voting patterns in each category. Although textual components can either increase subsystemic solidarity or, conversely, account for ''deviations'' from the anticipated voting pattern of specific states, they still form only one dimension of the multitude of factors which affect similarities or differences in voting behavior. While this research has not set out to explore in depth all these factors and their relative impact on voting behavior, it is still desirable to examine the composition of each cluster again. At this stage the aim of such an exercise is to find out whether common features exist among single African states within each of the five clusters, which explain their similar voting behavior. Such an inductive analysis has led to the results presented in Table 6:

Cluster A

Of the ten countries included, eight have generally followed a radical foreign policy: Burundi, Congo (Brazzaville), Equatorial Guinea, Guinea, Mali,

Tanzania, Uganda and Zambia.[24] The other two, Nigeria and Senegal, have generally been more moderate in their foreign policy orientations. All of the states, except Equatorial Guinea, which is relatively small, had fairly significant diplomatic representation in the Arab states, which was reciprocated. In contrast, none of the states, except Congo (B) until 1972, had diplomatic representation in Israel, although Israel had diplomatic representation in all the countries besides Guinea (which broke diplomatic relations immediately after the Six-Day War). Israel offered technical assistance to all of the states except Equatorial Guinea. In contrast, the Arabs extended financial assistance to only four states (Guinea, Nigeria, Senegal and Uganda), and at least in one case, they used the amount of their gifts as a political weapon (notably in Uganda in 1972).

The influence which the Arabs might have exerted through territorial contiguity touched only two countries, Mali and Uganda, and therefore cannot be seen as having a significant effect on voting behavior within this cluster. Tanzania and Guinea, which have no common borders with any Arab states, indicated the same pro-Egyptian voting record (93 percent X votes) as Mali, which borders Algeria.

Another factor which should not be overlooked is the existence of large Muslim populations. Three states (Guinea, Mali and Senegal) have over 50 percent Muslim populations, while three other states have many adherents. On the other hand, eight states have notable Christian populations, of which four have been led by men known to have strong religious affiliations.[25] It should be stressed that religion per se did not play a significant role in determining foreign policy until it was directly activated. This applies particularly to Islam, which became a more significant factor as Arab states within the OAU increasingly pressured their coreligionists in Africa to support them in their conflict with Israel.

The most salient common denominators for Cluster A have been radical foreign policies, active diplomatic exchanges with the Arabs, and the potentiality to appeal to countries with substantial Muslim populations.

Cluster B

None of the eight states in this category was classified as being radical during 1967-72. All have been moderate and, on the whole, pro-West in their foreign policy orientations. The exchange of diplomatic representation with the Arabs has been slight, especially in comparison with Cluster A. All the states had Israeli missions located within their own countries and five of them had diplomatic representation in Israel. Four of them located their embassies in Jerusalem so as to recognize its de jure status as Israel's capital.[26] All of them have received technical assistance from Israel, with some states, such as the Ivory Coast and Malawi, receiving comparatively

TABLE 6 Major Explanatory Factors

Cluster & African State		Diplomatic Representation				Aid		Con-tigu-ity	Prominent Religious Community	
	Radi-cal	Israel in SAS	SAS in Israel	Arab in SAS¶	SAS in Arab¶	From Israel‡	From Arabs**		Mosl.	Christ.
Cluster A										
1 Burundi	yes	yes	no	yes(1)	yes(1)	yes	no	no	no	yes
2 Congo(B)	yes	yes	yes†	yes(2)	yes(4)	yes	no	no	no	yes
3 Eq. Guinea	yes	yes	no	no	no	no	no	no	no	yes
4 Guinea	yes	no	no	yes(6)	yes(10)	yes	yes	no	yes*	no
5 Mali	yes	yes	no	yes(5)	yes(7)	yes	no	yes	yes*	no
6 Nigeria	no	yes	no	yes(8)	yes(7)	yes	yes	no	yes	yes
7 Senegal	no	yes	no	yes(6)	yes(7)	yes	yes	no	yes*	yes
8 Tanzania	yes	yes	no	yes(4)	yes(4)	yes	no	no	yes	yes
9 Uganda	yes	yes	no	yes(3)	yes(2)	yes	yes	yes	yes	yes
10 Zambia	yes	yes	no	yes(3)	yes(1)	yes	no	yes	yes	yes
11 Botswana	no	yes	no	no	no	yes	no	no	no	yes
12 Dahomey	no	yes	yes†	yes(3)	yes(1)	yes	no	no	yes	yes
13 Ivory Coast	no	yes	yes†	yes(1)	yes(1)	yes	yes	no	yes	yes
14 Lesotho	no	yes	no	no	no	yes	no	no	no	yes
15 Liberia	no	yes	yes†	yes(4)	yes(3)	yes	no	no	yes	yes
16 Madagascar	no	yes	yes†	no	yes(1)	yes	no	no	no	yes
17 Malawi	no	yes	yes	no	yes(1)	yes	no	no	no	yes
18 Rwanda	no	yes	no	yes(1)	no	yes	no	no	no	yes

Cluster Cx										
19 Cameroun	no	yes	no	yes(5)	yes(6)	yes	yes	no	yes	yes
20 Chad	no	yes	no	yes(7)	yes(4)	yes	yes	yes	yes	yes
21 Ethiopia	no	yes	no	yes(7)	yes(9)	yes	no	yes	yes	yes
22 Kenya	no	yes	yes	yes(4)	yes(2)	yes	no	yes	yes	yes
23 Mauritius	no	yes	no	no	no	yes	no	no	yes	yes
24 Niger	no	yes	yes†	yes(5)	yes(2)	yes	yes	yes	yes*	no
Cluster Cy										
25 Gabon	no	yes	yes†	yes(1)	yes(1)	yes	no	no	no	yes
26 Gambia	no	yes	no	yes(1)	no	yes	no	yes	yes	no
27 Ghana	no	yes	yes	yes(8)	yes(9)	yes	no	yes	yes	yes
28 Swaziland	no	yes	no	no	no	yes	no	no	no	yes
Cluster Cz										
29 C.A. Rep.	no	yes	yes(J)	yes(2)	yes(3)	yes	yes	yes	yes	no
30 Sierra Leone	no	yes	yes	yes(3)	yes(2)	yes	no	no	yes	yes
31 Togo	no	yes	no	yes(3)	no	yes	no	no	yes	yes
32 Upper Volta	no	yes	yes(J)	yes(1)	yes(1)	yes	no	no	yes	yes
33 Zaire	yes(?)	yes	yes(J)	yes(3)	yes(4)	yes	yes	yes	yes	yes

Notes: * Over 50%
†Jerusalem
**Given mainly in the form of financial assistance
‡Given mainly in the form of technical assistance
¶Numbers in parentheses refer to the number of Arab missions represented

Sources: The Middle East and North Africa, 1972-1973 (London: Europa, 1972); *Africa, 1972-1973* (London: Europa, 1972); *Africa, 1971* (New York: Africana, 1970); Division for International Cooperation, *Israel's Programme of International Cooperation* (Jerusalem: Ministry for Foreign Affairs, December 1971).

large amounts. Only the Ivory Coast received financial aid from the Arabs.

None of the states borders on Arab countries and therefore none was under potential or actual pressure from insistent neighbors.[27] Only three of these states have notable Muslim populations, but these have not been particularly significant politically. All eight states have substantial Christian populations and are led by Christian ruling elites.[28]

The major characteristics for Cluster B were a moderate foreign policy, more extensive diplomatic and aid ties with Israel than with the Arabs, and the prominence of Christians within the general populations and especially within the ruling groups. The apparent influence of contiguity with Arabs or Islam was negligible.

Cluster Cx

All the six countries classified in this group have generally followed a moderate foreign policy, although Kenya and Ethiopia have at times sided with the more radical states on the question of southern Africa.[29] Members of this group have the greatest level of diplomatic representation with the Arabs after those in Cluster A. Israel was represented in all of them before 1973; but only Niger maintained an embassy in Israel, in Jerusalem. All the states, and Ethiopia in particular, received aid from Israel; in contrast, only half of the group (Cameroon, Chad and Niger) benefitted from Arab assistance.

Most states (Chad, Ethiopia, Kenya and Niger) share borders with the Arabs. This has been significant particularly where subversive or irridentist Muslim groups within the countries or on their borders have looked for support to the Arab neighbors and others. The National Liberation Front (Frolinat) in Northern Chad received help from Libya during the early seventies, while the Eritrean Liberation Front (ELF) has benefitted from both Sudanese and Syrian support in particular. Somalia has received Arab assistance in its efforts to possess territories with substantial Somali populations now located within Ethiopia and Kenya.[30] In regard to religion, both Islam and Christianity have made a strong impact in each of the countries, but only in Niger does Islam predominate numerically and culturally. In Ethiopia Christianity is more significant both in numbers and political influence, despite the efforts of an active Islamic minority.

The states in Cluster Cx offer a mixed profile. They are generally moderate, have rather extensive diplomatic ties with the Arabs, but have also maintained friendly connections with Israel. Contiguity with the Arab states played a more prominent role here than in any of the other groups. Religion was balanced in almost every country between Islam and Christianity, so that it may not have exerted a strong influence on voting behavior.

Cluster Cy

The four members of the group: Gabon, Gambia, Ghana and Swaziland, resemble the states in Cluster B in their moderate foreign policy orientations, the good diplomatic and aid relations they maintained with Israel, and the relative absence of factors such as Islamic activism and contiguity with Arab states.[31]

Cluster Cz

Most of the determining factors here are largely similar to those in Cluster Cy. None of the states was radical; and, on the whole, all were known to follow moderate policies both at home and abroad during the discussed period.[32] On the diplomatic level, all (apart from Togo, which had no Middle East representation) had exchanges of envoys with both the Arabs and Israel, and three states established embassies in Jerusalem. Contiguity with Arab countries was a factor which applied geographically to only two states. There were no indications that such a factor had any direct impact on the decision-making elites in those states. The same may be said about the religious factor.

The similarity of determining factors with Cluster Cy and the dissimilarity in voting behavior, suggests the possibility that states in this cluster preferred for various reasons to remain as uncommitted as possible on Middle East issues. The fact that the operational significance of their votes (high percentage of Z votes) was favorable to Israel was perhaps only secondary to their desire to avoid disagreements with either Arab African states or Israel. Z votes (abstention or absence) was the most suitable procedural method to do so. The preceding observations suggest a number of inferences applicable to the period under discussion:

1. Radical regimes tended to support other states with similar political orientations. In this case, the radical African states almost automatically supported Egypt, which had been active in this group since the Casablanca meeting of January 1961. Moderate, more pro-Western regimes tended to be less rigid in their voting behavior and were thus also willing at times, depending on the issues discussed, to vote in a manner favorable to Israel.

2. Diplomatic representation was a good indicator of likely voting behavior.[33] States which had a salient diplomatic presence in Arab capitals also tended to support the Egyptian position strongly, while those which had established diplomatic missions in Israel, particularly in Jerusalem, also tended to vote directly or indirectly in favor of Israel.

3. Israeli technical assistance on a bilateral level did not have a noticeable effect on African voting behavior in multilateral forums. The distribution of

Arab financial aid, which was more restricted but generally of greater monetary value, tended to be a more visible indicator.[34]

4. Territorial contiguity was generally not an important indicator unless the Arabs supported dissident groups within the black African state or backed irridentist claims on neighboring states. Contiguity could subject an African state to Arab pressure, either real or imaginary. The possibility of such threats may have led to a more cautious stand by the SAS from its desire to avoid confrontation with its Arab neighbors. This was an even stronger motivation when a contiguous SAS confronted internal problems with ethnic or religious dimensions which could be intensified by support from adjacent Arab forces.

5. States with large Muslim populations were more likely to support the Arab cause, particularly when they were mobilized for this purpose by local leadership and by Arab OAU members. Countries with large Christian populations or Christian leaders were likely to cast a more balanced vote unless other factors, such as radical foreign policies, intervened.

Each of these factors could exist separately or in conjunction with others. Often the combination of two factors or more made the SAS's location within a particular cluster and the general voting pattern it could have been expected to adopt more discernible.

Conclusions

This research analysis has concentrated primarily upon the attitudes of members of the African subordinate state system at the United Nations toward the protagonists of the Middle East conflict during 1967-72. It has blended findings from voting records, the textual components of draft resolutions, and explanatory factors affecting the behavior of individual states. As a result of this study, it is possible to discern a variety of considerations which affected African voting behavior in practice.

1. At least until the end of the period discussed (1972), the Arab African states failed to channel the OAU's expressed desire to reach continental solidarity into the United Nations. This was despite Egypt's activities within the OAU (supported by five other Arab African states), which persistently tried to identify its struggle against Israel with that of Africa's struggle against colonialism and imperialism.

2. The absence of a united African front at the United Nations on the Arab-Israeli conflict was an impressive achievement for Israel's diplomacy in Africa. This accomplishment was due primarily to the special efforts which Israel invested in Africa during the early sixties (immediate recognition of newly independent states and technical assistance programs).

3. New dynamic factors, which affected the entire spectrum of African politics (radicalization of regimes, political activization of Islam, rap-

prochement between Arab and black Africa, and increasing vulnerability to economic pressures, for example), have intensified the corrosion of such achievements and have also succeeded in offsetting them over time. As a result, Israel's policy at the United Nations and elsewhere has been based essentially on a "rearguard" strategy, namely, slowing down the process of estrangement after having almost lost completely the ability to stop it.

4. Gradual disenchantment of black African states with Israel has been legitimized on the basis of substantive issues. By having acquired territories by force, Israel was seen to have violated one of Africa's most cherished continental principles, the integrity and sanctity of existing borders. The fact that part of these occupied territories belong to an African state (Egypt) added to the gravity of this violation, especially since during the discussed period Israel was not perceived as having declared itself committed to withdraw from the territories. The black African states have been increasingly insistent on the territorial issues since 1967, as the voting records in Category 2 have demonstrated.

5. Another substantive issue which received subsystemic consensus in the early seventies both at the OAU and the United Nations was the Palestinian problem. The increasing Arab emphasis on the right to self-determination touched upon a sensitive issue for Africans, although a consensus on the issue was not achieved immediately (see Category 3). While it has continued to be unlikely that black African states would endorse the extreme Palestinian interpretation of this "right" (dissolution of the State of Israel as a first step), it has also gradually become apparent that OAU members would not endorse Israel's policy of delay and postponement in the search for a solution to the Palestinian problem. The fact that Israel has not had a definite plan to deal with this dilemma may have contributed as well to the drastic changes of African voting patterns on this issue at the United Nations.

6. The combined effect of dynamic factors may have reenforced black African states' sensitivities toward conflict issues brought before the General Assembly. The exact connections between the two would form the basis for a separate study. In the meantime, the combined methods used for this research have helped to elucidate voting patterns and trends at both the continental and the individual state levels on issues which have been of major concern to members of another subsystem (although Egypt should be considered a member of both the Middle East and African subsystems).

7. African voting behavior delineated in this study has also been a fairly good predictor for countries that broke diplomatic relations with Israel before the 1973 Yom Kippur War.

Out of the nine countries to do so, five came from Cluster A (Burundi, Congo [B], Guinea, Mali and Uganda); two from Cluster Cx (Chad and Niger); and another two from Cz (Togo and Zaire). In contrast, when twenty

TABLE 7 Black African States Which Severed Diplomatic Relations With Israel, 1967-1973

African State	Date Broke Diplomatic Relations
Guinea	June 12, 1967
Uganda	March 30, 1972
Chad	November 28, 1972
Congo (B)	December 31, 1972
Niger	January 4, 1973
Mali	January 5, 1973
Burundi	May 16, 1973
Togo	September 21, 1973
Zaire	October 4, 1973
Dahomey	October 6, 1973
Rwanda	October 9, 1973
Cameroun	October 15, 1973
Equatorial Guinea	October 15, 1973
Upper Volta	October 18, 1973
Tanzania	October 18, 1973
Malagasy Republic	October 20, 1973
Central African Republic	October 21, 1973
Sierra Leone	October 22, 1973
Ethiopia	October 23, 1973
Nigeria	October 25, 1973
Zambia	October 25, 1973
Gambia	October 25, 1973
Ghana	October 27, 1973
Senegal	October 27, 1973
Gabon	October 29, 1973
Kenya	November 1, 1973
Liberia	November 2, 1973
Ivory Coast	November 8, 1973
Botswana	November 13, 1973

African states finally severed diplomatic ties following the October war, the three last countries to do so were Liberia, the Ivory Coast and Botswana, all of which were grouped in Cluster B. The few states which had not cut off ties with Israel by the beginning of 1974 came from Clusters B (Lesotho and Malawi), Cy (Swaziland) and Cx (Mauritius). The designated patterns also were useful for classifying the ten states which abstained or were absent on the central vote at the General Assembly in 1973 on A/Res. 3151 (XXVIII) condemning the "unholy alliance between Portuguese colonialism, South African racism, Zionism and Israeli imperialism." Five states came from Cluster B (Botswana, Dahomey, the Ivory Coast, Lesotho and Malawi); two from Cy (Gambia and Swaziland); another two from Cz (Central African Republic and Upper Volta); and one from Cx (Mauritius). The 1973 voting patterns appear in Table 8.

TABLE 8 SAS Votes at the 28th (1973) U.N. General Assembly (Votes Translated into their Operational Significance)

No. & State	Res. 3089 Displaced Inhabitants and Gaza	Res. 3090 Palestinian Rights	Res. 3092 Territories	Res. 3151 Apartheid and Zionism
1 Botswana	X	Z	X	Z
2 Burundi	X	X	X	X
3 Cameroun	X	X	X	X
4 Cent. Afr. Rep.	X	X	X	Z
5 Chad	X	X	X	X
6 Congo (B)	X	X	X	X
7 Dahomey	X	X	X	Z
8 Eq. Guinea	X	X	X	X
9 Ethiopia	X	X	X	X
10 Gabon	X	X	X	X
11 Gambia	X	X	X	Z
12 Ghana	X	X	X	X
13 Guinea	X	X	X	X
14 Iv. Coast	X	X	X	Z
15 Kenya	X	X	X	X
16 Lesotho	X	Z	X	Z
17 Liberia	X	X	X	X
18 Madagascar	X	X	X	X
19 Malawi	Z	Z	Z	Z
20 Mali	X	X	X	X
21 Mauritius	Z	Z	Z	Z
22 Niger	X	X	X	X
23 Nigeria	X	X	X	X
24 Rwanda	X	X	X	X
25 Senegal	X	X	X	X
26 Sierra Leone	X	X	X	X
27 Swaziland	Z	Z	Z	Z
28 Tanzania	X	X	X	X
29 Togo	X	X	X	X
30 Uganda	X	X	X	X
31 Upper Volta	X	X	X	Z
32 Zaire	X	X	X	X
33 Zambia	X	X	X	X

Future African voting behavior at the United Nations on the Middle East conflict will depend upon further developments within the Middle East itself, especially between Egypt and Israel, as well as within Africa, particularly between Arab and black Africa. It will help understand events if one analyzes them through a similar combination of substantive and quantitative methods, including the operational significance of voting patterns, the textual components of draft resolutions, and the explanatory factors affecting individual states.

NOTES

The authors would like to thank the Leonard Davis Institute for International Relations for its support, Yitzhak Eldan for his research assistance, and Naomi Chazan for her comments. This article originally appeared in the *Jerusalem Journal of International Relations*, 1, no. 2 (1975).

1. For a definition of the concept of subordinate systems, see Michael Brecher, et al., "A Framework for Research on Foreign Policy Behavior," *Journal of Conflict Resolution* 13, no. 1 (March 1969): 83.

2. See for example Susan Aurelia Gitelson, "The Linkages Between External and Domestic Policies: Israel's Experience with Ghana and Nigeria," *Sage International Yearbook of Foreign Policy Studies* (Beverly Hills: Sage, 1976).

3. Some quantitative analyses of African voting behavior at the UN, often including reference to the Middle East conflict, were produced on roll call votes from the sixties, for instance, in Hayward R. Alker, Jr. and Bruce M. Russett, *World Politics in the General Assembly* (New Haven and London, 1965); Thomas Hovet, Jr., *Africa in the United Nations* (Evanston, Ill., 1963); Kathleen Maas Weigert and Robert E. Riggs, "Africa and United Nations Elections: An Aggregate Data Analysis," *International Organization* 23, no. 1 (Winter 1969): 1-19; and Dorothy Dodge, "African Voting Cohesion in the UN," *Africa Report* 12, no. 7 (October 1967): 58-59. The specific issue of concern here, African attitudes toward the Middle East, has been analyzed mainly in relation to the Six-Day War of 1967, as for example in Samuel Decalo, "Israeli Foreign Policy and the Third World," *Orbis* 11, no. 3 (Fall 1967): 724-45.

4. See David A. Kay. "The Impact of African States on the United Nations," *International Organization* 23, no. 1 (Winter 1967): 20-47. The UN is preferable to the continental OAU as a testing area for black Africa's views on the core issues of the Middle East conflict mainly because of the emphasis within the OAU on continental solidarity, on the one hand, and the reluctance to publicize differences among its members, on the other. See Jon Woronoff, *Organizing African Unity* (Metuchen, N.J.: Scarecrow, 1970). In addition, some Arab states within the Middle East subsystem are also members of the OAU.

5. Whereas the chief issues before the Six-Day War of 1967 had centered mostly around the 1948 refugee problem (as a result of the first Israeli-Arab war), after 1967 the focus shifted primarily to the occupied territories (Sinai, the West Bank and the Golan Heights), as well as to the repercussions from that conflict.

6. African voting attitudes during the 28th meeting of the UN General Assembly were omitted from this discussion for two main reasons. First, the session terminated its deliberations after the October 1973 war. Second, the war marked the culmination

of a rupture in diplomatic relations by the majority of black African states with Israel, which affected the votes they cast.

7. The six Arab North African states (Algeria, Egypt, Libya, Morocco, the Sudan and Tunisia), all of which are active members of the Arab League, have been excluded for obvious reasons. In addition, two predominantly Muslim states, Mauritania and Somalia, were left out since both states have declared their allegiance to Arab League principles and have voted similarly to Egypt and the other Arab states.

8. A resolution with a purely humanitarian focus usually includes the following elements: (1) appeals for special and generous contributions to the UN Relief and Works Agency (UNRWA); and (2) requests support for the Working Group on the financing of UNRWA, etc. These resolutions often enjoy UN majority support. See for instance A/Res. 2341 (22) para. A, of December 11, 1967; A/Res. 2535 (24) para. C of December 12, 1969; A/Res. 2672 (25) para. A and B of January 4, 1971.

9. Egypt was chosen to represent the Arab attitudes at the UN since it is the chief protagonist in the Arab-Israeli conflict, and other Arab states tend to vote identically with Egypt.

10. Absence is being interpreted by the authors as taking a deliberate stand operationally similar to absention. See discussion below on the significance of Z votes.

11. In view of the automatic support which Egypt can expect from both the communist and the Muslim worlds, abstention or absence by any Third World country is viewed by Israel as an achievement, according to a responsible official of the Israeli Foreign Ministry, Jerusalem, December, 1972.

12. For background on the OAU involvement in the Middle East conflict, see Susan Aurelia Gitelson, "The OAU Mission and the Middle East Conflict," *International Organization* 27, no. 2 (Summer 1973): 413-29; and Ran Kochan, "An African Peace Mission in the Middle East," *African Affairs* 72, no. 287 (April 1973): 186-96. The precipitous break in diplomatic relations is analyzed in Susan Aurelia Gitelson, "Israel's African Setback in Perspective," *Jerusalem Papers on Peace Problems* no. 6 (May 1974); and id., "Why do Small States Break Diplomatic Relations with Outside Powers? Lessons from the African Experience," *International Studies Quarterly* 18, no. 4 (December 1974): 451-84.

13. Scores have been allocated to each vote according to the following key: X and Y votes—2 scores each (explicit expression of support) and Z vote—1 score only (implicit expression of stand taken). Since Y and Z have a common operational significance, they have been considered as a single voting unit (2Y + Z).

14. These two types have been grouped together because the offsetting effect within the balancing SAS is operationally similar to the SAS which chooses to maintain a consistent record of abstention.

15. For example, see the Soviet draft resolution A/L 519, 5th Emergency Session, July 1967, which was finally rejected by a majority of General Assembly members.

16. For example, see A/Res. 2628 (XXV) of November 5, 1970.

17. For example, see A/Res. 2672 (XXV), para. 6, December 12, 1970.

18. See A/Res. 2535 (XXIV), December 10, 1969, para. A and C are humanitarian, while para. B belongs to Category 1.

19. Issues falling into the category of "important questions" (according to Article 18, paragraph 2 of the UN Charter) can be endorsed only if a two-thirds majority of the members present vote for their adoption. All other issues come under the heading "other questions" (Article 18(3) of the Charter) may be adopted by a

simple majority of the members present and voting. Israel has often objected to the change in status from "important" to "other" questions because this would have enhanced the adoption of resolutions backed or initiated by Egypt. For example, see A/L 584 (XXIV) December 12, 1969, and A/L 619 (XXV) December 8, 1970.

20. The Latin American draft contained most of the textual components agreeable to the African states (Category 1). The fact that it was proposed by a group of states usually known to vote in a manner favorable to Israel, coupled with the fact that the draft had been aimed at counteracting the Asian-African draft, led to a different voting pattern (Category 4). See A/L 604 (XXV), November 11, 1970.

21. This can be seen particularly in A/Res. 3151 (XXVIII) on the "Situation in South Africa Resulting from the Policies of Apartheid" adapted at the 2201st Plenary meeting, December 14, 1973.

22. Compare A/Res. 2463 (XXVII), para. E, with the resolution on Palestinian rights in the 28th Assembly of December 1973, A/Res. 3090 (XXVIII) (see Appendix 2).

23. In Category 2, for example, the average number of states voting X rose to 23. Marked changes were also noticeable in Categories 3 and 4. See Table 4.

24. Woronoff points out quite correctly that membership in radical or moderate groups in Africa is very fluid because the "tenure of office is at best uncertain; a *coup d'état* can alter the official policy of a country overnight or rarely, a gradual change could bring a country from one coup to another" (*Organizing African Unity*, p. 601). In spite of these objective difficulties, specialists in African affairs often refer to the following black African countries as being "radical," particularly during most of the period discussed: Burundi, Congo (B), Equatorial Guinea, Guinea, Mali, Tanzania, Uganda and Zambia. For an illuminating attempt to define radical and moderate states, see Immanuel Wallerstein, "The Range of Choice: Constraints on the Policies of Governments of Contemporary African Independent States," in *The State of the Nations*, ed. Michael F. Lofchie (Berkeley and Los Angeles: 1971), esp. pp. 28, 31.

25. Julius Nyerere of Tanzania and Leopold Senghor of Senegal are Catholics and Yakubu Gowon of Nigeria and Kenneth Kaunda of Zambia are Protestants (both are sons of ministers).

26. Many states which have diplomatic relations with Israel have located their embassies in Tel Aviv rather than in Jerusalem. Such an act follows the lines suggested by the UN partition Plan of 1947, according to which Jerusalem was supposed to become an internationalized city rather than the capital of either Israel or Jordan. Establishing an embassy in Jerusalem, the self-proclaimed capital of Israel, and not in Tel Aviv, has always been considered by Israeli policymakers as an expression of friendship towards Israel.

27. Three countries—Botswana, Lesotho and Malawi—while nominally independent, are geographically and politically linked to South Africa and frequently tend to follow that country's lead on many foreign policy issues.

28. Religion may not be a dominant factor in policy formulation. The fact that the State of Israel has been associated with the Holy Land, however, has been mentioned on occasion as having affected the attachment of some black African leaders to Israel.

29. For black African views on the Southern African problem, see, for example, Yashpal Tandon, "South Africa and the OAU: The Dialogue on the Dialogue Issue," *Mawazo*, (Makerere University, Kampala) 3, no. 2 (December 1971): 3-16.

30. See Christopher Clapham, "Ethiopia and Somalia," *Adelphi Papers*, no. 93 (December 1972): 1-23; Catherine Hoskyns, *Case Studies in African Diplomacy: 2, The Ethiopia-Somali-Kenya Dispute, 1960-1967* (Dar es Salaam: Oxford University

Press, 1969); Saadia Touval, *The Boundary Politics of Independent Africa* (Cambridge, Mass.: Harvard University Press, 1972), and their bibliographies.

31. Although Ghana has become somewhat more radical since the National Redemption Council assumed power in January 1972. See West Africa and article on Ghana in *Africa Contemporary Record, 1972-73*, ed. Colin Legum (New York: Africana, 1973), pp. B595-B614. Ghana's voting behavior followed suit, until by 1972 it had moved almost entirely to X votes.

32. Although Colin Legum indicated more radical manifestations in Zaire since 1971. Colin Legum, ed., *Africa Contemporary Record*, pp. B560-B572. Also see Sam Uba, "Zaire's New Image," *Africa*, no. 30 (February 1974): 12-15.

33. See Melvin Small and J. David Singer, "The Diplomatic Importance of States, 1816-1970: An Extension and Refinement of the Indicator," *World Politics* 25, no. 4 (July 1973): 577-99, on the significance of diplomatic missions for attesting political proclivities.

34. Israel's technical assistance to African countries during the early sixties was a determining factor in many black African states' attitudes toward Israel. Nonetheless, this aid was always moderate in scope and it became increasingly less significant compared to the rapidly growing demands and needs of African states. When this process coincided with the reduction in foreign aid by traditional patrons, many black African states became willing to turn to any new source of financial aid. This reality was well understood by some Arab countries (particularly Libya and Saudi Arabia), which were ready to exchange financial aid for political support on the Israeli-Arab conflict. On Israel's assistance programs to African countries in the early sixties, see Leopold Laufer, *Israel and the Developing Countries* (New York, 1967); and Mordechai E. Kreinin, *Israel and Africa: A Study in Technical Cooperation* (New York, 1964).

35. Shifts in voting behavior by Dahomey, Madagascar and Rwanda in Cluster B were primarily due to internal changes in their regimes and preceded the more drastic act of severing diplomatic relations with Israel. See *Africa Research Bulletin* (1972).

22

Meron Medzini

ASIAN VOTING PATTERNS ON THE MIDDLE EAST AT THE U N GENERAL ASSEMBLY

Any effort to describe and explain the policy of a number of Asian nations towards Israel as seen exclusively by their voting record and speeches at the UN, is bound to be both erroneous and misleading. The voting habits of certain Asian nations, primarily those "neutral" in their attitude to the Arab-Israeli conflict, did not necessarily reflect their relations with Israel. Until the Yom Kippur War of October 1973, Asian nations friendly to Israel sought to separate their UN voting from the maintenance of normal bilateral relations with Israel. They stressed the bilateral element particularly when their vote was unfriendly to Israel.

Few Asian nations ever voted in the United Nations on matters that concerned the Arab-Israeli conflict with any degree of impartiality, preferring not to judge the issue strictly by its merits. In most cases their voting was the result of many factors, most of them not directly connected with the Arab-Israeli dispute but with other factors, such as loyalty to the Third World, their relations with Arab states, the degree of their dependence on Middle Eastern oil, and their ties with either Moscow or Peking. Much of the effort was concentrated in the General Assembly, where there was no great power veto. Another important reason for voting against Israel on most issues had to do with the need for Arab and African votes in the United Nations on matters that concerned certain Asian nations directly, such as the Indo-Pakistani conflict and the Indonesian-Dutch conflict in the late 1940s and early 1960s over Western Irian.

Unlike African nations, veteran Asian states have not shown much trust in the United Nations, and expressed little belief that it would help solve their problems. Disillusionment with the United Nations which became evident to African nations in the early 1970s, was not that noticeable to Asian states which had little expectations from the world body. For analytical purposes it is helpful to divide Asian nations members of the United Nations into three groups, and study their relations with Israel and their voting patterns at the United Nations.

MUSLIM STATES

No relations have ever existed between Israel and the chief Muslim states of Asia. Afghanistan, Pakistan, Indonesia and Malaysia (and later Bangladesh), consistently refused to establish any ties with Israel. Afghanistan voted consistently against partition of Palestine, admission of Israel to membership in the United Nations, and during the 1956 Sinai War, the 1967 Six-Day War and after the 1973 Yom Kippur War, voted against Israel in all the resolutions tabled before the General Assembly. The few occasions on which Afghanistan abstained had to do with extension of the mandate of the United Nations Emergency Force (UNEF) that functioned along the Israeli-Egyptian Armistice Demarcation Lines from November 1956 to May 1967. Similar consistent anti-Israel voting was that of Pakistan. In addition to being a Muslim nation, it needed Arab support in its struggle against India. Thus there were never any surprises when it came to Pakistan. Even after the establishment of Bangladesh, and its recognition by Israel in February 1972, the former did not respond and the Israeli initiative went unanswered. Indonesia was a somewhat different matter. Israel extended recognition to Indonesia in January 1950 and there were hopes that ties would be established. Israeli visitors were admitted to Indonesia until 1953, but from 1954 Indonesia refrained from any ties, although it was one of the moderate Asian and Muslim nations when it came to expressing its views in the General Assembly. In later years, Indonesia would need Arab votes for its quarrel with Holland over Western Irian and later when it fought with neighboring Malaysia, and for a time left the United Nations altogether. Malaysia and Israel maintained unofficial ties in 1957-58. But Arab pressure became too much and these ties were broken off in 1959. Malaysia was also consistent in its anti-Israel voting.

COMMUNIST STATES

Israel recognized the People's Republic of China as early as January 1950, but no ties have been established due to many factors. Until it entered the United Nations 1971, Peking showed little interest in UN resolutions on

Palestine. But it needed Arab votes for the time when it would be seated instead of Nationalist China, and those votes had to be cultivated. In 1965 China recognized the Palestine Liberation Organization (PLO) and permitted it to open offices in Peking. Throughout the years Israel abstained on the issue of the legitimacy of the Nationalist Chinese representation, thus earning the rebuke of both Taiwan and Peking. Finally it voted to seat Peking in the United Nations and opposed the expulsion of Taiwan. Since its admission to the United Nations, Communist China has either voted against Israel or abstained, particularly in the Security Council.

Israel never maintained relations with the People's Republic of Mongolia, and it was to be expected that the latter would vote against Israel in the United Nations, which it did soon after it was admitted to the world body. Although they have not been members of the United Nations, Israel never had any diplomatic or other ties with North Korea and North Vietnam (but had an embassy in Saigan and has one in Seoul). Whether the former were closer to Moscow or to Peking, they were bound to be hostile to Israel and friendly to the Arabs. Israel was seen as a friend of U.S. imperialism and Zionism was equated with colonialism.

"NEUTRAL" STATES

The position of "neutral" states was dictated by a multitude of considerations. India voted against partition of Palestine and recommended establishment of a federal regime in that country. India based its attitude to Israel on its own bitter experiences following partition of the Indian subcontinent and the establishment of Pakistan on purely religious grounds. India needed Arab votes in the United Nations because for many years the Indo-Pakistani conflict was on the agenda of either the General Assembly or the Security Council. India needed the Arabs for economic reasons and, finally, there was a large Muslim majority in India that the Delhi government could not ignore. It took India more than two years to recognize Israel (September 1950), but diplomatic relations were never established. Israel had to contend with a Consulate General in Bombay, while India refused to dispatch any representative to Israel. Indian voting has been consistently anti-Israeli. The late Pandit Nehru was a leading figure in Third World politics with Nasser and Tito, and he would not bow to Indian public opinion, as expressed in the Indian press, to become more friendly to Israel. Israeli expectations stemming from similar colonial experiences, a socialist ideology and Indian protestations of justice and equality were bound to be dashed. Even support for India against China in 1962 was not publicly acknowledged or appreciated. It was clear to Israel that India was a "tone setter" among the nonaligned nations of Asia, and many would look to India before they cast their votes—in addition to the idea of bloc solidarity. Nationalist China was irked at Israel's recognition of the People's Republic of China, and it needed

Arab votes to help it in the annual struggle to defeat attempts to seat Peking. These attempts were finally unsuccessful and Taiwan was, for all intents and purposes, expelled from the United Nations. Having abstained in the crucial partition vote, Nationalist China then either voted against Israel or abstained. It never used its veto in Security Council voting, but in that body too, China voted against Israel.

The position of Japan was the most difficult among Asian nations. Its dependence on Middle Eastern oil made it highly vulnerable to any trouble in that area. Since Japan is the most industrialized nation in Asia, the Tokyo government would have to be very careful not to antagonize the Arab states. It found a simple solution in its votes—it declared that Japan upheld the United Nations and its resolutions on the Palestine question. Thus Japan, since it was admitted to the United Nations in 1956, either voted against Israel or abstained. In the wake of the Yom Kippur War, the Arab oil embargo and the quadrupling of the price of oil, Japan felt it had to follow a far more careful policy. In the 1974 General Assembly that invited the PLO and dealt with the rights of Palestinians, Japan abstained in the voting. It realized that Israel still had some influence when it came to the export and sale of Japanese goods abroad. It also understood that by voting blindly with the Arabs it was opening itself up for additional pressure.

Relations between Israel and Cambodia were cordial until the late 1960s. Israel recognized the independence of Cambodia in 1955, it opened an embassy in Phnom Penh in 1967 and Foreign Minister Eban visited that country in that year. But following the 1967 war and above all, the aspirations of Prince Norodom Sihanouk to play a major role in the Third World, he began to move his country towards the Arab line. When he was deposed in 1970, the succeeding government maintained ties with Israel, but in the United Nations it either voted against Israel or abstained. This was normally explained by the Khmer government as being unimportant and irrelevent to good relations between itself and Israel. Similar explanation was given to Israel by Laos, which on rare occasions voted with Israel, but preferred to go along with the majority of Asian nations. Since relations between Israel and Laos were never very close—there was no Israeli ambassador resident in Vientiane—Israel could not expect a different attitude.

Nepal is another country that has been very friendly to Israel, and the recipient of large-scale Israeli technical and military aid. An Israeli president visited Nepal in 1966 in response to the state visit to Israel of King Mahendra V. But Nepal preferred to maintain its ties with Israel on two levels. In the United Nations to support anti-Israel resolutions, while retaining good bilateral relations. Singapore, another Asian nation which was the recipient of Israeli military and technological aid, voted against Israel on a number of occasions, but asked that this not be debited to it, as UN votes did not necessarily reflect its true attitude to Israel. Ceylon voted against Israel since

1956, although it maintained diplomatic ties with Jerusalem until 1970.

Two Asian countries tried to play a more independent role in their UN voting. One was the Philippines, the only Asian nation that voted for partition of Palestine and the establishment of a Jewish state. The other was Thailand. But on the whole, the performance of the two can also be said to have followed the general line of Asian nations, not to rock the boat, not to be overly independent and above all, not to ascribe much importance to UN voting.

Table 2 shows that on the whole, Asian nations did not vote in favor of Israel. They were not too interested in General Assembly voting, knowing well that votes there had only limited value, and Assembly decisions, unlike Security Council decisions, were basically recommendations. A number of Asian governments were annoyed with Israel for asking them to vote for pro-Israel resolutions. Here, Israel at times said that UN votes did not amount to much, but on the other hand, persistently asked for votes. Israeli diplomats often reported to Jerusalem that it was impossible to get the votes of Asian states and that the effort was wasteful and caused embarrassment to all sides concerned. Israel's effort to get Asian nations to join an Afro-Latin American initiative in 1961 toward direct Arab-Israeli talks, met with failure.

CONCLUSIONS

Israel's position in the United Nations reflected its international standing only partially. The makeup of the United Nations was bound to make it an anti-Israel body. Bloc solidarity, Arab pressure, the need for Arab votes, the desire to hit at a country they considered closely aligned to the United States, all these considerations played a role in the Asian voting pattern. The United Nations was a more remote organization to most Asian nations and their expectations of it were minimal compared with African or Latin American hopes. Not all of them were aware of the "Jewish question" in the past, knew either nothing or very little of the special ties of Jews to the Land of Israel, and the concept of human rights had different meaning to different Asian nations. All this was seen in their UN voting, which was consistently anti-Israel. Israel did not even express public regret over the manner in which certain Asian nations voted. Israel too was more interested in bilateral relations and tried to nurture these more than it cared about UN voting, which was sometimes a nuisance for Israeli representatives serving in Asia.

Israel understood that Asia was part of the Third World, but it also realized that certain states in the continent did not consider themselves wholly committed to bloc politics. In the final analysis, when it came to voting, they were pressured into bloc voting. There were not too many surprises in the Asian voting, but it does not always reflect the voting pattern of the Third World.

TABLE 1 Israeli-Asian Diplomatic Relations

Country	Recognition of Israel de facto	de jure	Recognition by Israel	State of Relations
Afghanistan				
Bangladesh				
Burma	Dec. 5, 1949		Feb. 4, 1972	Embassies in Rangoon and Tel Aviv
China (Nationalist)		March 2, 1949		
China (People's Rep.)				
India		Sep. 18, 1950	Jan. 9, 1950	Israeli Consulate General in Bombay
Indonesia			Jan. 13, 1950	
Japan			May 15, 1952	Embassies in Tokyo and Tel Aviv
Khmer (Cambodia)			Feb. 15, 1955	Relations broken, April 1975
Laos			Feb. 13, 1955	Israeli Embassy in Vientiane, non-resident Laotian ambassador
Malaysia			Sep. 17, 1963	
Maldives			Sep. 22, 1963	Relations suspended, May 1975
Mongolia				
Nepal		Sep. 7, 1950		Israeli Embassy in Katmandu, nonresident Nepalese ambassador
Pakistan				
Philippines		April 1, 1949		Embassies in Manila and Tel Aviv
Singapore			Aug. 9, 1965	Israeli Embassy in Singapore
Sri-Lanka (Ceylon)	March 24, 1949	Sep. 18, 1957		Relations broken, Aug. 20, 1970
Thailand		Sep. 25, 1950		Israeli Embassy in Bangkok, nonresident Thai ambassador

Note: Israel also has an embassy in Seoul, South Korea, and had an embassy in Saigon until the communist takeover in April 1975.

TABLE 2

Session Number	SI	II	III	III	IV	ESI	ESI	ESI	ESI
Date	5/15/47	11/29/47	12/11/48	5/11/49	12/9/49	11/2/56	11/4/56	11/5/56	11/7/56
Resolution	106	181	194	273	303	997	998	1000	1001
Afghanistan	N	N	N	N	Y	Y	Y	Y	Y
Bangladesh	—	—	—	—	—	—	—	—	—
Bhutan	—	—	—	—	—	—	—	—	—
Burma	—	—	A	N	Y	Y	Y	Y	Y
China (Nat.)	Y	A	Y	Y	Y	Y	Y	Y	Y
China (P.R.)	—	—	—	—	—	—	—	—	—
India	Y	N	A	N	Y	Y	Y	Y	Y
Indonesia	—	—	—	—	—	Y	Y	Y	Y
Japan	—	—	—	—	—	—	—	—	—
Khmer*	—	—	—	—	—	Y	Y	Y	Y
Laos	—	—	—	—	—	A	A	A	Y
Malaysia	—	—	—	—	—	—	—	—	—
Maldives	—	—	—	—	—	—	—	—	—
Mongolia	—	—	—	—	—	—	—	—	—
Nepal	—	—	—	—	—	Y	Y	Y	Y
Pakistan	—	N	N	N	Y	Y	Y	Y	Y
Philippines	B	Y	Y	Y	Y	Y	Y	Y	Y
Singapore	—	—	—	—	—	—	—	—	—
Sri-Lanka†	—	—	—	—	—	Y	Y	Y	Y
Thailand	A	B	Y	A	A	Y	Y	Y	Y

Key: *(Cambodia)   †(Ceylon)   Y = Yes   N = No   A = Abstain   B = Absent

Resolution Code:
106   Creation of a Special Committee on Palestine (UNSCOP).
181   Future government of Palestine (Partition Resolution).
194   Creation of a conciliation commission, Arab refugees.
273   Israel's admission to the United Nations.
303   International regime for Jerusalem and the Holy Places.
997   Immediate cease-fire.
998   Plan for setting up UN Emergency Force (UNEF).
1000   Establishment of a United Nations Force.
1001   Authority of United Nations Force.
1002   Immediate withdrawal of Israeli, British, and French troops from Egypt.
1120   Calls upon Israel, Britain, and France to evacuate their forces from Egypt.
1122   Administrative and financial arrangements for UNEF.
1123   Immediate withdrawal of Israeli forces from Sinai.
1124   Demand for the completion of Israeli withdrawal from Sinai.

TABLE 2 (Continued)

ESI 11/7/56 1002	XI 11/24/56 1120	XI 11/26/56 1122	XI 6/19/57 1123	XI 2/2/57 1124	XII 2/2/57 1125	XIV 12/5/59 1441	XV 4/24/61 1604	XVI 12/20/61 1725	XVI 12/20/61 1733
Y	Y	Y	Y	Y	Y	A	Y	Y	A
—	—	—	—	—	—	—	—	—	—
—	—	—	—	—	—	—	—	—	—
Y	Y	Y	Y	Y	Y	Y	Y	A	Y
Y	A	Y	Y	Y	Y	A	A	Y	A
—	—	—	—	—	—	—	—	—	—
Y	Y	Y	Y	Y	Y	Y	Y	Y	Y
Y	Y	Y	Y	Y	Y	Y	Y	A	Y
—	—	—	Y	Y	Y	Y	A	Y	Y
Y	Y	A	Y	Y	Y	Y	Y	A	Y
A	Y	B	Y	Y	Y	Y	A	Y	Y
—	—	—	—	—	—	Y	N	Y	Y
—	—	—	—	—	—	—	—	—	—
—	—	—	—	—	—	—	—	A	N
Y	Y	Y	Y	Y	Y	A	Y	A	Y
Y	Y	Y	Y	Y	Y	Y	Y	Y	Y
Y	Y	B	Y	Y	Y	Y	Y	A	A
—	—	—	—	—	—	—	—	—	—
Y	Y	Y	Y	Y	Y	Y	A	Y	Y
Y	Y	Y	Y	Y	Y	Y	A	A	Y

1125	Restoration of Armistice after Israeli withdrawal from Sinai.
1441	Financial arrangements for UNEF during 1960.
1604	Report of director of UNRWA on Palestinian refugees.
1725	Report of director of UNRWA on Palestinian refugees.
1733	Cost and maintenance of UNEF.
A/519	Soviet draft resolution following the Six-Day War.
A/523	Latin American draft resolution following the Six-Day War.
A/522	Yugoslav draft resolution after the Six-Day War.
2253	Israel to rescind all measures taken on Jerusalem.
3210	Palestine Liberation Organization (PLO) to be invited to the General Assembly.
3230	Limits on the rights of speech in the General Assembly.
3236	Rights of Palestinians.
3237	Status of the PLO as observer.
3240	Situation in the territories.
3246	Rights of displaced persons.

TABLE 2 (Continued)

ESV 6/19/67 A519	ESV 6/30/67 A523	ESV 7/3/67 A522	ESV 7/4/67 2253	XXIX 10/14/74 3210	XXIX 11/14/74 3220	XXIX 11/22/74 3236	XXIX 11/22/74 3237	XXIX 11/29/74 3240	XXIX 12/17/74 3246
Y	N	Y	Y	Y	Y	Y	Y	Y	Y
—	—	—	—	Y	Y	Y	Y	Y	Y
—	—	—	—	Y	B	Y	Y	Y	Y
A	A	Y	Y	A	B	Y	Y	Y	Y
A	Y	A	Y	—	—	—	—	—	—
—	—	—	—	Y	Y	Y	Y	Y	Y
Y	N	Y	Y	Y	Y	Y	Y	Y	Y
Y	N	Y	Y	Y	Y	Y	Y	Y	Y
N	Y	Y	Y	Y	A	A	A	A	Y
Y	A	Y	Y	Y	A	Y	Y	Y	Y
N	A	A	Y	A	B	A	A	A	Y
Y	N	Y	Y	Y	Y	Y	Y	Y	Y
—	B	B	B	B	B	B	B	B	B
Y	N	Y	Y	Y	Y	Y	Y	Y	Y
A	A	Y	Y	Y	A	A	Y	Y	Y
Y	N	Y	Y	Y	Y	Y	Y	Y	Y
N	Y	N	Y	Y	Y	Y	Y	Y	Y
A	A	A	Y	Y	B	A	Y	Y	Y
A	N	Y	Y	Y	Y	Y	Y	Y	Y
A	Y	A	Y	Y	Y	Y	A	Y	Y

23

Benjamin Rivlin

and Jacques Fomerand

CHANGING THIRD WORLD PERSPECTIVES AND POLICIES TOWARDS ISRAEL

Israel's image among countries of the Third World has not always been a positive one, but it was never so uniformly negative as manifested in the fall 1974 debate in the United Nations General Assembly (UNGA). In the past, although Israel has had its detractors among Third World states, it has also had its friends. About a decade ago Israel's Third World friends far outnumbered its non-Arab detractors. Now to all intents and purposes, Israel has been completely isolated from the Third World and has been paired with South Africa as the leading public enemy of this amorphous bloc of states. How has this change taken place? Why? What is the current perspective of Israel held by the non-Arab states of the Third World? Is it a monolithic attitude? Is it subject to change?

THIRD WORLD STRUCTURE AND ORIENTATION

The Third World as we know it today in international politics is a loose tricontinental coalition of Asian, African and Latin American states. It is made up of so disparate a group of states that it would seem difficult, if not impossible, to discern a common psychological and social frame of images throughout its length and breadth. The Third World literally girdles the globe, mostly in the Southern Hemisphere and includes within it every climatic, cultural, racial and political difference in the world. Despite these disparities and contradictions, certain Third World psychological and social predispositions can be discerned, whose distinctiveness critically affects the perception these countries and their leaders have of Israel and of the Arabs. What Third World states have in common is their recent emergence on the international scene as independent actors, representing states generally lacking in industrialization and crippled by social and economic underdevelopment. Most Third World states have had little experience as independent international actors, having been passive subjects of the politics of others rather than active participants themselves.

There is a common experience of political subordination and economic poverty implanted within the peoples of the Third World and their elites—bitter memories of having been victimized by foreign exploiters and white racists. Such memories provide the foundation for the emergence of anticolonialism and antiimperialism as the dominant ideology of nationalist struggles for self-determination and independence. It is characteristic of this ideology to be concerned about the fate of all oppressed colonial peoples. Thus, as soon as a significant number of former colonies attained independence and membership in the United Nations, they launched a campaign for decolonization.

The "founding fathers" of the Third World coalition were the Asian states, which were in the United Nations almost from the beginning of the organization and provided most of the leadership and participants in the 1955 Bandung Afro-Asian Conference. A significant part of this group was composed of nine Middle East Arab states (including Egypt, Libya and Sudan, technically not Asian states). From 1956, African states became independent in increasing numbers. They immediately attained membership in the United Nations and entered into contact with the Asian states there. The existence of a half dozen North African Arab states among the African bloc constituted a bridge between Africans and Asians. This bridge was strengthened after 1962 when the newly independent Algeria joined this group since it had achieved preeminence in the Third World because it won its freedom from a major power after a protracted struggle.

Although Latin American states are the oldest in terms of political independence and membership in the United Nations, they became the last adherents to the Third World movement. Having enjoyed political independence since the early nineteenth century, most Latin American countries, particularly their elites, did not perceive themselves in this camp until more recently. In 1949 when the UNGA was deciding the fate of Italy's former colonies in Africa, the Latin American bloc of nineteen states favored the return of Tripolitania and Somaliland to Italian rule under trusteeship, perceiving itself as the protector of fellow Latin (Italian) interests in Africa.[1] Anticolonialism and antiimperialism seemed remote from their consciousness at the time. It was only after the Castro revolution in Cuba and the spread of Castro-like "progressive revolutionary" forces throughout Latin

America, stressing the image of Latin America as the victim of U.S. economic imperialism, that a common ideological framework emerged, welding Latin America into the Third World bloc.

THIRD WORLD PREDISPOSITIONS TOWARDS ISRAEL AND THE ARABS

In seeking to understand Third World perspectives of the Arab-Israeli dispute, anticolonialist/antiimperialist ideology must be recognized as the lens through which the Third World views this conflict. But, who would be perceived as the oppressed victim of colonialism—Jews or Arabs?

Israel's Third World Profile

Located geographically on the Asian continent, and sharing many major attributes of Third World states, Israel could have been perceived as part of the Third World. Given the diversity within this heterogeneous group of states, Israel's credentials could conceivably meet Third World criteria. Long victimized and oppressed, the Jews fought a war of national liberation in Palestine against a colonial regime in fulfillment of the principle of self-determination. At independence, Israel faced problems of economic development, social mobilization, political integration and modernization— the same problems that challenge Third World states. Although its leaders are primarily of Western Ashkenazic heritage, the majority of its people are oriental in origin, with traditional societal and cultural moorings that have been cut under the impact of modernism, as were those of most Third World peoples. Internationally, Israel started out its life as an independent state hoping to pursue a policy of nonalignment with both the United States and the Soviet Union.[2] Despite these apparent similarities, and some effort and desire to be identified as part of ths Third World, Israel was not accorded such recognition.

The Heritage of Colonialism and Imperialism

Israel's failure in this regard stems from the fact that Jews in Palestine were not viewed as natives but as foreigners, exponents of Western culture and agents of Western imperialism. Although Jews in Palestine fought the British colonial master, their struggle for independence was not accepted by the Third World as part of the struggle of dependent peoples in Asia and Africa against colonialism. On the contrary, Israel was viewed by key leaders of the emerging Third World as thwarting a colonial people, the Arabs of Palestine, in their fight for independence. Despite a sympathetic attitude towards Jews and even Zionist achievement in Palestine—Gandhi called Jews the "untouchables of Christianity" and denounced the "unenviable plight" of Jews in Europe, while Nehru acknowledged that "it is a fact that Jewish immigrants there [Palestine] had improved the country, introduced industries and raised standards of living"—the two great leaders of Indian nationalism came down unequivocably on the side of the Arabs. Both called Zionism "an accomplice of British imperialism" and viewed the Arabs as the aggrieved party. As Nehru stated in *Glimpses of World History*, "We must remember that Palestine is essentially an Arab country, and must remain so, and the Arabs must not be crushed and suppressed within their own homeland . . . ."[3]

Gandhi and Nehru were articulating a view that emerged directly from India's own struggle for independence and their attitude, expressed prior to the establishment of Israel, bears remarkable resemblance to the current Third World attitude towards Israel. In subsequent years, as increasing Asian and African colonies became engaged in their own anticolonialist struggle, quite understandably they manifested similar attitudes towards the Palestine problem. The anticolonialist/antiimperialist ideological lens directed the Third World toward a pro-Palestinian Arab and anti-Israeli position. This was reinforced by the largely Western bourgeois style of life that developed in Israel, by the treatment of the Arab minority, and by the collusion with Great Britain and France, the arch imperialists, in the 1956 Suez operation. Since 1967, Israel's heavy reliance upon the United States for military and economic aid eventually sharpened the negative image of Israel among Third World states.

Islamic and Judaic Heritage

While the anticolonialist/antiimperialist ideological orientation of the Third World constitutes the primary basis for anti-Israeli feelings in the Third World, it is by no means the only one. In evoking a sympathetic response, the Arabs have distinct advantage because of their Muslim religion. Islam is the predominant religion of many non-Arab states of Asia and Africa, in addition to being the faith of sizeable minorities in many others. Consciousness of Islamic solidarity has increased significantly as more African and Asian colonies have become independent. Since decolonization, there has been a sharp increase in contacts among the elite at world Islamic meetings, through the exchange of diplomatic representation, and at the United Nations. Communication has also taken place on the mass level, notably through the hajj. The preeminent place of Islam in the weltanschauung of this important segment of the Third World influences these states toward an anti-Israeli stance and establishes a solid core of pro-Arab sentiment within the Third World movement.

Lack of contact with Jews and unfamiliarity with their historical travail impede the development of a sympathetic understanding of Zionism and the rationale for the return of Jews to Palestine and establishment of the State of Israel. This is in marked contrast to the situation in the Western world, where Jewish identification with the Holy Land is readily comprehensible to Bible-reading Christians, and where guilt feelings over the pernicious effects of anti-Semitism have contributed to a sympathetic view of Israel. Most Third World countries have not had large Jewish populations in their midst and could not be expected to react to the Jews' plight in Europe as Westerners did. The Inquisition, the Dreyfus case, the pogroms of Eastern Europe and Hitlerian Germany were not part of their close experiences. Even with awareness and understanding of Jewish history, as noted in the case of Western-educated Mahatma Gandhi, affinity to the Arab experience and the desire to keep Muslims and Hindus united within the Congress movement overcame any potential sympathy for Zionist aspirations.

Sources of Perspective Diversity

Given the fact that some twenty Third World states are Arab and the centrality of the Palestine cause to the Arab world, it is not surprising that the Third World has become largely anti-Israeli. What is surprising is the length of time it has taken the Arabs to mobilize the Third World against Israel. Facing this potential opposition, one may ask how Israel managed to establish such close relations with large numbers of Third World states and maintain them over so long a period. The answer lies in the historical, cultural and experiential diversity within the Third World-to-be; this was evident at the time that Palestine partition was voted at the United Nations and over the next few years, in the differing perceptions and attitudes, not all unfavorable to Israel nor all favorable to the Arabs.

Of the three continental components of the Third World, Latin American states were most remote geographically from the Middle East. Unlike Africans and Asians they lacked any significant ties to the area. Until they recognized, under the impact of the Third World's radicalization, their common interests with Asian and Africa, Latin American states, while not hostile towards Arabs and Palestinians, were generally favorably predisposed towards the Jews and Israel. Their elites were primarily Christian and European in origin and in the area of foreign policy, particularly on more remote issues, Latin American perspectives were very much influenced by the position of the United States. Consequently, Latin American states shared the favorable attitude of Europeans towards Zionism and the establishment of Israel. When the Palestine partition resolution was adopted by the UNGA in 1947, Latin America provided thirteen out of the thirty-three affirmative votes with only one negative vote. Inasmuch as the partition plan passed by the barest two-thirds majority, each of these votes, plus the six Latin American delegations which abstained, were crucial in setting the stage for the establishment of the State of Israel.

The votes of the eight non-Arab Asian states in the United Nations in 1947 almost thwarted the adoption of the partition plan. Working closely with the Arab delegations, five Asian states voted against partition. Four out of the five were Muslim (Afghanistan, Iran, Pakistan and Turkey) and the fifth, India, boasted a Muslim population many times larger than that of most Arab states. Nationalist China abstained; Thailand was absent; and only the Philippines, just emerging from dependence status under the United States and still very much under American influence, voted for the resolution.

In contrast to the Asians and Latin Americans, only two black African states—Ethiopia and Liberia—were members of the United Nations at the time. Liberia, closely identified with the United States, voted in favor of partition while Ethiopia, having a large Muslim population, abstained. The Arabs' image among non-Arab Afro-Asian countries, including some Islamic states, was not an untarnished one. If the non-Arab Afro-Asians were unfamiliar with the Jews, many of them were all too familiar with Arabs, frequently holding them in contempt. Turks and Iranians were Muslims, but there exists a long-standing mutual antipathy between each of them and the Arabs, based on religious and cultural differences. More recently, geopolitical considerations have reinforced this antagonism so much so that Turkey and Iran could at times have been considered to be friendly, not merely ambivalent, towards Israel. Similarly, those parts of black Africa that have had pre-twentieth-century experience with the Arabs—and this includes all the states bordering on the Sahara, the central and East African states—retain "haunting memories" of Arab slave trade and of Arab raids into the regions located on the southern fringes of the Sahara.[4]

Augmenting this negative image held by black Africans of Arabs is the presence of substantial numbers of Arab immigrants (mostly Lebanese and Syrian) in a good number of African countries south of the Sahara. It has been pointed out that "most of these immigrants, for long a wealthy and privileged group, were viewed as symbols of foreign exploitation and were targets of the growing African nationalism. The tension between them and the emerging indigenous elites was considerable."[5]

Although most of these black African states were Muslim and antiimperialist, memories of unpleasant experiences with Arabs in the past and their dislike for contemporary Arabs in their midst made them suspicious of Arabs, and permitted them to pursue an independent policy toward the Palestine problem, which at times was quite friendly toward Israel.

EARLY ASIAN PERSPECTIVES

Diplomatic Normalcy and Neutrality

When the modern state of Israel was established in 1948, the independent Third World was almost entirely Asian in composition. These states had adhered to the Arab position in the UN voting on partition and on the admission of Israel. Within two years, the Philippines, Turkey, Iran, Nationalist China, Burma, Thailand and India—most of which had voted against Israel—recognized the new Jewish state. These actions were not a volte-face; these Asian states did not abruptly become friends of Israel and enemies of the Arabs. These were acts of recognition under international law, which merely imply that the states involved agree to behave toward each other as states normally do in international life.

The Asian states' recognition of Israel cannot be interpreted as having been anti-Arab. The Arab states had gone to war against Israel and had entered into armistice agreements with Israel—thus in a sense granting de facto recognition to the Jewish state. The intensity of Arab feelings, while understood, was not perceived at the time as being adamantly against a negotiated settlement with Israel. If normal international precedents were to be followed, Asian states could have expected that the Israeli-Arab armistice agreement would sooner or later be followed by negotiated peace treaties. The Asian states acted accordingly, not out of any special consideration for Israel, nor out of any antipathy towards the Arabs. Turkey tried to pursue a policy of "cordial relations with both the Arab States and Israel,"[6] while India explained its recognition of Israel as being in part motivated by its desire to serve, possibly in the "role of intermediary" between Israel and the Arab states. In a similar vein, Prime Minister U Nu of Burma, which became more friendly toward Israel than any other Asian state, said "We recognized Israel because it is a living reality." U Nu spoke of "our Arab friends" and our "Israeli friends," urging both to end their deadlock.[7] Recognition, ranging from full ambassadorial and ministerial exchange to the reciprocal establishment of consular and trade representatives, was accorded to Israel, not only from the five aforementioned Asian UN members (India, Burma, the Philippines, Iran and Turkey), but also by Ceylon, Laos, Cambodia, Japan and South Vietnam, not then members of the world organization. Through these acts, Israel was being accepted into the family of Asian nations. Pakistan, Indonesia and Afghanistan—unlike Turkey and Iran, their fellow Islamic Asian states—supported the Arab position, and refused to enter into any relations with Israel. The Asian states that entered into relations with Israel did so for varying reasons, under diverse circumstances and in differing degrees.

India

As a matter of principle, India advocated recognition of all states in the international arena. Ideological differences were no basis for nonrecognition. As far as India's relations with Israel were concerned, the government found it difficult to live up to its principles because it was subject to contradictory pulls from its tense Hindu-Muslim populations[8] while having to keep an eye on Pakistani reactions and their effects upon significant Arab bloc votes in the United Nations during the many debates on Kashmir. After procrastinating for a year, India finally recognized Israel but did not exchange ambassadors. Negotiations for an Israeli legation in Delhi did take place but they were never consummated because Israel insisted on reciprocity. The Indian government could not go this far, weighing the single state of Israel against the numerous Arab states and fearing an Arab-Pakistani rapprochement.[9] To this day, relations between India and Israel have never gone beyond some limited trade and consular representation.

Turkey

In the case of Turkey, the government acted in terms of political and economic self-interest, and in accordance with its Kemalist, laic self-image. "When it became clear that the issue [Palestine] involved factors which Turkey regarded as of vital concern to her own interests . . . [and] that the United States supported Zionist claims as an integral part of her own policy, Turkey had no qualms in promptly abandoning her support of the Arabs." Turkey found Israel to be a "profitable outlet for Turkish produce."[10] The Islamic appeal had little effect in drawing the Turks to the side of the Arabs. Internally, Turkey was in its most secularist phase. Upon joining the Baghdad Pact in April 1955, Turkey yielded to pressure from Iraq and relations with Israel cooled but were not broken; Turkey continued to recognize Israel and carry on normal relations. Turkey became Israel's most active trading partner in the Third World until it enlisted Arab support in the Cyprus dispute in 1969 and trade with Israel declined sharply.[11]

Iran

. Islam was by no means downgraded as a force within Iran, as it had been in Turkey. However, it did not prove to be an insurmountable obstacle to the development of significant relations with Israel, beginning in 1949 with the recognition of Israel, albeit on a de facto basis. Lack of formal diplomatic relations did not prevent Iran from becoming the major supplier of Israel's petroleum needs, nor did it impede the development of extensive Israeli technical assistance and training projects in Iran, in such areas as agriculture, tourism and rural cooperatives. Trade and exchange visits of academicians and students developed, and one of the earliest and most important collaborations between Israel and Iran involved "quiet ties between intelligence services,"[12] military liaison on a staff level, and military training. Iranian-Israeli relations hardly seem to be the kind of interstate relations entered into merely on a de facto basis. Yet, this is as far as the Shah would go in spite of his positive perceptions of the Jewish state itself[13] and a strong Israeli desire for full diplomatic relations. Attention to internal Muslim sensibilities and to intense pressure from Arab states, influenced the Iranian government not to establish de jure relations with Israel. These fundamental Muslim predispositions were not strong enough to overcome other factors such as Iran's traditional rivalry with neighboring Arab states, and its suspicion of certain Arab radical leaders, including Nasser, who were friendly with Iran's arch enemy, the Soviet Union.

Iran and Turkey shared similar geopolitical motivations for entering into relations with Israel, despite strong Arab objections. Both saw in Israel a useful counterweight to potentially threatening Arab strength which they viewed as inimical to their own interests. Both eventually shifted away from Israel and toward the Arabs when their interests dictated a change. In January 1975, during a trip to Egypt and Jordan, the Shah called for complete Israeli withdrawal from Arab territories and recognized the Palestine Liberation Organization (PLO) as the legitimate representative of Palestinians. Similarly, Turkey expressed support for the Palestinian people's "liberation struggle" and for the "right of the Arab countries to regain their occupied lands by all means."[14]

Burma

Neither geopolitical considerations nor traditional antipathy towards the Arabs figured in Burma's perception of Israel. The catalyst that brought these most unlikely partners together was their common adherence to the ideology of democratic socialism. Contact first took place on the trade union level in 1950 at the International Trade Union Congress in Belgrade. Within two years a delegation of Burmese socialists visited Israel and in 1953 Israel's Labor party, Mapai, participated as a full-fledged member at the First Asian Socialist Conference held in Rangoon. There, high-ranking Israeli and Burmese officials laid down the foundations of what eventually turned out to be the most fruitful and friendly relations that Israel was to have with any Asian state. Burma and Israel faced many similar problems and viewed them from the same ideological perspective. Israel was willing to extend technical assistance and enter into economic relations on the basis of reciprocity, without the threat of political and economic domination. Both countries exchanged diplomats and the ministerial level shortly after the First Asian Socialist Conference. On the economic and social level, a complex technical assistance program developed. On the diplomatic level, close ties were established and Burma repeatedly demonstrated a remarkable understanding of the Israeli position for any state to have, certainly a state from the Third World. For example, Burma, as one of the sponsors of the Afro-Asian conference at Bandung, fought unsuccessfully to have Israel invited to this first parley of the emerging Third World. At the conference itself, it tried to prevent discussion of issues involving Israel in Israel's absence. Later, while U Nu criticized Israel's preventive war in 1956, he stated publicly that Israel could plead "extenuating circumstances for her attack on Egypt." U Nu squarely attributed the lack of peace in the Middle East to the Arabs' unwillingness "to accept the fact of Israel."[15]

Bandung

By the time of the first Asian-African Conference in April 1955, Israel had succeeded in being recognized by many Asian states, most of which had opposed establishment of the revived Jewish state. Israel seemed certain of being invited to this conference conceived by its sponsoring powers— Burma, Ceylon, India, Indonesia and Pakistan—as being open to every independent state of Asia and Africa. Since many of the countries invited were unfriendly with other invitees and, in some instances, had not even extended diplomatic recognition to one another, the conference sponsors agreed that any state's acceptance of an invitation "would in no way involve or even imply any change in its views of the status of any other country."[16] Invitations were extended to states whose close identification with the West or Communist China made them controversial. Communist China and states which did not recognize its regime and even opposed its admission to the United Nations, were able to participate at the conference. Despite this pragmatic acknowledgement that a nation's ideology or legitimacy would not be compromised by participating in the meeting, Israel alone was not invited. As already noted, Burma pressed for Israel's participation. India, too in keeping with the principle of a conference open to all independent Asian states, favored Israel's inclusion. Ceylon took no stand on the question, but Pakistan and Indonesia were unalterably opposed, arguing that if Israel were invited, the Arab states, (which would constitute one-third of the participants) would boycott the conference. U Nu and Nehru acceded to the anti-Israeli pressure. Nehru admitted that "we felt that logically Israel should be invited, but when we saw that the consequences of that invitation would be that many others would not be able to come, then we agreed."[17] The failure to be invited was a severe setback for Israel, because it meant that Israel's claim as an Asian state with a right to participate in the formation of a nonaligned group of new nations was rejected.[18] It also revealed Israel's weakness in the Third World conference setting. A dozen participating states

at Bandung had relations with Israel of one form or another—ranging from
Burma's warm friendship, to India's begrudging acceptance. Their varying
attitudes could not be translated into a collective Third World (in this case
Asian) acceptance of Israel. On the whole Asia's attitude towards Israel was
at best ambivalent presenting "a curious pattern encompassing relationship,
semi-relationship and non-relationship," and being "an indication of the
fact that Israel's credentials for admission to the Asian community are
seriously questioned by many of its members and only gingerly endorsed by
some."[19]

Bandung was just the first of many future Third World meetings and
conferences at which a negative image of Israel would prevail. The joint
communiqué issued at the end of the Bandung Conference failed to mention
Israel at all, and supported "the rights of the Arab people of Palestine,"
while "calling for the implementation of the United Nations resolutions on
Palestine and the peaceful settlement of the Palestine question."[20] Although
the Arab delegations were unable to have a resolution accepted that branded
Israel "an illegitimate state and aggressor," in the words of Walter Eytan,
the Bandung Conference was "a blow from which Israel's standing in Asia
could not quickly recover."[21]

AFRICAN PERSPECTIVES, 1957-1973

Opportune Friend and Hopeful Model

The Bandung anti-Israeli perspective of the Palestine problem did not
carry over to Africa. Ironically, the one black African colony represented at
Bandung, the Gold Coast—in two years to become independent as
Ghana—was the first black African state to befriend Israel. As with Burma,
there were no cultural or historical ties that would bring these two widely
separated states together. Fortuitous circumstances contributed to Israel's
ability to establish close relations with Ghana. First, Israel had a consulate in
Accra, carried over from British colonial days, and thus had a representative
at Ghana's independence celebration. Egypt, later to be so much involved in
the Third World movement with Ghana, was not even invited. The Israeli
consul, Chanan Yavor, acted quickly and deftly in developing friendships
among Ghanaians. Second, a group of young Ghanians stopping off in Israel
on the way home from a conference in Indonesia extended their stay, having
been significantly impressed with what they had seen. John Tettegah,
Ghana's trade union leader, said in 1957 that during a ten-day visit to Israel
he had "learned more about trade unionism that he could have learned in a
British university in ten years, and that he decided to model Ghana's on the
Israeli Histadrut."[22] Third, a man of great influence in Ghana at the time
was the Pan-Africanist George Padmore, who felt profound sympathy for

the Jews and who had little use for Nasser, whom he considered to be a tool of the Russians. Most important, President Kwame Nkrumah played a unique and decisive role in the rapprochement between Israel and Ghana, which established a pattern to be emulated elsewhere in black Africa. Nkrumah's three major preoccupations as Ghana's president, as prime mover of Pan-Africanism, and as a Third World leader, not only shaped Ghana's attitude and policy towards Israel but also significantly influenced the development of friendly relations between many black African states and Israel.

Upon leading his nation to independence, Nkrumah was anxious to create a state that had not merely achieved token freedom. To avoid this, it was necessary to minimize dependence on the former mother country or on any other powerful external state. This posed a dilemma. Ghana's top priority was economic development, which required outside technical and economic assistance since the nation's colonial heritage left it inadequately prepared to undertake such development on its own. Confronted with this situation, Israel represented a most opportune friend to Nkrumah. Capable of providing much technical assistance as well as some financial help, Israel loomed as an attractive source of such aid. In the words of an Israeli diplomat, "he [Nkrumah] thought he could do much" and that "we could do much to help him. Indeed, his ideas of what we could provide were grandiose." [23]

The series of economic and technical assistance programs entered into between Ghana and Israel, beginning in 1957, were impressive. Cooperative programs were developed in four areas: trade, technical assistance, capital investment and exchange programs. Within one year Israeli trade, which had been virtually nonexistent with the Gold Coast, showed exports to Ghana exceeding $100,000 with imports reaching $300,000. Important trade agreements were signed in 1958 providing for a four-year program of exchange of Israeli manufactured goods for Ghanaian raw materials. A prominent feature of Israeli-Ghanaian relations was the establishment of joint economic enterprises, such as the Black Star Line and the Ghana National Construction Company, Ltd. In these companies, Ghana retained majority ownership while Israeli interests, ZIM navigation company and Histadrut's Solel Boneh were given minority shares which eventually were taken over by Ghana. In both instances, an important part of the agreements involved training for a potentially completely Ghanaian-run operation. With Israel's experience in the kibbutzim and moshavim serving as models, Israel provided technical assistance in city planning, irrigation and water development, cooperative farming, marketing and consumer cooperatives. This brief list does not fully describe the nature and intricacies of the Ghanaian-Israeli relationship. It does suggest the outline of this very fruitful relationship, which later was duplicated and expanded in many other African countries. [24]

In the decade between Ghana's independence and the 1967 Six-Day War, thirty black African countries gained independence and emulated Ghana by entering into a friendly relationship with Israel. Given Nkrumah's stature as a Pan-African leader, the relations and programs he established with Israel were bound to attract attention and serve as a model for other African states. Shortly after Ghana gained independence, Accra served as a Mecca for dissident nationalists, soon to assume leadership in their own newly independent states. A significant number of these leaders, such as Tom Mboya, Julius Nyerere, Hastings Banda and Kenneth Kaunda, were introduced to Israel by Nkrumah. In this way, Nkrumah was vouching for Israel as a legitimate friend of Africa's newly independent states. As a direct result of Nkrumah's introductions, numerous African nationalists visited Israel, and were impressed by what they saw.

While fairly ubiquitous and involving nearly every newly independent black African state, Israeli programs were modest, in keeping with the small size and limited capabilities of Israel, and relied on organization and motivation rather than on heavy machinery.[25] The type of Israeli aid programs throughout the continent south of the Sahara, generally followed the pattern originally established in Ghana. To these were added a number of military and paramilitary assistance projects, ranging from the training of pilots and parachutists to Nahal and Gadna-type programs, which combined military and specialized agricultural training.[26] As of 1966, twenty-one African states had received training or instruction in Nahal-type programs. Among the parachutists and officers receiving training in Israel were Mobutu Sese Soko of Zaire and Idi Amin of Uganda, both of whom eventually took over the leadership of their countries. In addition to these much publicized examples of Israel's military aid to Africa, there were several secret arrangements under which Israel provided assistance in particularly sensitive areas as well as nonmilitary training programs established in Israel for Africans.

At its height about 1965, between five hundred and six hundred African trainees in agriculture, science, medicine and cooperative management were in Israel at one time. All told, some six thousand Africans have been trained in Israel and some sixteen hundred Israeli experts have served in Africa. Every country south of the Sahara, except for Somalia, Mauritania and Guinea, established diplomatic relations with Israel. Somalia and Mauritania desisted because of their close affiliation with the Arab League, while Guinea's failure is attributable to its sharp break with France and its turn towards the Soviet Union for technical assistance and economic aid at independence. As for the overwhelming part of black Africa, Israel seemed to be very popular. Why? With the possible exception of Ethiopia, where the royal family and the Amharic elite claimed historic ties to Biblical Hebrews and felt very close to modern Israelis, most of black Africa had little direct knowledge of, or contact with, Israel. The rapid development of mutual cooperation between Israel and the new states of black Africa reflected specific needs of both parties. As did Ghana, all African states which successively became independent faced the problem of economic development and the need for outside help. Introduced by Nkrumah to Israel and cognizant of Israel's successful ventures in Ghana, they turned to the Jewish state with hope that they would be assisted and confident that they would not be dominated by a more powerful partner. What attracted Africans was that Israel was a small state that had created a variety of innovative socioeconomic institutions as it coped with problems of social mobilization and economic development. At this time, they perceived Israel as they perceived themselves—underdogs who had persevered despite adversity in the struggle for national existence. The words of Africans themselves provide the best testimony of the positive impression Africans had of Israel in these early days of their relationship. One African scholar is quoted as saying, "In the United States I can study the history of economic development; in Israel I can see economic development in action." [27] Tom Mboya, upon his return from a visit to Israel, wrote: "New African States have naturally shown great interest in Israeli experiments with different forms of cooperatives. . . . Any African who tours Israel cannot fail to be impressed by the achievements made in such a short time from such poor soil and with so few natural resources. We all tended to come away most excited and eager to return to our own countries and repeat all these experiments."[28] Julius Nyerere succinctly expressed the perception of Israel as an appropriate model for Africa when he said: "Israel is a small country . . . but it can offer a lot to a country like mine. We can learn a great deal because the problems of Tanganyika are similar to Israel's. . . . What are our problems? . . . two major tasks: building the nation and changing the face of the land, physically and economically."[29]

Israel's positive image in Africa was enhanced by the type of people it sent to carry out its programs. A number of African leaders have testified to the extraordinary contribution made by Israel's representatives to their countries. For example, in Ghana, "Israel's achievement . . . was the result of one man's diplomacy," Ambassador Ehud Avriel.[30] In Kenya, Tom Mboya wrote "Kenya has been fortunate in having the Israeli, Deputy Director of Agriculture, Arie Amir, to advise us . . ."[31] On the whole, Israel carefully selected only the most highly competent economic advisers for service in Africa, and their performance was favorably received by the host governments. Israel's programs were accomplished expeditiously with a minimum of red tape and in dealing with Africa, Israel avoided getting overextended and emphasized small projects that could be carried out efficiently.[32] Doudou Thiam, former foreign minister of Senegal, provided this assessment of Israel's achievement: "By an extremely able diplomacy, by concluding agreements for cooperation and technical assistance, and by the successes of its policy of economic development, Israel has become recognized as a valuable partner for the newly independent states of Africa."[33]

Complementing these positive evaluations of Israel and its technical assistance programs were some early negative images of the Arabs. As noted above, there existed memories in large parts of black Africa that established a tendency for a suspicious attitude towards Arabs. This suspicion, combined with gross unfamiliarity with the details of the Palestine problem and almost total ignorance of the existence of a human tragedy involving the Arabs of Palestine, provided a climate favorable to Israel in Africa. Black Africans, having found in the Jewish state a helpful and useful friend, resented efforts on the part of the Arabs to undermine Israeli-black African relations. Black Africans' resentment of Arabs formed part of a rivalry that for a time worked to the advantage of Israel.

Arab-black African rivalry, overplayed by some analysts and downplayed by others, was manifested in the jockeying between Kwame Nkrumah and Gamal Abdul Nasser for African leadership. Nasser's ambitions for Egypt were clearly enunciated in this book *Egypt's Liberation: The Philosophy of the Revolution*. Reminiscent of the European imperialist's civilizing mission argument, Nasser wrote: "We will never in any circumstances be able to relinquish our responsibility to support, with all our might, the spread of enlightenment and civilization to the remotest depths of the jungle."[34] Nkrumah, in opening the All-African People's Conference in Accra later in 1958, alluded to Nasser's African interest when he declared: "Do not let us forget that colonialism and imperialism may come to us yet in a different guise, not necessarily from Europe. We must alert ourselves to be able to recognize this when it rears its head and prepare ourselves to fight against it."[35] Certainly, Nasser's efforts to assume the role of top African leader brought him into conflict with Nkrumah, whose star was rising as black Africa's leading nationalist. The situation was described in these words: "The very stridency of the Egyptian claim for leadership repels many Africans, and this claim is often seen in Ghana as a challenge to the leadership of Africa."[36] Nasser moved on a wide front to establish himself as an African leader, notably supporting liberation movements from Algeria to the Congo. Our concern here is his use of the Palestine issue to gain a foothold in African affairs. At the outset, the Palestine issue was never considered by Africans on its own merits but rather as a manifestation of Nasser's designs to "lead" or "dominate" Africa. Accordingly, black Africans resisted becoming involved in the Palestine dispute on the side of the Arabs. At the very first Conference of Independent African States, in which five of the eight states participating were Arab (U.A.R., Libya,

Tunisia, Morocco, and Sudan), the Egyptians tried to press the Palestine question and the condemnation of Israel. They were thwarted in these efforts by Ghana. Before the year was out, the December 1958 All-African People's Conference, also meeting in Accra and attended by representatives of African parties, trade unions and nationalist organizations, "firmly resisted Egyptian efforts to label Israel an 'imperialist' state along with the United Kingdom and France."[37] Black Africans, notably Ghana, resented the intense Arab hostility towards Israel being made an issue at African conferences. They viewed Arab efforts as an attempt to involve them in a matter alien to them, and as a threat to their independence in that it challenged their right to have good relations with Israel. Tom Mboya, when questioned by Arab friends as to why he turned to Israel and not to the Arabs for aid, clearly stated the case for African independence from Arab interference when he said: "It would be morally wrong . . . if Kenya were to make enemies on the basis of other peoples' judgements."[38]

Israel: Expendable "Friend" vs. New-Found Arab "Brothers"

It would be a serious mistake to assume that during this period of black Africa's friendship, Israel was able to maintain an untarnished image or that the Arabs and their attitude on Palestine were uniformly held in low esteem. Nkrumah, steeped in the worldwide anticolonialist/antiimperialist struggle, was well aware of the way in which the modern State of Israel was established in Palestine, considering the country "as an imperialist enclave, but not an artificially created one, like Rhodesia."[39] Nyerere described "the establishment of the State of Israel" as "an act of aggression against the Arab people," even though he recognized that the international community, except for the Arabs, accepted the establishment of the Jewish state in Palestine following the holocaust in Europe.[40] Even the appropriateness of the Israeli model for African development was questioned. Tom Mboya, who first looked enthusiastically to Israel as a model, observed: " . . . but when you come to look at the Israeli systems coolly and dispassionately later, you find their introduction into Africa will not be as easy as you first thought."[41] The truth of Mboya's observation was substantiated in Israeli programs which failed to take root in Africa. One such program was the Mwanza land settlement project in Tanzania. Here, Israel tried to do something too quickly and at too high cost in a setting and under circumstances not appropriate to implementing the moshav and Lachish concepts.[42] The failure in Tanzania did not enhance Israel's image and may well have contributed to the outspoken opposition to Israel taken by President Nyerere.

The Nasser-Nkrumah rivalry never did develop into a deep-seated acrimonious affair. Rather, it took the form of subtle competition that was held under control because both sides saw advantages in uniting the African continent and playing down differences between North and South. This situation affected black African attitudes towards Israel and their perspective of the Palestinian problem. As rapprochement grew between the Arab North and black South, the latter's positive image of Israel was weakened, while the Palestinian's cause moved into the consciousness of black Africa. Nasser and Nkrumah headed opposing sides in this rivalry. Nasser was not the sole exponent of the Arab cause; he was joined by the other Arab states of North Africa, Morocco, Tunisia, Algeria, and Libya. In the South, joining Nkrumah as spokesmen for black Africa, were Leopold Senghor, Jomo Kenyatta, Julius Nyerere, Kenneth Kaunda, Sékou Touré, and others.

The shift in black Africa's attitude towards Israel did not take place abruptly. North Africans were anxious to be part of an evolving African community, and sought to avoid antagonizing the South unnecessarily. Nasser, particularly, was interested in being in the mainstream of African affairs. Nkrumah never acted to exclude North Africa nor Egypt from African affairs. On the contrary, he visited Egypt several times, was married to an Egyptian, and sought to build bridges between black Africa and Arab affairs. It has been suggested that Nkrumah viewed friendship with Nasser as aiding his own position of leadership in Africa. Developing friendly relations with Nasser meant loosening ties with Israel and accepting the Palestine issue as a legitimate concern of black Africa.[43]

The goal of the Arabs, insofar as Israel and Palestine were concerned, was to cultivate black African support for their position, but to do so without risking continental unity. They pursued a policy of education and political pressure aimed at bringing black Africans around to their position sooner or later. Serving as arenas for these efforts generally were frequent African unity conferences, and the African bloc at the UNGA.

The breakthrough for the Arabs came at the Casablanca Conference held in January 1961 and attended by six African states—Ghana, Guinea, Libya, Mali, Morocco and the United Arab Republic—and the Provisional Government of the Algerian Republic (G.P.R.A.). Although generally thought of as giving birth to the bloc of radical African states, the Casablanca Conference was ideologically mixed. Ghana, Guinea, Mali, U.A.R. and the G.P.R.A. gave the conference its radical stamp, while Morocco and Libya (then under King Idris) represented a conservative traditionalist orientation. Similarly, the primary issues that brought each of these countries to Casablanca varied. The radical states' aim was to organize a countervailing force to the French-dominated Union of African States and Madagascar, formed some months earlier in Brazzaville. Morocco saw utility in joining the radicals since to its chagrin the Brazzaville group had sponsored Mauritania's membership in the United Nations. The Congo, notably the question of

Lumumba and the issue over continuation of the UN forces, concerned all the conferees, although there were significant differences among them, notably between Ghana and the other radical states. All participants were equally concerned over France's use of the Sahara for nuclear testing and the war in Algeria. The problem of Palestine was not on the original agenda which, according to the call for the conference by Mohammed V, was "to help the Congo and Algeria in their struggle against imperialism, and to study the special case of the African states that will achieve independence in the near future." [44] The question of Palestine and Israel was uppermost in the minds of Arab participants, who were led by Nasser on this issue. To get favorable action, Nkrumah's friendship with Israel had to be circumvented. Nasser was able to achieve this as the interplay of conflicting goals and diverse interests was played out at the conference. In a classic example of log rolling, each participant succeeded in having the conference endorse his primary concern. Nkrumah got his African Charter, Morocco support for its Mauritanian position, the radical states their Congo resolution and Nasser a resolution that condemned Israel "as an instrument in the service of imperialism and neo-colonialist not only in the Middle East but also in Africa and Asia" and expressed deep concern over "depriving the Arabs of Palestine of their legitimate rights." [45] Israel was branded as "imperialist" not only in the Middle East but in Africa as well. Israel's position on basic African issues, for which this conference had been called, helped bring this about. Because of Algeria and the Sahara nuclear tests, France was a major object of concern at Casablanca. France, as Israel's major ally and supplier of arms at the time, was supported by Israel particularly in voting at the United Nations. Israel favored Tshombe over Lumumba in the Congo and was viewed as siding with apartheid because of the influential Jewish population in South Africa. In Israel's attitudes on African issues there was "enough to make African radicals suspicious of Israel even if these black radicals had no special Pan-African links with North Africans." [46]

The Casablanca Conference witnessed an interplay of diverse interests working to the disadvantage of Israel and demonstrating, as did Bandung before it, the great advantage held by the Arabs in conference settings. As Colin Legum pointed out: "Ghana was the only member which could have resisted the UAR's demand for branding Israel as an 'imperialist base,' as it had done at other conferences. But after the Congo debate, Dr. Nkrumah was unwilling to isolate himself on yet another point. Casablanca was the first occasion where a group of African States agreed to the UAR resolution on Israel." [47]

Agreeing to the anti-Israeli resolution did not automatically lead to an abandonment of friendly relations with Israel by the three sub-Saharan states. According to Mazrui, Nkrumah's reasons for accepting the condemnation of Israel were "Pan-African rather than anti-Israel," it was "a question of denouncing Israel to please North African friends, rather than out of genuine antagonism against Israel."[48] After the conference, Ghana, Guinea and Mali continued their dealings with Israel as though nothing had happened. Israel was still viewed as a beneficial partner in the economic and technical sphere; although adhering to the anti-Israeli resolution for politically expedient reasons, by their actions they rejected a total break with Israel. Nor did the Arabs seek such a break, no matter how much they may have preferred to have Israel cut off from black Africa. Neither did Israelis consider withdrawing their aid from Africa, even though some of their specialists foresaw a changing black African attitude towards Israel as a result of Arab pressures and changing world conditions.[49] In the years following Casablanca, both Arabs and Israelis considered it in their respective interests to avoid making demands that black Africans would feel as impinging upon their freedom of action as independent states. This did not prevent Arabs from waging a steady effort to undermine Israel's position in Africa and to commit black Africa to the side of the Palestinians, nor did it stop Israelis from trying to maintain and broaden their relations with African states.

The position of black African states was that the Arab-Israeli dispute was of no direct concern to them. Rather than taking one side or the other, their role was to maintain friendship with both sides and not permit either the Arabs or Israelis to undermine their relationship with the other. The Arabs, trying to dislodge Israel, were more aggressive in their efforts. Black Africans let it be known that they were unhappy with Arab, particularly U.A.R., efforts to introduce the Arab-Israeli problem at the Organization of African Unity Conference. In deference to African sensibilities, the Arabs, notably Nasser, did not press to have the matter discussed at OAU meetings for several years.[50] This changed after the 1967 Six-Day War. African states could no longer resist Egyptian pressure for support, especially when the issue was presented in terms of African territory—the Sinai—occupied by the aggressor state, Israel. Both within the OAU and the UNGA, African states had to confront the Arab-Israeli dispute. They could no longer avoid getting involved, if only to express an opinion through a vote. Despite a highly charged atmosphere and tremendous pressure for continental solidarity, black African states were not stampeded into supporting the Arabs and the UAR. At the Fifth Emergency Session of the UNGA, called immediately after hostilities ceased, two resolutions may be taken as indicative of pro-Arab and pro-Israeli sentiment, although both were anti-Israeli in the sense that they called for Israel's withdrawal from occupied territories. The resolution sponsored by eighteen Latin American states was considered to be less anti-Israeli because it coupled Israel's withdrawal with the Arab states ending the state of belligerency. The Yugoslavian resolution, cosponsored by seventeen Afro-Asian states including nine African—Burundi, Congo (Brazzaville), Guinea, Kenya, Mali, Senegal, Tanzania and Zambia—was considered to be pro-Arab. Excluding the six North African Arab states, as well as Somalia and Mauritania, the votes of the thirty black African states were distributed as follows:[51]

	Yugoslavian Resolution	Latin American Resolution
Yes	12	17
No	8	8
Abstention	10	5

African opinion was clearly divided. On the whole it could be considered favorable to Israel, since abstentions in these votes had a decidedly anti-Arab effect. An analysis of nine votes in the GA taken on a series of Cuban, Albanian, Russian and Yugoslavian resolutions and amendments that were clearly pro-Arab and hence anti-Israeli reveal the following breakdown of the 226 African votes cast:[52]

	No	Percent
Pro-Arab	46	17.2
Pro-Israeli	110	41.4
Abstention	110	41.4

Votes at the United Nations may not be revealing of true feelings but they provide clues where full statements are not available. A number of black African states expressed themselves on the subject and here, too, one encounters a variety of attitudes. One extreme is Malawi's President Hastings Banda's total support of Israel: "Israel did the right thing; to suggest that Israel was the aggressor was not only a distortion, but a prostitution of truth." In contrast is Guinea's breaking off diplomatic relations with Israel and its expression of full support for the Arab cause.[53]

Beginning with the OAU's fifth session in Algiers in 1968, Israel's friends had increasing difficulty preventing the organization from responding positively to the fraternal antiimperialist/colonialist appeal of Egypt and its other more radical members. Under the relentless pressure of Egypt, Algeria and others, the OAU passed resolutions calling upon Israel to withdraw from occupied territories in conformity with the celebrated UN Resolution 242 of November 1967. Each succeeding year OAU resolutions assumed an increasingly sharper tone of condemnation of Israel.[54] Despite these resolutions, most bilateral arrangements between black African states and Israel were not disturbed. Seeing utility in their continued relations with Israel in the economic and technical fields, these states did not turn their backs on Israel. In some instances such as Uganda, Chad, Ethiopia and Nigeria, bilateral arrangements were intensified. While in agreement with the pro-Arab lobby that Israel was wrong in not returning occupied territories, pro-Israeli states would not accede to Egypt's maneuver of having the OAU condemn Israel more sharply. Led by Kenneth Kaunda of Zambia, at the Eighth Summit Meeting in Addis Ababa in 1971, these states succeeded in having the OAU assume a more neutral stance by creating a special OAU mediation committee of Ten Wise Men.[55] This committee, consisting of ten African heads of state, sent a mission of four presidents from black African states—Senghor of Senegal (chairman), Ahidjo of Cameroon, Gowon of Nigeria, and Mobutu of Zaire—to Jerusalem and Cairo. The futile efforts of this mission have been fully discussed elsewhere;[56] for our purposes the point to be stressed is that as late as 1971, Israel was not without friends in the OAU. Although a number of states such as Tanzania, Congo (Brazzaville) and Mali became more critical of Israel, only Guinea severed relations. In the four years following the Six-Day War, Israel's image in black Africa seemed to have been enhanced rather than weakened. Israel's African position, described "as sound as ever" by one observer in 1971, soon began to deteriorate.[57] A number of diverse factors combined to bring about this reversal. The failure of the OAU presidents' mediation mission was one of the turning points in 1971. The mission came away from Israel with the distinct impression (whether correct or not) that Israel was not prepared to agree unequivocally to the return of occupied territories. Israel's African friends had hoped to find Israel more cooperative on this point. Instead they encountered an unyielding position which left them with a "dismayed" feeling that "they had been misled and deceived by Jerusalem," so much so that "the Arab thesis, accordingly, became credible among African leaders."[58] They concluded that Israel intended to hold on to some of the conquered territory for security reasons. A direct consequence of the failure of the presidents' mission was the passage, without a single vote in opposition of "the toughest anti-Israeli resolution on record" at the Rabat OAU summit meeting in 1972. Striking evidence of Israel's deteriorating position was that the resolution was moved by the foreign minister of the Ivory Coast—"one of Israel's staunchest defenders in Africa."[59]

Simultaneously with this changing view of Israel was a changing image of the Palestinians. For years Palestinians were perceived as hapless refugees, to be pitied and minimally sustained. With the PLO escalating its activities after 1969 and gaining widespread attention, Palestinians came to be perceived not merely as refugees, but as a subjugated people fighting for national liberation, with Israel viewed as the oppressor. An Arab Palestinian struggle for national liberation struck a responsive chord in Africa, as African consciousness was focused on its own still unrequited national liberation movements in the Portuguese colonies, Rhodesia and South Africa. First advocated by a number of radical black African states—Guinea, Tanzania and Congo (Brazzaville)—the Palestine national liberation cause was soon taken up among more móderate states such as Senegal, the Ivory Coast and Zaire. President Mobutu of Zaire, long a friend of Israel, reflected the viewpoint of the increasing number of defecting friends of Israel when he told the United Nations in 1973 " . . . the Palestinians had the same right as the Israeli people—to have a homeland and live in peace. The Jewish people which had suffered under Nazism and racism, should understand better than any other people the sufferings of the Palestinian refugees, who for a quarter-century had been without a homeland."[60]

Pro-Israeli sentiment eroded in Africa. Ideological and emotional appeals pointed to Israel's "aggressive behavior" and its "unjust treatment" of Palestinians. This developed empathetic identification with the Palestinian national liberation movement throughout the increasingly radicalized African continent. The representative of Chad, in a statement echoed by many other African delegates, told the UNGA that " . . . the dispossessed peoples of South Africa, Mozambique, Angola, Guinea (Bissau) and Zimbabwe were martyrs to the cause of freedom and . . . the liberation movements which were struggling in Africa and Palestine were its heroes."[61] Compounding Israel's dereliction in the eyes of Africans was Israel's friendly relations with white Southern Africa at a time when the African community was mobilizing world opinion against the racist and colonialist regimes of South Africa, Rhodesia and Portugal. Added to this was a heightened suspiciousness of Israel because of its closeness to the United States for whom disillusionment had set in among African leaders.

Faring badly in the chambers of the OAU represented a setback for Israel. This was not totally unexpected given Israel's weakness in the setting of international meetings. The U.A.R. was a founding member of the OAU, had many Arab and radical friends as fellow members, and had been carrying on a skillful and relentless diplomatic offensive against Israel. It is surprising that Israel had competed so effectively with Egypt in the OAU, succeeding for so long to stave off passage of strong condemnatory resolutions. Losing out in this competition did not necessarily mean an end to Israel's positive image in Africa. What damaged it critically was the sudden deterioration of some of Israel's most successful bilateral arrangements, notably Uganda, Chad, Gabon, Zaire and Ethiopia. While each case has a uniqueness of its own, in all instances Israel suffered because it could not compete diplomatically, financially or ideologically with the Arabs in the three years before the Yom Kippur War.[62]

The 1973 October War and Its Aftermath in Africa

Israel's image among African states reached its nadir in the aftermath of the Yom Kippur War when, in early November, seventeen countries broke relations with the Jewish state. Israel's military inroads into "African soil" were undoubtedly a key psychological factor in cementing hostile African attitudes that had been building up. The 1973 Israeli occupation of a portion of Egyptian territory on the West bank of the Suez Canal provided Arabs, particularly the Egyptians, with a new talking point: the Arab-Israeli conflict was no longer purely regional; it had become an issue affecting the entire African continent because of Israel's "threat to African soil." Statements justifying diplomatic breaks with Israel are replete with this argument.

Not only did the Arabs exploit the issue of Israeli occupation of African territory, their propaganda also appealed to other burning African sensitivities by linking Israel with Africa's most hated enemies. There was probably more fantasy than reality in the Arab argument that South Africa had assisted the Israeli air force during the war. More plausible and devastating in its impact on African attitudes was Arab emphasis on the fact that Portuguese possessions had been used by the United States to resupply Israel. The Arabs were in a position to lend a degree of credibility to a line they had repeatedly used in multilateral diplomatic settings: that Israel and South Africa were both nations of alien settlers oppressing indigenous populations and serving as outposts of imperialist ventures against the Africans.

Arabs and black Africans had seemingly reached total agreement on the matter of Israel. Africans broke relations with Israel, even when it may have hurt. They denounced Israel and acclaimed the Palestinians. They talked of their Arab brothers. The Arabs had won a stunning victory in Africa at the expense of Israel.[63] But it soon became clear that the victory was not total. Cracks were appearing in the links of solidarity between black Africans and Arabs. In siding with the Arabs, one might question the extent to which black Africans were governed by emotional appeal rather than by more practical considerations posed by the new-found Arab oil power. Judging by African criticism of Arab lack of reciprocal concern over the impact of staggering increase in the price of oil on their economies, African acceptance of the Arab position was primarily dictated by practical economic considerations rather than emotional ideological rhetoric.[64] As President Senghor of Senegal aptly stressed, "The Arabs have the numbers, space and oil. In the Third World, they outweigh Israel."[65]

THIRD WORLD COALESCENCE AGAINST ISRAEL

Isolating Israel

Simultaneous with the change in African attitudes towards Israel came the emergence of a coalesced Third World anti-Israeli and pro-Palestinian position. The first attempt to speak for the Third World as a whole came at

Bandung in 1955. This conference of mainly Asian and Arab states at the behest of Nasser excluded Israel and adopted resolutions unfavorable to it. It was not until 1973 that the Arabs finally succeeded in isolating Israel behind an effective *cordon sanitaire* to Third World nations.

The development of a Third World qua Third World attitude towards Israel and the Palestinians only took place as the concept of the Third World took organizational and institutional shape. This involved a slow evolutionary process. At early Third World meetings, such as the 1961 and 1964 Conferences of Nonaligned Nations in Belgrade and Cairo, the Middle East was among the few issues upon which agreement could be reached in an atmosphere marked by personal clashes and dissension. Although not condemned by name, Israel was the target of resolutions condemning "imperialist policies in the Middle East" and calling for "the complete reinstatement of the Arab people in Palestine in all their rights to their country as well as their inalienable right of self-determination."[66]

Until a year or two after the 1967 Six-Day War, Israel was not the object of combined and common Third World disparagement. The Arab diplomatic machine had not yet been successful in mobilizing the Third World to accept the position that challenged the very legitimacy and existence of Israel and totally accepted Arafat and the PLO. Focusing on the plight of the refugees, the Arabs had only been able to have the Middle East problem defined as a humanitarian issue rather than a political one. Although the 1967 war was initiated by Israel, Third World nations shared the general feeling that the Jewish state had been unduly provoked by the rash and intemperate actions and statements of Arab leaders. In contrast to the post-Yom Kippur War, Israel had not been condemned universally after 1967.

The perceptual maps of Third World leaders started to change after 1967. Israel's stunning military feat and the Arabs' crushing defeat definitely undermined the Jewish state's image as the valiant Biblical David fighting against impossible odds. A growing number of Third World statesmen slowly came to the conclusion that the balance of power in the Middle East had tilted in favor of Israel, viewed as militarily invincible. This view emerged just as the Third World was being transformed into a cohesive coalition of the underdog and underprivileged peoples of the world. Included in this were not only Asian and African states but also Latin American states. The common ground for this coalition was the growing frustration of these Third World countries at their inability to bridge the gap with the rich industrialized world. The watchword of this Third World coalition was antiimperialism and anticolonialism directed primarily against the United States and its allies.

Instrumental in bringing about the coalescence of the three component parts of the Third World was UNCTAD (United Nations Conference on

Trade and Development), which had its origin in the group of 77 Developing Countries in 1963.[67] Asian, African and Latin American states determined to alter the terms of trade and economic relations between themselves and the industrial world, came together for the first time in Geneva in 1964 to pursue these aims. Although never directly involved in the problems of the Middle East, UNCTAD, because of its very existence, had a significant bearing on the processes which cast Israel into the role of an international political villain, as perceived by the Third World. The nature of the group system which emerged with the creation of UNCTAD confirmed that Israel was still not being considered as a member of the Third World. The Group of 77 which today includes more than a hundred nations, consists of those countries which signed the 1964 Declaration and any additional members acceptable to its regional groupings. Israel and Cuba which, at the time, were not acceptable to the Arab and Latin American groupings, were excluded in 1964. Cuba has since been accepted but Israel has been specifically excluded from the group's proceedings during the conferences of Geneva, New Delhi and Santiago de Chile as well as from the preparatory meeting prior to each conference.

UNCTAD served as a center of communication and as an agency of socialization into Third World ideology. It helped bridge the gap between Latin America on the one hand and Asia and Africa on the other. Latin American countries have always been full-fledged participants in UNCTAD and in its setting they came into contact with the militant antiimperialist and anticolonialist ideology of the Third World. Latin America had long proclaimed its own brand of anticolonialism and antiimperialism, determined by its juxtaposition with the United States and largely juridical in nature. In the early days of the United Nations, this orientation did not prevent Latin American states from siding with colonial powers in the matter of disposition of the Italian colonies and with the United States on the issue of Palestine partition. The UNCTAD setting, coupled with the radicalization of several key countries in Latin America, added a dimension to their anticolonialist and antiimperialist ideology, an important part of which was a manifestation of solidarity with the other sectors of the Third World. As part of this expression of solidarity, Latin American states eventually shifted their position on the Middle East, adhering instead to one more closely in line with that of the Arabs.

The Arabs took great advantage of the coalescing of the Third World in the years following the 1967 war, developing an effective lobbying technique focused upon Israel's diplomatic "obduracy" and the resurgence of an autonomous Palestinian nationalist movement. The Arabs thus brought the issue of Israel's "aggressive" behavior to the Third Nonaligned Summit Conference in Lusaka on September 8-10, 1970. There for the first time, they found a majority willing to brand the Jewish state as an aggressor, colonialist and racist state.

The significance of this fourth parley of nonaligned states cannot be underestimated. For the Arabs, the conference provided sympathetic and receptive interstate forum. The Lusaka meeting gave the Arabs a considerably broadened audience whose ranks were inflated by the *entrée en force* of Latin American states in the Third World camp: Cuba, Guyana, Jamaica and Trinidad were full-fledged participants in the conference; Barbados, Bolivia, Brazil, Chile, Peru, Uruguay and Venezuela were present as observers.[68] The militancy of the Third World reached its peak during the conference. The pervading themes of deliberations revolved around condemnation of Western powers for complicity in aggravating international tensions and supporting reactionary regimes in the Third World. A majority of participants clamored for the adoption of unequivocal stands on Vietnam, South Africa and the Arab-Israeli conflict.[69] Following a now well-established ritual, the resolution on the Middle East demanded the immediate withdrawal of Israel from land occupied after June 5, 1967 and reaffirmed the inadmissibility of territorial seizures by force. The remainder of the resolution was far more disquieting for Israel. Anticipating a similar UNGA decision in the Fall, the chiefs of state of nonaligned nations first praised the Palestinian national liberation struggle against "colonialism" and "racism." They also stressed that respect for their "inalienable right" including their right to a "homeland" was a prerequisite for a political settlement in the Middle East. In another breakthrough for Arab diplomacy, the conference accused Israel of obstructing the way toward "a peace based on justice" and asked for "appropriate measures against the Jewish State if it were to continue its occupation of Arab lands."

In order to appease Israel's dwindling number of allies, the original draft of the resolution which called for sanctions was considerably moderated. Only twenty-six delegations voted against it and subsequent failures of the Jarring Mission and the mediation of the Ten Wise Men which were attributed to Israel's diplomatic immobilism, soon enabled the Arabs to intensify their pressure.

The Turning Point: Algiers, September 1973

The 1973 Algiers Conference of Nonaligned Nations, meeting just one month prior to the Yom Kippur War, demonstrated at one and the same time the solidarity of the Third World on the issue of Israel and the uniqueness of this consensus. Despite the claim of the conference's host and chairman, President Houari Boumediènne, that this "biggest international assembly in the history after the United Nations" would provide a "new impetus to the joint struggle of our peoples for the consolidation of their national independence, the consecration of their legitimate aspirations and the strengthening of their solidarity,"[70] the conference bogged down in disagreement and squabbling among delegates; most notably between Qaddafi and Castro. The Third World was finding it difficult to speak with a single voice and the conference appeared on the verge of collapse.[71] The meeting was extended by one day and a good deal of face was saved when the question of the Middle East enabled all participants to end the conference on a note of agreement, at least on one issue—condemnation of Israel. Israel was unambiguously bracketed with Portugal, South Africa and Rhodesia as a colonialist and racist state; and the Palestinians with liberation movements in Africa and Southeast Asia. Peace in the Middle East, said the resolution, depended on the immediate and unconditional withdrawal of Israel from occupied Arab territories and the restoration of the Palestinians' "national rights in their entirety."

Israel was also condemned for its "violations of human rights" in the occupied territories. Such violations as well as Israel's "refusal to apply the 1949 Geneva Convention at the time of war" and "policy aimed at changing the nature of the occupied territories" were all assessed as "war crimes" and "challenges to mankind." Finally, the conference delegates pledged "full support of Egypt, Syria, and Jordan in their struggle, by all means, to recover their occupied territories," welcomed "the decision of some countries to sever diplomatic relations with Israel" and called on all other member countries "to work on diplomatic, economic, military and cultural boycott of Israel."[72]

Israel's condemnation at the Algiers Conference represented the culmination of a series of diplomatic setbacks in the Third World experienced before the Yom Kippur War. It was only after the Yom Kippur War that the Arabs were able to apply their new economic power in escalating their international influence. The Arabs succeeded in isolating Israel from the Third World by their incessant hammering at the need to maintain a united front against imperialist and neocolonialist forces.

United Nations: Instrument of the Third World

The various nonaligned conferences were not the only settings in which the Arabs could mobilize the Third World against Israel. Since decolonization and the swelling of the United Nations membership to over 130 states, the international organization, most notably, the GA, had become an instrument of the Third World. By virtue of their overwhelming majority, Third World states dominated the GA and controlled its agenda. The Arabs used this arena most effectively. They garnered maximum publicity for their criticism of Israel, mobilizing against it rapidly growing majorities—predominantly Third World states—built up after patient negotiations, lengthy bargaining and extensive vote trading. Ever since the establishment of Israel, the Palestine question had been on the agenda of the GA, usually concerned with the plight of Arab refugees and the status of Jerusalem. Arab strategy had been directed toward embarassing Israel and keeping the issue alive. Beginning in 1968, the Arabs, buttressed by the support of some Third World states, embarked on a more aggressive strategy. In 1968, the GA established a three-state (Sri Lanka, Senegal, and Yugoslavia) Committee to Investigate Israeli Practices Affecting the Human Rights of the Populations of the Occupied Territories, with power to monitor the situation in regard to human rights in the territories under Israeli occupation throughout the year. The committee's activities and most particularly its hearings of carefully screened Palestinians who related grim stories of mass arrests, administrative detention, expropriations, deportations and torture, all dramatically condemned Israel's moral integrity.[73]

By the time of the 1974 GA session, the Third World states were unanimously and completely on the side of the Arabs. On the eve of the 1974 GA debate, Yosef Tekoah, Israel's ambassador to the United Nations, acknowledged the diplomatic isolation of Israel when he observed: "The Palestine Organization has the delegations of the 20 Arab states at its disposal and the Arab states are the moving force in the non-aligned group which comes close to 100 countries; in addition, the Soviet group is going along with the Arabs. [Facing such an impressive numerical majority] . . . there is only one Jewish state."[74]

For Israel, the 1974 GA session was a rout. Not only was the PLO granted observer status. Yasir Arafat was received in the assembly with all the trappings accorded to heads of state. Delegates from non-Third World states, many of whom were critical of Israel, were not necessarily in accord with this unprecedented violation of UN protocol, but they were forced to stand by idly in face of Third World majority. Speakers from the Third World seemed to be competing with each other in extolling the Palestinians as freedom fighters and in denouncing Israel as an imperialist aggressor. The anti-Israeli bandwagon was rolling in the GA and all the Third World states were on it. Even the minority of Third World states who were traditionally more moderate and balanced on the issue, always concluded their remarks by stressing the need to satisfy unrequited rights of the Palestinians. In the contagious setting of the GA hall little pro-Israeli sentiment was expressed by Third World states.

The failure of the 1974-75 diplomatic efforts to bring about some tangible movement towards peace insures the continuation of Arab efforts at the thirtieth session of the UNGA to have the Third World states espouse even more hostile attitudes towards Israel. Having carried their battle against

Israel to the halls of UNESCO and other UN agencies, the Arabs are bent on escalating the pressure on Israel in the United Nations with the aid of Third World countries. Steps have been taken for a possible consideration of the suspension of Israel, as was done to South Africa, and for the application of sanctions against Israel. Meeting in Cuba in April 1975, the seventeen nations constituting the steering committee of the tricontinental coalition of nonaligned forces postponed action until August on a Syrian-sponsored resolution demanding the expulsion of Israel from the United Nations. The Havana Declaration adopted by the Seventeen did condemn the Jewish state for its military occupation of foreign lands and stressed that "the time [was] ripe for the non-aligned countries to consider broader measures against Israel" within the framework of the UN Charter.[75] Radical Third World states and the PLO sought to have the ouster of Israel from the United Nations included in the final communiqué of the Nonaligned National Conference held in August in Lima (Peru). Their efforts might have succeeded had not Kissinger been able to bring about a second interim agreement between Israel and Egypt. Instead, the eighty-two participants to the meeting, led by Egypt, Yugoslavia and several black African delegations, adopted a more moderate text which invoked Chapter Seven of the UN Charter and called on the Security Council "to take all necessary measures" to force Israel to comply with the UN resolutions on the Middle East.[76]

The multilateral settings of the OAU, the Conferences of Nonaligned Nations and the United Nations provided Arabs with arenas in which to challenge and change Israel's international image and reputation, by giving unprecedented legitimacy to Palestinian nationalist aims. There they forged the present tricontinental anti-Israeli coalition. Focusing attention on the apparent contradictions of Israel's policy, the Arabs contrasted Israel's peaceful declarations to its diplomatic immobilism, reprisal raids and policy in the occupied territories. They underlined the clash between Israel's democratic ideals and its treatment of Palestinians while stressing the Jewish state's close links with the arch enemies of the Third World. In presenting their case to the Third World, the Arabs always carefully articulated their arguments within the framework of a language and a set of symbols which were easily identifiable and likely to elicit sympathetic reactions. They made constant references to the lofty principles of the UN Charter and international law and to the specters of neocolonialism and imperialism. Moving back and forth from regional to larger, global diplomatic multilateral settings, the Arabs, over the years, generated a slow but almost irresistible cumulative process in which the fear of isolation and the risks of siding with Israel made the overwhelming majority of Third World states fall into line in spite of a variety of political divisions.

CONCLUSION

This paper addressed three basic questions: What are the factors over the years which altered Third World perception of Israel? To what extent does the present attitude of the Third World toward the Jewish state reflect the existence of a genuine and monolithic support of the Arabs? Are the attitudes toward Israel likely to change in the future?

Factors Altering Third World Perspective

Four key structural developments in the evolution of the international system since the establishment of the State of Israel have undermined Israel's image and position: (1) the changing international system; (2) emergence of the Third World movement and its radicalization; (3) Arab ascendancy in the Third World; and (4) resurgence of Palestinian nationalism.

1. The Changing International System. Since World War II, international society has undergone drastic alterations which have increasingly isolated Israel. Bipolarity has given way to a looser pentagonal structure numerically overshadowed by Third World nations. Too often it is overlooked that Israel was created prior to the emergence of the Third World in international politics and that it owes its birth certificate, in part, to the structural simplicity of the world in the late forties. The United Nations was then dominated by Western nations which had been traumatized by the war and the Nazi holocaust of European Jewry. In this environment, the handful of Asian and African states sitting in the GA had little influence. Had the United Nations included a greater number of Third World states, if both the USSR and the United States had not favored the Palestine partition plan, the resolution would never have been adopted. In more recent years, Israel's reputation in the Third World has been further damaged by its increasing military and economic reliance and dependence on the United States. In many respects, the Jewish state has been a major casualty of the anti-American perception so dominantly in vogue throughout the Third World.

2. Emergence of the Third World. The emergence of an increasingly cohesive and institutionalized Third World movement had a damaging impact on Israel. As long as the Third World remained a collection of unorganized, unconnected and heterogeneous actors in international politics, there were no major obstacles to the development of cordial relations between Jerusalem and the capitals of numerous Asian and African states. Israel's network of bilateral economic and political ties with the Third World were built prior to the emergence of a strong Third World movement. But in a decolonized, radicalized and organized Third World system, the Jewish state became ipso facto a potential pariah. In a great number of cases, the anticolonialist and antiimperialist creed which cements the Third World (and does not preclude a considerable degree of political opportunism) led to perceptions of Israel either as a manifestation of hard dying colonialism or, at best, as a phenomenon alien to the Third World and its self defined interests. In more general terms, we found ample evidence showing that the operational code of Third World leaders never predisposed them to accept Israel unconditionally as one of their peers.

3. Arab Ascendancy. The Arab states have been catapulted into an unprecedented position of influence within the Third World. Until several years after the Six-Day War, a significant portion of the Third World perceived Israel as the legitimately aggrieved party and the Arabs as obstinate malefactors for not recognizing Israel and for threatening to drive the Israelis into the sea. By 1973, these perceptions were reversed. The Arabs were the aggrieved party and Israel the obstinate malefactor for its reluctance to withdraw from conquered territories. The ascendancy of the Arabs was complete when they effectively used the oil weapon during and after the Yom Kippur War. The Arabs achieved a position of influence in the corridors of the Third World far beyond any influence heretofore exercised by them and far more significant than that of any other group of Third World states.

4. Palestinian Resurgence. Finally, there is the political significance of the resurgence of an autonomous Palestinian nationalist movement. For many years, Palestinians were the forgotten people of the Middle East. Viewed as hapless refugees in UN camps, as quiescent subjects in Israel and the occupied territories, and as discordant irritants in neighboring Arab countries, Palestinians were passive participants in the dispute— manipulated and controlled by others. All this has changed in the past decade. By their organization and actions, Palestinians have become active participants, central to any resolution of the tangled affairs of the region. This development has refocused the Third World perception of the Arab-Israeli conflict and given salience to key problems which were hitherto largely ignored. The resurgence of Palestinians has drawn attention to the conflict, as one between two nationalisms competing for the same land. By the same token, while the claims of Palestinians receive greater attention, those of Israel are bound to be downgraded or sharply questioned. In the eyes of many Third World ideologues, the Israelis are viewed as interlopers, whose very legitimacy is challenged.

How Isolated Is Israel?

These global, regional and local changes in the structure of the international system have weakened Israel's position in the international community and in the Third World in particular. But the next question which must be raised is to what extent does Israel's present diplomatic isolation entail a general acceptance of the Arab definition of the Middle East conflict.

The public and overt behavior of Third World leaders may suggest that they share the Arab viewpoint, and their statement indeed abound in references to and criticisms of Israel's violations of human rights in the occupied territories, its diplomatic immobilism and rigidity as well as apparent unwillingness to return to the pre-1967 war borders. But public speeches do not tell the whole story. The decision to break diplomatic relations with Israel was often dictated by purely domestic considerations such as the existence of a restive or important Muslim minority within a state, or foreign aid and technical assistance needs which were well beyond Israel's meager means. In numerous cases, the Third World attitude and perception of the Jewish state had thus little to do with the intrinsic merits of the Arab-Israeli dispute.

Arab statements with regard to the future of the Middle East are clouded with ambiguity. A few "moderates" (President Sadat and King Hussein) have hinted, somewhat elusively, that they might accept a political settlement based in part on the recognition of Israel within its pre-1967 borders. Radical Arab spokesmen (Palestinians, Iraqis, Syrians and Qaddafi) do not seem to have altogether abandoned the original Arab policy of the mid-forties rejecting the right of Jews to have a state in Palestine. No Arab statesman or leader has yet unequivocally stated that he accepts the legitimacy of Israel's existence as a state. Taking into account Arab reluctance to accept the State of Israel as part of an overall settlement of the conflict, it might be inferred that the Arabs' present diplomatic strategy includes an ultimate goal, entailing the elimination of Israel. If the Arabs openly sought to reach this goal in Palestine, to what extent would they be supported by the present Third World coalition? The Arabs would undoubtedly find support in the radical wing of the Third World but they might also create a wave of sympathy in favor of Israel among their less enthusiastic and unconditional followers. Fear of losing a considerable number of allies and of opening new and deep fissures in the Third World movement probably explains why the Arabs have been content with the pursuit of "reasonable" incremental claims and demands. The very heterogeneity of the Third World thus emerges as an important variable which may determine whether Israel will remain isolated in the future.

The Third World shares a common past of colonial exploitation as well as a series of common economic grievances. Not unlike the European proletariat which, in the last decades of the nineteenth century understood that political power and change could be achieved only through collective action, the proletarian nations of the twentieth century realize that they can successfully press for a more equitable economic order only if they act as a bloc. Hence the unrelenting efforts of Asian, African and more recently, Latin American leaders to uphold unity within the OAU, the nonaligned meetings and the United Nations and act through these instrumentalities. As long as Third World leadership believes that concessions from the rich countries can be won by exerting collective pressure in multilateral settings, the Third World is not likely to disintegrate and it will tend to rally around anti-Israeli slogans.

The significance of the Third World's internal divisions cannot be underestimated. Much of the Third World's cohesion also depends upon the manner in which the Arabs will use their newly gained economic power. There are already indications that growing Arab economic power has aroused fears of a nascent "petrodollar imperialism." This is true for black Africa in particular: several states have bitterly expressed disappointment at the economic support received from the Arabs; economic agreements have been abrogated and fierce power struggles have erupted in the OAU. As a Kenyan professor of political science aptly put it, "[the Africans] expected a *quid pro quo*. They found that the Arabs agreed to sharing enemies but not energy." [77]

In the balance, Israel's image will probably continue to evolve along a continuum of perceptions reflecting the internal dynamics of the Third World. Should tensions within the Third World be exacerbated, Israel's image would undoubtedly be enhanced. The present combination of political, economic and cultural factors and, in particular, the dominant role of the Arabs in Third World councils, point at predominantly negative attitudes toward the Jewish state. But for how long and up to what point can Third World states continue to use anti-Israeli slogans for the purpose of defining and then reconciling their collective and individual identity and interests? Would the Third World still be cohesive if the Arab states "misused" their petro-dollars and if Israeli decision makers took the bold initiative of relinquishing most of the territories seized in 1967? How would a majority of Third World leaders be affected by such developments and how would they reconcile their new perception of Palestinians with a more favorable image of Israeli? The next chapter in the unfolding drama of the Third World's changing perception of Israel remains to be written.

NOTES

1. See Benjamin Rivlin, *The United Nations and the Italian Colonies* (New York: Carnegie Endowment for International Peace, 1950), pp. 33-41.

2. One of the initial five principles of Israeli foreign policy approved by the Knesset on March 11, 1949 spoke of "nonidentification" with either of the two superpowers. See Michael Brecher, *The New States of Asia* (New York: Oxford University Press, 1966), p. 129.

3. All the foregoing quotes by Gandhi and Nehru are from *India and Palestine* (New Dehli: The Statesman Press, published by the Ministry of External Affairs, n.d.), pp. 11-13.

4. Pierre Chauleur, "Afrique 1974," *Etudes* (June 1974): 838-39. Ralph Uwechue, the Nigerian editor of *Africa* also wrote: "Black Africa and the Arab world are linked by territory but, in spite of the common tie through the Muslim religion, they remain separated by many historical and psychological factors. Memories of Arab slave hunts are a painful reminder of the erstwhile relationship between the Black and the Arabs of the African continent." Quoted in Colin Legum, "Africa, the Arabs and the Middle East," *Africa Contemporary Record, 1973-1974* (London, 1974): A14-A15. See also Aryeh Oded, "Slaves and Oil: The Arab Image in Black Africa," *The Wiener Library Bulletin* n.s. 27, no. 32 (1974):35-36.

5. Fouad Ajami and Martin H. Sours, "Israel and Sub-Saharan Africa: A Study of Interaction," *African Studies Review* (December 1970): 407.

6. J.C. Hurewitz, *Middle East Dilemmas: The Background to U.S. Policy* (New York: Harper, 1953), 157.

7. Quoted in Richard J. Kozicki, "Burma and Israel: A Study in Friendly Asian Relations," *Middle Eastern Affairs* 10, no. 3 (March 1959): 115.

8. For an elaborate discussion of this point, see Onkar S. Marwah, "India's Relations with the West Asian-North African Countries," *Middle East Information Series* 22 (February 1973): 24, 22.

9. For a full analysis of early Indian-Israeli relations, see Richard J. Kozicki, "India and Israel: A Problem in Asian Politics," *Middle Eastern Affairs* 9, no. 5 (May 1958): 162-72.

10. Lewis V. Thomas, *The United States and Turkey and Iran* (Cambridge, Mass.: Harvard University Press, 1952), pp. 130-31.

11. Brecher, *New States*, p. 136; and Leopold Laufer, "Israel and the Third World," *Political Science Quarterly* no. 4 (December 1972): 263.

12. E.A. Bayne, *Four Ways of Politics: State and Nation in Italy, Somalia, Israel, Iran* (New York: American Universities Field Staff, 1965), p. 247.

13. Ibid., p. 212; and Brecher, *New States*, p. 137.

14. *New York Times*, January 20, 1975.

15. Kozicki, "Burma and Israel," p. 111.

16. George McTurnan Kahin, *The Asian-African Conference: Bandung, Indonesia, April 1955* (Ithaca: Cornell University Press, 1956), p. 3.

17. Brecher, *New States*, p. 133.

18. Meron Medzini, "Reflections on Israel's Asian Policy," *Midstream* (June/July 1972): 25-26.

19. M.S. Agwani, "The Palestine Conflict in Asian Perspective," in *The Transformation of Palestine: Essays on the Origin and Development of the Arab-Israel Conflict*, ed. Ibrahim Abu-Lughod (Evanston: Northwestern University Press, 1971), p. 457.

20. Text in Kahin, *Asian-African Conference*, p. 82.

21. Walter Eytan, *The First Ten Years* (New York: Simon and Schuster, 1958), p. 188.

22. W. Scott Thompson, *Ghana's Foreign Policy: 1957-1966* (Princeton: Princeton University Press), p. 47.

23. Ibid.

24. For further details see Arnold Rivkin, "Israel and the Afro-Asian World," *Foreign Affairs* 37, no. 3 (April 1959).

25. *Africa Report* (February 1970): 7.

26. See Irving Heymont, "The Israeli Nahal Program," *The Middle East Journal* 21, no. 3 (Summer 1967).

27. Ibid.

28. Tom Mboya, *Freedom and After* (Boston: Little, Brown and Co., 1963), pp. 173-74.

29. Quoted in Bernard Reich, "Israel's Policy in Africa," *The Middle East Journal* 18, no. 1 (Winter 1964): 19.

30. Thompson, *Ghana's Foreign Policy*, p. 48.

31. Mboya, *Freedom and After*.

32. *Africa Report* (April 1972): 14.

33. Doudou Thiam, *The Foreign Policy of African States* (New York: Praeger, 1965), p. 62.

34. Gamal Abdul Nasser, *Egypt's Liberation: The Philosophy of the Revolution* (Washington: Public Affairs Press, 1955), p. 110.

35. *New York Times*, December 9, 1958.

36. John Hatch, *A History of Postwar Africa* (New York: Praeger, 1965), p. 277. For differing interpretations of the Nasser-Nkrumah rivalry see Tareq Y. Ismael, *The U.A.R. in Africa: Egypt's Policy Under Nasser* (Evanston: Northwestern University Press, 1971), p. 32.

37. Rivkin, "Israel and the Afro-Asian World," p. 487.

38. Mboya, *Freedom and After*, p. 23.

39. Thompson, *Ghana's Foreign Policy*, p. 47.

40. Julius K. Nyerere, *Freedom and Socialism: A Selection from Writings and Speeches, 1965-1967* (Dar es Salaam: Oxford University Press), p. 371.

41. Mboya, *Freedom and After*, p. 174.

42. For a full discussion of this failure, see Abel Jacob, "Foreign Aid in Agriculture: Introducing Israel's Land Settlement Schemes to Tanzania," *African Affairs* 71, no. 283 (April 1972): 186-94.

43. For example, Ghana replaced the importing of Israeli cement with Egyptian cement for its Israeli-built cement works "as Kwame Nkrumah, in his quest for African leadership, attempted to strengthen relations with Nasser." Laufer, "Israel and the Third World," p. 623.

44. *Al Ahram*, December 21, 1960, quoted in Ismael, *U.A.R. in Africa*, p. 53.

45. See Legum, *Pan-Africanism: A Short Political Guide*, ed. (New York: Praeger, 1965), pp. 205-10 for documents on the Casablanca Conference.

46. Ali Mazrui, *Violence and Thought: Essays on Social Tensions in Africa* (London: Longmans, 1969), p. 248.

47. Legum, *Pan-Africanism*, p. 51.

48. Mazrui, *Violence and Thought*, p. 247.

49. See Thompson, *Ghana's Foreign Policy*, p. 55.

50. See Ismael, *U.A.R. in Africa*, pp. 67-74, passim.

51. For a detailed account of the voting on the two resolutions, see Samuel Decalo, "Israeli Foreign Policy and the Third World," *Orbis* (Fall 1967): 7-12; for texts of the resolutions as well as an account of the debates, see Arthur Lall, *The U.N. and the Middle East Crisis: 1967* (New York: Columbia University Press, 1968).

52. Ajami and Sours, *"Israel and Sub-Saharan Africa."*

53. Ibid.

54. For the resolution texts, see *Africa Contemporary Record, 1969-1970* and *1972-1973*.

55. See Legum, "Africa, the Arabs and the Middle East," *Africa Contemporary Record, 1972-1973* (1973): A123-A133.

56. Susan Aurelia Gitelson, "The O.A.U. Mission and the Middle East Conflict," *International Organization* 27, no. 3 (Summer 1973).

57. J. Bowyer Bell, "Israel's Setbacks in Africa," *Middle East International*

(London), no. 21 (March 1973): 22.

58. *Maghreb* (Paris), no. 64 (July-August 1974). In July 1967, Golda Meir is reported to have assured President Houphouet-Boigny of the Ivory Coast, at a secret meeting in Bavaria, that Israel had no territorial ambitions.

59. Legum, "Africa, the Arabs and the Middle East" (1973): A132; text in document section: C23.

60. *United Nations Chronicle* 10 no. 10 (November 1973): 71-72.

61. UNGA, 27th Session, Provisional A/C.3 SR 1957, November 22, 1972, pp. 14-15.

62. For details on the fate of Israel's assistance programs in Uganda, see Legum, "Africa, the Arabs and the Middle East" (1973): A134; for Chad, see *New York Times*, January 12, 1973; for Gabon, *Le Monde Diplomatique* (July 1974): 23; and Zaire and Ethiopia, UNGA, 17th Session, Provisional A/PV 2101, December 6, 1972, pp. 71-72 and Legum, "Africa, the Arabs and the Middle East" (1974): A4-5.

63. Ibid.

64. Ibid.: A13-14. See also Oded, "Slaves and Oil."

65. *Le Monde Diplomatique* (February 1974): 23.

66. For a summary of the proceedings of both conferences and the text of resolutions, see *Keesing's Contemporary Archives* (February 17-24, 1962): 18601-18605 and (November 28-December 5, 1964): 20431-20434.

67. On UNCTAD see Charles L. Robertson, "The Creation of UNCTAD," in *The Politics of International Organization*, ed. Robert Cox (New York 1969), pp. 258-74; and Robert S. Walters, "International Organizations and Political Communications: The Use of UNCTAD by Less Developed Countries," by *International Organization* 25, no. 4 (1971).

68. *Africa Research Bulletin* (September 1970): 1877-78.

69. As noted by Aniruha Gupta, "The Lusaka Meeting: An Assessment," *Africa Quarterly* 10 (October-December 1970): 194-200.

70. *Africa Research Bulletin* (September 1973): 2975. The conference was attended by 76 states, 8 "observers" (Barbados, Bolivia, Brazil, Colombia, Ecuador, Mexico, Panama, Uruguay and Venezuela), 8 "guests" (Austria, Finland, Sweden, the AAPSO, the Arab League, the OAU, the Puerto Rican Socialist party and a UN representative) and 6 liberation movements (FRELIMO, PAIGC, PLO, MPLA, SWAPO, and ZAPU). Ibid.: 2979-80. Twenty-five states and 3 observers attended the Belgrade conference. The 1964 Cairo conference gathered 47 nations and 10 observers. For the Lusaka meeting, the figures were 52 states and 11 observers, respectively.

71. For more detail on the political disputes which flared up at the Algiers conference, see *The Economist* (September 15, 1973); *Le Monde* (September 6, 9, 10, 1973); and *The New York Times* (September 6, 7, 8, 9, 1973).

72. *Africa Research Bulletin* (September 1973): 2978-79.

73. For a summary of the committee's most recent hearings, see *United Nations Monthly Chronicle* 12, no. 4 (April 1975): 23, 27.

74. *New York Times*, November 12, 1974.

75. *New York Times*, April 1, 1975.

76. For a summary of the conference's proceedings, see *New York Times*, August 26, 28, 29 and 31, 1975.

77. Quoted in Oded, "Slaves and Oil," p. 47.

24

Irving Louis Horowitz

FROM PARIAH PEOPLE TO PARIAH NATION: JEWS, ISRAELIS AND THE THIRD WORLD

There were two essential tactics in the pre-Israel period of Jewish life: assimilationism and Zionism. Both had as their essential premise a belief in the need to destroy the ghetto in which Jews had been incarcerated through-out most of their exile period. Both cosmopolitanism and nationalism have been absorbed within Israeli society, but neither inherited approach to the "Jewish problem" anticipated that Israel itself would be transformed into a national ghetto. Theodore Herzl assumed that once Jews implanted the national plan, once the "Jewish Company" had been formed, immediate relief would ensue.[1] Despite its achievement of national sovereignty and linguistic identity, in its twenty-seven years of existence, Israel has suffered the same problems of isolation that have characterized so much of modern Jewish history.[2] The purpose of this essay is to examine how a pariah people has been transformed into a pariah nation; and specifically what this situation augurs with respect to Israel's position in world affairs and in the Third World with which its fate is entwined.

With the emergence of the Middle East as a crucial crisis area, Israel becomes a central focus in world affairs. In consequence of this, Jewish communities throughout the world have increased their "particularistic" interests in Israel, often at the expense of their "universalistic" concerns for others. Israel unifies the Jewish community worldwide, giving it a sense of solidarity that transcends psychological anxieties and geographical differ-ences, however sharp or obscure. Old alliances and allegiances have broken

*I should like to thank The Memorial Foundation for Jewish Culture for the financial support which enabled me to prepare this study.

down, not simply within the international environment at large, but within the Jewish community in particular. The quality of Jewish radicalism or conservatism in the Diaspora is presently tempered by the needs of the sovereign power called Israel. Impulses toward Jewish solidarity are heightened by the growing isolation of Israel in world affairs. The existence of a Jewish community, the capacity to be a Jew, radical, conservative, or nonpolitical, comes to depend on the existence of Israel: not because of Israel's perfection or even perfectability, but because it has become a nationalized ghetto. If the fate of that ghetto is to be the same as that of Warsaw in 1943-44, then the second holacaust of the century will have occurred. As a result, to be a Jew would become impossible, or at best, an anachronism. This shared awareness among Diaspora and Israeli Jews has served to create linkages where none previously existed.[3]

What has confused and confounded the general perception of Israel as a Third World nation are its specific linkages with the American Jewish community as the underwriter of Israeli economic development, and with the American state as protector of military parity in the Middle East.[4] Many sectors of world Jewry, or at least those sectors extending from Western Europe to South Africa, have served, inadvertently or otherwise, to conservatize Israeli national policy. Israeli authorities, in deference to such foreign pressures (religious and political), have muted their critique of Soviet anti-Semitism, suppressed the multiracial and multiethnic character of their society, and have hardly dared to challenge directly the small but vocal theological elements within Israel, much less external elements who might withdraw their fiscal support or religious legitimation. These operational constraints imposed upon Israel by virtue of its isolation, have only deepened it. Radical critics join with their conservative opponents in denouncing Israel as a threat to international harmony and tranquility, which in turn only leads to deepening insularity and isolation.

There is a curious parallel between the emergence of European nationalism in the nineteenth century and Third World nationalism in the twentieth century. The past century witnessed a movement away from universal notions of human emancipation and even religious notions of ethnic, racial, class, and even tribal emancipation. A glance back indicates that the suspicion in which the Jews were held with respect to nationalism is by no means a current invention of the Arab bloc or the Third World.

The words of Edouard Drumont, writing in the *fin de siècle* on "The Soul of Dreyfus," indicate traditional French attitudes toward the Jew and the national question:

> In order for a man to betray his country, it is necessary first of all that he has a country, and that country cannot be acquired by an act of

naturalization. That country is the land of one's forefathers. Barrès expressed it in excellent fashion: "One understands by a nation a group of men united by common legends, with a tradition, with habits fashioned during a more or less long series of ancestors. Naturalization is a legal fiction which is used for the advantage of a nation, but which cannot give it character." What is needed is a law making it a prerequisite for nationality at least three generations of French descent. In resisting this idea the Jews are preparing for their own destruction. All the maneuvers of Jewdom are directed against the invincible resistance of the national element, the very soul of France. In insisting impudently upon imposing on us their own conception of equality, the Jews have prepared with their own hands the most frightful catastrophe of their tragic history.[5]

In Germany the same sorts of secular nationalist anti-Semitism emerged at the close of the past century.[6] The school of Eugen Dühring was particularly ferocious in asserting that German culture must liberate itself from the corrupt heritage of the Old and New Testament alike and assert the "peculiar, superior national character of the Germans." This was expressed in precise terms by a follower of Dühring, A.S. Danzig, writing in 1892, or two years earlier than Drumont in France:

Christianity has no practical ethical precept that is unambiguously useful and salutary. Hence, the nations will rid themselves of the Semitic spirit only after they succeed in uprooting this second manifestation of Hebraism as well . . . . To go forth today to combat racial Judaism from the standpoint of Christianity is to attempt to turn evil into non-evil by means of one of its own offshoots, that is, by means of itself. Those who desire to strengthen the Christian tradition are in no position to combat Judaism with vigor. A Christian who understand himself cannot be a serious anti-Semite. The Nordic idols and the Nordic God contain a natural kernel and no thousand-year-old distraction can remove it from the world. Here has reigned an imaginative spirit incomparably superior to the Jewish slave imagination.[7]

Virtual isolation was imposed upon Jews even at that time in European history when liberal enlightenment forces were at their peak. Such a retrospective glance also permits us to be more appreciative of those Jews and Israelis who take small comfort from past events in Western Europe and doubt that the Third World will provide sustenance for demands of Jewish survival. Although juridical conditions are now different—Israel seeks a role as a nation among nations rather than a pariah people in a world of alien nations—this legitimation of Judaism has not staved off attacks on either Zionism or Israel; and to complete the cycle, on Judaism once again.

Throughout the world, a wave of nationalism has overshadowed considerations of class. Certainly the "national question," rather than dissolving under the impact of the Soviet Revolution, has been accentuated by the emergence of socialism. Jews, historically presumed to be marginal citizens, test the egalitarian premises of socialism no less than those of capitalism. The question of dual or multiple national allegiances, and the appropriate posture of the individual in relation to the state, have once more become central, this time in the Third World rather than Western Europe. The Jew has come to represent the collective outsider, uniquely capable of withstanding the impact of newer forms of militant nationalism. At the same time, Israeli nationalism in the form of the Zionist movement also demands a central set of loyalties. Israeli authorities not only encourage migration of Jews from all parts of the world, but some clearly intimate that no Jewish culture can long survive elsewhere,[8] even in the democratic societies of the West. A mediating position increasingly expressed, is that the Diaspora Jew will survive only if Israel exists as a viable state. In the tension between claims of ethnic identification over national loyalty, the Jew once more performs a central role in the quest for extending democracy.

A major factor in any consideration of the Jews in the Soviet Union is how the Jewish question has become firmly linked to the national question. Specifically, the issue of Jewish liberation has been couched in larger civil libertarian terms. Leaders of Soviet communism have always understood the importance and used the Jewish question to measure the quantum of freedom in the Soviet Union. Events such as Jewish martyrdom at Babi Yar were incorporated into Russian cultural struggles rather than remaining mechanisms for Jewish survival. In the past, concern for the survival of the Jewish people could be deflected from Soviet repressive mechanisms onto German Nazi sources of repression and destruction. Beyond that, earlier concerns about the Jewish condition took for granted a national-socialist solution within the boundaries of the Soviet Union, whereas in the present it is precisely the freedom of the Jews apart from Soviet society, to practice their faith and to exercise their natural rights of migration to Israel or elsewhere, that has converted the earlier period of Jewish quiescence into a contemporary expression of defiant militance.

If a new element favorable to Soviet Jewry has been the broad gauged dialogue among its intelligentsia on the nature of Soviet society, a far more ominous element has been the rise of a multinational political economy. The aims of realpolitik as expressed in the Soviet-American détente, threaten to overwhelm earlier humanitarian considerations. The high irony of the present situation is that the existence of the Cold War made the Jews of the

Soviet Union an element in an East-West struggle. The decline of the Cold War, the growing fusion of interests between the two international superpowers in the wake of the Vietnamese debacle, and threats to the existing hegemony of each superpower—from Western Europe in the West and China in the East—have made the condition of the Jews a far less prominent concern. The moral claims of Jews for the rights to emigrate, when viewed in the context of economic advantages for the superpowers in muting their own political differences, will likely yield less overt protest and more quiet diplomacy. Add to this the growth of U.S. commercial investments in the Soviet Union and Eastern Europe at a time of shrinking U.S. overseas markets and domestic purchasing power, and the condition of Jews in the Soviet Union becomes an even more remote consideration in the fashioning of American foreign policy. Many past Soviet Jewish appeals have been directed at the United States in the expectation that the cold war would provide an impetus for their support. This emphasis will probably be compelled to shift or at least extend to Jews throughout the world, if for no other reason than the growing isomorphism between the Soviet Union and the United States.

West issues, from wartime cooperation in the forties, cold war in the fifties and sixties, to détente in the seventies, it is clear that Jews have been on both sides of most big-power struggles. They have both supported and opposed the world wars, socialism, the Third World and the conflict in Southeast Asia. In past eras whether or not one was a Jew could not and did not predict attitudes toward other global issues. Even fascism in Italy had its Jewish adherents, and Nazism, while lacking Jewish support, was able to mobilize a portion of the Jewish community to organize its own destruction. Pluralism of Jewish communities in the Diaspora led them to see positive and negative aspects in each of the struggles mentioned above. The Jew as word master expressed ideological beliefs on both sides, and played a valuable role in the political rationalization of the Western world. Prior to the emergence of Israel, and lacking a center of ideological gravity, Jews accommodated diverse interests. Pluralism became linked to liberalism. The Jews in this manner emphasized many causes as their own. Zionism was but one expression of a Jewish fondness for alternatives. The emergence of Israel dramatically changed this situation.

A central fact about social change and international development in the twentieth century is that events have become so compressed as to make generalizations on a centennial level less than convincing. It may be somewhat fatuous to talk about the seventeenth century as the century of technology, the eighteenth century as the age of reason, or the nineteenth century as the age of romanticism—but it is at least plausible to do so. Similar efforts to characterize this century, i.e., the age of analysis, of miniaturization, of communication, are flat and lack universal applicability. This may reflect weakness in our social science theories, or the need for shorter time spans in which we make historic and analytic generalizations.

Empirically, the first half of this century was still confined to the European orbit. The period 1910-20 may be defined by the war of imperialism—World War I. The period 1920-30 can best be characterized by the rise of socialism in one country, and the emergence of the Soviet Union as a world empire as well as a social system of unique dimensions. The years 1930-40 are overwhelmingly dominated by the emergence of fascism, or what might be termed the response and the counterresponse to socialism. The period 1940-50 was dominated by World War II. Its aftermath virtually obliterated fascism as a formal political system, but also revealed serious strains within and between capitalism and socialism.

The end of the war brought about not just an end to empire, but an end to European preeminence in world affairs. 1950-60 may be characterized as the period of the breakup of world empires, the emergence of the Third World with the establishment of new nationalisms throughout Asia and Africa and the emergence of Latin America as an independent category. The very reshaping of the map during this period is at least as dramatic as the geographic terror carried out during the two world wars and the rise of socialism and fascism. The importance of events within each decade of the twentieth century is attested to by a flintlike geographic territoriality; who owns what turf and when. The period 1960-70 is clearly dominated by the Far East, by the emergence of China and Japan as leading examples of Asian socialism and capitalism respectively, and above all, by the tragic war in Vietnam which mirrored the militarization of the Third World as a whole.

By all odds, the Middle East is the dominant area of contention in world affairs in the 1970s. Because of the oil embargo that region's struggles have already impacted American domestic affairs more directly than did the Far East struggles of the sixties. Related questions of energy resources, foreign investments in U.S. industry, and price structures in general, directly affect American citizens in a manner unknown during Vietnam. Gasoline shortages and decisions to increase prices or ration inevitably result from the assumption that a government foreign policy, in this case the decision not to abandon American commitments to Israel's survival and sovereignty, must be met, whatever the short-term consequences of economic hardships. In the long run, the tendency is to reverse U.S. foreign policy toward Israel and avoid an artificial energy crisis.

Local, particularistic issues also impinge upon, and in turn are affected by, the Middle East conflict. The Basque separatist movement extends formal identification and recognition of the Palestine Liberation Organization (PLO) and decries the Jewish conspiracy. The Dutch are deprived of oil for refusing to sever their historic ties with the Israelis and for keeping faith with their own democratic traditions. India denies entry to Israeli ping-pong players closing out sports as a diplomatic maneuver as assuredly as it was opened up several years ago by the People's Republic of China. The Chinese attempt (unsuccessfully) to hold a press conference in Washington at which Israeli and South African reporters are excluded from previewing China's latest archeological diggings. The United Nations Educational and Scientific Commission (UNESCO) refuses Israel regional membership in that international forum. A veritable deluge of other indignities of relative peripheral political importance directly involve Jewish communities throughout the world. The treatment of Jews often reveals official, government anti-Semitism, and hence involves matters of state rather than simple issues of personal conscience. In these ways a pariah people is transformed into a pariah nation.

The 1970s witnessed, in part as a result of the isolation of Israel, the adoption by Jews of what might be called an interest-group model. This represents an unusual development, for it is a well-established fact that in the past Jews have transcended the politics of self-interest. Whether because of their prophetic Jewish tradition or simply a belief that the good things of society should be equally distributed, Jews have uniquely demonstrated their fidelity to the democratic tradition of each person counting for no more and no less than one. The termination of such democratic universalism is evident in the United States. In the new America group demands upon the political system are answerable only insofar as the group has ethnic cohesion. Jews as a group have been quite restrained, although organizationally they are better capable of exercising an interest-group posture than are many. Demands for the rights of blacks, ethnics, students, women, etc., and the conversion of a democratic universal dream of brotherhood and equality into a series of particular demands on America have finally been adopted by Jews and articulated in a series of ethnic alliances, racial agreements, and political bargains which are all intended to prove that Jews are like everyone else. This result may at best be termed a mixed blessing. The Jewish community has now assumed an attitude of being for themselves before others, taking on the interest-group model of the American political system.

Jewish communities have taken on this interest-group model somewhat abashedly and timidly, but with a skill and intelligence acquired in their struggles in other movements. This new self-awareness has had a price, specifically the reintroduction by Arab spokesmen of the old canard that Jewish loyalties to any national structure (outside of Israel) are of dubious value. And more than faint echoes are now heard about Jewish cosmopolitanism as nothing more than a snare and a delusion, a means of weakening loyalties to the nations in which Jews reside. In short, Jewish life in the Diaspora continues to be plagued by a contradiction: whether to give uniform and unstinting support to the national system at the expense of Israel, or to provide support for Israel (usually in monetary and intellectual terms) and be sharply rebuked for less than total loyalty to the national state. The problem dissolves the moment one appreciates the fact that pluralistic activities and multiple allegiances are a veritable hallmark of the democratic credo; and characterize many ethnic groups such as the Irish, blacks, and all other peoples undergoing similar travails in their searches for independence. It is plain that the tolerance permitted to other peoples and groupings is by no means extended to world Jewry.

Arab propagandists are embarked on an effort to play on American fears of another military involvement similar to the one in Southeast Asia. American support for Israel is being challenged on the grounds that what is in the self interest of Jews may not be in the self-interest of Americans, that the linkage of Israeli survival with American foreign policy is spurious and dangerous. It is argued that listening to Jews on the question of the Middle East is pointless, that they are blinded by self-interest. This concerted effort at isolation of Israel also entails a revision of Arab tactics with regard to world Jewry. Far from being defined as different in substance from Israelis, Jews are now portrayed as the vanguard of Israeli interests. Although this argument is transparent to most—Israel is not a divided nation like Vietnam and does not seek, indeed rejects, foreign troops intervening—it serves to crystallize opposition to Israel by giving up the charade that anti-Zionism is qualitatively different from anti-Semitism. The new Arab tactics are a rather grim reminder of holocausts past.

The history of the 1970s has become interlocked with the condition, indeed the very existence of world Jewry. In such a situation, small cruelties count for less than the larger issues of whether Israel and the Jew shall survive. Until recently, Arab rhetoricians distinguished between the cause of Zionism and the rights of the Jewish people. That sharp separation partially accounts for the considerable propaganda success of the Arabs after their defeat in the Six-Day War. But as if to demonstrate that this distinction was a transitory strategem rather than a fundamental axiom, these same Arab sources, in the post-Round Four context, assert that Jews have a problem of dual allegiance, and that they must be "helped" to make a decision in terms of their new nation and acknowledge that the Arab-Israeli conflict is outside their sphere of influence or participation.

At this point a slightly argumentative digression is called for, since beyond the fact that modern democracy is defined by its pluralistic capabilities, is the essential series of commitments by Jews to a trinitarianism all their own: to Providence, Torah, and Israel—or more specifically, to a God who provides ethical precepts, and a national homeland for the Jewish people. As a result of this trinitarianism, or better, the selective identification with these three aspects of the Jewish experience, Judaism is at one and the same time a theological, ethical and political experience. Secularization or mystification of Judaism, while creating an inevitable number of disputations, hardly leads to the destruction of Jewish life. For this reason, propaganda urging religious conversion or simply Jewish indifference to Israel, has proven fruitless among Jews, but has managed to sow considerable bitter harvest among non-Jews.

The right of Jewish citizens to emigrate from the Soviet Union to Israel typifies the complex issues which define the relationship between a nation-state and a national religion. Beyond that, it indicates how necessary liberal, democratic societies are to continuing Jewish survival. The right of people to free movement is upheld by Jews, but no effort has been made to form a common front. The threat of a domino effect is genuine: if Jews have the right of free movement to and from other nations, then this right must be extended by normal political logic to all other peoples. The Israeli position (like that of other democracies) is that the individual has an absolute right to emigrate outward rather than necessarily to immigrate inward. Israel, like all other nations, makes specific demands upon those who would seek Israeli citizenship, and the "right of return" applies only to Jewish people. Exclusivism and even triumphalism enter into Israeli calculations for citizenship, as they do in many nations. A series of problems arise, more abstract than real, but theoretically thorny enough to sow the seeds of doubt and confusion concerning Jewish national loyalties.

Beyond the international question of the free movement of peoples and their rights to self-determination, are problems connected to subnational, or for that matter transnational, forms of identification. These are far from clearly articulated rights in most political systems, particularly in those Third World nations still attempting to work out the parameters of legitimacy and sovereignty. While the United States and the Soviet Union long ago formulated rather sophisticated doctrines of the rights of minorities to national self-identification, the weaknesses in these formulas soon became apparent. The basic Third World response was to insist that every minority should have the rights of nationhood per se, and not just equality within large national units. Ironically, this potential point of contact between Third World and Israeli postures has been lost in the rush of geopolitical events and pragmatic considerations.

A new wave of anti-Semitism has merged with anti-Israeli sentiment in a Left-Right crossfire to create a pariah state, as the older social movements of socialism, capitalism, and nationalism—ideological formations and social systems in which Jews have widely participated—also threaten Jewish survival. How is it that the Jew, so central to the formation of capitalism and socialism, nationalism and internationalism, the essential pattern variables of the past four hundred years has shared so little in the rewards of these reformist and revolutionary movements? Why does the Jewish question continue to play a central role so long after the formal emancipation of Jews by the leading secular system of this age? Why does this particular period reveal so little consensus about what it means to be a Jew? One recalls Marx's comments on the Enlightenment: that it came about as a universal demand for equity and justice and ended as a special interest claim for the bourgeoisie. Socialism has also claimed the mantle of universal equity and justice, but it too has been found wanting. The current animosity of radical elements for Jews, inside and outside of Israel, stems in no small part from the central role Jewish communities in the Soviet Union and Eastern Europe have played in unmasking pretentious socialist claims for universal justice and equality and defrocking its leaders as something other than the special heroes of modern history. Inevitably, socialism's asking price of Jewish emancipation was emancipation from being Jewish—the traditional demand of anti-Semitic movements.

If the fear of dual or multiple loyalties took on fearful proportions in the development of European socialism these fears have become downright xenophobic in a Third World context. The nationalist and anticolonialist origins of the new nations of the Third World have made them especially intolerant of such accentuated differences. Many new nations within the Third World, having fought their way to independence not only against foreign colonial powers but internal tribal, religious and racial powers, are profoundly suspicious of any calls for pluralism or cultural decentralization. The rise of militarism and bureaucratic centralism have further reduced the capacity of Third World leaders to absorb such forms of socioeconomic marginality that form the historical baggage of Jewish communities the world over. And the Third World response is in terms of either total absorption or total expulsion—a posture which also contributes to the sense of isolation faced by Israel in its dealings with other nations.

What has occurred in the political relationship between Israel and the Third World to offset their structural similarities? There is little in the twenty-seven-year history of Israel to suggest reasons for its present isolation. At the outset, Israel was accepted as a model for burgeoning national movements everywhere except within the Arab bloc. The Israeli political posture toward the Third World and the response of that world can be divided into five periods.

At first, Israel took a posture of nonalignment with respect to the controversies and cold war between the United States and the Soviet Union. The joint sponsorship of Israel by both the Soviet Union and the United States made political nonalignment necessary as well as advantageous. Israel scrupulously avoided participation in cold war rhetoric, and selectively emphasized to the West its adherence to the principles and premises of popular democracy, and to the East its labor socialism. During the late 1940s the Third World itself hardly existed. There were instead nations such as India, just undergoing its own independence revolution; Yugoslavia, in the midst of gaining a measure of independence and sovereignty outside the Soviet bloc; and Mexico, which had long since had its revolution but remained very much within the U.S. orbit. During this period Israel joined a cluster of nations that are best described as nonaligned with regard to the cold war, politically democratic, and vaguely, or precisely, socialist.

The policy of nonalignment showed its limits with respect to shifting attitudes toward Israel. The necessity for choice was imposed by the needs of many nations for technology, or food, or both. Two choices had to be made, and both reflected an increasing image of Israeli dependence upon the United States. First, Israel supported the U.S. position on Korea in the United Nations, specifically backing intervention into that national civil war on the side of the South Korean regime. Second, Israel delayed diplomatic recognition to the People's Republic of China, despite the fact that most Israelis recognized that the Kuomintang regime was finished, and that supporting the Taiwan group might create grave political problems in the long run. But again, pressure from the United States was strong enough to cancel any inclination to dissent, and as a result, Israel was increasingly seen, rightfully or otherwise, as in the U.S. camp. Third World response was to phase out Israel from the Bandung Conference, which was a unique event during this period, setting forth guiding principles for the Third World as a whole. Israel was first invited, then disinvited from the Bandung Conference. The decision on China, even more than the decision on Korea, undoubtedly led to this response. During this period too, a rapprochement emerged between Asia and Africa and the Arab nations, a rapprochement considerably accelerated by the extent of Israeli dependence on both European and American military aid.

Michael Brecher's reconstruction of Israel's foreign policy and its implications for the Third World as well as itself, is of unparalled importance; it deserves extensive citation:

> The recognition of Peking helped to sustain the unique phase (1948-50) of parallel US and Soviet support for Israel. Indeed, the Korean War marks the great divide in Israel's foreign policy, the shift from non-identification to alignment with the U.S. Her entry into the Western camp did not affect the balance of global power; it merely added one more vote to the already large—and unreal—Western majority in the UN General Assembly. Rather, it initiated Israel's

declining stature in the global system, a by-product of the end of the early phase of autonomous behaviour on issues outside the Near East Core. Similarly, the image of Israel in the Third World was rapidly transformed into that of a Western camp follower. Ironically, Israel's move away from non-alignment occurred at a time when it was a thriving international pressure group, making important contributions to the solution—or at least easing—of international conflicts, notably the Korean and first Indo-China Wars. Israel's membership in the non-aligned group, always challenged by her Arab enemies and their Muslim friends, had been affirmed by the policy of non-alignment. By 1953-4, all the epithets of "Zionism as a puppet of Imperialism," "Western beachhead in the Near East," etc., found a more receptive audience in the Third World, especially in Asia.

In the long run, the effect of Israel's Korea decisions was even greater on the psychological environment of her decision-makers. The swing to the West was accompanied by, and accentuated, an image of Israel's vital interests as linked indissolubly with those of the West. Sharett's image of the global system now became identical to that of Washington; that is, a tight bipolar system dominated by the conflict between the "free world" and the Communists. Looking back historically, the decision not to recognize China was a serious mistake. It would have been a first-class move. It might have transformed Israel's position in Asia and the Third World generally.

A decisive positive response to Peking's overtures in March 1955, or even better, in January, May or November 1954, would almost certainly have created a friendly Chinese predisposition towards Israel's claim to participate in the Bandung Conference. China could have—and, it is reasonable to surmise, would have—used her influence to persuade Nehru not to yield to Arab pressure on the Colombo Powers to exclude Israel. Chou En-Lai's advocacy of Israel's rightful place at Bandung as an Asian state—it is illogical to assert he would not have done so immediately after diplomatic relations were established with Israel—might have been the decisive input into the wrangle over Israel's invitation. Burma's U Nu sponsored her—but Burma alone was not strong enough to turn the tide.[9]

That period of time ranging from the Sinai to the Six-Day War, revealed that Israel was acting in concert with many European powers wishing to maintain their foothold in North Africa, and with the United States similarly wishing to establish a foothold in the area. We are ignoring for the moment the legitimacy of each of these conflicts, or what they meant to Israel, in order to indicate the growing military posture within Israel, and its identification with the camp of the First World of the United States and Western Europe, rather than the Second World of the Soviet Union and Eastern Europe, or the Third World, including China. Yet, during this period Israel had a tremendous impact on Africa. Economic missions, diplomatic missions, and political intercourse in general between Israel and the Third World was then at its peak, despite Arab efforts at blockade and boycott. The consolidation of Israel was considered a model for the Third World. Beyond that, Israel was considered small enough not to be a threat economically or technologically, yet sophisticated and rich enough in manpower resources to be of real assistance in the evolution of African and Asian societies. De jure, Israel had not progressed much beyond the interested outsider. De facto, Israel was actively involved in the Third World and its overtures were responded to in kind.

The period beginning with the Six-Day War and terminating with the Yom Kippur War was one of deepening isolation from the Third World. During this period Israelis developed a much higher sensitivity, as a result of military need if nothing else, to Jews the world over. Israeli consolidation took place on a worldwide basis, with renewed hopes that Zionism might attract the needy from the Soviet world and the hopeful from the Western world. This neoisolationism did not mean a lessening of overseas technological performance, but a less vigorous pursuit of de jure recognition. Uganda, after Amin's coup in January 1971, promised to establish diplomatic representation in Jerusalem.

Jewish consolidation thus came to mean stronger relationships with the Jewish communities in Argentina, South Africa, Canada and elsewhere, with relatively scant attention to the needs of the Third World, or even its remnant Jewish groupings. Given the antagonistic turn of events in the Third World, this also meant drawing back from overseas involvements in development planning generally. Beyond that, the initially rather warm relationship between Israel and South Africa, and their continuing strong relationship, further isolated Israel from the Third World, an isolation the Arab powers were quick to convert into the idea that Israel and South Africa were "settler" powers, and hence must exercise their authority by illegal military control of a local population. Charges against Israel for its racial and religious policies became fused with the earlier attack on Israel as an American imperialist outpost.

Whatever the military consequences of Round Four might have been and there can be no question that the military in Israel once again comported themselves quite well in the battlefield, the losses were disastrous, and the isolation of Israel from the Third World became de facto as well as de jure. One after another, the African nations, in response to Arab economic and political pressures, ceased diplomatic and economic relations with Israel.

Indian-Israeli friendship societies were dismantled. Even in nations with a large Jewish population, such as Argentina and Brazil, some strong hurts were dealt. Zionism, as an exclusive ideology, was attacked throughout the Third World as antinationalistic in character, and the U.N. voting patterns during this period reflected intensification of diplomatic, political and economic isolation of Israel from the Third World.

On the African continent, struggles between the Muslim North African regimes and the Christian and secular sub-Saharan regimes, have sharpened considerably in the recent past. The Organization of African Unity (OAU) only papered over the sharp dichotomization between North Africa and sub-Saharan Africa. The Sudanese struggle lasted over one hundred years, and saw a black Christian and pagan majority fighting a brown Muslim minority, eventually to be defeated by that minority although in a compromised fashion. The struggle between Ethiopia and Eritrea is clearly marked by a Christian-Muslim essence in which secession is directly tied to the interests and needs of the Muslim minority and the desires of the Arab world as a whole. To sever Eritrea from the military regime of Ethiopia is to firmly segregate Muslim and Christian states in Africa. In Uganda, the 6 or 7 percent Arab minority is so highly represented in military and political circles that it seems to dominate the overwhelming Christian majority. Such events have been viewed with suspicion within the sub-Saharan African world. Despite their interest in receiving petrodollars from the Organization of Petroleum Exporting Countries (OPEC), the Africans are not willing to translate that support into armed activity against Israel. The risk factor for African states is so small that they can cancel relationships with Israel without intending this to reveal any great passion for the Arab majority opinion on the nature and structure of the Middle East conflict. Should loans to developing countries decrease from their present 4 percent—as well they might, should oil export decline generally—or should there be a manifest threat to sub-Saharan, non-Muslim States, one can expect sharp diplomatic and military changes in the Middle Eastern situation.

A useful indicator of how much of a pariah state Israel has become is the fact that the only time that the African states have acted with diplomatic solidarity was with respect to Israel in the aftermath of the October 1973 conflict. While there had been breaks previously, one in 1967 when Guinea broke relations with Israel after the Six-Day War, and the other in 1972 when Uganda and several other nations which underwent internal coups broke relations, there was no concerted action against Israel. This took place only after the Yom Kippur War. The only developing states that failed to break diplomatic relations were Lesotho, Malawi, Swaziland and Mauritius, and these exceptions only proved the totality of Israeli isolation from the Third World, since three of them are uniquely dependent upon South Africa.

The immediate gains for the Africans were soon evident. The Arabs established an African Development Bank at their Algiers conference of November 1973, with an initial capitalization of almost $200 million. In addition, they showed that they would increase the offensive against southern Africa by extending their oil boycott and presumably strengthening their diplomatic pressure. The Africans were thus indicating continental solidarity without incurring the threat of substantial losses to themselves, as they had feared from Great Britain at UDI. For the long run the African leaders may have erred, however. They have lost their maneuverability, which was possible only when they were comparatively "nonaligned" on the Middle East question. They were probably more valuable to the Arabs when there was a possibility that they might break relations than they could be after they had actually done so. After all, what else of importance did they have to offer to the Arabs? That the Arabs would not risk their own vital interests for the Africans was evident by their initial unwillingness to reduce the oil prices to the poorer, developing countries from those demanded of their ostensible targets, the industrialized states. In effect, the Arabs apparently tried to step into a patron-client relationship, for which they had always criticized the Western countries. They would be glad to charge high prices for their goods and then offer financial assistance on their own terms to the Africans. Under these circumstances, the Africans would have been wiser to keep their options among the Middle East protagonists open by merely threatening to break relations with Israel rather than actually doing so.[10]

Just how profound Arab penetration of sub-Saharan Africa has been can be gleaned from the Ugandan case. According to the last official census of the 6.5 million inhabitants of Uganda, 34.5 percent were Catholic, 28.2 percent were Protestant, 5.6 percent were Muslim, and 31.7 percent were of other faiths. Despite this heavily Christian and secular background, the country is now ruled by a Muslim military chief; one who totally reversed the posture of Uganda with respect to Israel and became the first African nation to explicitly revoke the possibility of diplomatic relations because of the Arab influence in 1972.

The importance which the present regime in Uganda attributes to the Muslim religion is also reflected in its foreign policy. The Muslim factor was one of the causes of Amin's shift towards the Arab states and the severance of Uganda's relations with Israel in the hope that the Muslim countries would support his regime financially and politically. Thus, in the joint Amin-Qadhafi communique issued in Tripoli in February 13, 1972, both leaders undertook to base their respective revolutions and the development of their countries on the foundation of Islamic ideals (Uganda News, 15 February 1972). In June 1972, Amin visited nine Arab countries and that same year he twice made the pilgrimage to Mecca. Islamic activities such as Amin's participation in *Juma* prayers and *maulidi* (festivals marking the anniversary of the Prophet's birthday), and the construction of new mosques, occupy a prominent place in Uganda newspapers. In July 1972, the *Chief Qadi* announced that it was decided to translate the Qur'an into Luganda.... In contrast to the movement of Islam, the main axis of European colonial and Christian penetration in West Africa was from south to north. Thus the coastal nations like Liberia, Ivory Coast and Ghana retained their traditional religions, exhibited relatively weak Muslim influence, and came under stronger Christian impact. The drawing of religious lines between north and south is particularly visible in Nigeria, where the north of the country is mainly Muslim, while the south is generally non-Muslim. In East Africa, however, the main axis of Muslim penetration was from east to west, from the coast to the interior. Christianity later expanded in the same direction, following the very routes which had been established by the Arab traders. In this sense the Muslims indirectly aided the diffusion of Christianity in Africa.[11]

   In Asia, a similar situation is evident, namely, low risk for Asian nations criticizing Israel, and exceptionally high risk for those which cut themselves off from Arab oil supplies. Nonetheless, there are definite signs of internal threats and strains that may modify Asian opposition to Israel. There is genuine opposition within India to Indira Gandhi's anti-Israeli position, while in other Asian nations relationships have become far more ambiguous than the Arabs have hoped. Long-held feelings of distrust by Indonesia against external Arab policy provides little potential for crystallization of an anti-Israeli position. In some countries, such as Taiwan and Indochina, strong anticommunist positions lead to potential support of Israel, if not as an ally, at least not as a particularly meaningful opposition. Religious and social factors predominate in the policies of Muslim nations whereas in Asia, the major powers fill their own myriad national objectives, with scant regard to Middle Eastern global religious concerns. Beyond that, on almost every indicator of public opinion there is real disparity between governmental policies of opposition to Israel and public interest support for Israel. Mass public opinion tends to be far more sympathetic to Israel than to Arab causes;

and this too seems to dampen overt manifestations of opposition to Israel.

Southeast Asian attitudes toward the Arab-israeli struggle have been at least as ambiguous as Israeli attitudes toward the Southeast Asian struggle. It is true that the government of Israel, along with Muslim regimes such as Turkey, Iran, Jordan and Lebanon, were sympathetic to Saigon, whereas the others were mostly sympathetic to Hanoi in the Vietnamese struggle. Israel very clearly hedged its bets and maintained a considerable distance from the South Vietnamese government in Saigon insofar as this was possible. Indo-China perhaps is a good example of the ambiguous nature of the Southeast Asian response:

> Indonesian preferences on Arab-Israeli issues too have undergone a change in emphasis since the present Suharto regime has come to power. The current government, strongly anti-communist in doctrine and practice, is firmly opposed to Sino-Soviet regional objectives and is suspicious of left-wing oriented governments. Indonesia, which took a radical position on foreign policy in the Sukarno years has now become discreet, conservative and Western-oriented in its outlook. Israel's military performance in defeating the Russian-equipped Arab countries, and its open society, has elicited admiration by a number of key governmental officials. Yet the country is overwhelmingly, even if nominally, Muslim and tends, like its neighbor Malaysia, to consider Islam as a potential trans-regional ideology. Both views of Israel as a powerful force in the Middle East and a strong belief that religious values have been the cement of Muslim society throughout the centuries—have tempered Indonesian perspectives. Indonesian support for the Arab nations in international forums must take in account long-held and deepseated Javanese fears of external Islamic and Arabic influences intruding on national, secular matters.[12]

The situation in Latin America has probably changed less over time than elsewhere in the Third World. The participation of countries like Venezuela in OPEC and the growing political radicalization of the hemisphere as a whole, have led to a more positive feeling toward the Arab position. However, large and articulate Jewish minorities in Argentina and Uruguay, and the somewhat smaller Jewish minorities in Brazil and Mexico, have helped support a far more balanced attitude in Latin America toward the Israelis than elsewhere, if for no other reason than the presence of Jews as a real economic factor. Outside of Cuba, which has simply adhered to the Soviet position, the nations of the hemisphere have maintained economic, diplomatic and political ties with Israel, so that Latin America, while clearly reacting to a vigorous Arab campaign against Zionism by expanding trade relationships with the Arab bloc, has nonetheless not pursued any manifest anti-Israeli position either within the United Nations or in direct diplomatic negotiations with both sides.

A serious problem has arisen in Third World ideology with the policy of nonalignment, which has been compounded by the Arab-Israeli struggles. Whether through choice or necessity, nations such as Yugoslavia and India, which have identified the Third World ideology as nonalignment in the internal affairs of the First and Second Worlds, have committed themselves at least in principle, to the Second World posture toward the Arab-Israeli struggle. Tito espouses the radical Arab position on the entire complex of Middle East issues because it is the posture necessary for European Yugoslavia to retain its standing among the key non-European countries of the Third World. But this adaptation conflicts with the promotion of the Yugoslav conception of nonalignment.[13] The Middle East conflict has helped to move Third World ideology away from nonalignment and toward partisan support for the Soviet position. How much this ideological persuasion translates into organizational support is determined by the extent of dependency upon the Soviet Union.

Who is to blame and who is responsible, and what decisions might have led to more favorable pacific outcomes, will be debated for years to come. It is important to introduce the meaning of Third World opposition, and what that might imply for further Arab-Israeli hostilities. One can be relatively secure in the knowledge that the Third World will not, indeed cannot, act as a unified phalanx against Israeli interests. There are preliminary indications that the severance of diplomatic relationships with Israel may have been considered premature in some African-Asian capitals. There are further indications of profound economic schisms in the Arab nations.

In the 1970s we have had intensified polarization within each bloc: the United States in contrast to Western Europe, the Soviet Union in contrast to China, and the Middle East in contrast to Asia and sub-Saharan Africa. This intensified polarization has provided cushion and caution with respect to Third World policies toward Israel. Israelis would welcome diplomatic openings to any part of the Third World from which they are now sealed off, but the price of such openings is still not clear. Israel cannot respond the way Portugal did with respect to its African colonies. It cannot purchase goodwill by relinquishing colonies, for it has none. Nor can Israel's position be that of countries like Canada or Brazil which pick and choose alliances from the blocs on the basis of their natural mineral wealth. The question becomes whether Israel is willing (or able) to live as a small nation within the Third World, or whether it can survive as a relatively powerful nation in the Middle East outside of that Third World.

The morphology of Israel shows stark parallels with the rest of the Third

World: high militarization, with the armed forces functioning as the mark of national sovereignty no less than a response mechanism to a threat of any major international sort; high capitalization, in which every effort is bent toward increasing the gross national profit while holding constant individual forms of private wealth; centralized political authority in which, despite the particular nuances of the political party and parliamentary network, decision making is lodged in a well-defined group with long-standing firm leadership roles. Israel shares with the Third World a mixed societal pattern: Keynesian mechanisms of regulation in the economic sector, Leninist mechanisms of domination in the political sector, topped off by strong social welfare and social reform orientations toward the individual in society.

There are other parallels: Israel's struggle against colonialism in the 1940s was essentially a prototype of guerrilla warfare. Second, Israel's unity is based on ethnicity, religious values, and a strong egalitarian background— all necessary mobilizing components for economic development. Third, as with any successfully developing country in the twentieth century, Israel has had very strong external support for its development, in this case, an overseas ethnic-religious group. Many overseas Jews have prospered in the advanced nations and are able to provide material support and technological know-how at a low cost and on a temporary or permanent resettlement basis.

The morphological parallels between Israel and other Third World nations are great. For example, both India and Israel have borne the stress and strain of absorbing a high refugee influx; both have undergone the anguish of partition; and the anxiety of a national leadership based on a single-party mechanism which encourages smaller peripheral parties to survive and grow. Both also reveal the existence of a general federation of labor in which organized union activity serves as a pressure group attuned and parallel to the military and political systems as such.

Israel has a strong professional military group as do developing nations elsewhere. The recruitment process is from the middle sectors of society rather than its upper or distinctly ethnic sector. Professional training is often based on models from advanced European countries, including both the Soviet Union and the United States. Above all, Israel's military is held within strict boundaries of professionalism, which means that they maintain the national system and respond to and take orders from the political sector. Although the military is often a stepping stone to political careers, as it is throughout the Third World, during the period of actual military service there is a strict distinction between military and civilian tasks. So much so that different agencies are involved at a decision-making level. What is remarkable is not Israel's high sense of professional military activity, but the ability of that military network to contain itself so that it does not become an undue burden upon the political system.

The military in Israel is a touchstone for the Third World generally. The standing army is small, but the number of men capable of being rapidly mobilized is large. The Israeli armed forces are quite large; Israel has the highest proportion of men in uniform in the Mid East—a higher percentage of the total population than the United States and most other countries as well. The professional cadre numbers only about twelve thousand; but the high degree of militarization, despite its asymmetry with Jewish culture which eschews and even repudiates military means, has become a primary factor in defining Israeli society.

> The army does more than reassure Israelis. It undertakes explicit responsibilities in education and integration, and it simplicitly pro- vides the most manifest symbol of Israel's nationhood, undiluted by political debate, unencumbered by ideological baggage, unblemished by scandal. There is no question that the army is seen as the most "pure" and certainly most efficient of Israel's institutions. However bewildering, Israel has managed to maintain its military forces as a citizens' army. Although some Israelis believe that in the early years of statehood there was a minor possibility of military putsch, it is hardly likely that anyone in Israel today is seriously concerned with such a possibility. It is so far from likely, so almost literally inconceiv- able, that it is totally discounted.[14]

The performance of the Israeli armed forces (Zahal) in specifically military feats has been well recorded. Equally important is the function of the military as a means of integrating ethnic minority groups, religious factions, educational activities, and reducing deviance. Again, each of these problems is typical of developing nations, and Israel is no exception. Like other armed forces, Zahal has pioneered in racial and religious integration, and has promoted the idea of mass mobilization without at the same time inviting separate political units. In short, the Israeli armed forces are like those of Third World countries, but with an added feature: their military functions as professional fighting forces in the advanced industrial countries is a necessary component to a national unit fighting for survival throughout its youthful history. Professionalism, rather than praetorianism, has made the difference in Israeli campaigns against the Arab bloc.[15] And the conver- sion of its guerrilla-like Haganah forces into regular army units has paid handsome dividends—both in maintaining military morale and in retaining civilian controls.[16]

Israel exhibits strong characteristics of the Third World in its political structure. The country formally has a multiparty structure but actually has a uniparty operational apparatus that runs the country within the framework of democratic centralism. There may be a greater degree of Leninism in Israel than there presently is in the Soviet Union—if one takes seriously the intention of building a democracy based on broad class criteria rather than party bureaucracy. Israeli politicians certainly take class consciousness seriously; this is evidenced by the high degree of interest-group jockeying before and after electoral procedures.

The founders of Israel emanated from European struggles for economic emancipation, while looking toward the New World for their models of political and economic growth. They faced problems of building a new nation and overcoming the humiliation of anti-Semitism. The European and American context of Jewish ethnicity was primary for the founder generation. The sons, for their part, in reaction to the settler generation, tended to turn inward and deal with problems of Israeli development as if there were no international context, certainly no Third World, but rather a world of friends (the Jews) and enemies (the Arabs). Even Jews outside of Israel were oftentimes slighted in the calculations for Israeli survival. Hence it is that the dialectic of Israeli development tended to exclude considerations of the Third World as a prime item in the social agenda.[17]

It is exceedingly important to recognize the dialectic of generational conflict. Not only is there an internal struggle between a founder generation and their offspring sabra generation, who are now rulers of Israel, but in the very act of world Jewry becoming an accessory to Jewish settlement in Israel, a schism occurs between generations, among international Jewry specifically, with respect to the Israeli situation vis-à-vis the Third World.

This great identification of the Jewish community with Israel that is, to a certain extent, producing a withdrawal among part of the younger generation of Jews who, in rebelling against their Establishment-oriented parents are also rebelling against the identification of the present generation with Israel. These nuances also combine with the authentic sympathy, the struggle of the Arabs sometimes evokes in the New Left, the Israel-Arab struggle being viewed in terms of struggle between the Third World and European colonialism. If we may add to this the social anti-Semitism which sometimes manifests itself among the leadership of Black Power in the U.S., together with the disintegration of some of the classic premises of American pluralism, there is no doubt that since the Six-Day War a situation of polarization has come into being, which I think will become increasingly acute. In place of general apathy diluted with non-commital sympathy for Israel, there is now crystallizing a situation in which powerful, deep and intensive sympathy on the one hand is being confronted with severe criticism, if not revulsion, among portions of the younger generation, on the other.[18]

Only in the third decade of Israel's existence has there been some recognition of possible comparisons of Israeli society with other societies which developed from religious, national or political movements (like India, Pakistan and Indonesia). An important statement on this subject has been made by S.N. Eisenstadt:

> A further criterion of comparison is that with "underdeveloped" or "developing" nations and with "new states." This comparison is twofold. Firstly, it is concerned with the problems of economic development which are of great importance also in Israel, particularly in view of the flow of immigrants from traditional backgrounds. Secondly, the development of Israeli society may be compared with that of other "new" sovereign states which emerged through the institutionalization of socio-political movements, the transformation of the leadership of such movements into a ruling elite, and the establishment of a new political regime, stemming from various colonizing and "social movement" beginnings. These broad trends enable us to analyze the development of Israel as one among the crystallizing modern societies. The development of Israeli society can be seen as the encounter between these initial starting points and three crucial social processes. The first of these was the "natural" development of a different and complex social structure emerging from pioneering beginnings. Second were the changes in this structure, caused by the establishment of the State of Israel and its transformation into a full-fledged State and society. The third process was the influx of immigrants with new attitudes and motivations and their encounter with the merging social structure.[19]

The cornerstone of Israeli policy toward the Third World prior to Round Four was to provide the undeveloped and developing areas with know-how rather than finished product. Israel exported experts and imported trainees, rather than export commodity goods or import raw material. This is an appropriate posture for a small nation such as Israel in search of diplomatic legitimation. Beyond that, the Israeli effort can be divided into three substrategies: the attack on poverty; the interpretation of development in educational rather than political terms; and the use of young people to act as a kind of Peace Corps. These young people were called *madrichim*, or guides:

> It is above all a matter of social structures, of adequate bureaucracies, of dedicated elites. Efforts, therefore, must be made on a comprehensive scale to combat poverty, and not in single packages, only in one direction or the other. Development—the process of catching up—

must create hope. Hope can be instilled through ideology and through example. Israel could export some ideological jargon of a socialist type, but not a revolutionary ideology. It did, however, have a large reserve of people who could set an example in the field of cooperation, a real "army" of trained carriers of know-how, of innovation, who could help to stimulate imitations and activate the potential skills of the local traditional elites, who would, in turn, influence their own societies.... It was only when Israel began going out to the new countries of Africa and looking for the right men to send there that it realized the value of *madrichim* for technical cooperation and made them one of its resources in the field of assistance to development.[20]

Prior to the outbreak of Round Four, Israelis not only developed considerable flexibility in their foreign aid trade program with respect to the Third World, but also an appropriate ideological scale. The concept was based on appropriateness of small-nation help to other developing nations, enabling them to avoid the pitfalls of macro-aid, or large-scale direct financial assistance. A pioneer leader of Israeli aid to the Third World summarizes the Israeli approach as follows:

Micro-cooperation is not an independent system of aid-to-development. It is a claim for the integration into existing aid programmes of appropriate "ignition" systems or circuits, to help start the engines of any development plan. In this sense, micro-cooperation is only one of the many tools available for international cooperation, and has no programmatic purpose of its own. Micro-cooperation—that is, the coordinated effort of aid-to-development through the close cooperation of the men-in-the-middle and the members of the elites legitimizing the diffusion of their imported innovation—can be justified both by the accumulated experience of aid-advisers in the field and by new theoretical approaches in the social sciences. Foreign aid which is not able to promote self-help cannot really be regarded as aid-to-development. It still remains in the category of charity, which is so frustrating because so often it seems unending. To turn charity into aid, something else is needed; namely the translation into practice of the consciousness that every acquisition of a new technique, or any new use of an old technique, regardless of its origin, alters man's social ecology. To be acceptable, an innovation demands the restoration of a balance between man and environment. Micro-cooperation may not create new environments but it can, if properly handled, compensate for or help to repair the damage done by breaking an established harmony.[21]

A distinct paradox of the present wave of small-country nationalism is that Israeli claims to Third World status have been systematically denied. One might anticipate that Zionism would be perceived as a vanguard form of nationalism having distinctive religious and ethnic dimensions like other post-World War II, Third World nationalisms rather than more strictly defined economic goals of more recent national uprisings. But nothing of the sort has happened. Israel has been defined as a pariah nation, suited to harboring a "settler people." Instead of being scientifically compared to countries like Cuba, in terms of its mass military mobilization, or India, in terms of its single-party democracy, or Egypt, in terms of a theocratic component to national liberation, critics of Israel have reduced that country to pariah status by placing Israel firmly under the imperial umbrella, as if no other national liberation movement is hampered by big-power constraints and dependencies.

A major consequence of the post-October 1973 war was immediate reconsideration of Israeli attitudes toward the Third World. The broad-scale suspension of diplomatic and trade relations with Israel by Third World nations of Africa and Asia has given prima facie substance to the long simmering charges of conservative Israeli elements (not to mention their supporters in the West) that Israeli cultivation of African and Asian states represented a total waste of effort, and a violation of national self-interest, not to mention Jewish interests. As one Third World nation after the other capitulated to Arab pressures, the magnitude of Israeli isolation became manifest. One can appreciate the genuine belief of many Israeli conservatives that the only certain support of Israel in its time of travail is world Jewry; and that post-Round Four energies would best be directed toward strengthening the linkages of world Jewry, rather than cultivating powerless Third World nations that turn out to be graceless as well.

The primary response to the post-Round Four stalemate, and the consequent diplomatic debacle, has been renewed emphasis on the unity of the Jewish people at the expense of identification with the Third World:

> Israel alone in the Middle East does not have the capacity to survive. Israel plus the Jewish people throughout the world is a different condition. In the next decade, we must repair this demographic weakness. Our vulnerability is that we are 3 million and not 4 million. Our goal is the immigration of 25,000 Americans to Israel each year. Aliyah contains the answer to our future security and to our image of permanence. It is perhaps the most single and crucial way Israel's horizons can be transformed. America was built by immigrants and pioneers.[22]

This represents a slightly more blunt phrasing of the situation than diplomatic circles have admitted to; but certainly few would deny that this has been the operational code book of Israeli leadership since October 1973. During this period ties with South Africa, the United States, and countries of South America such as Brazil, that maintained a truly evenhanded standpoint, have been strengthened. A selective foreign policy, rather than one based on any set of broad principles, has dominated Israeli short-run thinking. While one can hardly fault Israelis for such a short-run policy posture, the Third World lurks in the backyard of Israel. This amorphous entity must be dealt with no less than the Soviet bloc or the Western European community. And it is the contention of this analysis that a positive reconsideration of Israeli policy toward the Third World is inevitable given the geopolitical realities which Israel must confront. The lack of economic dependency of the Third World upon Israel, and vice versa, could assist, rather than postpone such a policy reevaluation.

Historically, and the present century is no exception, Jews have been in the liberal vanguard of class revolution, social justice and racial comity. They have constantly asserted the need for universal equity. Implicit in this Jewish ideological behavior was a trickle-down theory in which defense of the rights of blacks, for example, is ultimately a defense of the rights of Jews. Affirmative action for women would mean employment opportunities for Jewish women. Open access to higher education for minorities would mean greater equity in the treatment of Jews within the university structure. But in their struggle for the rights of others, Jews discovered that the trickle-down theory was limited or, at times, counterproductive. Black animosity for Jews remained high despite the Mississippi Freedom marches and despite philanthropic endeavors on behalf of black colleges by the Jewish middle class. Equity for minorities and for women grouped under the general rubric of affirmative action, developed as an implicit target displacing male strength within academic environments, which disproportionately affected Jewish males concentrated in the arts and sciences. The radical movements which Jews had been part of in the sixties, became anti-Jewish movements, at least in the eyes of the Jewish establishment. The customary liberal posture, while still intact, became strained, and these painful setbacks were reflected in increasing class voting and decreasing support for minority groups across the land.

Israel remains the only example of formal democracy in the entire Middle East, the only country in the area where extremes of wealth and poverty are muted, it not absent. The disjunction between nationalism and radicalism in the Middle East has fragmented if not entirely confused old alliances and allegiances. The old New Left has been thrown into a painful defense of feudal capitalism in nations such as Iran and Saudi Arabia as the price of antiimperialism. Beyond that, Israel represents advanced political values that cannot easily be dismissed or submerged under the rhetoric of Third World solidarity. Attempts to apply 1960s categories used in relation to Southeast Asia to the Middle East reveal an intellectual confusion that no amount of religious fervor or special moral pleading can obscure. The articulation by the New Left of a pro-Arab standpoint represents little more than a relocation of good and evil by equating the Middle East with the Far East. The implausibility of such a mechanical transplant has shocked some radical critics into realizing that the world has changed dramatically, and that prophets of the previous decade are the pompous bores of the present. Moral fervor has not perished; rather moral certitude has given way to political ambiguity. The political parameters of the 1970s are sufficiently different from those of the sixties to create immobilism among leaders and uncertainty among the citizenry. Even within Jewish community life the moral edge has shifted from radicalism to conservatism: from a critique of America to that of the Soviet Union (or at least parallel criticisms); from defense of collective revolution in the Far East to defense of a singular democratic system in the Middle East. This transformation of values has led to considerable empirical confusion. Historically, Jews have been on both sides of the fence: they have authored books of scholarship and kept the books of high finance; they have exhibited the moral passion of the prophets and the moral degeneracy of the slum lord. Jewish politicians expose inhuman conditions in homes for the aged while Jewish rabbis reap profits from such homes. The fact that Jews occupy both the high ground and the low ground makes it inevitable that to some extent this ambiguous legacy will be transferred to the Israelis.

In any interaction, political as well as personal, there are the interests of two sides to contend with. When these appear irreconcilable, then new (or old) coalitions are created. In the short run, the interests of the Israelis require deep and continuing identification with world Jewry. Israel has one military ally at this point: the reluctant dragon known as the United States. Nations such as South Africa and Brazil can be counted among the friends of Israel, but they have no corresponding military potential. For its part, the Third World, in drawing closer to the interests of the Arab bloc and identifying ideologically with the Palestine Liberation effort, has also moved under the overall umbrella of the Soviet Union. This has converted the earlier 1960s notion of the Third World as a nonaligned bloc, into the concept of these nations as an antiimperial bloc. This has reaped considerable benefits for the Third World in the form of additional aid from the OPEC nations to compensate for a falling off of assistance from the OECD nations. Empirically there can be little expectation of a rapprochement between Israel and the Third World for the present.

Far from any movement toward reconciliation, the current period clearly represents the nadir in Third World Israeli relationships. The final declaration of the Third Ministerial Meeting of the Coordinating Bureau of Nonaligned Nations (a cluster of seventeen nations providing a reasonably representative cross-section of Third World official opinion) contained some key items: it affixed the entire blame and responsibility for the Middle East crisis upon Israel, and it threatened collective economic and political sanctions. These can hardly be dismissed as sheer propaganda in view of the current economic boycott and diplomatic isolation Israel is currently being made to endure.

> The threat of the renewal of hostilities is due to the persistence of Israel in its aggressive, expansionist and occupational policy, as well as its refusal to recognize the rights of the Palestinian people and its contempt for the United Nations' Charter and resolutions . . . . The Bureau believes the time is ripe for the nonaligned countries to consider broader measures against Israel, in compliance with the Charter of the United Nations, including such measures as the implementation of sanctions, the dismissal from the United Nations, etc.[23]

Given such categorical and unqualified support for the Arab posture, one can scarcely treat the "etc." with a sense of equanimity. The fact that the ministerial conference was held in Havana, Cuba; and that the forthcoming meeting of this same body is to be held in Lima, Peru, serves to underscore the global context of Arab efforts to solicit support for its cause. The effect to defeat Israel in diplomacy is not confined to a proximate locale, but extends to the most remote parts of the Third World. That Latin America is not simply the scene of this condemnation rituals, but the one sphere of the Third World containing large clusters of Jewish people, must also be reckoned with in any future dealings between Israel and the Third World.

In the long run, if there is a long run, the Israelis will have to adapt to the realities of their area, and these include the overall needs of the Third World. Israel was moving toward that end between Rounds Three and Four. One might argue that the Arab effort, diplomatically as well as on the propaganda front, was oriented precisely to prevent the successful conclusion of this policy. The Third World can derive only short-term benefits from recognizing Israel, that is, in the material sense of aid and trade. In the larger sense, the Third World provides a unique morphology of growth which is remarkably well illustrated by Israel's development. While it would be wishful thinking to imagine that similitudes in size or structure would tilt the balance of the Third World in favor of Israel and against the Arab bloc, there are a sufficient number of disquieting features in the present situation of the Third

World to provide Israel with some rays of hope for a more balanced posture in the future.

Above all, there is a question of the solidarity of the Third World itself, or more precisely, even if there are similar global tendencies toward the militarization of the Third World, this does not eliminate the existence of profound differences, even schisms, between Arab Africa and sub-Saharan Africa. Likewise, tendencies toward polarization of all sorts exist within Latin America and Southeast Asia. In at least some of these instances recognition of Israel makes possible a wider latitude of policy options for those Third World nations in a position to run short-term risks imposed by an oil embargo or the suspension of aid from the OPEC nations. Given the expansion of the oil-producing bloc to include Venezuela and Nigeria itself offers some interesting long-range possibilities.

The one overriding theme common to both Israel and the Third World is an animosity, even a flat rejection, of big-power imperial domination and settlement of international disputes. In this shared belief in national autonomy, the rights of each nation to self-determination, and the juridical and military importance of sovereignty, a common kernel of truth continues to link Israel to the Third World despite the magnitude of the current split. One can only anticipate that if such a long-run perspective is feasible, that perspective might well include as a scenario first the reestablishment of trade linkages (which even now have not been entirely severed), and then a merging of Israeli interests with those concerns characteristic of the Third World as a whole.

If such an appraisal is hardly calculated to satisfy those who continue to believe that Israel's primary linkage is with Diaspora Jewry, or equally, those who maintain that the Third World's essential linkage is with the Left, these concerns will simply have to be put to the test of time—not ideology or theology. Prospects for Israeli linkages with the Third World are neither grim nor necessarily euphoric. But there is a middle ground which offers not only a hope for the pacification of the Middle East, but also a more definite expectation for the participation of Israel in the Third World. Such a development alone offers Israel an opportunity of a final break with a pariah status that has plagued it throughout its brief history.

POSTSCRIPT

The aftermath of the Yom Kippur War witnessed greatly increased efforts on the part of the Arab bloc to consign Israel to a pariah status. What was denied to it on the battlefield, outright victory, the Arab bloc sought and partially realized on the diplomatic turf. Despite the Israeli-Egyptian accords of 1975, no Arab state was prepared to offer *de jure* status to Israel. It might well be argued that intensified efforts against Israel at a *de facto* level increased. The vote in October 1975, taken by the Social, Humanitarian and Cultural Committee of the United Nations, to condemn Zionism "as a form of racism and racial discrimination" represents more than a shameful form of hypocrisy and distortion. The resolution makes Israel in effect, the first member of the United Nations to have its particular doctrine of nationalism and national liberation defamed and condemned by other member states. In this singular fact, one senses the victory of the Arab policy of isolating Israel and then following this up with an enforced pariah status.

The unity of Arab sentiment and policy concerning the future of Israel has been fully documented. More important, 1975 marked the first full-scale effort to reach out to the rest of the Third World for support of their maximalist posture. The African nations in particular have been subject to Arab pressures. While nations of sub-Saharan Africa are ready to grant that they have no intrinsic reasons for opposing Israel on either economic or diplomatic grounds, the fact that Israel is a bargaining chip Africans can play in their efforts to gain material advantages from the oil producing Arab states, has become a factor in present-day Middle Eastern affairs. Mitigating African willingness to support the Arab policy is the clear favoritism of Arab states, which pour aid only into areas with significant Islamic populations (the Philippines, Pakistan, Bangladesh, Ghana, the Sudan and Uganda) at the expense of the rest of sub-Saharan Africa (especially Tanzania, Liberia, Zambia, Malawi, Kenya and the Ivory Coast). This has led some black African states to reconsider a policy that would make Israel a pariah nation with no measurable returns to Africa other than a homogenous policy endorsing Muslim aims.

If anti-Semitism has properly been termed "the socialism of fools," anti-Zionism might well be termed "the nationalism of fools." Anti-Zionism is the one post-war nationalist movement which has managed to unite such extraordinary opposites as the Cuban government of Comandante Castro, which co-sponsored the United Nations draft resolution linking Zionism with racism, and the Chilean government of General Pinochet, reputed to have sold its United Nations vote to the Arab powers in exchange for Arab support in Chile's efforts to avoid being condemned for genocidal practices. One would be hard put to find another issue that would link the Chilean military Right with the Cuban military Left. This in itself is indicative of how the Jew continues to serve as the whipping-boy for everyone else's frustrations: national no less than personal.

Yet, an uncomfortable, if as yet unarticulated awareness of the non-rational sources of anti-Zionism has occasioned reconsideration on the part of many member nations of the Third World that would otherwise stand united. While seventy nations favored the draft resolution, twenty-nine opposed the resolution, twenty-seven abstained, and sixteen more absented themselves, for a total of seventy-two that did not vote for the resolution. This is indicative of the continuing struggles involved, not simply between Israel and its Arab neighbors, but between the larger question of democratic and authoritarian forms of rule within the Third World. For the Jew in his person, in his marginality, represents a continuing sense of options. By extension, it is not unreasonable to claim that Israel in its own legal person represents a similar sense of options in the political realm. As a result, the effort to convert Israel from a pariah people to a pariah nation is part of the historic dilemma of nationalism as such. It is also part of the specific dilemma of Jewish nationalism: namely, whether one can any longer speak of center and periphery in the same way as in past ages. For if Jewish nationalism is like all nationalisms, any special claims to Israeli citizenship by Jews the world over becomes questionable. On the other hand, if Jewish nationalism is different than all others, the question then becomes whether the Israeli State is also different than all other states. Issues of such magnitude remain to be asked and answered in the next period of history—one which hopefully fully and finally resolves the pariah status which the tragic past of the Jewish peoples has bequeathed to the Israeli nation.

NOTES

1. Theodor Herzl, "The Jewish State," in *The Zionist Idea: A Historical Analysis and Reader*, ed. Arthur Hertzberg (New York and Philadelphia: Meridiam Books and The Jewish Publication Society of America, 1960), pp. 224-25.

2. Cf. Jacob Talmon, *The Unique and The Universal: Some Historical Reflections* (New York: George Braziller, 1965), pp. 64-90.

3. Cf. Irving Louis Horowitz, *Israeli Ecstasies/Jewish Agonies* (New York and London: Oxford University Press, 1974), pp. 75-85.

4. Cf. Theodore Draper, "The United States and Israel," *Commentary* 59, no. 4 (April 1975): 29-45.

5. Cf. Louis I. Snyder, *The Dreyfus Case: A Documentary History* (New Brunswick: Rutgers University Press, 1973), pp. 92-98.

6. George L. Mosse, *The Nationalization of the Masses* (New York: Howard Fertig-Publishers, 1975), pp. 198-99.

7. Uriel Tal, *Christians and Jews in Germany*, trans. Noah Jonathan Jacobs (Ithaca and London: Cornell University Press, 1975), pp. 265-66.

8. Amos Elon, *The Israelis: Founders and Sons* (New York: Holt, Reinhart and Winston, 1971), pp. 323-24.

9. Michael Brecher, *Decisions in Israel's Foreign Policy* (New Haven: Yale University Press, 1975), pp. 165-69.

10. Susan Aurelia Gitelson, "Why Do Small States Break Diplomatic Relations with Outside Powers? Lesson from the African Experience," *International Studies Quarterly* 18, no. 4 (December 1974): 451-84.

11. Arye Oded, *Islam in Uganda: Islamization Through a Centralized State in Pre-Colonial Africa* (Jerusalem and New York: Israel Universities Press and John Wiley & Sons, 1974), pp. 315 and 5 respectively.

12. Rene Peritz, "The Middle East and Southeast Asia: Linkages and Interactions," *Middle East Information Series*, whole no. 22 (February 1973): 30-39.

13. Alvin Z. Rubinstein, "Yugoslavia and the Middle East," *Middle East Information Series*, whole no. 21 (December 1972): 30-33.

14. Leonard J. Fein, *Israel: Politics and People* (Boston: Little, Brown and Company, 1968), pp. 269-70.

15. Amos Perlmutter, *Egypt: The Praetorian State* (New Brunswick: Transaction Books, 1974), pp. 177-81.

16. Cf. Edward Bernard Glick, *Between Israel and Death* (Harrisburg, Pa.: Stackpole Books, 1974), pp. 125-35.

17. Elon, *The Israelis*.

18. Shlomo Avineri, "Subjugation of the Means to the State's Ends?" in *Unease in Zion*, ed. Ehud Ben Ezer (New York and Jerusalem: Quadrangle Books and Jerusalem Academic Press, 1974), p. 64.

19. S.N. Eisenstadt, *Israeli Society* (New York: Basic Books, 1967), pp. 5-6.

20. Dan V. Segre, "Israel and the Third World," *Middle East Information Series*, no. 22 (February 1973): 10.

21. Dan V. Segre, *The High Road and the Low: A Study in Legitimacy, Authority and Technical Aid* (London: Allen Lane Publishers, 1974), pp. 145-48.

22. Abba Eban, "Eban Calls for 'Pioneers,'" *The Star Ledger*, March 3, 1975.

23. "Final Declaration of the Third Ministerial Meeting of the Coordinating Bureau of Nonaligned Countries," *Granma* (Havana) 10, no. 13 (March 30, 1975): 7.

APPENDIX

ISRAELI FOREIGN AID PROJECTS

As of 1970, the State of Israel was engaged in the following foreign aid projects around the world:

ASIA AND THE MEDITERRANEAN AREA

Cambodia

Prek Thnot: experimental farm for field and vegetable crops, with demonstration plots established in villages, and furtherance of agricultural services.

Cyprus

Medical program in ophthalmology and plastic surgery (ninth year), including visits by Israeli specialists. Continued cooperation between the medical departments and the Ministries of Health in the two countries.

Korea

Exploratory state of water drilling and irrigation by Tahal.

Laos

Experimental farm at Hatdokkao, linked with crop demonstration on many farms and introduction of simple farm implements.

Establishment of agricultural cooperative society and agricultural services.

Malta

Advice on afforestation.
Advice on cattle and milk.
Survey of local cheese industry.

Nepal

Comprehensive regional agricultural development program in Nawalpur for 800 families.

Regional development scheme in Nepalgang for 1,000 families in eight villages, together with development of water resources.

Philippines

Survey of the establishment of a model coopeative village at Ario-Riketta.

Singapore

Advice on Hydroponics (soilless cultivation).
Lecturer in sociology at the University of Singapore.
Project to establish national symphony orchestra (second year).

Thailand

Program of irrigation, introduction of new crops, communal organization, training and settlement in Hop-Topang (fourth year).

Irrigation and agricultural planning for the Faculty of Agriculture farm in Kon-Ken (second year).

AFRICA

Botswana

Eradication of tuberculosis (five-year program).
Survey of eye disease.

Cameroon

Young Pioneer agricultural settlement program at Obala and Garoua.
Advice on urban youth clubs.
Management of two agricultural training centers and the settling of two new village centers (fifth year).
Vegetable growing and marketing program at Fonban.
Preparation of youth-training teachers at teachers' college.

Central African Republic

Advice on six cooperative villages and management of two model farms.
National youth movement and agricultural extension services.
Advice on youth.

Congo (Brazzaville)

Poultry farm scheme (third year).

Dahomey

Pioneering youth training.
Advice to government on information and broadcasting service.
Advice on State Lottery.
Experimental and demonstration citrus farm.

Ethiopia

Fisheries development program.
Advice on road construction.
Advice on traffic engineering problems.
Advice on port maintenance.
Cotton farm at Abadir (second year).
Management and training at school for hotel management.
Establishment of blood banks in cooperation with the Ethiopian Red Cross.
Geological survey and mapping with Ethiopian teams led by Israeli geologists.
Development of pharmaceutical services.
Adoption of Natural Sciences Faculty at Haile Selassie I University of Addis Ababa by Hebrew University of Jerusalem, for a period of five years.
Advice on organization and the marketing of handicrafts.
Agricultural advice in Tigre Province.

Gabon

Civic, rural and professional training center (fifth year).
Civic-physical education and handicrafts in schools.

Gambia

Advice in agriculture.
Course on argricultural extension services.

Ghana

Cattle-raising at Tadzewu.
Advice and training at the laboratory of the Medical School.
Advice on textiles in the Bureau of Standards.

Ivory Coast

Joint Israeli-Ivory Coast corporation dealing with heavy equipment and farm machinery.
Country-wide pioneer training program (6,500 men and women).
Pioneering training center at Bouaké.
Twenty pioneering youth centers.
Cattle farm at Gangara.

Kenya

Lecturer in biochemistry at the University of Nairobi.
Social Work Center.

Lesotho

Several soil conservation programs (third and last years, respectively).
Advice to government on youth organization.

Liberia

Training farm at Harrisburg.
Urban youth club program.
Eye clinic.

Malagasy Republic

Citrus program in Morondava (third year).
Establishment of agricultural training center and regional settlement scheme.
Advice on women's organization.

Malawi

Youth training (Malawi Young Pioneers).
Direction of central school for youth instructors.
Direction of eye clinic.

Mauritius

Agricultural instruction to Young Farmers' Organization (second year).
Advice on bacteriology in Central Laboratory.
Lecturer in cooperation at College of Mauritius.

Niger

Training program for youth movement.
Advice to government for establishment of training farm at Dalol Boso.

Rwanda

Direction of ophthalmic service (with ambulant services).
Management of school of nursing.
Youth training program.
Advice on dental clinic.

Senegal

Bee-raising program
Advice on youth program.

Sierra Leone

Advice on electrical engineering.
Preliminary survey on establishment of experimental farm at the University of Argriculture, Najela.

Swaziland

Youth training (third year).
Course for youth instructors.

Tchad

Management of youth training farm at Candoul (fifth year).
Youth training and management of Young Pioneer farm.
Management of model farm (third year).
Afforestation program.
Management of government printing press.

Togo

Advice to government on juvenile delinquency.
Advice on pineapple growing and its industrialization.
Agricultural training center for young pioneers in Glidji.
450 Young Pioneers cultivating more than 500 acres in thirty-two agricultural clubs.
Model cooperative village at Togodo, established by graduates from Glidji.

Uganda

Citrus planting in four areas.
Lecturer in zoology at University of Makerere.
Consultant psychiatrist to Ministry of Health. (Program terminated in early 1972.)

Upper Volta

Management of pediatrics department at Ouagadougou Hospital.
Advice on State Lottery.
Participation in polyvalent farm at Maturkos.

Zaire

Poultry. farm.

Zambia

Comprehensive development scheme in Kafubu and Kafulafuta (fourth year).
Survey for comprehensive development scheme in Western Province.

LATIN AMERICA

Bolivia

Agricultural advice to six pioneer centers.
Advice on organization of courses in agricultural training and cooperation.

Barbados

Advice on port development.

Brazil

Lameiro (State of Piaui): Regional development of program involving 500 families of farmers (third year).
Establishment of two experimental and demonstration stations.
Calderon: First stage of regional development project.

Chile

Cooperative marketing program for farms supplying Santiago and environs (fourth year).
Choapa-Ovalle-Serana: Program of agricultural advice, introduction of irrigation methods and cooperative organizations within the framework of agrarian reform (for 3,000 families).

Colombia

Boyaca: Three programs to modernize the farming practices and auxiliary services in an area of 35,000 acres (fourth year).

Costa Rica

National Youth Movement in capital and inner regions of the country throughout thirty-five branches.

Dominican Republic

El Sisal (Azua): Regional development program involving the settlement of 360 families, preparation of tillage for new villages and direction of model farm for cotton and vegetable production (fourth year).

Ecuador

Tenguel: Parcellation of land, construction of homes and provision of agricultural extension services for 150 families.
San Augustin: Housing of 80 families in two villages, in similar scheme (third year).
Cayambe: First stage towards realization of settlement program, as future settlers belonging to Ecuadorian Young Pioneers complete agricultural training.

Guatemala

Development of agricultural extension services for beneficiaries of agrarian reform in Zapaca (second year).

Guyana

First survey of avocado project.

Haiti

Demonstration farm specializing in export crops (second year).
Organization of 150 families in cooperatives.

Honduras

Monjaras Buena Vista: Regional development scheme to embrace 500 families in village cooperatives, and including village institutions and agricultural extension services (third year).
San Bernardo: First stage of advice and agricultural training in regional development scheme.

Nicaragua

Colonia Israel (Ato Grande): Comprehensive plan of development for 170 families on 50,000 acres, including the establishment of farm homes and village institutions and the introduction of supervised credit (third year).
Rigoberto Cabezas: Advice and agricultural training in scheme to settle 170 families.

Panama

Advice and agricultural training in small irrigation projects and several settlement schemes.

Paraguay

First stage of project to establish a national supervised credit system.

Peru

La Joya: Completion of the first two villages of 100 settlers each, in regional development scheme planned jointly by the OAS, Peru and Israel.
Project aiming at the unification of transport cooperatives in the Lima region and the organization of professional courses for cooperatives.

Trinidad

Advice to the Ministry of Agriculture on dairy extension services. Cattle-feeding program (fourth year).

Uruguay

National cattle-breeding program.
Advice on agricultural development.

Venezuela

Completion of supervised credit program, extending to 15,000 farmers in 220 villages.

Advice to government on expansion of agricultural exports (second year).

Advice on national agricultural mechanization project, including advice to two cooperatives on the formation of regional mechanization instructors.

Guarapiche: First stage of regional development scheme in northeastern region of Venezuela.

CONTRIBUTORS

Moshe Alpan is Director of Koor Intertrade Company.

Shimeon Amir is Senior Lecturer on Development and Cooperation Programs at Tel Aviv University.

Ehud Avriel is Consul General in Chicago and former Ambassador to Ghana.

Joel Barromi is Director, U.N. Department of the Ministry for Foreign Affairs, Israel.

Michael Brecher is Professor of International Relations, McGill University.

Michael Curtis is Professor of Political Science, Rutgers University.

Samuel Decalo is Associate Professor of Political Science, the New School for Social Research.

Ephraim Dubek is an official and former member of the Department of International Relations, the Hebrew University.

Akiva Eger is Director of the Afro-Asian Institute.

Jacques Fomerand is Research Associate at C.U.N.Y. Graduate School and University Center.

Eli Ginzberg is A. Barton Hepburn Professor of Economics and Director of the Conservation of Human Resources, Columbia University.

Susan Aurelia Gitelson is Research Associate at the Middle East Institute, Columbia University.

Irving Louis Horowitz is Professor of Sociology and Political Sociology, Rutgers University.

Eliyahu Kanovsky is Professor of Economics at S.U.N.Y., Stony Brook.

Edy Kaufman is a member of the Department of International Relations, the Hebrew University.

Ran Kochan is a member of the Department of International Relations, the Hebrew University.

401

Mordechai E. Kreinin is Professor of Economics, Michigan State University.

Netanel Lorch is Secretary General of the Knesset.

Meron Medzini is an Israeli political scientist and journalist.

Benjamin Rivlin is Dean of University and Special Programs and Professor of Political Science, C.U.N.Y. Graduate School and University Center.

Dan Segre is Professor of International Relations, the Hebrew University, and Editor of the Jerusalem Journal of International Relations.

Yoram Shapira is a member of the Latin American Studies Department, the Hebrew University.

Yaacov Shimoni is Deputy Director General, Ministry for Foreign Affairs, Israel.

INDEX